WRITING TALK

WRITING TALK

Sentences and Paragraphs with Readings

FIFTH EDITION

Anthony C. Winkler

Jo Ray McCuen-Metherell
Glendale Community College

PEARSON
Prentice Hall

Upper Saddle River, New Jersey 07458

Library of Congress Cataloging-in-Publication Data

Winkler, Anthony C.

Writing talk. Sentences and paragraphs with readings / Anthony C. Winkler, Jo Ray McCuen.-- 5th ed.

p. cm.

Includes index.

ISBN-13: 978-0-13-500880-5

ISBN-10: 0-13-500880-8

1. English language--Sentences--Problems, exercises, etc. 2. English language--Paragraphs--Problems, exercises, etc. 3. English language--Grammar--Problems, exercises, etc. 4. Report writing--Problems, exercises, etc. 5. College readers. I. Title: Sentences and paragraphs with readings. II. McCuen, Jo Ray, 1929- III. Title.

PE1441.W57 2008

808'.042

2008008629

Editorial Director: Leah Jewell
Editor in Chief: Craig Campanella
Executive Marketing Manager: Megan Galvin-Fak
Marketing Manager: Thomas DeMarco
Marketing Assistant: Sara Fry
Senior Operations Supervisor: Sherry Lewis
Operations Specialist: Christina Amato
Text Permissions Specialist: Kathleen Karcher
Permissions Assistant: Peggy Davis
Director, Image Resource Center: Melinda Patelli
Manager, Image Rights and Permissions: Zina Arabia
Manager, Visual Research: Beth Brenzel
Image Permissions Coordinator: Craig A. Jones
Associate Director for Central Design: Jayne Conte
Cover Designer: Bruce Kenselaar
Cover Art: Nicholas Wilton/Jan Collier Represents/Zocolo
Senior Art Director: Nancy Wells
Full-Service Project Management: Aptara, Inc./ Sarvesh Mehrotra
Copyeditor: Brian Baker
Composition: Aptara, Inc.
Printer/Binder: RR Donnelley
Cover Printer: RR Donnelley
Text Font: 11/13 New Century Schoolbook

Credits and acknowledgments for material borrowed from other sources and reproduced, with permission, in this textbook appear on page 525.

Pearson Education Ltd., London
Pearson Education Singapore, Pte. Ltd
Pearson Education Canada, Inc.
Pearson Education—Japan
Pearson Education Australia PTY, Limited
Pearson Education North Asia, Ltd., Hong Kong
Pearson Educación de Mexico, S.A. de C.V.
Pearson Education Malaysia, Pte. Ltd.
Pearson Education, Upper Saddle River, New Jersey

PEARSON
Prentice Hall

10 9 8 7 6
ISBN 13: 978-0-13-500880-5
ISBN 10: 0-13-500880-8

CONTENTS

Preface to the Fifth Edition

The fifth edition of *Writing Talk: Sentences and Paragraphs with Readings,* like its four predecessors, takes for granted that grammar is a built-in skill for native speakers, not a book-learned one, and that the speaker's ear for the mother tongue is therefore the best judge of grammatical correctness. Yet as English teachers we know that many of our students neither speak nor write what we have been trained to call "good grammar." Students use fragments; they punctuate badly; they misplace modifiers and garble sentences; they use the wrong case or tense; they speak and write slang. How can we say that a speaker's ear is the best judge of grammar when all around us we have evidence to the contrary?

The answer is simple: Much of the time students don't make errors of bad grammar but of inappropriate usage. If you are raised hearing *ain't* used every day, you will grow up using *ain't* in your own speaking and writing. But because *ain't* is regarded as nonstandard and unacceptable usage in formal writing, it is our job as English teachers to wean students off that word when the circumstances demand the formality of standard English.

Usage variations aside, it is still a fact that all native speakers, as well as those who have spoken English for years, have within them an ear for English grammar that students for whom English is a second language (ESL) do not share.

This assumption was thought by some to make previous editions of this book suitable for native speakers but not for ESL students. Nevertheless, regardless of the differences between native speakers and ESL students, many school systems, because of budgetary pressures, freely mix both populations in the same classroom, making no distinction between them. The upshot is that many teachers have asked us to include both groups, native speakers as well as ESL students. That is exactly what we have done beginning with the fourth edition and continuing in this fifth.

In coping with both audiences, we take a dual approach. We begin with a candid admission that ESL students and native speakers have different strengths and weaknesses. For the native speaker, the advantage is an ear that is finely tuned to the mother tongue. On the other hand, ESL students who come to English as adults or near-adults often bring to the table a solid grounding in the grammatical basics of their adopted tongue. Gradually, as they progress in fluency, they will acquire what to the native speaker is a birthright, namely an ear for the language.

Until that happens, foreign speakers learning English often make mistakes in phrasing that would rarely, if ever, be made by a native speaker. For example, recently we overheard a foreign student say to another student who was about to take a test, "Have a good luck." This sentence is not ungrammatical; it is unidiomatic. But it is also the sort of sentence no native speaker would use. People say to one another, "Good luck," all the time. But they never say, "Have a good luck." On the other hand, no native speaker would say, "Have good day," but would immediately know to say "Have a good day." Yet if you ask one hundred such speakers why "a" goes before "day" but not before "luck," you'd truly have a good luck if you find one who can tell you.

Yet native speakers do make mistakes. Here is a sentence that is typical: "The men at the baseball park was talking throughout the game." This sentence confuses the prepositional phrase "at the baseball park" for the subject and commits a classic subject–verb agreement error. In short, both groups commonly make mistakes in English usage. But they make different mistakes.

With these differences in mind, we have adapted the pedagogy of this book to take into account many of the known difficulties that ESL students have with English as well as many of the common errors that all students make. Where appropriate, we issue an ESL Advice notice, alerting students that this particular usage is one that often baffles ESL students.

This dual approach is aimed at both audiences, whose superficial differences cannot alter the fact that they have a common goal this book can help them reach: namely, mastery of English.

There are occasions when, no matter what the background of the student, the ear is at odds with the formal rule and of no help whatsoever in deciding what is right and appropriate. A case in point is the infamous "between you and I." Although used by a surprising array of prominent men and women in the media, this construction is incorrect. Yet the right form, "between you and me," often sounds wrong. We flag such cases with a unique feature of the Writing Talk series, namely, an Ear Alert warning. We first explain the formal rule for the benefit of both groups, but particularly for the ESL student; we then show how its practice in everyday speech varies from the rule. Finally, the Ear Alert label and distinctive icon in the margin warn everyone that this is a point of grammar on which no one's ear can be trusted.

Writing Talk: Sentences and Paragraphs with Readings is the first book in a series of two, and it covers the following topics:

- *Common Myths and Standard Written English.* We dispel some common and discouraging myths that students believe about writing. Writing is hard for everybody (no doubt rare exceptions exist, but we can't think of any offhand). We also know that the fumbling and revision that goes with writing is not a sign of ineptness, but a universal condition of the discipline. Many students do not understand how difficult writing is and tend to misinterpret the normal tedium of composing as a sign that they cannot write.

- *Paragraph Writing Assignments in Every Sentence Unit.* Grammar by itself can be a grim, unmerciful, seemingly pointless business. By including paragraph writing assignments at the end of every sentence unit, we emphasize that grammar is a means to an end rather than an end in itself.

Throughout, our explanations of grammar rules

- emphasize functional problems, not descriptive grammar.
- use a minimum of terminology.
- give short, pointed explanations with a light touch.
- are followed by immediate practice.
- come with abundant exercises that include paragraphs for editing and sentences for reading aloud.
- are followed by a short summary of every main point (In a Nutshell).

Organization of the Fifth Edition

Previous users of this text will immediately notice in the Contents that there has been a massive reorganization of the unit topics. The entire book has been reorganized so that the topics now proceed from the smaller to the larger. In Part One, newly entitled Getting Started, we still deal with the differences between the ESL students and native speakers. Each group has its strengths and weaknesses and we discuss them separately and together.

However, in spite of the reorganization of the Contents, all the well-known features that users of earlier editions particularly liked have been retained. Every chapter still has a Talk–Write Assignment that gives students practice in translating oral dialogue into its written formal equivalent. Each assignment presents a dialogue that might be overheard in an informal discussion and then asks students to write the equivalent in a more formal style.

As before, this new edition ends most chapters with the following five types of exercises:

- A *Unit Test* that tests mastery of the chapter. This is now a feature of virtually every unit.
- A *Unit Talk–Write Assignment* that reinforces the difference between spoken and written language.
- A *Unit Collaborative Assignment* that gives students an opportunity to interact in group sessions and put their ear to use in practicing the contents of the chapter.
- A *Unit Writing Assignment* that gives students a chance to apply the writing principles they have just learned.
- A *Photo Writing Assignment* that asks students to write on a topic suggested by a photograph. We have changed some of the assignments and some of the photographs.

We have also added some new features to the fifth edition.

- We have added a section to Unit One explaining why it is important to speak and write correctly.
- We have updated the slang and other student expressions in the Talk–Write Assignments.
- We have added more exercises on the use of the apostrophe with plural nouns.
- We have enlarged our discussion of verb problems in Unit Ten.
- At the request of some reviewers, we have added to the discussion of indefinite pronouns.
- We have added to our discussion of direct objects.
- We have laboriously combed through every exercise of every chapter and made additions where we felt they were necessary. For some peculiar reason exercises generally occur in multiples of five, and this edition contains hundreds of exercises that hammer home some principle of grammar or writing. All exercises push the students' understanding of some particular point and help reinforce their memory of what was taught. Instructors know the value of repetitive exercises as a learning technique, but we also understand that exercises and drills walk a fine line between usefulness and tedium. Each chapter now has more numerous and varied exercises that reinforce every concept taught. We have tried to write exercises that are interesting to do and require a variety of responses.

Throughout the entire book we've also made many microscopic changes to the textual explanations. Always, we've tried to be simpler and more direct, and where the opportunity presented itself, to add some humor to what might otherwise seem to the student to be a typically grim exposition of grammatical principles. Teaching grammar is a serious enterprise, but it does not deserve the graveyard sobriety of tone it is so often given.

Finally, we have changed three selections in the Readings section. New to this edition is an essay discussing how lawyers today restrict the access ice skaters used to have to government lakes and ponds during the winter. We have also added that classic piece by Mark Twain, "The War Prayer," which speaks to our own day as it did to readers in 1905. The final new essay, "Welcome Our Planet, Ourselves," makes an impassioned plea for us to do something about global warming. The readings in *Writing Talk: Sentences and Paragraphs* are, as before, thematically organized. Some instructors like to teach principles and then show them in practice, exactly what the readings in this book are meant to do.

Each reading is prefaced by a headnote and followed by Vocabulary, comprehension questions (Understanding What You Have Read), and thought-provoking questions (Thinking About What You Have Read). Finally, two Writing Assignments are included for each reading.

Throughout both our books, we have tried to make the explanations simple but concise so that they will be understandable to both ESL and native students, to explain everything step-by-step, to provide exercises immediately after explaining any rule or principle, and to respect and encourage the student's "ear" for grammar, whether it exists by birthright or was acquired by an accumulated study of English.

Acknowledgments

Our thanks to Craig Campanella, editor in chief at Prentice Hall, who oversaw this revision, and to the production and manufacturing staff at Prentice Hall.

We would also like to thank the following reviewers:

Roy Bond, *Richland College*
Donald Brotherton, *College of Lane County*
Donna Deaton, *Carl Albert State College*
Beverly Dile, *Elizabethtown Comm & Tech*
Deborah Fuller, *Bunker Hill CC*
Billy Jones, *Miami Dade College-Kendall*
Joanne Krueger, *Arizona W. College*
Joan Reeves, *NE Alabama CC*
Bonnie Ronson, *Hillsborough Comm. College*
Vicki Strunk, *National College*
Malik Toms, *Estrella Mountain CC*

Anthony C. Winkler
Jo Ray McCuen-Metherell

WRITING TALK

1 The ESL Student and the Native Speaker

"Having an ear for the language means that you're usually able to tell when something doesn't sound right, even though you can't say why."

Language typically consists of two main parts: sounds and rules. Its sounds are the way the language is spoken—its **pronunciation.** Its rules are its **grammar.** Part of learning a language involves mastering the rules. But odd as it may seem, if you are a native speaker, you already know, and correctly observe, many rules of the language simply by the way it sounds. For example, do you see anything wrong with this sentence?

> She will speaking with you be later.

Most likely, you immediately saw that the verb *be* was out of place. The sentence should have read,

> She will be speaking with you later.

This is just one example of a basic truth: You know more about your language than you think. For instance, did you know that you know how to use the future progressive tense? If you say you don't, you're wrong. The construction "She will be speaking" is in the future progressive tense. If you haven't spoken it today, you probably will later. It is a very complex tense, yet nearly every day, you use it flawlessly, as you do many other parts of speech. You do not need to know the formal definition of a preposition to correctly use one. Practically no native speaker would make this mistake:

> I put book the table on.

It does not look right. But more importantly, it just does not sound right. Whether or not you know the formal rule that the preposition comes before the object that it modifies, you still practice it. And you do that entirely by the way the construction sounds—strictly by ear.

Differences Between Native Speakers and ESL Students

We bring this up to help explain the differences that exist between a native speaker of English and an ESL (English as a Second Language) student. Both can learn to master English by using this book. However, although both have the same goal—to learn to speak and write English well—they do not begin at the same place and therefore cannot learn English the same way. The main difference between them is this: The native speaker, from having heard English spoken since birth, has an ear for it. *Having an ear for a language* means that you're usually able to tell when something doesn't sound right, even though you can't say why. Nearly all native speakers have this ability. It exists even if they mainly speak a dialect of the language. Most native speakers, for example, will automatically say "If I were you" without knowing the formal rule behind that expression. If an ESL student says "If I were you," it is most likely because he or she has learned the formal rule governing the subjunctive.

ESL students face different challenges than do native speakers. Indeed, the difficulties that most ESL students have when learning English generally fall into three broad categories: pronunciation, grammar, and idioms.

Pronunciation

Many words in English will take on a different meaning, depending on how they are pronounced. From experience, native speakers know, recognize, and use these differences almost instinctively. For example, place the emphasis on the first syllable of the word *present* and it means "a gift" ("Thank you for that terrific birthday present") or "a time period" ("There's no time like the present"). However, place the emphasis on the second syllable of *present* and it means "to introduce" ("Ladies and gentlemen, I would like to present the president of the United States"). Another example is the word *invalid.* If spoken with an emphasis on the second syllable, this word means "legally no good" ("Her check was invalid"). But when the emphasis is on the first syllable, *invalid* means "a sick person."

Here are some other examples of meanings that depend purely on sound:

> The lovely white <u>dove</u> flew from a branch just as I <u>dove</u> into the river.
>
> Nancy was <u>close</u> to fainting, so the nurse asked us to <u>close</u> the door.
>
> The <u>wind</u> was so powerful that the sailors could not <u>wind</u> the sails.

Many other examples of words that shift their meanings with sound can be found in English.

PRACTICE 1

Working in a small group, explain the difference in the meanings of the underlined words in the sentences that follow.

1. U.S. farms <u>produce</u> huge volumes of <u>produce</u> every year.

 ____

2. Why <u>object</u> to such a beautiful <u>object</u> just because it is old?

 ____

3. I <u>refuse</u> to clean the yard because it is full of <u>refuse.</u>

 ____

4. The <u>sewer</u> tripped and fell down the <u>sewer.</u>

 ____

5. These homeowners <u>lead</u> the campaign to get the <u>lead</u> out of drinking water.

 ____

6. There was a <u>row</u> in the third <u>row</u> of seats.

 ____

7. The bandage was <u>wound</u> around the <u>wound.</u>

 ____

8. Please <u>relay</u> the results of the <u>relay</u> to me.

 ____

9. They <u>polish</u> the sign that said they were <u>Polish.</u>

 ____

10. The mating stag <u>does</u> a dance when he sees the <u>does.</u>

 ____

Homonyms

Occasionally, two words may sound alike but have different meanings. Such words are called **homonyms.** Here are some examples with the homonyms underlined.

> <u>They're</u> much too difficult for the students. <u>Their</u> homes are out of town. Place the book over <u>there.</u>
>
> Give the peach <u>to</u> your brother. He owns <u>two</u> motorcycles. I, <u>too,</u> love cats.
>
> <u>You're</u> about to win $300. Have you checked with <u>your</u> boss?

In the case of homonyms, however, the spelling always determines the meaning.

PRACTICE 2

Circle the correct homonym in parentheses.

1. The (souls, soles) of his shoes were worn out.
2. We have every (right, write) to complain about so many blackouts.
3. (It's, Its) better to have loved and lost than never to have loved at all.
4. They'll simply have to wait for (they're, their) turn.
5. I can't see that (theirs, there's) any difference between them.
6. I can't (bear, bare) to face the truth.
7. The students had (sheer, shear) luck on their side.
8. After a long war, finally, we had (piece, peace).
9. Every evening for a full year, she took an (our, hour) of conversational French.
10. She told us the story to (lesson, lessen) our grief.

Context

Some words, although spelled and pronounced the same way, still take on different meanings, depending on the **context** in which they're used. Consider these examples:

> The burglar was *shot* by the police.
>
> After the sales meeting, my whole day was *shot*.
>
> He gave me a *shot* of whiskey.

Most native speakers would immediately grasp from the context the different meanings of *shot* in these sentences. In the first example, *shot* means "gunshot"; in the second, it means "ruined"; in the third, it means "measure" or "portion." Depending on how much or how little English they know, many students would find these different meanings baffling.

Here are some other examples of words whose meanings change with context:

> When he heard the news, he went into *shock*.
>
> His freckled face was topped by a *shock* of red hair.
>
> Let me just *lie* here on the green grass.
>
> What that man just told you is a big *lie*.

In the first example, *shock* means "a state of profound depression of the vital processes of the body"; in the second, it means "a thick mass." In its first use, *lie* means "to be in a reclining position"; in the second example, it means "an untruth."

IN A NUTSHELL

- Language consists of two main parts: pronunciation and grammar.
- If you're a native speaker, you know more about grammar than you think.
- Native speakers and ESL students face different problems in learning how to write English well.
- Some English words get their meanings from the way they are pronounced.
- *Homonyms* are words that sound alike but have different meanings.
- Context often determines the meanings of words.

PRACTICE 3

Working with a partner, define the underlined words whose meanings change with context.

1. The foreign student carried a single grip./Her grip was surprisingly firm.

   ____

   ____

2. The bird's wing was broken./The vote of the right wing was behind her.

   ____

   ____

3. She said she was fed up./The dogs were well fed.

   ____

   ____

4. He spread the jam carefully./Her ranch was quite a spread.

   ____

   ____

5. The team beat us badly./I love the beat of their latest hit.

   ____

   ____

6. Last year net profits were down./He caught ten fish with a net.

   ____

   ____

7. No one is safe around drunk drivers./I keep my passport in a safe.

____

____

8. What a joint!/My knee joint hurt after I played tennis.

____

____

9. He told her to stop trying to cow him./My uncle owns a milk cow.

____

____

10. After nine innings, the score was dead even./Sundays are usually dead.

____

____

Grammar

English grammar is a difficult subject. Even professional grammarians often disagree about its rules, many of which sometimes seem ridiculous. The native speaker, who may know no more grammar than the ESL student, at least has the advantage of being able to recognize the usual and customary place for nouns and verbs in a sentence. It is the rare native speaker, for example, who would say, "I to the store now go," putting the verb in the wrong place. Likewise, native speakers are unlikely to make prepositional errors such as saying, "Peggy stayed her room," leaving out the preposition *in*. Of course, native speakers do make grammatical errors. They're just likely to make errors of a different kind.

On the other hand, the proper use of prepositions and articles often baffles ESL students. An ESL student might say, "I must run to store," leaving out the "the"—an error that a native speaker is unlikely to make. Yet another difficulty often encountered by ESL students is in the use of pronouns. A **pronoun** is a word that takes the place of a noun. ESL students tend to omit pronouns, as in the putative sentence "The students shouted when won the football game," leaving out the pronoun *they*. Another tendency that ESL students have is to use both a noun and a pronoun referring to the noun in the same sentence, as in "My boss, she increased my hourly pay." The ear of most native speakers would immediately detect this error.

Many foreign students, especially those from countries such as China, Japan, and Russia, where the grammar of the native language is totally different from English, find it hard to write English correctly. We have had students complain in mournful tones, "I go over my writing again and again in order to make sure that I have corrected all grammar errors, but my teacher always finds more." Take heart, because millions of immigrants have arrived in America knowing absolutely no English and still have mastered it sufficiently not only to survive, but to prosper.

In this book, we will teach English grammar while addressing the basic differences between the ESL student and the native speaker. When we come across a usage that ESL students are known to have trouble with, we will issue an **ESL Advice,** warning students to be particularly careful. We will then follow up that warning with numerous drills. When the ear is an unreliable guide to a particular item of usage, we will issue an **Ear Alert,** warning the native speaker that the rule must be mastered.

Both populations should benefit from this dual approach. The native speaker, who has the ear but probably lacks grounding in the formal rules, will benefit from the extra drills. On the other hand, the ESL student, who may lack the ear but is getting solid training in the formal rules, will gradually become familiar with ordinary idiomatic usage. In either case, the goal is the same: to learn to write and speak English better. And in both cases, whoever you are, if you apply yourself to this book, you will reach that goal.

PRACTICE 4

Using your ear or your grasp of the rules, correct the grammar mistakes in the following sentences. If the sentence is correctly written, mark a *C* beside it.

1. Yesterday I went to church.
2. I believe she breaked my skateboard.
3. Foreign students are special people.
4. Television in the living room needs fixing.
5. He opened up heart to her.
6. He must buy broom.
7. He said he was lonely and needed friend.
8. Last night he the book tried to read.
9. Come to me, my melancholy baby.
10. You everything very well understand.

Idioms

An **idiom** is a phrase or expression that means something different than what it seems to say. For example, the sentence "That guy is a fish out of water" does not mean that the person being described actually resembles a beached fish. It means, instead, that the person is in an uncomfortable position. Likewise, to say "I felt my heart leap into my throat" does not mean that the speaker's heart actually moved. Rather, it means that the speaker was terrified. Native speakers immediately get these meanings; ESL students may or may not, depending on their familiarity with such idioms.

To the ESL student, idioms can be a nightmare. The problem is that while there is sometimes a natural logic to an idiom, just as often there is not. For example, to say that someone is a "fifth wheel"—meaning "unnecessary"—immediately brings to mind an image of uselessness, which is exactly what a fifth wheel would be, giving a natural logic to that particular expression. But what does "kick the bucket," which means "to die," have to do with dying? No doubt, there was once a logical connection between the two. But it has long been lost to most of us. What we are left with is an expression that is common in conversational English but means something totally different from what its individual words would suggest. That is the trademark of an idiom.

It is not only the colorful phrases of idioms that ESL students find troublesome. What is also hard for them is learning how words are customarily grouped to make up conversational expressions. For example, we heard a foreign student say to another who was about to take a test, "Have a good luck!" What the student meant was clear, and strictly speaking, there was nothing ungrammatical about what she had said. It's just that no native speaker would ever phrase it that way. What a native speaker would have said was, "Good luck!" In another example, an ESL student wrote in an essay, "I altered my mind on this question," whereas a native speaker would write, "I changed my mind on this question." The phrase "altered my mind" is not technically wrong; however, it is unidiomatic.

Here, for example, is a letter written by a European travel agent to an American client:

> I have received your dated fax May 3. I communicate to you that we are in accord on the appointment for Friday, May 25. We request you contact us the same day to be at the hour that is convenient. The place of the appointment, if you believe it opportune, can be in our office. Receive a cordial greeting as we transmit our best wishes.
>
> Manuel Ortega

No word in this brief letter is misspelled, and the grammar is not wrong. Still, the letter sounds foreign because the writer has not mastered idiomatic English. Rewritten in everyday English, the letter might sound like this:

> I received your fax dated May 3 and wish to confirm our appointment on Friday, May 25. We ask that you contact us on that day to

arrange for a convenient meeting time. If you don't mind, we can meet in our office.

Cordially, sending our best wishes,

Manuel Ortega

Yet, as difficult as it might be, with practice and exposure to conversational English, ESL students will gradually gain a mastery over the idioms of their adopted language.

IN A NUTSHELL

- ESL students and native speakers often make different kinds of mistakes.
- Idioms often give ESL students trouble.
- This book takes a dual approach that helps both the ESL student and the native speaker.

PRACTICE 5

In the space provided, check the sentence that is in idiomatic English.

1. ____ (a) In obedience with the laws of New York, we must stop using so much electricity.

   ____ (b) In accordance with the laws of New York, we must stop using so much electricity.

2. ____ (a) What a weeping shame that she didn't graduate from Chico High.

   ____ (b) What a crying shame that she didn't graduate from Chico High.

3. ____ (a) If it takes me a thousand years, I'll get even to that thief.

   ____ (b) If it takes me a thousand years, I'll get even with that thief.

4. ____ (a) By asking her that question, he really put her on the spot.

   ____ (b) By asking her that question, he really put her in the spot.

5. ____ (a) Henry decided to stick to his guns by telling her not to call him again.

   ____ (b) Henry decided to make his guns stick by telling her not to call him again.

6. ____ (a) She gives off an air of suffering.

   ____ (b) She gives off a breeze of suffering.

7. ____ (a) He said that he would try as difficult as he could.

____ (b) He said that he would try as hard as he could.

8. ____ (a) All the effort she made on our behalf came to nothing.

____ (b) All the effort she made in our behalf arrived at nothing.

9. ____ (a) She plays checkers, but she's better at chess.

____ (b) She plays checkers, but she's better in chess.

10. ____ (a) My mother is a treasure.

____ (b) My mother is a fortune.

PRACTICE 6

On the lines provided, write the meanings of the following idiomatic sentences.

1. He's a penny pincher.

____

2. When it comes to that question, we're night and day.

____

3. She said that she had had her nose to the grindstone.

____

4. Lately, my friend Jim has been burning the midnight oil.

____

5. Keep your eyes peeled for Connecticut Street.

____

6. This is a far cry from what you said you'd do.

____

7. The pitch that he hit for a home run was right in his strike zone.

____

8. His generosity floored us.

____

9. Our negotiations have hit a stone wall.

____

10. The Wilsons spent a pretty penny remodeling their home.

____

The Importance of Speaking and Writing Well

Why is it important that you speak and write well? Realizing that we're on shaky ground to even bring the subject up, we still think that the question deserves an answer. In a free society where people are entitled to talk the way they choose, to insist that everyone read and write according to some academic standard might seem like snobbery. But in fact, although our society is indeed free, people still judge one another by their style of talking and writing. Many stories from ancient times have hammered home this truth. There is the story, for example, of a rich Greek merchant who takes his son to meet a renowned philosopher and head of a distinguished school to which the father hopes his son will be admitted. Looking at the boy standing no more than five feet away from him, the philosopher says, "Speak, so I can see you."

It may seem to be a puzzling remark, but in fact, its meaning is quite plain. The outer man or woman can disguise with stylish clothes what he or she is really like. But the clothes worn by the inner person is language, and language is see-through clothing. If the boy had answered, "What you talkin' 'bout, man? You blind or something? You think you be some kind o' big shot?" his language would have painted him in a very bad light.

Every time you open your mouth or put pen to paper, you say something about someone or some topic and also about yourself. You reveal your level of education. You make a statement about your ability to reason and to think. Napoleon, when presented with a candidate for a certain office, asked, "Has he written anything? Let me see his style." Whether or not the story is true, it unmistakably belongs to the same tradition as the one about the philosopher and says the same thing: How you speak and write matters more than you might think.

Language exists in a continuous chain of usage that runs from the most conventional standards to ghetto speak. You do not have to speak or write from one particular part of the chain all the time. Depending on the context of communication, everyone is free to move up and down the usage chain, in both writing and speaking. You would not talk to your senior professor of philosophy in the same way you would to your best friend. Common sense suggests that it is not only sensible to adjust what you say and how you say it before different audiences, it is also necessary.

Many of us use different variations of English throughout a typical day. Some people, Jamaicans for example, speak among themselves a kind of English that is utterly incomprehensible to a non-user. Can you tell what this means?

> Me a go left unu. (deep patois)

If you're baffled, it's no wonder. That sentence is from the deepest *patois* that Jamaicans speak. (*Patois,* a French word that means *dialect,* is what Jamaicans call the language they speak among each other.) The same thought can be expressed in many different ways by variations in the usage chain. For example, what does this mean?

> Me a go leave unu. (moderate patois)

Probably, you still don't know what this means. Here's the same sentence expressed in different variations:

> Me going leave you. (lighter patois)
>
> I go leave you. (informal English)
>
> I'm going to leave you. (standard English)
>
> ("Unu" is the Jamaican patois equivalent of *you.*)

A similar ranking can be applied to any language. The educated speaker or writer can move among the variations of language as necessary. The uneducated writer or speaker, however, is stuck at one level. Education always teaches alternatives, and the practical effect of having alternative varieties of English is that you can adjust your language, depending on whom you are speaking to or why.

So why is it important that you learn to speak and write standard English? It is important because you do not want to be stereotyped by the way you write or talk. Language is supposed to be race neutral and class neutral, but in fact, it isn't. We judge each other by the way we write and talk. Language is also used to indicate a belongingness to a certain people or group. The Jamaican taxi driver who has an American passenger will speak standard English. Transporting a Jamaican passenger, the same driver would probably speak a variation of patois. The point of being educated is to use and understand alternatives. The person who speaks and understands "Me a go left unu," as well as "I'm going to leave you," has more options for expressing him- or herself than a person who is stuck at one level.

So, for the time being, "Me a go left unu."

But I'll be back in the next chapter.

IN A NUTSHELL

The language you speak and write helps define you as a person to others.

Unit Test

In each pair of sentences, check the sentence that is correct.

Example: _____ **(a)** Native speakers often have an ear for correct language, but don't know the rules.

_____ **(b)** Non-native speakers usually have a better ear for correct English than do native speakers.

1. _____ **(a)** The two main parts of language are mind and tongue.

_____ **(b)** The two main parts of language are sounds and rules.

2. ______ **(a)** Both native and non-native speakers begin learning the English language at the same place.

______ **(b)** Native and non-native speakers do not begin at the same place in learning English.

3. ______ **(a)** The non-native speaker often knows the rules of grammar better than the native speaker.

______ **(b)** It is impossible to teach adult ESL students correct English.

4. ______ **(a)** Many words in English take on a different meaning, depending on how they are pronounced.

______ **(b)** Once you know how to pronounce a word, you will know what it means.

5. ______ **(a)** In the case of homonyms, spelling is not important.

______ **(b)** In the case of homonyms, spelling determines the meaning.

6. ______ **(a)** The rules of English grammar are completely consistent.

______ **(b)** Even professional grammarians don't agree on all grammar rules.

7. ______ **(a)** When your ear fails to give you the correct English, you must memorize the rule.

______ **(b)** Always trust your ear to point out the correct English.

8. ______ **(a)** "I paid top dollar for that coat" is an idiomatic expression.

______ **(b)** One should never use idiomatic expressions.

9. ______ **(a)** "I live in the United States" is an idiomatic expression.

______ **(b)** "Let's drum up support for the candidate" is an idiomatic expression.

10. ______ **(a)** Most foreign students say that they find English difficult to learn.

______ **(b)** Most foreign students say that they find English easy to learn.

Unit Talk–Write Assignment

An ESL student and a native speaker have a talk about English. Correct any mistakes you find in any of the sentences. Rewrite any that you think are too idiomatic to be understood by a foreign speaker familiar only with textbook English.

TALK	WRITE
Student No. 1: For me, English it is very difficult.	______________________ ______________________

Student No. 2: Nah, man. It's a piece of cake.

Student No. 1: But how can that be? It is not food.

Student No. 2: What I mean is that it's a snap. Nothing to it. I could do it in my sleep.

Student No. 1: Do you talk in sleep?

Student No. 2: We're not on the same wavelength, man. You're not with the program.

Student No. 1: What program you mean?

Student No. 2: No program, dude. You're just missing the mark.

Student No. 1: Where is this missing mark?

Student No. 2: You're driving me nuts. I'm trying to tell you something, but you keep missing the boat!

Student No. 1: What exactly you trying say?

Student No. 2: Nothing, man. A big fat zero.

Student No. 1: I was saying that, for me, English is hard.

Student No. 2: You got that right! Things are tough all over.

Student No. 1: What things you mean?

Student No. 2: Gimme a break, man.

Student No. 1: Yes, it is lunchtime.

Student No. 2: What's cooking in your English class today, man?

Student No. 1: I think prepositions are cooking.

Student No. 2: That's cool.

Unit Collaborative Assignment

Get together with three other students. Take turns having one student read aloud the questions that follow to the other three in the group. Listen to how, one by one, each of the three students responds casually to the question, perhaps even using idiomatic expressions. The one who has asked the question will write down the answers given. After all five questions have been answered, sit down with the group and rewrite the answers in formal English, avoiding idiomatic expressions that might be confusing to ESL students.

1. How important is the Internet to the present generation of college students?
2. What is your opinion of people who want to climb Mount Everest when it is known to be so dangerous?
3. What do you think the most popular mode of transportation will be in the year 2100?
4. What do you think of the philosophical admonition "Be yourself; do your best"?
5. What is your opinion of same-sex marriage?

Unit Writing Assignment

Write a paragraph in which you explain what an idiom is. Use examples to clarify your definition.

Photo Writing Assignment

Look carefully at this photo of two students from widely different cultures studying on the same campus, perhaps even taking the same courses. Then write a paragraph about what practical steps both American students and foreign students can take to bridge the existing culture gap between them. Consider such gestures of friendship as meeting to learn about each other's religion, or hosting a get-together where students can mingle and discuss their cultural differences.

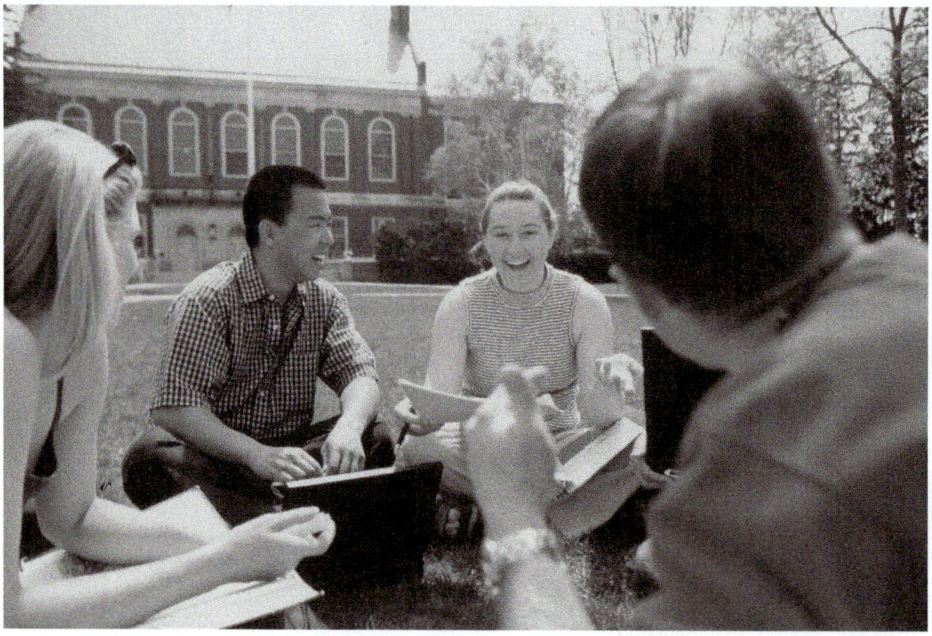

2 Myths About Writing

"Anyone who's not dead has something to write about."

If you can "talk" English, you can learn to write it. Indeed, you already know more about writing than you think. If you are like most students, though, you probably believe some common and harmful myths about writing—our own students often do. Most likely, you use these myths to belittle your natural writing skills.

If a myth leads you to think that you write badly, you'll probably try to avoid writing. Practice makes perfect in writing (as in nearly everything else), so if you avoid writing, you won't get any better at it. To think that you are naturally bad at writing is to plant a nagging critic inside your head who will scold every sentence you scribble. No one works well with constant scolding; everyone works better if encouraged. Human nature swims on "You can!" and drowns on "You can't!"

We begin, then, with a discussion of some myths about writing and how believing them can stunt your growth as a writer.

Myths About Writing

A **myth** is a popular but false belief. Among the many myths that students believe about writing are the following:

- I have nothing to write about.
- I can't write the way you're supposed to—with big words and long sentences.
- I hate to write because I make too many mistakes.

We will take up these myths, one by one, in order.

I Have Nothing to Write About

Anyone who's not dead has something to write about. All of us have opinions that can be used as writing topics. The problem is that students often think that only stuffy, academic topics are suitable for college essays.

However, you can write about many topics that are neither academic nor stuffy. You can write about an everyday event in your life, such as dating, or an idea that interests you. You can write about a friend, a hobby, or your job. You can tell about an exciting experience, a favorite teacher, a kindly uncle, or a nasty neighbor. One student we know wrote a funny essay about a goldfish. Another wrote a moving essay about burying a hamster. Everyone alive is interested in something; that something is what you can write about.

To see that you have ideas worth writing about, do the following activity, which we call Practice. Chances are that everyone in your group will be able to come up with an idea suitable for a paragraph.

PRACTICE 1

Form a group of three or four students. Choose one topic from the list that follows. Everyone in the group should take turns talking about the same topic. The purpose of this exercise is to get you involved enough to offer your opinions and to comment on the opinions of others.

If the discussion is slow to start, you might break the ice by asking a general question such as, "Has anyone here seen any good movies recently?" Or, "How do you feel about building a wall between the United States and Mexico to keep out illegal immigrants?" Or, "Which of your uncles, aunts, or cousins do you like most and why?" Keep asking questions until your group is engaged in a lively discussion.

1. A movie I recently saw
2. My favorite television show
3. An event much discussed in the news media
4. My favorite relative
5. One of the worst problems in our society

I can't write the way you're supposed to—with big words and long sentences.

The first aim of any writer is to communicate. If using big words and long sentences will get a message across, a writer will use them. Ask yourself, though, how often do big words and long sentences help anyone communicate? The answer is *almost never*. Writers use big words and long sentences only when small words and short sentences will not do the job. Small words and short sentences often make the point as well as, if not better than, big words and long sentences.

Writers mainly want to get a message across, and few people like reading big words clumped together in jaw-breaking sentences. Understanding such writing simply takes too much effort. Look at the following passages, for example. Which one do you think is better written and easier to understand?

> The audience was lachrymose at the termination of the drama, especially expressing a predilection for the heroine's experienced reunification with her long-lost progeny.

> The audience was tearful at the end of the play. They especially liked when the heroine was reunited with her long-lost children.

The first passage consists of big words in one python-long sentence; the second uses simple words and two straightforward sentences. The second passage, by being direct and clear, is better than the first because it is easier to read and understand.

Directness and clarity are desirable qualities of good writing, not big words and long sentences. This book will teach you how to write clearly, directly, and always understandably.

PRACTICE 2

Get together in a small group. Each student should choose one topic from the list that follows and "talk a paragraph" about it for a minute or less. More than one person in the group may select the same topic. When it is your turn to speak, be as clear and direct as you can. Don't try to sound wise or scholarly; just be yourself. You might want to write down a few ideas in advance so you won't ramble or beat around the bush.

1. A cause that has caught my attention
2. The best way to make new friends at college
3. A teacher whom I particularly admire
4. A teacher whom I particularly dislike
5. A college course I enjoy

PRACTICE 3

In the blank provided, check the sentence that is simpler and better.

1. ____ (a) The trees assumed a verdant hue because of heavy precipitation.

   ____ (b) The trees looked green because of the heavy rain last week.

2. ____ (a) We are planning to have a quick snack in the student cafeteria.

   ____ (b) We are devising a scheme to have a quick snack in the student cafeteria.

3. ____ (a) Henry was laid off because the garage where he worked went bankrupt.

____ (b) Henry experienced an involuntary termination when his place of employment was beset by financial reversals.

4. ____ (a) Can I persuade you to purchase this previously owned automotive vehicle?

____ (b) Can I talk you into buying this used car?

5. ____ (a) This cosmetic product will conceal the blemishes that commonly erupt on the skin of adolescents.

____ (b) This makeup will hide all of the pimples that tend to break out on teenagers' skin.

6. ____ (a) Jack was unmoved by my words, and he hung up in anger.

____ (b) Jack was indifferent to my verbal harangue, and he hung up in fury.

7. ____ (a) As you assist other humans, you diminish your own anguish.

____ (b) As you help others, you lessen your own pain.

8. ____ (a) Our trepidations often outweigh the situational actuality.

____ (b) Our fears are often worse than the reality.

9. ____ (a) My dad would rather work on his computer than talk with me.

____ (b) My dad reveals a preference for his computer over conversing with me.

10. ____ (a) One morning he perceived the peculiar sound of crutches outside his dormitory room.

____ (b) One morning he heard the unmistakable thump of crutches outside his dorm room.

I hate to write because I make too many mistakes.

Everyone who writes or talks occasionally makes mistakes. We came across this sentence, for example, in a scholarly book about the Civil War's Union General William Tecumseh Sherman:

> When victory was achieved, however, [the army should] stop the bloodshed and destruction immediately and help those in need irregardless of any oaths of allegiance.

Irregardless is not a standard word. If you check your dictionary, you'll see that the author should have written *regardless.*

In speech, every one of us has at one time or another mispronounced a word, addressed someone by a wrong name, or misspoken a common phrase. Mistakes in speech are so common that many even have names. Here, for example, is a **spoonerism,** a mistake where a speaker mixes up the initial letters of words:

Will someone please hick up my pat?

What the speaker meant was, *Will someone please pick up my hat?*

Grammatical mistakes can be occasionally found in the most improbable places. The odd thing about grammar is that we're seldom praised for being grammatically correct but are far more likely to be criticized when we are not. Using good grammar does not make us virtuous or holier than thou, but it does help us make ourselves understood. For example, many people will say, "He *snuck* into my room," which is understandable to a native speaker but not necessarily to a nonnative speaker since "sneaked" not "snuck" is the past tense of the verb "to sneak." The correct sentence is "He *sneaked* into my room." Many grammatical errors involve such small matters of misusage. *Unintended errors* can creep into our language, both in speaking and writing. For instance, you might say, "I'm proud of my Indian posterity," when you really meant "ancestry," not "posterity." Good grammar is like good table manners; it is missed only when it's absent.

Everyone makes an occasional grammatical error. As we pointed out earlier, English offers a wide range of alternatives for the expression of almost any idea. This flexibility makes it easy for anyone to misspeak. Here is an example taken from a note that a student's father recently received from a business in Beijing: "We sorry for mistake. Please you be patient and wait to receiving the right jade horse." In perfect English, the letter might have read something like this: "We apologize for the mistake. Please be patient until we send you the right jade horse." In spite of all the obstacles, ESL students are quick to pick up and practice the rules of grammar to an extent we often find amazing.

The bottom line is that no one knows everything about the language. Like the rest of us, you have your strengths and weaknesses. If you are a native speaker, this book can teach you how to use your natural ear for the language to help your writing. If you are an ESL student, it will tell you what you need to know about English to write and speak it well.

Let us begin with what you know. Take the following quiz. We think you will be pleasantly surprised to find out how much you already naturally know about English.

PRACTICE 4

Using your ear for the language, check the space in front of any sentence that you think is incorrect. If you think a sentence is correct, leave the space blank.

1. ____ Johnny is bad boy.
2. ____ Atlanta is the capital of Georgia.
3. ____ My mother has never went college.
4. ____ You see what I have to put up with?
5. ____ I speak quick because I be nervous.
6. ____ You out the door go.
7. ____ Where are you going today?
8. ____ That ticket costed me $5.00.

9. ____ Go to your room.
10. ____ She is a better cook than me is.

Here are the correct sentences:

1. Johnny is a bad boy. (original omits the *a*)
2. Atlanta is the capital of Georgia. (correct as written)
3. My mother never went to college. (should be *went to*)
4. You see what I have to put up with? (correct as written)
5. I speak quickly because I'm nervous. (should be *quickly* and *I'm*)
6. You go out the door. (verb *go* is in the wrong place)
7. Where are you going today? (correct as written)
8. That ticket cost me $5.00. (*costed* is not a word)
9. Go to your room. (correct as written)
10. She is a better cook than I am. (not *me is*)

To sum up, don't approach writing as if it were a kind of communication utterly different from the speaking that you normally do. See it first as a kind of speech—but on paper. Remember, also, that if English is your mother tongue, you can use your native ear to become a better writer. And if you are an ESL student, you can learn the rules of grammar until you, too, acquire an ear for spoken English.

IN A NUTSHELL

There are three common myths about writing:

- I have nothing to write about.
- I can't write the way you're supposed to—with big words and long sentences.
- I hate to write because I make too many mistakes.

PRACTICE 5

State what you believe to be the three most serious difficulties you have with writing. State each in a separate sentence.

1. ______________________________
2. ______________________________
3. ______________________________

PRACTICE 6

Form a small group of three or four classmates and discuss the difficulties you have with writing and what you might do about them. Refer to your answers from Practice 4. Choose a person to summarize your discussion for the other groups in your class.

Standard English

If you can speak English well, why do you sometimes have trouble writing it? The answer is simple. Writing is, for the most part, done in standard English, which is not the English we commonly speak.

Standard English is English that is universally found in dictionaries and accepted by respected authorities. It is the English that all people who speak and understand English can use to communicate. Just as plumbing pipes have standard sizes and fittings, so standard English has a standard vocabulary—no slang or street talk—and a standard grammar. Without standards, English would become so regional that a New Yorker might have a hard time communicating with a Californian or a Georgian. With standard English, however, all who speak the language can make themselves understood, at least on one level.

Consider, for examples, these pairs of sentences, labeled *standard* and *nonstandard*:

Standard: What's happening?
Nonstandard: What's cooking?

Standard: Last night we had fun.
Nonstandard: Last night we got wasted.

Standard: Isn't it a shame that Jody was arrested by the police?
Nonstandard: Ain't it awful that Jody got busted by the cops?

Realistically, which sentence in each pair do you think, say, a native Russian who speaks only textbook English would be more likely to understand? The nonstandard sentences would be understandable only to those who have an ear for nonstandard English.

Even if you speak mainly nonstandard English, you also have an ear for standard English. Every day, you hear it in television and radio newscasts and you read it in magazines and newspapers. Even the supermarket tabloids with their alien three-headed babies and prowling Bigfoots are written in standard English. In fact, you are more likely to read this standard English headline in a tabloid,

> Bigfoot Spotted by Campers in Yosemite!

than this nonstandard one:

> Campers Scope Out Bigfoot in Yosemite!

Your ear, however, cannot help you with some finer points of standard English. For example, is this sentence correct?

> Between you and I, she can't spell.

The answer is *no*. The *I* is wrong. The correct sentence would read,

> Between you and me, she can't spell.

Yet practically every day we hear people say *between you and I*. In standard English, that is wrong.

Do you see anything wrong with this statement?

> Tomorrow I am going to ask my dad to loan me $100.

In standard English, the word *loan* is a noun and is not used as a verb. The sentence in standard English is this:

> Tomorrow I am going to ask my dad to lend me $100.

or

> Tomorrow I am going to ask my dad for a $100 loan.

To sum up, use your ear for the language to help you with your writing, but remember that your ear can sometimes mislead you. To become the best writer you can be, you must also learn certain ground rules for works written in standard English. You must avoid slang, or the dialect of everyday conversation. You must learn the rules of capitalization and punctuation and how to use prepositions correctly (*between you and me*), adverbs (*I speak quickly,* not *I speak quick*), and verbs (*cost,* not *costed*). Whether you're a native speaker or an ESL student, learning even a teaspoon of grammar will help your writing.

IN A NUTSHELL

- Standard English is English that is found universally in dictionaries and accepted by respected authorities.
- Even if you speak nonstandard English, you still have an ear for standard English.
- This ear can usually help you with your writing. When it can't, this book will help you.

PRACTICE 7

From the following pairs of sentences, check the ones written in standard English.

1. ____ **(a)** You ain't gotta convince me, Joe.

____ **(b)** You aren't going to convince me, Joe.

2. ____ (a) It seems strange that no one has any homework.

____ (b) It seems awful fishy that no one has any homework.

3. ____ (a) Mrs. Lopez is tough about discipline; she don't mess around with rude students.

____ (b) Mrs. Lopez is strict about discipline; she doesn't tolerate rude students.

4. ____ (a) Don't be difficult.

____ (b) Don't be such a pain.

5. ____ (a) He doesn't care the slightest whether or not I have money.

____ (b) He doesn't give a damn about whether or not I have money.

6. ____ (a) I'm fixing to bake a pie.

____ (b) I am getting ready to bake a pie.

7. ____ (a) Old bags like us don't need all that hip shakin' no more.

____ (b) Old women like us don't need all that dancing anymore.

8. ____ (a) Practice hard and you'll be the big man on campus.

____ (b) Practice hard and you'll stand out from the others.

9. ____ (a) I would appreciate your driving me to the store.

____ (b) I'd appreciate it if you'd take me to the store.

10. ____ (a) We all wish she'd mellow out.

____ (b) We all wish she'd be less nervous.

PRACTICE 8

Below are two paragraphs from a newspaper interview with Tyson Beckford, one of the most popular African-American male models working today. Underline the sentences or phrases that are nonstandard English. Then rewrite both paragraphs in standard English.

I had just dropped out of college, Rockland Community College in Rockland, N.Y. I was just kicking back, no job, nothing. College wasn't for me. . . . I wanted to get into the entertainment field, either entertainment or acting. I never thought of modeling, never that. When that took off, I was like, "Wow." Modeling wasn't known as something masculine, something cool to do.

____

____

____

____

____

I was just chillin' in Washington Square Park in New York. And a fashion editor for *Source* magazine came up to me and asked me to model. I said no. And with some convincing they got me to do it. I didn't think it was real. They just told me where it could lead to, like acting. So I was, like, "OK, that's cool, I'll do it." The photo shoot was easy. I was like, "They pay you to do this? I can do this."

PRACTICE 9

On a separate sheet of paper, write two paragraphs on one of the topics that follow. In the first paragraph, feel free to use nonstandard English. In the second, use only standard English.

1. A person who is not famous whom I admire
2. What I like to do in my spare time
3. Something memorable that once happened to me
4. The value of difficult times in my life
5. Why so many people believe in superstitions

Unit Test

In the blank provided, mark *T* if the statement is true, or *F* if the statement is false.

1. _____ A myth is the same as a fact.
2. _____ If you can speak English, you can learn to write it.
3. _____ Even people who are dead have something to write about.

4. ______ To write well, you must use big words and long sentences.
5. ______ The first aim of a writer is to impress the reader.
6. ______ Directness and clarity are desirable qualities of good writing.
7. ______ Everyone who writes or speaks occasionally makes mistakes.
8. ______ Standard English is what you hear spoken on the streets.
9. ______ The purpose of standard English is to have a common way for English-speaking people to communicate.
10. ______ When your ear is of no help, you have to go by the rules of standard English.

Unit Talk–Write Assignment

The *Talk* column on the left side of this page contains sentences from a student's casual conversation with a friend. Many of these sentences use nonstandard phrases, suitable for casual speech but not for formal writing. Rewrite the sentences in the blanks provided under the *Write* column, converting the nonstandard phrases into their standard English equivalents. If a sentence does not need to be corrected, leave the space blank.

TALK	WRITE
1. Between you and I, Dr. Mudd, my math prof, is, like, a real flake.	______________________
2. He lets the cute chicks in the class get away with murder, but he dumps on all of us guys.	______________________
3. Math is tough to start with, so when you got a teacher who don't give a damn, how can you learn?	______________________
4. When it comes to teaching math, Popeye, as we call him, missed the boat.	______________________

5. He acts like he is a genius, dude.

6. Last Thursday, I asked him politely to explain the word problem.

7. Good old Popeye bawled me out in front of the whole class, yelling, "If you'd listened, I wouldn't have to waste class time repeating."

8. Don't this creep realize how lousy he is?

9. I mean, gimme a break. A teacher ought to be patient.

10. I mean, like, you know?

Unit Collaborative Assignment

Get together with a classmate and describe to him or her a job you now or once had and how you feel about it. Then use your discussion to write about the job in standard English.

Unit Writing Assignment

Project 10 years into the future. Write about who you would like to be and what work you would like to be doing by then. Use standard English.

Here is how one student accomplished the assignment:

Ten years from now I would like to be a famous costume designer. That is, I would like to be the kind of costume designer that movie studios hire to research what clothes people were wearing at a certain time in history. For instance, the movie *Gone with the Wind* required female gowns with lace bodices, taffeta petticoats, and broad-brimmed hats. It required male frock coats, stiff shirts, and top hats. I can't imagine a bigger thrill than to have my name called during an Academy Award ceremony and to be asked to walk up to the stage to receive an Oscar for the Best Costume Design. I see myself owning my own design studio, with dozens of helpers to execute my designs. But I would always do the mock-ups myself, to make sure that the details are perfect. This is my dream, but sometimes dreams come true, don't they?

Photo Writing Assignment

Natural disasters are unfortunate facts of life. The following photo depicts the horrors of one such catastrophic event. Think about the impact that such random disasters have on everyday life, along with the terrible consequences they leave behind: death, injury, grief, financial burdens, and increased health costs. After mulling over such ideas, write a paragraph expressing how you feel about any recent natural disaster. Did it make you angry? Whom do you blame? What lessons can be learned? How can one prepare for such a calamity? Use only standard English.

3 How to Start Writing

"In their working habits, writers tend to resemble baseball pitchers. For both, warming up is essential."

Before you begin writing, you should understand that learning how to write is not a topic but a process. What is the difference between the two? A topic can be learned from a book. A process seldom can be. The history of the bicycle is a topic. Learning how to ride a bicycle is a process.

There are some obvious differences between studying a topic and learning a process. You can learn about the history of the bicycle by reading books on the topic. But reading a thousand books about the bicycle won't teach you how to ride one. That's because riding the bicycle is a process you learn only by doing.

It is the same with writing. You learn how to write by writing. Learning how to write is a process that involves many variations. Some people are what is known as "distillers." They sit and think and work out everything in their minds before they begin to write. When they have the first draft down on paper, they rewrite it repeatedly. Other writers are "gushers." They blow up like a volcano, splattering all their thoughts over the page. They seldom go back over what they've written.

We do not recommend *gushing* as a method of writing. It works better for fiction or other emotional writing than for factual prose. The best way to approach college writing is to commit yourself in advance to doing at least three drafts. Obviously, for an in-class assignment, doing three drafts is not practical. But if you have the opportunity to work at home on the assignment, you should write at least three drafts.

The first draft you can do any way you want. If you feel like gushing, you should gush. If you feel like thinking about the topic and then writing about it, go ahead. Instructors seldom see a first draft. It can be as neat or as messy as you please. In it, you are simply trying to get down the basics—how you feel about the topic, what opinions you have on it, and what facts you have learned about it. Your paper should look like a document written by a committee. It should be scribbled over from top to bottom and have lots of marginal rewriting.

Your second draft is when you begin finishing the material. You read it with as much openness and honesty as you can, correcting as you go. You change paragraphs, you rewrite sentences, you choose better words, and you might even add or remove some facts. If you have done your job well, the paper by now looks respectable. It is not dressed up enough to attend a formal dinner party, but it is presentable enough to go out in public.

Your third draft is where you polish what you have written. You correct misspelled words. You add punctuation to increase the clarity or flow of your writing. You delete useless words or phrases that bloat your paper. You check your grammar. In short, you do all you can to repair and polish up your work.

But the process is not yet done. What you might find as you complete the third draft is that you made a horrible mistake, such as leaving out some significant information. Or you might find that the source you depended on most heavily was flawed, making your entire opinion wrong. The only way to repair the mistake is to start writing the paper all over again.

The process of writing does not proceed in a straight line. Laboratory studies of composing writers have confirmed that composing is a circular process. We begin a paragraph, scribble a few lines, go back to the opening sentence and fuss with it for a while, then we resume where we left off. If you find yourself doing that, you are working like a real writer.

IN A NUTSHELL

Writing is a circular process.

Writing is always hardest at the beginning, when the page is blank. We start to write, find the going slow, and imagine that our secret fears about our inability to write are confirmed.

The truth is that for nearly everyone, writing is hard and slow work. The only solution to the slow start is to get started quickly. Once the words are flowing, self-doubt will give way to the practical business of writing.

In their working habits, writers tend to resemble baseball pitchers. For both, warming up is essential. Pitchers throw practice balls to flex their arms; similarly, writers warm up their writing skills by scribbling words on the page. Indeed, the longer you sit and write, the better you will gradually find yourself getting at it.

There are four things that you can do to start writing:

- Freewrite
- Keep a journal
- Brainstorm
- Cluster

All four activities will help you to warm up, get ideas, and arrive at a suitable writing topic.

Freewriting

A good warm-up exercise for the writer is freewriting. To **freewrite** is to write about a topic for a timed period of about 10 minutes. Forget about grammar, spelling, and punctuation. Just sit and write freely. If you have nothing to say, write, "I have nothing to say," until you do say something. The result of such freewriting will be sense mixed with nonsense, but you'll gradually find yourself warming up to the topic.

Here is an example of student freewriting:

> I go to school every day. Then I go to work. I have no time for myself. It's rough. What'd I say now? I can't think of anything to say. That reminds me, I do my best thinking in the bathroom. I like to think in the bathroom because when you are in their you can close the door shut and everyone leaves you alone. I don't know what else to say. The cat keeps out of there and so do the dog. This sounds weird, but I tend to be a weird type of guy with a lot in my head some days. I hate going straight from school to work. I feel like I'm jumping from one planet to another. This is a really, really weird paragraph. I wish I was going to a movie with Maria tonight. She's good for getting my mind off school. But she gotta go to work too. So what can I say?

Notice that the paragraph contains many spelling and grammatical errors. For example, in the sentence, "*I* like to think in the bathroom because when *you* are in *their* you can close the door shut and everyone leaves you alone," the writer misuses *their* for *there,* and shifts the point of view from *I* to *you.* The sentence "The cat keeps out of there and so *do* the dog" should really read, "The cat keeps out of there and so *does* the dog." These kinds of errors are normal and expected in freewriting.

The writer's thinking might also strike you as jumbled. Some of what he says makes sense—that he does his best thinking in the bathroom, for example—but other sentences seem to hop aimlessly from this to that. In freewriting, this mix of sense and nonsense is always a good sign. It shows that you are writing and thinking freely, which is what you are supposed to do in a loosening-up exercise.

Your own attempts at freewriting should be similarly loose. Don't try to correct your mistakes, control your writing, or muzzle your thoughts. Freewriting should be as free and uncontrolled as a pitcher's warm-up tosses. The aim in both cases is the same: to warm up, whether the arm or the brain.

Keeping a Journal

A good way to practice your writing skills is to keep a journal. A **journal** is private writing intended for your eyes only. Regularly keeping a journal teaches some good habits. First, you'll get in the habit of writing freely without fear of criticism or disapproval. Second, keeping a journal can lead to surprising self-discoveries. Often, writers do not really know how they feel about a topic until they try writing about it. You may be surprised when you try to express your feelings in a journal to find out how you really feel about a topic. Finally, keeping a journal will get you into the habit of writing regularly. If you are like most students, you write mainly under pressure—for example, when you have to take a test or do an assignment. Anything done only under pressure can hardly be fun. Journal writing can at least get you used to the idea of writing as a means of relaxation rather than a constant source of stress.

Your journal does not have to be a diary. That is, it does not have to faithfully record everything that happened during the day. You can include anything you have read that impressed you, a wise piece of advice by someone you admire, newsclippings, and even photos if they stimulate ideas for your writing. Here is an example of a useful journal entry:

> Today Fran kept complaining about her boyfriend Luke and how he always tries to make her feel jealous by flirting with other girls. I thought to myself, "Fran, quit giving him the power to make you jealous. If you didn't react to his flirting, he would probably quit." Once you learn not to react to people's provocations, they'll stop.

That journal entry is a good start to an essay on jealousy.

IN A NUTSHELL

- Writing is most difficult in the beginning.
- Warming up is critical for the writer.
- You can warm up by freewriting.
- Keeping a journal can help your writing.

PRACTICE 1

Freewrite for 5 to 10 minutes on one of the topics below.

1. Something you would like to own
2. The smells in your neighborhood
3. Your favorite season of the year
4. A scary incident
5. Recurring daydreams
6. Modern music
7. A movie
8. Your career hopes
9. The qualities of a good pet
10. Your feelings about dating

PRACTICE 2

Choose any topic that pops into your mind. Fill up the freewriting box below with your own words. Use every line, even if you have to write a filler sentence such as "I can't think of anything to write."

PRACTICE 3

In this exercise, you're going to talk to yourself on paper, which is another way of saying that you'll be pretending to write a journal. Since you're writing basically for yourself, feel free to experiment and to get your feelings off your chest. Whatever you write will be read by no one else. Get in the habit of writing for yourself regularly, and you'll find it easier to write on more formal occasions.

Since this writing exercise is intended only for your eyes, you may say anything you want to and in any manner you wish. You may simply tell how the day went, jotting down its highlights and low points. Or, if you can't think of anything to say, you may write your thoughts down about one of these topics:

- Something that was most significant about the day
- Something boring that you did
- Something you saw
- An argument you had with someone
- A newspaper headline that disturbed you

- A movie ad you found atrocious (or fascinating)
- A comment about life made by one of your parents
- An attitude you had toward a certain teacher
- A discussion you had with a classmate
- How the weather affected your mood

Brainstorming

The aim of freewriting is just to get you writing. Once you're warmed up and ready to write, you need to focus on finding ideas to put down on paper. One especially good technique for finding ideas is brainstorming.

Brainstorming is an exercise in thinking. List every thought that comes to mind about a subject. Jot down words and phrases. Don't try to write in sentences or worry about logic, style, punctuation, and grammar. Above all, don't judge your ideas as they flow onto the page. Later, after the storm has passed, you can decide which ideas are worthwhile. Here is an example of brainstorming on "my neighborhood":

noisy

lots of traffic

corner stores

people don't know one another

there're few trees

a city worker told me that an oak on the corner was a hundred years old

most people take the bus to work

a few drive cars

the houses are old

some are 70 years old

my grandparents used to live in our house

we have three bedrooms

a park is down the street

many old people live there

Mrs. Ramirez is 90

Mr. Goldstein is 82

at least my parents own their home

I wished I lived in the country

Brainstorming produces a random list of ideas. When you are finished brainstorming, look over the ideas scribbled on the page and find out what you really think about the topic. As we said earlier, odd as it may seem, many writers learn what they really think about a topic only when they try writing about it.

For example, this student noticed that she kept mentioning the age of her neighborhood in her brainstorming session. Until then, she hadn't really consciously thought about its age. She decided to write a paragraph on the age of her neighborhood, using as examples its ancient oak tree, old homes, and elderly residents. Brainstorming will often give you this kind of new slant on a topic.

IN A NUTSHELL

Brainstorming is the technique of freely jotting down ideas about a topic.

PRACTICE 4

Brainstorm on one or more of the topics below. Don't worry about grammar or logic. Simply write down any idea that comes to mind, but don't stray away from the topic.

1. Your girlfriend, boyfriend, spouse, child, parent, or sibling
2. Work
3. A favorite book, magazine, or TV show
4. Clothing styles
5. Your favorite class
6. Why you love (or hate) English classes
7. Coping with problems
8. Problems that overwhelm you
9. A favorite sport
10. The role of money

Clustering

Clustering goes a step beyond brainstorming because it groups—Cluster—related ideas. You take the big subject in the middle and reduce it to a smaller idea that you put at the end of a spoke. From this smaller idea, you can branch off another idea that is even smaller. Eventually, you will not only find an idea small enough to be a manageable topic, you will also find that you have much to say about it. For example, in the clustering diagram on page 40, the topic "Fair weather friends" even suggests two names that you think belong here. These names, in turn, will no doubt bring to mind many details of these fair-weather friendships."

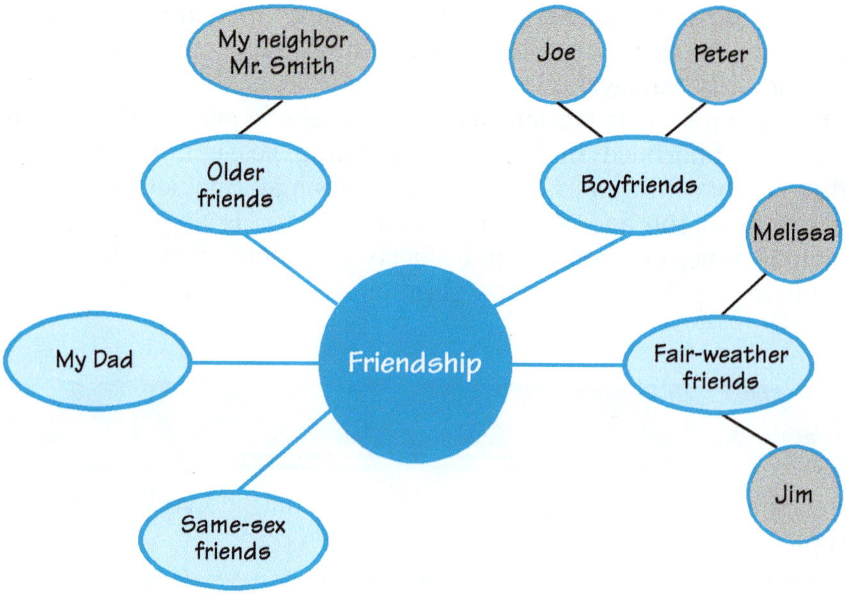

IN A NUTSHELL

Clustering is using a diagram to think about your topic.

PRACTICE 5

Do a cluster on one of the topics below.

1. Lovers
2. Malls
3. Cars
4. Runaway kids
5. Advertising
6. Graduation requirements
7. Instructors
8. Politics
9. Housework
10. Money

The Topic Sentence

You have a topic, some ideas about it, and are now ready to write your paragraph. How do you begin? You begin at the beginning—by writing a topic sentence.

The **topic sentence** is a single sentence that sums up the main point of your paragraph. It is usually the opening sentence and must not be a dry, narrow statement of fact. Rather, it should have a **discussible point** that gives you something to write about. Here is an example of weak and strong topic sentences:

Weak:	I own a blue Honda Civic.
Strong:	A Honda Civic is an ideal car for a student.

A weak topic sentence is a dead end and difficult to write about. For example, after you say that you own a blue Honda Civic, what else can you say? Nothing comes to mind without head-scratching effort.

On the other hand, notice the momentum in this topic sentence, "A Honda Civic is an ideal car for a student." The question "Why?" immediately comes to mind, and you could easily write a paragraph answering it. You could also write about what you mean by an "ideal car." Many other possibilities exist.

How can you tell if your topic sentence is discussible enough for a paragraph? You can tell by using your common sense. If your topic sentence offers nothing to discuss, you'll have trouble writing the paragraph. You'll suffer head scratching and pen chewing, and find yourself digging for something to say. The obvious thing to do when you see these signs is to rewrite your topic sentence.

ESL Advice!

Be sure to use the full verb and correct tense in your topic sentence. Don't leave out important articles in front of nouns. (Study the Revising Checklist inside the front cover of this book.)

NOT THIS:	My aunt, Pham Phong, live through the hell of watch her village destroyed during the Vietnam War.
BUT THIS:	My aunt, Pham Phong, lived through the hell of watching her village being destroyed during the Vietnam War.
NOT THIS:	From her home in Darjeeling, I had beautiful view of Kanchenjunga, one of tallest mountains in world.
BUT THIS:	From her home in Darjeeling, I had a beautiful view of Kanchenjunga, one of the tallest mountains in the world.

IN A NUTSHELL

The topic sentence of a paragraph should make a discussible point.

PRACTICE 6

Place a checkmark by the topic sentence in each group that would be easiest to write a paragraph about.

1. ____ (a) Blueberries are a nourishing food.
   ____ (b) Last week I ate a bowl of fresh blueberries.
   ____ (c) Sometimes blueberries don't taste ripe.
2. ____ (a) The primary school is in an adobe building.
   ____ (b) You get out of school what you put into it.
   ____ (c) I went to school yesterday.
3. ____ (a) Scouting builds character.
   ____ (b) The scout told me that he was happy.
   ____ (c) I have a Tenderfoot scouting badge.
4. ____ (a) The trail goes through the Sierra Madre Mountains.
   ____ (b) Rain falls every day in the Sierra Madres.
   ____ (c) The Sierra Madre Mountains are a hiker's paradise.
5. ____ (a) She told me a white lie.
   ____ (b) There are three kinds of lies.
   ____ (c) They repeated her lie.
6. ____ (a) Sometimes quitting is the right choice to make.
   ____ (b) George quit his job without telling me.
   ____ (c) The job George had was making sandwiches.
7. ____ (a) Most prisons have chaplains.
   ____ (b) Prison chaplains have changed criminals for the better.
   ____ (c) Prison chaplains don't wear uniforms.
8. ____ (a) My dog Courage is a Great Dane.
   ____ (b) My Great Dane, Courage, loves a big, hearty meal.
   ____ (c) Despite his severe arthritis, my Great Dane, Courage, lives up to his name.
9. ____ (a) Yesterday I had an X-ray taken of my ankle.
   ____ (b) It took 5 minutes to x-ray my ankle.
   ____ (c) X-ray technology helps save limbs and lives.
10. ____ (a) My sister chops up veggies when she has a lull in the day.
    ____ (b) Use downtime to accomplish small tasks that need to be done.
    ____ (c) It takes me 20 minutes to answer an average e-mail.

PRACTICE 7

Below are some topics for paragraphs. Write weak and strong topic sentences for each.

1. **Topic:** Television shows

   Weak topic sentence: ______________________________

   ____

   Strong topic sentence: ______________________________

   ____

2. **Topic:** Credit cards

   Weak topic sentence: ______________________________

   ____

   Strong topic sentence: ______________________________

   ____

3. **Topic:** Professional athletes

   Weak topic sentence: ______________________________

   ____

   Strong topic sentence: ______________________________

   ____

4. **Topic:** Housework

   Weak topic sentence: ______________________________

   ____

   Strong topic sentence: ______________________________

   ____

5. **Topic:** A Halloween memory

   Weak topic sentence: ______________________________

   ____

   Strong topic sentence: ______________________________

   ____

6. **Topic:** Messy roommates

   Weak topic sentence: ______________________________

   ____

   Strong topic sentence: ______________________________

   ____

7. **Topic:** Wearing seat belts

   Weak topic sentence: ______________________________

   ____

Strong topic sentence: ______________________________

____

8. **Topic:** Junk food

Weak topic sentence: ______________________________

____

Strong topic sentence: ______________________________

____

9. **Topic:** Tattoos

Weak topic sentence: ______________________________

____

Strong topic sentence: ______________________________

____

10. **Topic:** Restaurants

Weak topic sentence: ______________________________

____

Strong topic sentence: ______________________________

____

Unit Test

Underline the word(s) in parentheses that best completes the meaning of the sentence.

Example: Free writing is writing (free from personal worries/without paying attention to grammar, punctuation, or spelling).

1. Writing is a (circular process/topic) that can be learned from a book.
2. Writing is always most difficult when you are trying to find a (beginning/ending).
3. One helpful way to get started writing is to use a diagram to think about your topic. This technique is called (outlining/clustering).
4. Like most athletes, writers need to (warm up/take vitamin pills).
5. Once your writing flows, (your confidence will decrease/your confidence will increase).
6. The topic sentence of a paragraph (hints at what you have to say/sums up the main point of your paragraph).
7. "A hammer is used for hitting nails" is (excellent/weak) as a topic sentence.

8. The best kind of topic sentence is one (that has a discussible point/that appeals to you).
9. A weak topic sentence is one that (opens many possibilities for writing about it/leads to a dead end).
10. "Being lost in a foreign city is a frightening experience" makes a strong topic sentence because (you need not say anything more/it cries out for further explanation).

Unit Talk–Write Assignment

The *Talk* column on the left side of this page contains sentences from a student's conversation with a friend about writing. The selection includes nonstandard phrases and irrelevant material. Rewrite the sentences in the blanks provided under *Write,* making sure that you use standard English and that you stick to the point you are trying to make.

TALK	WRITE
1. I used to think writing was a bummer.	
2. But biology is even worse than writing.	
3. Brainstorming has helped me fight my fear of writing because it's so cool suddenly to get ideas that might work.	
4. When other students whine, "I'm going to crash on this assignment," I tell them to chill 'cause writing ain't as bad as they think.	
5. My roommate Jeff, who's a terrific athlete, used to freak out when he had to write an essay.	

6. But I shown him how to brainstorm, and now he thinks he's a hotshot writer.

7. Brainstorming is better than freewriting because you gotta concentrate on one topic.

8. If I freewrite, I don't get nowhere because I blab all over the place, and I just keep saying, "I can't think of nothing to say."

9. Clustering is just flat out too logical and tangled up.

10. I got me a B on my last essay because I got some good ideas brainstorming on the topic of white lies. I am beginning to kinda like writing.

Unit Collaborative Assignment

Get together with a partner and brainstorm on two of the subjects listed below.

1. Summertime memories
2. Role models
3. Anger
4. Stress
5. Television commercials
6. Energy
7. Political enemies
8. Study abroad programs

9. Credit cards
10. Obesity

Unit Writing Assignment

Choose one of the above subjects that you brainstormed about and cluster, if necessary, to produce a manageable topic. Then write about it, beginning with a discussible topic sentence. Here is how one student handled the topic about role models:

Brainstorming Role Models

Mark Rettig is a good choice

he's pretty old, but that's O.K.

nobody has influenced me more—he's like a grandpa

he grew up during the Depression—attended Catholic school—made him serious

he used to scrap broken-down cars for salvage metal (always carried hammers, axes, picks, and crowbars)

he experimented with crystal radio set

owned a venetian blind shop

Dad and he carved me toys out of scrap lumber

I loved Mark's wife—a sweet, chubby lady—cupboard full of candy

they've been married for 52 years

he should slow down, but he doesn't

dedicated cabinet maker—clock and trunk

his precision and care inspire me still

a real craftsman

Paragraph

My friend, Mark Rettig, will always be an inspiration to me, no matter what career I choose. He is seventy-four years old and has been like my grandfather. He is a short man, about five feet four with wavy white hair. He is usually wearing a plaid, short-sleeved button-down shirt when I visit him. Mark grew up during the Depression. For most of his life he owned and operated a venetian blind shop. One of my fondest memories is visiting this shop, where Mark and my dad would make wonderful wooden toys from scraps of wood. In his spare time, Mark creates beautiful cabinet work. His living room displays an elegant grandfather clock, which he made. He also restored an old trunk for my family; it now sits proudly in our living room, housing all kinds of pictures and old keepsakes. What continues to inspire me about Mark is the way he carefully explained his methods of woodworking to me. He has taught me to work carefully and painstakingly on all of my projects, whether physical or intellectual. He has inspired me to be a real craftsman.

Photo Writing Assignment

Carefully study the photo below. Try to get a feel for the way the grandparent and grandchild are interacting. On a separate sheet of paper, brainstorm about the possible benefits of having caring grandparents. Simply pour out your thoughts without censoring them. Once you have ended your brainstorming session, review your ideas and underline those with the most promise for writing a good paragraph.

4 The Basic Sentence

"Every sentence—no matter how long and complex—contains a kernel sentence."

A **sentence** is a group of words that expresses a complete thought. This completeness is what your speaker's ear uses to recognize a sentence. If someone said to you, "Leaf," you'd probably reply, "What?" ("What do you mean?") However, if someone said, "A leaf fell," you'd probably reply, "So what?" meaning that you understand but don't care. You responded differently because the second statement is complete enough for you to understand it.

Subject and Verb

To be complete, every sentence must have a subject and a verb. In its simplest form, the **subject** is someone who does something:

John spoke.

Mary ran.

Jeannie laughed.

John, Mary, and *Jeannie* are the simple subjects of these sentences.

The subject of a sentence can also be something rather than someone.

The plane flew.

The ship sailed.

The house collapsed.

Plane, ship, and *house* are subjects.

The subject can even be intangible, such as *greed, jealousy,* or *liberty.*

Greed hurts.

Jealousy destroys.

Liberty releases the soul.

Greed, jealousy, and *liberty* are subjects.

The word that tells what the subject does or did is called the **verb.** From the examples above, we know that John *spoke,* Mary *ran,* and Jeannie *laughed.* We also know that the plane *flew,* the ship *sailed,* and the house *collapsed.* Additionally, we know that greed *hurts,* jealousy *destroys,* and liberty *releases* the soul.

Subjects and verbs are always linked, and the best way to distinguish one from the other is to find the verb first and then ask, "Who or what did that?" For instance, here is a typical sentence:

Roger Tash painted the entire cabin in one day.

The action word is *painted,* so that is the verb. To find the subject, you now simply ask, "Who or what painted? The answer is *Roger Tash.*

PRACTICE 1

In each of these sentences, underline the subject once and the verb twice.

Example: The bird chirped.

1. The house burned.
2. The car sputters.
3. Jane Alexandra Jones laughed.
4. Beauty comforts.
5. The thingamabob spins.
6. Computers crash.
7. Money talks.
8. Horses neigh.
9. Kings ruled.
10. Elves exist.

Kernel Sentences

Each of these examples is called a kernel sentence. A kernel sentence is the smallest sentence possible, consisting only of the subject and the verb, nothing more. Here are some other kernel sentences:

Run!

Halt!

Go!

These kernel sentences are commands. The subject (you) is implied:

> [You] run!
>
> [You] halt!
>
> [You] go!

Every sentence—no matter how long and complex—contains a kernel sentence. For example, consider this kernel sentence:

> John spoke.

We can add words to it, making it longer and more detailed. Its core will still be the same basic kernel sentence: *John spoke.* Here are some examples, with the kernel sentence italicized:

> At noon, before a crowd of students, *John spoke.*
>
> *John,* in a red plaid coat and checkered pants, *spoke.*
>
> Knowing the crowd was against him, *John spoke.*
>
> *John spoke* at 12 o'clock in the blazing sun.
>
> At 12 o'clock, *John spoke* in the blazing sun.

Here are some more italicized kernel sentences:

> The *doctor,* assisted by a nurse, helped the child.
>
> Wearing a big smile on his face, the *doctor left* the hospital.
>
> The *doctor spoke* the truth.
>
> The *doctor,* wearing his white jacket, *looked* straight down the hall.

When we read a sentence, we know who did what or what happened and to whom. Without the subject and verb of the kernel sentence, for example, each of the phrases below is incomplete:

At noon before a crowd of students.	**(What happened?)**
In a red plaid coat and checkered pants.	**(What are you talking about? What did he or she do?)**
Knowing the crowd was against him.	**(Who? What happened?)**
At 12 o'clock in the blazing sun.	**(What happened?)**

As mentioned earlier, to find the subject of a sentence, simply do this: Identify the verb. Then ask "Who?" or "What?" in front of it. The answer will be the subject. For example, in the sentence *John spoke,* we know that the verb is *spoke.* If we ask, "Who spoke?" the answer is the subject, John.

PRACTICE 2

Underline the kernel sentence in each sentence below.

1. Cell phones store an amazing amount of information.
2. Every Thursday, John misses the school bus.

3. Sally drives like a bat out of hell.
4. Many athletes exercise at home, not at the gym.
5. With his skateboard in hand, Jimmy crossed the street.
6. We study at the library just about every weekend.
7. Without signaling, he turned into the wrong lane.
8. Two tattered pillows covered the sofa.
9. Benjamin Franklin wrote a famous diary.
10. Loud noises during a movie annoy me.

Sentences Worded as Questions

This simple test will also help you find the subject of a sentence worded as a question. Consider these examples:

> When did John speak?
>
> Did John speak at noon?
>
> Why did John speak at noon?

If we ask, "Who?" before the verb "did speak," the answer is the same: John, John, and John. In a question, the verb often has a helping verb, such as *am, are, did, have, should, could, can, must, might,* or *would.* You should include the helping verb with the main verb when searching for the kernel sentence. We will have more on helping verbs later in this chapter.

PRACTICE 3

Underline the kernel sentence in each question.

Example: With interest rates so high, can I afford two credit cards?

1. Will he shut the door behind you?
2. Do they prefer hot chocolate for breakfast?
3. In this hot weather, can the electrician repair the air-conditioner?
4. Do you see your slippers under the bed?
5. With so much lightning in the sky, will the airplane be safe?
6. Have we ever seen such a dark sky?
7. Could Matt improve his tennis score?
8. Where on earth does Marcus live?
9. Must I unpack the car before tomorrow?
10. Can General Fillmore control the troops?

ESL Advice!

Don't leave off the helping verb in questions.

Wrong: You see the rainbow?

Right: <u>Did</u> you see the rainbow? or <u>Could</u> you see the rainbow?

IN A NUTSHELL

- **A sentence always expresses a complete thought.**
- **A sentence always includes a subject and verb.**
- **A kernel sentence is the smallest sentence possible.**

PRACTICE 4

Underline the kernel sentence in each of these sentences.

Example: Clutching her red handbag, the <u>woman ran</u> after the bus.

1. Masako jumped into the pool.
2. Looking hard in the mirror, John smiled proudly.
3. Keisha waved her little flag.
4. Jack Horner, a happy grin on his ugly face, ate.
5. Quite by accident, she bumped the chair.
6. The ship hit an iceberg.
7. We skied all day.
8. The trolls played under the bridge.
9. Admit it or not, he often lies.
10. We know a lot about the case.

PRACTICE 5

Write an *S* beside any construction that you think is a sentence and *NS* if you think the construction is not a sentence. If the construction is not a sentence, turn it into one in the space provided. Remember that a sentence must express a complete thought and contain a subject and verb.

1. ____ The green hat.

____

2. ____ Mice squeak.

____

3. ____ The black limousine with shiny tires.

____

4. ____ The bat slept.

____

5. ____ Sheila snored.

____

6. ____ Running fast.

____

7. ____ The ocean roared.

____

8. ____ Setting the table.

____

9. ____ Made her worried.

____

10. ____ Hear me, please!

____

Prepositional Phrases

Sometimes it is easy to spot the subject of a sentence, but sometimes it isn't. For example, what is the subject of this sentence?

> One of Mary's friends gave her a surprise party.

If we apply the test of asking "Who?" before *gave,* we find that *one* is the subject. Because the prepositional phrase *of Mary's friends* comes before the verb *gave,* you might mistake *Mary's friends* for the subject.

A **preposition** is a word that shows the relationship between two things; a **prepositional phrase** is a group of words beginning with a preposition. A preposition always has an **object**—usually a noun or pronoun—that follows it. Together, a preposition and its object make up a prepositional phrase. Here is an example:

> He put the book on the table.

Here, the preposition is *on,* and the object is *table.* Remember this formula:

PREPOSITION =	OBJECT =	PREPOSITIONAL PHRASE
on	the table	on the table
to	the sea	to the sea
of	the college	of the college
from	the store	from the store

Below is a list of the most common prepositions:

about	beside	inside	toward
above	besides	into	under
across	between	like	underneath
after	beyond	near	until
against	by	of	up
along	despite	off	upon
among	down	on	with
around	during	out	within
at	except	outside	without
before	for	over	throughout
behind	from	past	through
below	in	since	to
beneath			

One way to avoid mistaking a preposition for the subject of a sentence is to cross out all of the prepositional phrases in any sentence whose subject you're trying to find. Here are some examples:

The driver ~~of the car~~ spoke ~~to the officer~~.

The answers ~~to the test~~ were not given.

Every student ~~from our school~~ loves cold weather.

IN A NUTSHELL

- A preposition is a word that shows the relationship between two things; a prepositional phrase is a preposition and its object.
- Don't mistake a word in a prepositional phrase for the subject of a sentence.
- If in doubt, cross out the prepositional phrase.

PRACTICE 6

For each of the following prepositions, create a prepositional phrase. Then use the prepositional phrase to write a complete sentence.

1. above ______________________________
____
____
2. through ______________________________
____
____
3. inside ______________________________
____
____
4. during ______________________________
____
____
5. throughout ______________________________
____
____
6. underneath ______________________________
____
____
7. without ______________________________
____
____
8. toward ______________________________
____
____
9. around ______________________________
____
____
10. in ______________________________
____
____

PRACTICE 7

Exchange your answers for the Practice 5 exercise with a classmate. Underline the subject and verb in each of your partner's sentences. If you disagree about the subject and verb of any sentence, discuss it with other classmates.

PRACTICE 8

Cross out the prepositional phrase or phrases in each of the sentences below. Then identify the subject by circling it.

Example: The box is on the top shelf in the closet.

1. He jumped the fence and ran across the field.
2. The son of Nadia nodded.
3. After the singing, they went into the dining room for dinner.
4. I was at the library until 4:00.
5. She is a woman of her word.
6. For your love, I give everything.
7. We sat near Louise in the back row.
8. We sailed up the lazy river.
9. You put it on the shelf behind the suitcase.
10. She backed out of the driveway without looking both ways.

Action Verbs and Linking Verbs

Verbs tell us who did what action in a sentence. What action, though, does *is* describe? In fact, it describes no action because *is* is a linking verb.

Indeed, there are two main kinds of verbs: action verbs and linking verbs. **Action verbs** describe an action. They tell us that the subject performed a particular action. Here are examples:

Mary jumped off the chair.

Peter threw the ball.

Adam wrote an essay.

Each of these verbs describes a definite action: jumping, throwing, and writing. If someone asked you to mimic any of these actions, you could easily act out someone jumping, throwing, or writing. What if, however, someone asked you to mimic the action behind the verb *is?* You couldn't do it, because *is,* although a verb, describes no action and is instead a linking verb.

A **linking verb** connects the subject to other words that say something about it. Here are some examples of linking verbs in italics:

Cathy *is* an accountant.

Harry *looks* tired.

Mary *seems* happy to be home.

The linking verb *is* connects the subject *Cathy* to the words *an accountant,* which is Cathy's job. Likewise, *Harry* is linked to *tired* by the linking verb *looks,* and *Mary* is linked to *happy to be at home* by the linking verb *seems.* Linking verbs get their name because they link the subject to other words that tell us something about the subject. These other words are called **complements** because they "complete" the subject by renaming or describing it. So, *Cathy* is *an accountant* (another name for Cathy), and *Harry* looks *tired* (describes his appearance).

Here are some other examples of complements:

The whole day was a disaster.

The mayor is his mother.

The milk smells sour.

Granny is the youngest lawyer in the firm.

Old bones become brittle.

Here is a list of some common linking verbs:

am	feel
is	sound
are	look
has been	appear
was	seem
were	taste
become	smell

Don't mistake the complement of a sentence for its subject. Remember, to find the subject of a sentence, ask "Who?" or "What?" before the verb. The answer will be the subject. So, for example, in the sentence, *Granny is the youngest lawyer in the firm,* first identify the verb *is* and then ask, "Who is?" The answer, *Granny,* is the subject.

PRACTICE 9

In the space provided, write *AV* if the sentence contains an action verb and *LV* if it contains a linking verb.

1. ____ *Little Red Riding Hood* is a famous fairy tale.
2. ____ Those years seem so sad to me.

3. ____ The students shuffled into the auditorium.
4. ____ Jack tripped me on the football field.
5. ____ His father handed him the broom.
6. ____ The young minister looked awkward.
7. ____ All this was most upsetting.
8. ____ The colt nuzzled my hand.
9. ____ We explored the streams in the winter afternoons.
10. ____ The street was filled with potholes.

PRACTICE 10

In each of the following sentences, circle the linking verb and underline the complement.

Example: She [is] <u>lovely</u>.

1. They were careful.
2. Otto is a St. Bernard.
3. She was the team leader both years.
4. Her smile looked phony.
5. The judge's memory was not clear.
6. Does the cheese smell bad?
7. First graders often feel lonely.
8. The river looks murky.
9. Jealousy is a hurtful emotion.
10. Her purse is the size of a suitcase.

Helping Verbs

Verbs sometimes need additional words, called **helping verbs,** to express the past, present, and future. In the four sentences below, the complete verb is underlined:

The children <u>are eating</u> at noon.	**(present)**
The children <u>will eat</u> at noon.	**(future)**
The children <u>had eaten</u> before the storm arrived.	**(past)**
The children <u>were eating</u> when he knocked.	**(past)**

Here, for example, are some of the many forms of the verb *work.* Notice the many different helping verbs.

works	should have been working	will have worked
worked	can work	would have worked

is working	would have been working	should have worked
was working	will be working	must have worked
may work	had been working	having worked
should work	have worked	did work
will work	has worked	had worked
does work		

Occasionally, words that are not part of the complete verb will intrude between the helping verb and the main verb. Here are some examples, with the intruding words underlined:

> She has already left.
>
> They could have definitely fallen.
>
> All of us had quickly disappeared.
>
> We will surely help next time.

IN A NUTSHELL

- Action verbs are verbs that describe an action.
- Linking verbs are verbs that link a subject to its complement.
- Helping verbs are words such as *are, will,* and *had* that help a verb to express the past, present, and future.

PRACTICE 11

Underline the complete verb in the following sentences.

1. Dimitri had stopped his car a mile from camp.
2. Peter was waiting for her.
3. I will remember that picture.
4. She has begun to make the waffles.
5. They should have gone home earlier.
6. The accident was reported yesterday.
7. If only they had remained quiet!
8. The geese were honking full force.
9. My father is sitting at the head of the table.
10. You should eat more fresh vegetables.

PRACTICE 12

Underline only the complete verb in the following sentences. Do not underline words that come between the helping verb and the main verb.

Example: They <u>had</u> never <u>helped</u> their neighbors.

1. You must occasionally hurry.
2. They have often traveled to a foreign country.
3. Carlos should have deeply regretted his lie.
4. Few people can always smile.
5. He must never have been the tallest in his class.
6. He had usually rented an apartment.
7. You could have quickly run across the street.
8. The man should have patiently waited.
9. The party has just been canceled.
10. Carina will never go swimming again.

Verbals

Verbals are words that look like verbs but do not act like verbs. Verbals are of three kinds: gerunds, participles, and infinitives. We'll look at each separately.

Gerunds

Gerunds are words that end in *-ing* and act as nouns, meaning that they can be the subject of a sentence. How can you tell if an *-ing* word is a gerund or a verb? Easy: Look for the helping verb. For an *-ing* word to be a verb, it must have a helping verb. Look at these sentences:

We were swimming for fun.	**(were + -ing word = verb)**
Swimming is fun.	**(Swimming = subject = gerund)**
He is running in the Boston Marathon.	**(is + -ing word = verb)**
Running is good for you.	**(Running = subject = gerund)**

Apply the test for a subject by asking "Who?" or "What?" before the verb. "What" is good for you? Running (running = subject = gerund).

Weeding the garden can be hard work.

"What" can be hard work? Weeding (weeding = subject = gerund).

Another way to spot a gerund is to use the pronoun *it* in place of the suspect *-ing* word. If the *-ing* word is a gerund, this substitution is possible. If it is a verb, the substitution will seem ridiculous.

Swimming is fun.

It is fun.

The substitution makes sense: *swimming* is a gerund.

We were swimming for fun.

We were it for fun.

The sentence makes no sense: *swimming,* as used here, is not a gerund.

PRACTICE 13

Rewrite the following sentences by turning the italicized verb into a gerund. As the example shows, you will have to change the original sentence by adding or deleting words.

Example: Scientists *are finding* cures for many diseases.

Finding cures for many diseases keeps scientists busy.

1. Freddy *has been visiting* his grandparents.

____

2. He *was using* a ruler to keep the lines straight.

____

3. We *were hoping* for sunny weather.

____

4. The children *were eating* candy.

____

5. All year, I *had been avoiding* my homework.

____

6. John *was deciding* whether or not to join the team.

____

7. When was Meg *wearing* a black hat?

____

8. George and Ani *were watching* television.

____

9. He *was kicking* the seat to annoy us.

____

10. They *had been begging* us to paint the house green.

____

PRACTICE 14

Write a *V* next to the sentence when the *-ing* word is used as a verb, and circle the helping verb. Write a *G* when the *-ing* word is used as a gerund.

1. ____ I am missing two assignments.
2. ____ All of us were wearing glasses.
3. ____ Marrying too young is not a good idea.
4. ____ Ted is marrying Maria.
5. ____ The directions are confusing.
6. ____ Winning the lottery would be nice.
7. ____ The screaming was eerie.
8. ____ I am counting on him.
9. ____ The officer was enforcing the law.
10. ____ Driving out West with my sister was fun.

Participles

Participles are words that look like verbs but act like adjectives, meaning that they are descriptive. Present participles end in *-ing.* Past participles end in *-ed.* Here are some examples:

Jack is dancing with Linda.

Here, *dancing* is a verb telling what Jack was doing.

Jack is a dancing man.

Here, *dancing* is a present participle describing the man Jack.

We barbecued ribs for dinner.

Here, *barbecued* is a verb telling what we did to the ribs.

We ate barbecued ribs for dinner.

Here, *barbecued* is a past participle describing the ribs.

PRACTICE 15

In each of the following sentences, underline the participle.

Example: Jack has on a <u>battered</u> hat.

1. The hissing cat jumped off the table.
2. Howling winds kept us awake all night.
3. The sky looks like a painted ceiling.
4. My mother's dyed hair makes her look young.
5. None of the running horses belonged to the ranch.
6. With her head bowed, Georgia sighed.
7. The Assembly passed a modified version of the bill.
8. He watched a boring movie.
9. We had an uninterrupted view.
10. She is a moving target.

Infinitives

Infinitives consist of *to* plus a verb. Infinitives never act as verbs; they always serve some other function. Study these examples:

He wanted to disappear.

Here, the infinitive *to disappear* tells what he wanted. The verb is *wanted.*

He wanted a place to sleep.

Here, the infinitive *to sleep* tells what kind of place. The verb is *wanted.*

He waved to get her attention.

Here, *to get* tells why he waved. The verb is *waved.*

Be careful not to confuse an infinitive with the preposition *to* followed by a noun or a pronoun.

Infinitive: Pete wanted <u>to walk</u>.

Preposition: Pete gave the apple <u>to Fred</u>.

IN A NUTSHELL

- Verbals are words that look like verbs but do not act like verbs.
- Gerunds always end in *-ing* and act as nouns.
- Participles can end in *-ing* or *-ed;* they act as adjectives.
- An infinitive is *to* + a verb.

PRACTICE 16

Underline only the infinitives in the following sentences. Do not underline if the *to* is a preposition.

1. When do you plan to eat?
2. Margie gave her last dime to her sister.
3. Don't expect to see the lions.
4. We prefer to walk in the garden.
5. He whistled to the tune of "Yankee Doodle."
6. He listens only to his stomach.
7. He wanted to play every instrument in the band.
8. Carlita wanted to love her brother but couldn't.
9. Halfway to the store, he realized that he'd forgotten to wear his watch.
10. Giving money to his best friend turned out to be a mistake.

PRACTICE 17

In the following sentences, underline the verb and circle the infinitive

Example: The wind <u>began</u> [to blow].

1. I am going to buy a new suit for my interview.
2. Every single student wanted to go to the game.
3. My boyfriend loves to ski.
4. I need to change the oil in my car.
5. It will be difficult to be as cheerful as Olivia.
6. Finally, I have learned how to drive a stick shift.
7. Everyone must leave in order to clear the hallways.
8. He refuses to lose weight.
9. I want to be alone.
10. Why did you ask her to change your appointment?

Compound Subjects and Verbs

A sentence with more than one subject is said to have a **compound subject.** Here are some examples:

> John and Peter fished.
>
> The man and his son laughed.
>
> My wife and I knew.

In the first sentence, *John* and *Peter* are both subjects of the verb *fished*. In the second, the subjects are *man* and *son*. In the third, the subjects are *wife* and *I*.

A sentence may also have more than one verb—called a **compound verb.** Here are some examples:

> John fished and hunted.
>
> The man talked and laughed.
>
> I knew and understood.

The compound verbs are *fished* and *hunted* in the first sentence, *laughed* and *talked* in the second, and *knew* and *understood* in the third.

Naturally, compound subjects and verbs may occur in the same sentence:

> John, Peter, Tom, and Harry fished and hunted.
>
> The man and his son talked, laughed, and smiled.
>
> My wife and I knew, understood, and sympathized.

ESL Advice!

Compound subjects take a plural verb in the present tense (i.e., John and his son *talk* (not *talks*) about life).

If you are like the rest of us, you often use such compound subjects and verbs in your everyday speech, perhaps without knowing their formal names. Recently, a 4-year-old we know tearfully blurted out this sentence after an accident:

> I tripped and fell.

When it was pointed out to her that she had just used a compound verb, she was neither consoled nor amused.

IN A NUTSHELL

- A sentence with more than one subject has a compound subject.
- A sentence with more than one verb has a compound verb.

PRACTICE 18

Underline the compound subjects in the following sentences.

1. My teacher and I disagree.
2. My best friend and his wife came to dinner.
3. Fair weather and good company make the time fly.

4. Hope and love are both emotions.
5. Southern women and their diaries tell the story of the Civil War.
6. My dog, cat, and parakeet love one another.
7. Poetry and music are my twin loves.
8. Coffee, tea, and cookies were served.
9. Food and clothing are a big part of my budget.
10. A fool and his money are soon parted.

PRACTICE 19

Underline the compound verbs in the following sentences.

1. My heart sang and rejoiced at the victory.
2. He praised and rewarded my efforts.
3. Many people love and honor their roots.
4. The dog barked and howled all night.
5. She smiled and blew kisses to her fans.
6. I came and saw and conquered.
7. My husband scrimps and saves.
8. She said and did two different things.
9. The reporter talked and pointed to the map.
10. Terry had dusted and vacuumed the room.

Unit Test

In the following sentences, underline the subject once and the complete verb twice.

1. The poster showed the beauty of the garden.
2. Carlos had been riding his bicycle for 2 hours.
3. Do you want another chance?
4. The clouds above the mountains looked white and fluffy.
5. Fifty packed years of experience have taught us much.
6. My whole life has been a miracle.
7. They should have been working.
8. Angie and Dion operate the scoreboard.
9. The car sputtered and stopped.
10. The broken lamp has not been of any use.

In the following sentences, underline the prepositional phrases:

1. We found holes throughout the lace tablecloth.
2. It is difficult to complete college without extra money.
3. There stood Mr. Assadi, hiding behind the door.

From the verbs in parentheses, choose the correct one by underlining it.

1. Playing music (has been, have been) my great joy.
2. He and Marcy (is, are) having trouble communicating.
3. Tina and Josie (asks, ask) him the same question every day.
4. The men in the car (is, are) bothering the neighbors.
5. I often (pretends, pretend) to be rich and famous.
6. Giving the thumbs up sign (mean, means) that everything is fine.
7. What (were, was) you saying when I interrupted you?
8. Living without you (seem, seems) tedious.
9. Grasshoppers on the tree (sing, sings) me to sleep every night.
10. The young owner of the restaurants (speak, speaks) to my class today.

Unit Talk–Write Assignment

Underline all the verbals (gerunds, participles, and infinitives) in the *Talk* column below. Then, using the sentences in the *Talk* column, write a paragraph in the *Write* column. Most of the sentences need to be rewritten in standard English.

TALK	WRITE
1. Grandma, who died dirt poor, always made a big deal of having a nest egg for a rainy day.	
2. "Don't let spending dictate your finances; let finances dictate your spending," she used to say, pointing her arthritic finger at me.	

3. Then she'd dump her famous three rules on me:

4. First, "Don't own a credit card, but if you have to use one, pay it off at the end of every month so you aren't bothered by late fees or high interest payments."

5. Second, "Always have an emergency fund, no matter how teensy."

6. Third, "Set up a savings account and put something in it every month, even if it's just a nickel."

7. Grandma's rules used to really drive me nuts cause she kept hitting me over the head with them.

8. But I guess in the back of my mind I listened, because now, as a college sophomore, I do have a $100.00 emergency fund, a $1000.00 savings account, and nil as far as credit cards go.

9. Grandma's warning taught me a super lesson.

10. Personal finances can either drive you bananas or give you a sense of stability.

Unit Collaborative Assignment

Choose a partner to whom you will ask the questions below and who must then write down an answer in a full sentence. Exchange roles and have your partner ask you the same questions, to which you will write your answers in complete sentences. Exchange papers. Circle the subjects and underline the verbs in your partner's sentences, while your partner does the same to yours. Do you agree on all the subjects and verbs? In case of disagreement, ask your instructor.

1. What is your favorite restaurant?
2. Where is it located?
3. Why is it your favorite?
4. What is the decor like?
5. What kind of food does it serve?
6. What are your favorite dishes?
7. How expensive is it?
8. Whom do you go there with?
9. How do the waiters act?
10. How would you sum up your attitude toward this restaurant?

Unit Writing Assignment

Use the sentences you wrote in the Unit Collaborative Assignment to write a paragraph on your favorite restaurant. Pay particular attention to linking the sentences in your paragraph.

Photo Writing Assignment

Write an essay on any topic suggested by the following photo of a girls' basketball team. For example, you might write about encouraging girls to participate in sports dominated by males, such as soccer, football, basketball, or baseball. You could also write about the good effects of team sports—how they foster cooperation, ambition, and good health. If you don't like sports, you might try to argue that sports in public schools are a waste of taxpayers' money.

5 Building Sentences

"Your ear for the language is the best judge of whether a clause makes sense or not and is therefore independent or dependent."

Every sentence must have a subject and a verb; there is no exception to this rule. But not every construction with a subject and a verb is a sentence. It could be a dependent clause.

Dependent and Independent Clauses

A **clause** is a group of words with both a subject and a verb. If a clause makes sense on its own, it is called an **independent clause** and is a complete sentence. These are independent clauses and, therefore, complete sentences:

> They will pick up the dry cleaning.
>
> You can always go home for dinner.
>
> We are looking for a renter.

Each of the above has a subject (*they, you,* and *we*) and a verb (*will pick up, go,* and *are looking*). Moreover, as your speaker's ear will tell you, each makes sense on its own.

> However, what about the following?
>
> After you go to the bank.
>
> If it rains.
>
> Who has a steady income.

Each of the above clauses has a subject (*you, it,* and *who*) and a verb (*go, rains,* and *has*), but none makes complete sense. These are **dependent clauses**—a group of words with a subject and a verb that must be connected to an independent clause to make sense, as indicated below:

> Pick up the dry cleaning after you go to the bank.
>
> You can always go to the movies if it rains.
>
> We are looking for a renter who has a steady income.

Your ear for the language is the best judge of whether a clause makes sense or not and is therefore independent or dependent. Most speakers, for example, can immediately hear the differences between the following pairs of clauses:

Dependent:	Since David moved.
Independent:	I haven't been backpacking.
Combined:	Since David moved, I haven't been backpacking.
Dependent:	After they sang.
Independent:	The audience applauded.
Combined:	After they sang, the audience applauded.
Dependent:	Which is my hometown.
Independent:	We stopped in Denver.
Combined:	We stopped in Denver, which is my hometown.

ESL Advice!

If you haven't yet acquired an ear for English, memorize the definition of a sentence and study the options for combining sentences.

Many dependent clauses begin with a telltale sign—one of the following words. These words are called **relative pronouns** because they show how a dependent clause is related to a main clause.

who	whose	that
whom	which	what

A dependent clause may also begin with one of these words, called **subordinating conjunctions**:

after	if	so that	where
although	in order that	than	whenever
as if	now that	that	wherever
because	once	though	whether
before	provided that	unless	while
even if	rather than	until	why
even though	since	when	

Typically, it is these linking words that make a clause dependent. In fact, removing the subordinate conjunction changes a dependent clause into an independent clause. Here are some examples:

Dependent:	Since you left me.
Independent:	You left me.
Dependent:	Because you didn't study.
Independent:	You didn't study.
Dependent:	While you were on vacation.
Independent:	You were on vacation.
Dependent:	That he needs to work harder.
Independent:	He needs to work harder.

The obvious lesson to be learned is this: If you begin a sentence with one of the telltale words that make a clause dependent, be careful not to commit a dependent clause error.

IN A NUTSHELL

- A clause is a group of words that contains a subject and a verb.
- An independent clause makes sense on its own; a dependent clause does not.
- Only a clause that can stand by itself is a sentence.

PRACTICE 1

In the blanks provided, write *D* if the clause is dependent and *I* if the clause is independent. For each clause that you mark with a *D*, underline the word that makes the clause dependent.

1. ____ Who darted across the street like lightning.
2. ____ New brakes were needed.
3. ____ The trial will begin in a week.
4. ____ Because he was sad and depressed.
5. ____ While she was walking home.
6. ____ Though the soup was ready.
7. ____ Since no book can provide all the answers.
8. ____ That he never looked back.
9. ____ If war could have solved the problem.
10. ____ Creative thinkers make good leaders.

11. ____ Wherever he lived.
12. ____ Until we meet again.
13. ____ That quarrel was unnecessary.
14. ____ Good books contain real treasures.
15. ____ Loving your enemy will drive him crazy.

PRACTICE 2

In each blank, write an independent clause that could complete the sentence.

Example: Because he was only seventeen, ***he could not vote.***

1. If you wear a badge with your name on it, ____________
2. Before she moved to Idaho, ____________
3. ____________, where I found the wallet.
4. Unless you call before 2:00 P.M., ____________
5. Whenever time passed slowly, ____________
6. Mrs. Forsythe, who never spent a dime on Halloween treats, ____________
7. Although getting exercise is important, ____________
8. Because they won, ____________
9. Even if you visit George, ____________
10. Until television arrived, ____________

Three Basic Sentence Types

There are three basic sentence types: simple, compound, and complex. All three sentence types are commonly used in writing and talking. We shall discuss each separately.

The simple sentence

A **simple sentence** consists of a single independent clause. It is both the first sentence out of the mouth of babes, as well as the workhorse of daily writing. First graders routinely write simple sentences such as these:

Bobby fell down.

Sally is my friend.

I like my brother.

The simple sentence is commonly found in the Bible, where its simplicity is surprisingly powerful. Here, for example, is the first sentence of the Bible:

> In the beginning God created the heavens and the earth.

The simple sentence, in spite of its name, is not always simply written. Nor is it always short, crisp, and childlike. It can be expanded if it is given more than one subject or verb. Here are some examples:

Simple sentences with singular subjects:

> My mother has no ear for music.
>
> My father has no ear for music.

Simple sentences with more than one subject:

> My mother and father have no ear for music.
>
> The boy and man play together very well.
>
> The dog and the cat chased after the children.
>
> The sun and the rain help the vegetation.
>
> Cowards and liars defeat our goals.

Simple sentence with one subject and three verbs:

> The children laugh at the monkeys, run away from the tigers, and feed the goats.

Simple sentences with two subjects and one verb:

> The teammates and coach rehearse the play.
>
> The woman and child enter the room.
>
> The brother and sister often agree.

Simple sentence with three subjects and three verbs:

> The man, woman, and children laugh, chuckle, and point.

Another way to expand the simple sentence is to add **modifiers,** which are words that describe and explain the subject or verb. Here are some examples:

Simple sentence:	Jim lives in Windsor.
First expansion:	Jim, a star basketball player, lives in Windsor.
Second expansion:	Jim, a star basketball player and an excellent student, lives in Windsor, Canada, across from Detroit.

IN A NUTSHELL

- The simple sentence consists of one independent clause.
- It can be expanded with multiple subjects, verbs, or modifiers.

PRACTICE 3

In the following simple sentences, underline the subject(s) and verb(s):

Example: The cousins <u>Alberto</u> and <u>Carmen</u> often <u>play</u> in the school orchestra and <u>sing</u> in the choir.

1. José, a new student at school, is a very good striker at soccer.
2. The two dogs and the three cats played together surprisingly well in spite of the heat.
3. A victim of circumstances, the ship went down in the storm.
4. I, like many other people, watch television less and less every year.
5. Carina and Alphonso, two students from different countries, are surprisingly alike on political issues.
6. The party fished, caught crabs, played catch, and danced all night long.
7. Alfredo and Juanita, two Guatemalans, speak and write English very well.
8. I am always delighted at the bobbing and weaving of seabirds.
9. The Earth Shoe was in vogue a long time ago.
10. My uncle and aunt, military officers for 25 years, still arise at 6 A.M. every morning.

PRACTICE 4

Expand the simple sentences below by adding subjects, verbs, or modifiers. Be sure to limit the sentence to one independent clause.

Example: My father loves to fish.

Expanded by adding modifiers: My father, a retired firefighter, loves to fish in the stream near his house.

Expanded by adding an additional subject and verb: My father and my uncle like to hike and love to fish.

1. My house is green. ______________________________

____

2. The man denied the story. ______________________________

____

3. Many people keep diaries. ______________________________

____

4. Sailing is fun. ______________________________

____

5. She works at the thrift shop. ______________________________

____

6. The train was late. ______________________________

____

7. The boy chased the dog. ______________________________

____

8. She went shopping. ______________________________

____

9. Her appearance had changed. ______________________________

____

10. The room is full. ______________________________

____

11. John loves to waste time. ______________________________

____

12. Democracy is based on the will of the people. ______________________________

____

13. It is never too late to save money. ______________________________

____

14. The wind blew. ______________________________

____

15. The good life is inspired by love. ______________________________

____

The compound sentence

A **compound sentence** consists of two or more simple sentences joined by a **coordinating conjunction.** There are seven coordinating conjunctions: *and, but, for, or, nor, so,* and *yet.* A comma is placed immediately before a coordinating conjunction. The simple sentences in a compound sentence should express ideas of equal importance. Here are some examples:

Simple:	Face-lifts are not always successful. The operation is painful.
Compound:	Face-lifts are not always successful, <u>and</u> the operation is painful.
Simple:	He must pay the fine. He will go to jail.
Compound:	He must pay the fine, <u>or</u> he will go to jail.
Simple:	She didn't study. She got poor grades.
Compound:	She didn't study, <u>so</u> she got poor grades.

Notice that a comma comes immediately before the coordinating conjunction that joins the sentences.

IN A NUTSHELL

- A compound sentence consists of two or more simple sentences joined by a coordinating conjunction.
- The coordinating conjunctions are *and, but, for, or, nor, so,* and *yet.*
- A comma is placed immediately before the joining conjunction.

PRACTICE 5

Use a coordinating conjunction to join these paired simple sentences into a compound sentence. Don't forget the comma.

Example: My mother hates exercising. My father loves it.

<u>My mother hates exercising, but my father loves it.</u>

1. The band played loudly. The audience enjoyed it.

   ____

2. I saw my neighbor. We made a date for lunch.

   ____

3. I went to aerobics class and did 20 minutes on the treadmill. I'm exhausted.

   ____

4. Liza ran up the stairs. She made a telephone call.

   ____

5. I read the novel last night. I enjoyed it.

   ____

6. The dance music was old-fashioned. The students had a fine evening.

____

7. Bicarbonate of soda is good for an upset stomach. I often use it.

____

8. I reserved four tickets. That wasn't enough.

____

9. We met at Luigi's for dinner. Molly never showed up.

____

10. The bell rang. We filed out of the class.

____

The complex sentence

The **complex sentence** consists of one independent clause joined to one or more dependent clauses. Unlike the compound sentence, which connects two equal ideas, the complex sentence emphasizes one idea over the others. The less important idea or ideas are said to be subordinate. The more important idea is expressed in the independent clause:

> My toe hurts because John stepped on it.

The hurting toe is the main idea; the less important idea is why it hurts—because John stepped on it.

Here is another example of a complex sentence—this one with one independent and two dependent clauses:

> Tea has been shown to be good for you because it contains an ingredient in the leaf, although coffee drinkers dispute the evidence.

The main idea here is that tea is good for you. The less important ideas are that this is so because of an ingredient in the leaf and that coffee drinkers dispute the evidence.

Common sense and your ear for language will help you decide which of two ideas is more important and therefore belongs in the independent clause. If neither idea is clearly more important, you must decide which idea to emphasize. For example, here are two sentences:

> I drank a cup of hot chocolate. I went to bed.

If you want to emphasize *going to bed,* put it in the independent clause:

> After I drank a cup of hot chocolate, I went to bed.

If you want to emphasize *drinking hot chocolate,* put it in the independent clause:

> Before I went to bed, I drank a cup of hot chocolate.

Where you put the independent or dependent clause is a matter of personal style. But the placement of these clauses does affect the punctuation of the sentence. Here is the rule: If the dependent clause comes first, it must be followed by a comma; if the independent clause comes first, no comma is needed between clauses. Here are some examples:

Dependent clause first: While he sat in the dentist's office, Phillip felt nervous. *(Note the comma between clauses.)*

Independent clause first: Phillip felt nervous while he sat in the dentist's office. *(Note the absence of a comma.)*

Independent clause first: We could not see the stage because a dense crowd of people hid it from us.

Dependent clause first: Because a dense crowd of people hid it from us, we could not see the stage.

Exactly which idea you might choose to emphasize depends on what you want to say. Sometimes, however, it is clear which of two ideas is more important. Consider these two simple sentences:

The *Titanic* sank with a great loss of life. She struck an iceberg.

Common sense suggests that any complex sentence uniting these two ideas should emphasize the loss of life:

After she struck an iceberg, the *Titanic* sank with a great loss of life.

The reason that the *Titanic* sank is secondary and belongs in the dependent clause.

Bear in mind the words that signal a dependent clause. You may wish to review the relative pronouns and subordinating conjunctions on page 73 before you do the exercises.

IN A NUTSHELL

- A complex sentence consists of one independent clause joined to one or more dependent clauses.
- The more important idea is expressed in the independent clause.

PRACTICE 6

Join the following sentences into a complex sentence, using one of the linking words listed on Unit 5, page 73 sure to put the most important idea—or the one you choose to emphasize—in the independent clause.

Example: My mother hates her work. She finds it boring.

My mother hates her work because she finds it boring.

1. She felt sorry for the beggar. She gave him money.

   ____

2. The army retreated. It burned the bridges.

   ____

3. We will proceed with the job. You object to the charges.

   ____

4. You don't believe me. It is the truth.

   ____

5. You have been gone. I have not been the same.

   ____

6. The headmaster issued the uniforms. There was a complaint about them.

   ____

7. You explain your behavior. I will report the incident.

   ____

8. You were gone. The bill collector came.

   ____

9. You will be admitted to the intermediate-level course. You did well on the tests.

   ____

10. The band stopped playing. The program was over.

    ____

PRACTICE 7

In the space to the left of each of the following sentences, identify the sentence as simple, compound, or complex.

1. ____ The opera singer, clad in a magnificent costume, shrieked her lungs out during the aria.
2. ____ Baseball is so popular partly because it has a long, storied history.
3. ____ They didn't even ask management's permission to put the idea into effect.
4. ____ The Lifetime channel on cable TV is very popular with women.

5. ____ They ran into trouble from the very start, but they were too foolish to ask for help.

6. ____ Because I'm a bird-watcher, I'm often to be found tromping through the woods.

7. ____ Basking in popularity, the young quarterback became even vainer.

8. ____ Although she is young, she has a surprisingly mature grasp of the stock market.

9. ____ He could not do it no matter how hard he tried, so he threw his hands up in the air and gave up.

10. ____ The streets of Nice, France, are usually littered with dog droppings, yet the streets of Paris, a much bigger city, are surprisingly clean.

PRACTICE 8

Write a series of sentences on one of your favorite activities—something you really enjoy. Each sentence should be of the specific type listed below.

1. Simple sentence with more than one subject:

   ____

2. Simple sentence with more than one verb:

   ____

3. Simple sentence with modifiers:

   ____

4. Two compound sentences:

   (a). ______________________________

   ____

   (b). ______________________________

   ____

5. Three complex sentences:

   (a). ______________________________

   ____

   (b). ______________________________

   ____

   (c). ______________________________

   ____

PRACTICE 9

Exchange papers with a classmate and discuss the sentences you wrote in Practice 8. Help each other make any necessary corrections.

Sentence Variety

Writers seldom write in only one sentence type for the same reason that good cooks season their food with more than just salt. Any sentence pattern that is overused will quickly seem boring. Variety is the key to a good writing style and can be achieved easily if you use a mix of simple, compound, and complex sentences. Here is an example of a ho-hum passage:

> Rap music started during the 1970s. It comes from African chanting. It also comes from chatting. Rap music means "chat music." It contains . . .

This passage consists of a string of simple sentences. Note the immediate improvement when the sentences are varied:

> Rap music, which started during the 1970s, comes from African chanting. It also comes from chatting. Rap music means "chat music," and it contains . . .

This sort of sentence variation is exactly what you do instinctively in your everyday speech. It is what you must also try to do in your writing.

IN A NUTSHELL

For variety, use all three sentence types—simple, compound, and complex—in your writing.

PRACTICE 10

Rewrite each paragraph below to eliminate the choppy effect of too many simple sentences. First, read the sentences aloud to determine the relationship between them. Then reduce the number of simple sentences by combining some into compound and complex sentences.

1. On Monday, nothing seemed right. On Friday, Linda was pleased with her life. She had called her mother. Her mother had been feeling sick. On the phone, she sounded chipper. Linda felt relieved. She decided to go camping in the mountains. Her friend had a cabin there. She would fish all weekend. She would be alone. She liked being alone. The weekend would cost little. She would only have to buy groceries for herself. She had enough money. She had just gotten a paycheck. She would wear

old clothes. She would lounge by the river. She would sleep late. There would be no alarm clock. Nobody would bother her. Linda thought, "Everything turns out for the best."

2. Most college students juggle the hours in their day. They play sports and go to parties. Many also have jobs. They try to include serving on committees. They perform volunteer work. They go to lectures. The many options do evoke a great deal of anxiety. The choices are unlimited. The hours are limited. Students feel pressured to get good grades. They feel pressured to experience life fully. They have to decide how much time they can spare outside of class and work for general enrichment. That decision is not always easy to make.

3. This year I tried to be creative with my mom's Christmas present. She said that it was the best present she had ever received. I ordered it through a garden catalog. For $80, the catalog company shipped my mom six baskets of planted flower bulbs. She received a basket every month for 6 months. Each basket contained different flower bulbs. The first month was a large amaryllis. The next delivery was tulips. The next was daffodils. The next was hyacinths. The next was irises. The final month was a mixture of bulbs with riotous colors. All my mom had to do was open the package and water the basket. She then watched the flowers grow. In about a week, they were in full bloom. My mom appreciates beauty. She used the flowers for centerpieces on her dining room table. Several of my friends are going to give their mothers this kind of gift next year.

4. Velcro is one of the most underrated inventions of our modern world. Do you remember how we all used to tie our shoes with shoelaces? Also, we buttoned our jackets. Then Velcro came along and saved the day. Some years ago, my grandmother developed crippling arthritis in her hands. She could not button or zip any of her blouses or jackets. We replaced most of her buttons and zippers with Velcro. It was much easier for her to get dressed with Velcro closings. Also, my aunt has bunions on her feet. She has to wear really wide shoes. Slip-on shoes with Velcro closings are the only shoes she can wear comfortably. They can be adjusted to the most suitable width. Whoever invented Velcro deserves our praise and gratitude.

Unit Test

1. Write a simple sentence with modifiers.

____

____

____

2. Write a compound sentence by connecting two simple sentences with "but."

____

____

____

3. Write a complex sentence beginning with "Although." Be sure to place a comma following the dependent clause.

____

____

____

4. Use the pattern of the following sentence, but change the words to create your own sentence on any topic of your choice: "I will never forget my Aunt Stella because she was my favorite relative." What kind of sentence is this?

____

____

____

5. Identify each of the following sentences as simple, compound, or complex.

_____ **(a)** When John entered his astronomy class, he was embarrassed to find everyone staring at him.

_____ **(b)** Let's follow the instructions carefully, and then we'll compare what we've done with the picture.

_____ **(c)** If you hurry, you can probably catch her.

_____ **(d)** The umbrella, wet and dripping, stood in the corner of the hall.

_____ **(e)** Our neighborhood block party on Memorial Day is always fun.

_____ **(f)** Because we came late, we couldn't find seats together.

_____ **(g)** I know what it is to be hungry, but I have never been hungry for long.

_____ **(h)** Winning is not always important because sometimes defeat teaches more than winning.

_____ **(i)** I have discovered how to fool people.

_____ **(j)** I don't like to swim unless the water is really warm.

Unit Talk–Write Assignment

A political science class was asked whether court cases should ever be televised. The reaction was predictably mixed. One student, however, had very strong opinions and was not timid about expressing them. The student's ideas are in the *Talk* column.

First, study the *Talk* column to get an understanding of the student's opinion. Second, rewrite every sentence in the *Talk* column to make it suitable for inclusion in a written paragraph. Third, using a combination of the student's oral remarks and your own opinions, write a paragraph giving your own views on this topic..

TALK	WRITE
1. Court cases on television?	________________
2. How stupid.	________________
3. That may be within the law, but heck, I couldn't care less.	________________
4. Put a witness on the stand before television cameras and lights, and before you know it, the Bozo is acting like he's a movie star, cutting up for the director.	________________
5. The point is, you don't want a system that makes every jerk feel like the world is hanging onto his every word.	________________
6. Take the Anna Nicole Smith case—what a can of worms!	________________

7. You had the judge carrying on like he was at a circus—even sniffling and boohooing in front of the audience in the courtroom.

8. And whoever heard of everyone involved in the case being hounded by the moron paparazzi? If they could've, they would've paid a thousand bucks to take pictures of Anna Nicole's baby to spread all over the front page of their junk papers.

9. The whole thing was like a reality TV show —not a where-did-they-bury-the-corpse court case.

10. During a trial, the last thing you need is blown-up publicity. I'm totally against televising court cases.

Unit Collaborative Assignment

Get together with two or three classmates to talk about your pet peeves, such as drivers who can't make up their minds, people who refuse to take their turns in lines, and teachers who wait until halfway through the semester to give the first exam. When one student is speaking, the others should write down some of the sentences. When everyone has discussed his or her pet peeve, take turns presenting and classifying the written sentences as simple, compound, or complex.

Unit Writing Assignment

Using the ideas you accumulated during the Unit Collaborative Assignment, write about one of your pet peeves. Make a special effort to use sentence variety.

Photo Writing Assignment

Almost overnight, cell phones have become a global means of communication. You can hear cell phones ringing everywhere—in restaurants, on campus, at the airport, in offices, or even in churches. For emergencies, keeping in touch, or communicating to or from remote locations, the cell phone is a miracle of convenience. Yet, even a miracle can have its downside. Cell phones are frequently intrusive, encourage excessively loud and boastful chatter, and even help criminals do their dirty work. Write a paragraph in which you sum up the pluses and minuses of this invention. Make a special effort to use sentence variety.

6 Avoiding Non-Sentences

"If he blows up the world." "Fred is a flake no one likes him." "Last night I helped get supper, my potatoes were delicious."

You have already learned that a sentence is the same as an independent clause. It has a subject, a verb, and makes complete sense on its own. Non-sentences can be of two types—fragments and run-ons. We'll discuss fragments first.

Sentence Fragments

A **fragment** is only part of a sentence. It is a "wannabe" sentence that lacks either a subject or a verb and makes no sense; it fails to express a complete thought. Sometimes the omission occurs because the writer is "on a roll." It's fine to write fast and get all your thoughts down in a hurry, but then you must always proofread your work for errors.

Here are some examples of fragments that can occur in the rush of writing:

Has an 8 o'clock class.	**(Missing subject)**
Joe's sweater.	**(Missing verb)**
Especially when she is on a diet.	**(Not a complete thought)**

Most of us speak in fragments every day without being misunderstood. Consider, for example, the exchange that follows:

Josh: Get your schedule yet?
Max: Sure did.

Josh: Any 8 o'clock classes?
Max: One. Psych.

Josh: Grim.
Max: I know. And with Skrebniski, too.

This conversation in fragments strikes the ear as typical of daily speech. Yet, in spite of the fragments, Josh and Max obviously still understand each other. Their exchange moves along smoothly, and neither interrupts the other for any clarification.

We have learned, however, that formal writing aims for a universal audience and therefore requires the use of standard English—a standard vocabulary and complete sentences. Here is how Josh and Max's exchange would be written in standard English:

Josh: Have you gotten your schedule yet?
Max: Yes, I have.

Josh: Do you have any 8 o'clock classes?
Max: I have one—psychology.

Josh: That's grim.
Max: I know. And the class is with Skrebniski, too.

The standard English version may seem a little stiff, perhaps, compared with Josh and Max's informality. However, it is now understandable not only to Josh and Max, but to the millions of people around the world who read standard English.

IN A NUTSHELL

A fragment is a "wannabe" sentence that lacks either a subject or verb and fails to express a complete thought.

PRACTICE 1

Identify the fragments in the list of constructions below. Mark *F* for a fragment and *S* for a complete sentence. Using the lines provided, correct all of the fragments that you find by turning them into complete sentences.

Example: F Went to buy milk. *Jake went to buy milk.*

1. ____ Hoping to score big. ____________________
2. ____ He is a big man on campus. ____________________
3. ____ Let me call you sweetheart. ____________________
4. ____ To join the army. ____________________

5. ____ Crying all the time. ______________________________
6. ____ Give me a few dollars. ______________________________
7. ____ I saw you in the garden. ______________________________
8. ____ Who's sorry now? ______________________________
9. ____ Just in time. ______________________________
10. ____ Because it's my decision. ______________________________

Avoiding Sentence Fragments

A fragment can spring from one of several causes. If you learn to recognize these, you will be able to avoid fragments in your writing.

Fragments Caused by a Missing Subject

In the heat of writing, it is easy to write a verb but forget to write the subject. The result will be a fragment. Here are some examples:

> Kevin handed Marty two tickets for the playoffs. Then watched the look on his face.

> They're getting married in May. But not going on a honeymoon until September.

In these examples, the writer mistakenly thought that the subject of the first sentence also applied to the second group of words. It does—but the second thought must be formally joined to the first by a conjunction, such as *and*. If you omit the conjunction, you must write the two thoughts as separate, complete sentences:

> Kevin handed Marty two tickets for the playoffs, and then he watched the look on Marty's face.

or

> Kevin handed Marty two tickets for the playoffs. Then he watched the look on Marty's face.

> They're getting married in May, but are not going on a honeymoon until September.

or

> They're getting married in May. But they're not going on a honeymoon until September.

IN A NUTSHELL

Do not create a fragment by carelessly omitting the subject of the sentence.

PRACTICE 2

Correct the following fragments caused by a missing subject. You can either join the fragment to the sentence preceding it or rewrite it as a separate sentence.

Example: Maybe the universe is younger than we think. And was not caused by the Big Bang.

Joined: Maybe the universe is younger than we think, and it was not caused by the Big Bang.

or

Joined: Maybe the universe is younger than we think and was not caused by the Big Bang.

Note: Usually a comma is inserted before the coordinating conjunction (*and, but, or, nor, for, so,* and *yet*). However, if the clauses have the same subject and are short, the comma may be omitted. When in doubt, use the comma.

Rewritten: Maybe the universe is younger than we think. Maybe it was not caused by the Big Bang.

1. Larry announced that he was going to Finland. Then showed me his ticket.

   ____

   ____

2. For plotting to kill Queen Elizabeth I, Sir Walter Raleigh was dropped from the list of the Queen's lovers. Also was beheaded.

   ____

   ____

3. Mario learned to ski. And loved the sport.

   ____

   ____

4. They prepared to entertain. But forgot to buy wine.

   ____

   ____

5. The car blew a tire. Spun around into a lamppost. And landed in a ditch.

   ____

   ____

6. I find Alice's rudeness to servers irritating. And tell her so.

   ____

   ____

7. Our bookkeeper did the ledger. But didn't do the spreadsheets.

8. Mr. Gibson was always talking about politics. And was himself quite a politician.

9. He served a wonderful dinner. But burned the dessert.

10. Cathy was sorry. Or at least I think she was.

11. Blue Bay used to be a wonderful summer resort. But has become too commercial.

12. The trees swayed in the wind. And seemed to whisper secrets.

13. The Victorian Age required women to be extremely modest. Some rebelled and refused to follow all of the rules of behavior.

14. The neighborhood loves Mr. Zev. Serves lemonade free of charge to kids.

15. Manda was outside picking roses. Or feeding the chickens.

Fragments Due to *-ing* words

Some fragments are triggered by an *-ing* word, such as dancing. Here are some examples:

They celebrated. Dancing in the street.

The plane landed. Skidding to a halt.

Why beginning with an *-ing* word often leads to a fragment is something of a puzzle. Possibly, the writer mistakes the *-ing* word for a full verb, but it isn't. As you know from Unit 7, an *-ing* word can be a verb in a sentence only if it is paired with a helping verb.

To correct a fragment due to an *-ing* word, either join it to the sentence that went before it (use a comma to set off the first part of the sentence), or rewrite it as a separate sentence:

> They celebrated, dancing in the street.
>
> or
>
> They celebrated. They were dancing in the street.
>
> The plane landed, skidding to a halt.
>
> or
>
> The plane landed. It skidded to a halt.

IN A NUTSHELL

Be careful of creating a fragment with an *-ing* word.

PRACTICE 3

Correct the *-ing* fragments by rewriting the sentences below.

1. My parents wouldn't let me study the trumpet. Insisting that I should learn to play the piano.

   ____

   ____

2. He spent two summers on a farm. Picking vegetables in the heat of the day.

   ____

   ____

3. The coach lifted curfew. Believing the team members could discipline themselves.

   ____

   ____

4. His handwriting is filled with sharp points and angles. Classifying him as a mean and stingy person.

   ____

   ____

5. The director carefully observed the dancers. Looking for signs of exceptional talent.

____

____

6. He loves to read. Spending many hours in an armchair.

____

____

7. He attended to his father's business. Working long hours every day.

____

____

8. She was the star of the soccer team. Having scored the most goals.

____

____

9. He proposed to her one day. Getting down on one knee.

____

____

10. Many movies are violent. Appealing to the resentment people feel.

____

____

11. He left on the morning bus. Arriving in Arizona late that same night.

____

____

12. My parents use their DVD often. Always using the remote control.

____

____

13. We ambled down the street. Listening to rap music on our boom box.

____

____

14. The Ibarra family enjoys leisurely evenings. Watching TV and munching popcorn.

____

____

15. Rosie loves her job. Making it the center of her life.

____

____

Fragments Due to the Incorrect Use of Infinitives

A third common type of fragment is triggered by the incorrect use of infinitives (*to* + verb). (See Unit 4 to review infinitives.) Here is an example:

I am taking karate lessons. To build up my strength.

John went to a movie. To get his mind off of exams.

As before, you can correct this type of fragment by either joining it to the sentence before it or rewriting it as a separate and complete sentence:

Joined: I am taking karate lessons to build up my strength.

Rewritten: I am taking karate lessons. I want to build up my strength.

Joined: John went to a movie to get his mind off of exams.

Rewritten: John went to a movie. He needed to get his mind off of exams.

Note that you could also make the infinitive and the words around it into a dependent clause that you put either at the beginning or at the end of the combined sentence. If you put the dependent clause at the beginning of the new sentence, be sure to put a comma after it. No comma is necessary if the independent clause comes first.

To build up my strength, I am taking karate lessons.

To get his mind off of exams, John went to a movie. (Comma is necessary because the dependent clause comes first.)

but

I am taking karate lessons to build up my strength.

John went to a movie to get his mind off of exams. (No comma is necessary because the independent clause comes first.)

IN A NUTSHELL

Watch out for fragments caused by the incorrect use of infinitives.

PRACTICE 4

Correct each of the following *to* fragments by either joining the fragment to the sentence before it or rewriting the fragment as a separate sentence.

1. The students took out state educational loans. To get money at a low interest rate.

   ______

   ______

2. I, too, would like a wife. To tend to my every want and slightest need.

   ______

   ______

3. We screen our calls through our answering machine. To avoid telemarketers.

   ______

   ______

4. I bought some property outside of Phoenix. To build a cabin some day.

   ______

   ______

5. I used to live in San Antonio, Texas. To make a long story short.

   ______

   ______

6. He took the train home. To avoid the heavy traffic.

   ______

   ______

7. She read a novel. To wile away the time.

   ______

   ______

8. She took a summer job. To earn money for college.

   ______

   ______

9. You need a key. To start the engine.

   ______

   ______

10. He exercised all summer. To make the football team.

PRACTICE 5

Turn the following fragments due to incorrect use of *-ing* words or infinitives into complete sentences by adding an independent clause before or after the fragment.

Example: To make sure she got home safely.

Jack picked Carmen up after work every night to make sure she got home safely.

or

To make sure she got home safely, Jack picked Carmen up after work every night.

1. Being too tired to go to the theater.

2. To have her car repaired.

3. Showing the programmer the operation of the new computer.

4. Pretending it was otherwise.

5. Investing as a way of life.

6. To perform at a higher level of efficiency.

7. To fake it for the sake of the show.

8. Using a substitute for whalebone.

____

____

9. To laugh at our own weaknesses.

____

____

10. Boiling instead of frying.

____

____

Fragments Due to Dependent Words

You have learned about fragments caused by omitted subjects, *-ing* words, and the incorrect use of infinitives. You have also learned two ways of correcting fragments—by joining the fragment to the sentence before it or by rewriting the fragment as a separate sentence.

We come now to a fourth kind of fragment. This one is triggered by the misuse of relative pronouns and subordinate conjunctions, both of which we covered in Unit 4. This fourth type of fragment is corrected in only one way—by joining it to the sentence before it. Here is a list of relative pronouns that can cause fragments:

who	whose	that
whom	which	

Here are examples of fragments caused by unconnected relative pronouns:

We inspected the attic. <u>Which</u> had become a dumping ground for excess furniture.

Next month we must pay tribute to Coach Peters. <u>Who</u> helped us win the trophy.

Here are the corrections:

We inspected the attic, <u>which</u> had become a dumping ground for excess furniture.

Next month we must pay tribute to Coach Peters, <u>who</u> helped us win the trophy.

As you can see, each of the fragments was corrected by joining the fragment to the sentence before it. Indeed, both were caused by the writer's use of a period instead of a comma.

Similarly, a fragment can be caused by the misuse of a subordinate conjunction. Here is a list of subordinate conjunctions:

after	if	so that	whenever
although	in order that	than	where
as if	now that	that	wherever
because	once	though	whether
before	provided that	unless	while
even if	rather than	until	why
even though	since	when	

Here are some examples of fragments caused by unconnected subordinate conjunctions:

> Even though society seems to be increasingly concerned. Crime keeps rising.
>
> After the flood subsided. The corn started to grow again.

To correct such fragments, simply join them to the neighboring sentence:

> Even though society seems to be increasingly concerned, crime keeps rising.
>
> The corn started to grow again after the flood subsided.

Remember to use a comma following the dependent clause if it comes before the independent clause:

Incorrect: Since it was our anniversary. We ordered lobster.
Correct: Since it was our anniversary, we ordered lobster.
But: We ordered lobster since it was our anniversary.

IN A NUTSHELL

Subordinate conjunctions and relative pronouns can trigger sentence fragments. Correct these fragments by joining them to a neighboring sentence.

PRACTICE 6

Correct the following fragments by joining them to a neighboring sentence.

1. We shop at Piggly-Wiggly for most of our groceries. Although I prefer Dominick's for meats.

____

____

2. The words acquired new meaning. When he found out that they were spoken by Abraham Lincoln.

3. Now, let's look at the words *bull* and *cow*. Which are simply male and female equivalents.

4. Stop and take a rest. If your breathing becomes labored.

5. My favorite restaurant is the Fireside Inn. Which is near my grandparents' house.

6. The hills were alive with the voices of people. Whose laughter rang across the valley.

7. He plays several sports. Since he is quite athletic.

8. I want to leave the hustle and bustle of city life. Where every decision is one more frustration.

9. He worked hard and studied until midnight every night. In order to make the Dean's List.

10. Get one large pizza. Rather than two medium ones.

Fragments Due to Added Details

Details added to a sentence can also cause a fragment. Beware of the words listed below. They often lead to added-detail fragments.

especially	including
except, except for	not even
also	such as
in addition	for example

Here are three examples of fragments caused by added details:

The entire neighborhood was up in arms. Except the Johnson sisters.

The expedition leader warned of many hardships. Including freezing weather, lack of food, and difficult terrain.

Pottery made by the Acoma has very bold geometric designs. For example, horizontal and vertical lines, triangles, and diamonds.

To correct a fragment caused by added details, simply attach the details to the previous sentence (using a comma to set off the added details) and add any words necessary to complete the link:

The entire neighborhood was up in arms, except the Johnson sisters.

The expedition leader warned of many hardships, including freezing weather, lack of food, and difficult terrain.

If the fragment containing the additional details is long, you can make it into a separate sentence:

Pottery made by the Acoma has very bold geometric designs. These designs feature horizontal and vertical lines, triangles, and diamonds.

IN A NUTSHELL

Details added to a sentence as an afterthought can cause a fragment. Correct the fragment by connecting it to the previous sentence or by turning it into a complete sentence of its own.

PRACTICE 7

Correct the following fragments caused by added details by joining the fragment to the sentence before it.

1. Some of my favorite people are a little eccentric. For example, the woman who wears an evening gown to feed the pigeons.

____

____

2. Certain languages are more musical than others. Among them Italian and Spanish.

____

____

3. She received many gifts. Tickets to a Hawks game, a bracelet, and a couple of CDs.

____

____

4. No parent always makes the right decision. Not even with the best of intentions.

____

____

5. We encountered some minor difficulties. Including locking the keys in the car.

____

____

6. For appetizers, we'll have chips and salsa. Also, cheese and vegetables with dip.

____

____

7. The girls kept getting into trouble at the bus stop. Except for Mary, an A student.

____

____

8. Students should be encouraged to become intimate with their books. Even writing in the margins of pages.

____

____

9. The Boston Pops always puts on a great July 4th celebration. With fireworks and a cannon.

____

____

10. A good leader never leaves his followers without hope. Especially in times of serious trouble.

____

____

Run-on Sentences

A **run-on sentence** is actually two sentences mistaken for one. There are two main types of run-on sentences: the **fused sentence** and the **comma splice**.

The **fused sentence** consists of two sentences joined—or fused—without any punctuation between them:

> We toured General Grant's home it is in Illinois.

Here is how the sentence should be written:

> We toured General Grant's home. It is in Illinois.

The second type of run-on sentence is the **comma splice**—two full sentences separated by a comma instead of a period:

> The steak was gray and tough, the eggs tasted like rubber.

Here is the sentence, corrected:

> The steak was gray and tough. The eggs tasted like rubber.

ESL Advice!

If you learned British English, you were probably allowed to link independent clauses with a comma. When writing American English, you must follow the rules described in this chapter.

PRACTICE 8

In the blanks provided, indicate *FS* if the run-on sentence is fused and *CS* if it is spliced. If the sentence is correct, neither fused nor spliced, mark it with a checkmark.

Example: CS She is beautiful, she is too thin.

1. ____ Don't wait another minute to send your money now.
2. ____ He must attend class on Wednesday, a test will be given.
3. ____ Raspberries are tasty, they are expensive.
4. ____ You may be able to live on love you definitely can't retire on it.
5. ____ Scorpions are wary they rely on their natural camouflage to protect them from enemies.
6. ____ Mark Blumenstein is a modern artist who uses saws, gas nozzles, and scythe blades in his sculptures.
7. ____ Get relief from allergies use a steam inhalator.
8. ____ It was cold, windy, and dark the fish didn't bite.
9. ____ People from all walks of life play softball because it is our most democratic pastime.

10. ____ She wore a black turtleneck everyone wanted to know where she had bought it.

Correcting Run-on Sentences

There are four ways to correct run-on sentences. Take this one, for example:

Frank is outgoing Jeff is timid.

To correct it, you can do one of the following:

1. Put a period at the end of the first sentence:

   Frank is outgoing. Jeff is timid.

2. Put a semicolon at the end of the first sentence:

   Frank is outgoing; Jeff is timid.

3. Put a coordinating conjunction (with a comma before it) at the end of the first sentence:

   Frank is outgoing, but Jeff is timid.

4. Use a subordinating conjunction:

   Frank is outgoing although Jeff is timid.

   or

   Although Frank is outgoing, Jeff is timid.

IN A NUTSHELL

Two sentences that are run together as one create a run-on sentence. To correct a run-on sentence, do one of the following:

- Put a period between them.
- Put a semicolon between them.
- Put a coordinating conjunction between them. (Don't forget the comma.)
- Use a subordinating conjunction. (Put a comma after the subordinating conjunction if it is first.)

PRACTICE 9

Correct the following run-on sentences in all four possible ways.

1. He sent a dozen roses she still didn't forgive him.

   Insert a period: ______________________________

   ____

Insert a semicolon: ______________________________

____

Insert a coordinating conjunction and comma: ________

____

Insert a subordinating conjunction (with comma if needed): ______________________________

____

2. I've always wanted a pickup truck it's only a matter of time until I get one.

Insert a period: ______________________________

____

Insert a semicolon: ______________________________

____

Insert a coordinating conjunction and comma: ________

____

Insert a subordinating conjunction (with comma if needed): ______________________________

____

3. It rained all day, the yard was one big puddle.

Insert a period: ______________________________

____

Insert a semicolon: ______________________________

____

Insert a coordinating conjunction and comma: ________

____

Insert a subordinating conjunction (with comma if needed): ______________________________

____

4. Bring name tags and pens Mary always forgets them.

Insert a period: ______________________________

____

Insert a semicolon: ______________________________

____

Insert a coordinating conjunction and comma: ________

____

Insert a subordinating conjunction (with comma if needed): ______________________________

____

5. The children looked for shells their mother watched that they didn't wander far.

Insert a period: ______________________________

____

Insert a semicolon: ______________________________

____

Insert a coordinating conjunction and comma: __________

____

Insert a subordinating conjunction (with comma if needed): ______________________________

____

6. Our team has talent and trains hard our problem is injuries.

Insert a period: ______________________________

____

Insert a semicolon: ______________________________

____

Insert a coordinating conjunction and comma: __________

____

Insert a subordinating conjunction (with comma if needed): ______________________________

____

7. I love bright colors that liking doesn't include pea green.

Insert a period: ______________________________

____

Insert a semicolon: ______________________________

____

Insert a coordinating conjunction and comma: __________

____

Insert a subordinating conjunction (with comma if needed): ______________________________

____

8. People are having dinner on the patio I wish we had an umbrella to avoid the sun.

   Insert a period: ______________________________

   ____

   Insert a semicolon: ______________________________

   ____

   Insert a coordinating conjunction and comma: ________

   ____

   Insert a subordinating conjunction (with comma if needed): ______________________________

   ____

9. We were roommates for one year we got to know each other well.

   Insert a period: ______________________________

   ____

   Insert a semicolon: ______________________________

   ____

   Insert a coordinating conjunction and comma: ________

   ____

   Insert a subordinating conjunction (with comma if needed): ______________________________

   ____

10. I often get colds I have some home remedies that really help.

   Insert a period: ______________________________

   ____

   Insert a semicolon: ______________________________

   ____

   Insert a coordinating conjunction and comma: ________

   ____

   Insert a subordinating conjunction (with comma if needed): ______________________________

   ____

PRACTICE 10

In the space before each of the following run-on sentences, mark the error as a fused sentence *(FS)* or comma splice *(CS)*. Then, correct each sentence.

1. ____ Today is my birthday I still feel young.

____

____

2. ____ Rico wanted to go on vacation, his boss demanded the report by tomorrow.

____

____

3. ____ Bright red lipstick looks gaudy it isn't popular this summer.

____

____

4. ____ Our plane was delayed, the fog was too thick.

____

____

5. ____ Botany is difficult for me it involves much memory work.

____

____

6. ____ A computer is a mystery, I can't even imagine how it functions.

____

____

7. ____ My first date with Felice was a disaster, she wanted to dance, and I am a klutz.

____

____

8. ____ I made a plum pie it was juicy and sweet.

____

____

9. ____ I picked up my coat and ran to the front door my dad was patiently waiting.

____

____

10. ____ We had to watch 10 minutes of silly trailers the main movie did not begin until 7:15.

____

____

PRACTICE 11

Correct the following run-on sentences.

1. Chris has a good sense of humor he often laughs at himself.

2. Sandra is a striking child, with jet black ringlets framing her face, she looks like her mother.

3. The male butterfly attracts a mate by fluttering around and showing off his strategy doesn't always work.

4. The police log shows burglaries are down car theft is up, though.

5. Caterpillars are one of nature's great illusions who would ever think that these wormlike creatures become such beauties?

6. Sherry is totally unreliable, sometimes she arrives an hour or two late.

7. You cannot avoid cold germs simply by hiding from everyone, a better way is to strengthen your resistance.

8. I decided to change my approach I would pretend total indifference to her.

9. All of us like to show off at times no one is immune to the human need for attention.

10. Lip readers read each word slowly, on the other hand, speed readers drop diagonally down the page to catch the main ideas.

____

____

PRACTICE 12

Some of the sentences that follow are correct; others contain fragments or run-ons. If the sentence is correct, write *C* in the blank. If the sentence is incorrect, identify the error by writing *F* for fragment or *R* for run-on in the blank. Then rewrite the sentence to correct the error.

1. ____ I arrived at the park at noon, the sun was directly overhead, and a few random clouds were scattered across the sky.

____

____

2. ____ I brought nothing with me except a pen and a notebook for recording my thoughts I did not want to spoil the park's natural beauty with anything from the outside world.

____

____

3. ____ Other people had also decided to visit the park that day, we paid no attention to each other.

____

____

4. ____ I stood on a grassy knoll. Where I could observe and absorb everything around me.

____

____

5. ____ To the left of me was a small grove of orange trees. Including a tree so gnarled that it looked as if it had been transplanted from a witch's garden.

____

____

6. ____ Everywhere else, all I could see were mountains, mountains, mountains.

____

____

7. ____ As I walked toward the orange grove, I heard different birds calling to one another.

____

____

8. ____ Birds have a freedom that humans do not possess. The freedom to soar above the ground and see the world from a different perspective.

____

____

9. ____ I picked an orange from a low branch and peeled it so that I could squeeze the juice into my mouth.

____

____

10. ____ The sweetness trickled from my lips, it seemed like drops of some magical potion.

____

____

PRACTICE 13

The following paragraph contains fragments and run-on sentences. Rewrite it to correct each error by one of the methods described in this unit.

Two years had passed since I had last seen my grandmother. During this time, her condition had worsened, now she was completely bedridden. No longer able to get up and walk. She babbled without making sense, she had no idea who I was. Her gray eyes stared vacantly. As if she were half in another world unknown to me. All I could do was smile at her and hold her hand. Yet, I was struck by the fact that even in this hopelessly deteriorated state, she seemed to want to communicate with me she wanted a human connection. I decided that she was still my kind, beautiful grandmother inside, no matter how she appeared on the outside. Today I wonder what it will be like when I am old. Personally, I hope I don't live long enough to be in such a deteriorated condition. Unable to recognize loved ones. How frustrating it must be to be senile. To repeat the same questions and to remember nothing. Still, maybe science will some day find a cure for extreme senility, I hope so.

____

____

____

Unit Test

After each sentence, write *F* for fragment, *CS* for comma splice, or *FS* for fused sentences. Then correct each error. *(Note: One of the sentences contains two errors.)*

1. Diogenes was not a degenerate or a beggar he was a philosopher and poet. ______

2. Cheese macaroni is a quick and easy meal. Also spaghetti. ______

3. Political correctness has its downside, it may stop any honest debate about sensitive subjects. ______

4. I love our family farm. Because all of my childhood memories are connected with this piece of land. ______

5. History teaches us that rebels were often right they were not always crazy or radical. Consider, for example, George Washington, Martin Luther, and Galileo. ______

6. Most Americans get their news from television they read newspapers only for sports and human interest stories. ______

7. Rollerblading is good exercise you should wear kneepads when you're first learning. _____

8. The ice skater gracefully lifted his partner above his head the audience gasped. _____

9. The health food store closed, I guess it wasn't making money. _____

10. We drove from Cleveland to Pittsburgh and back. Filling up on gas only once. _____

Unit Talk–Write Assignment

Two freshman students are talking about the class they hated most in high school. They both agree that it was gym and take turns blasting it as a waste of time. Both students talk in everyday non-standard English filled with fragments and run-on sentences—the kind of speech you would use with a close friend but not in an English paper. Using the lines provided in the column on the right, turn all of the fragments into complete sentences that are written in standard English.

TALK	WRITE
1. Margie: Going to gym! What a waste of time.	
2. Cathy: To run up and down the basketball court until you sweat like a pig and doing it everyday.	

3. Margie: You know what I hated the most? After the stupid games like golf.

4. Cathy: The way some teachers took it seriously?

5. Margie: Not that. Bad enough already. The bowling. I told the teacher I can't do this I just had my nails done you can't expect me to go bowling with these nails. Know what he said?

6. Cathy: To forget about your nails?

7. Margie: He said a good bowler like me will sacrifice her nails for the game. Like I'm a good bowler. To think that about me!

8. Cathy: Like you care about bowling.

9. Margie: I said, you know how much these nails cost me you know how much a manicure runs these days?

10. Cathy: Probably as much as a bowling ball. Golf was what got me. Hated that game. Ridiculous running around hitting a stupid ball with a stick into a hole. To take a game like that so seriously!

11. Margie: To be always hitting the stupid ball into the bushes. And never being able to find it. I told the teacher. Let me throw the ball I can do better that way.

12. Cathy: Praying for rain every day so we have to stay inside.

13. Margie: Gym class—what a joke!

Unit Collaborative Assignment

Some of the sentences in the following paragraphs are correct, but some are fragments or run-ons. Correct all of the incorrect sentences. Then team up with a classmate, exchange books, and check each other's work. Discuss any sentences about which you disagree.

I am a file clerk in the office of a Denny's restaurant, I am required to file correctly. While this process may seem easy, it can actually become a real problem. If the proper filing rules are not followed. Nothing is more confusing and time wasting than lost files.

Here are some basic filing rules to follow: First, you need to know the correct order of the letters of the alphabet. Something you should have learned in grade school. Second, a file clerk must know that for each of the 26 letters there is a file cut, the file cut is the label part that extends above the rest of the file. These file cuts are right, left, and middle. Third, before you put files in a filing cabinet, you must take the time to alphabetize them so that you don't have to jump back and forth. From drawer to drawer. Fourth, while filing, you must never rush otherwise you are likely to misfile. Which may cause big trouble because lost files are hard to find later.

Finally, the order of filing is important and can be tricky. For instance, you must file by a person's last name. If two people have the same last name, then use the first name to distinguish between them. To stay in proper alphabetical order. For instance, "John Smith" comes after "Agnes Smith." Furthermore, a space in a name is treated as if the space were not there, for instance, "De Lang" precedes "Derring." Following these simple rules lessens the risk of making filing errors, and in the long run they will save you time and energy.

Unit Writing Assignment

Using freewriting, brainstorming, clustering, or any other method of prewriting, write about one of these subjects. Avoid sentence fragments and run-on sentences.

1. The person you are whom others seldom see
2. Your attitude toward practical jokes
3. Someone you think is terribly funny
4. Your favorite (or least favorite) exercise to keep in shape
5. A habit you would like to overcome

Photo Writing Assignment

The person in the following picture is eating alone. Brainstorm or freewrite to develop a paragraph about why you think the person is alone. Develop a discussible topic sentence, and support it with strong details. Check your sentences carefully to ensure that you have avoided fragments and run-on sentences. Use the Revising Checklist.

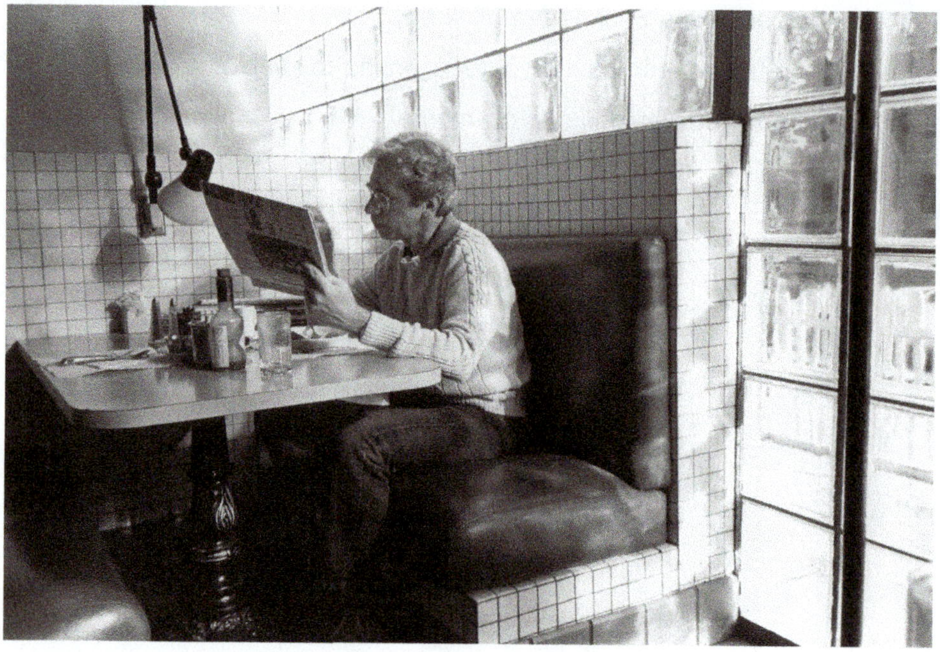

Here's a handy shortcut for recognizing sentence fragments:

Step 1: Check each possible sentence to make sure that it contains a subject and a verb.

Fragment: The girl in the long skirt. (Girl could be the subject of a sentence, but there is no verb.)

Correction: The girl in the long skirt spoke fluent Spanish. (Spoke now serves as a verb.)

Step 2: If you find a subject and a verb, check to make sure that the group of words makes a complete statement.

Fragment: After she stole all of his money. (This group of words has a subject and a verb, but it is a dependent clause and does not make a complete sentence.)

Correction: After she stole all of his money, she had the nerve to ask him to lend her $200. (Now the group of words makes a complete sentence because the independent clause was joined to an independent clause.)

7 VERBS—AN OVERVIEW

"They had danced when they were younger."

Verbs can be troublesome. Part of the problem is that we don't speak and write verbs the same way. In speech we sometimes drop the tense endings of verbs when we shouldn't, as in this sentence:

> She talk too much.

Or, we add an ending when we shouldn't:

> They talks too much.

In the first sentence, since *she* is singular, the verb must also be singular—*talks*. In the second sentence, since *they* is plural, the verb must also be plural—*talk*.

You can make these mistakes in everyday speech—we all occasionally do—and be forgiven. You should not, however, make them in writing. The standards for grammar are stricter in writing than in speech, meaning that you must always write verb tenses correctly.

There is good news: You already know more about verb tenses than you realize.

Twelve Tenses

English has 12 tenses. Of these 12 tenses, the most widely used are the simple present, past, and future. Here is a formal list of all the tenses and their functions:

TENSE	HOW IT IS USED	EXAMPLE
Present	For actions that are occurring now and are ongoing	I dance. Bill dances.
Simple past	For actions that took place in the past and do not extend into the present	We danced all night.
Future	For actions that will happen sometime after the present	I will dance at your wedding.
Present perfect	For actions that started in the past and have been completed in the present	I have just finished dancing.
Past perfect	For actions that were completed in the past before another action took place	Amazingly, she had often danced with him before he became president.
Future perfect	For actions that will happen in the future before some other specific future action	The couple will have danced twice before you leave.
Present progressive	For actions that are still in progress	They are dancing in the park.
Past progressive	For actions that were in progress in the past	She was dancing like a gypsy.
Future progressive	For future actions that will take place continuously	He will be dancing with you.
Present perfect progressive	For actions that started in the past and continue into the present	Madame François has been dancing lately.
Past perfect progressive	For actions that were in progress in the past before another past action took place	Everyone had been dancing until the music stopped.
Future progressive perfect	For actions that continue to take place before some other future action	The dancing will have been going on for a long time before you have to choose a winner.

ESL Advice!

Knowing the formal names of these tenses is unnecessary as long as you learn how to use them correctly.

Scanning this table of tenses should make you appreciate your instinctive sense of grammar—assuming that you're a native speaker. Indeed, many people to whom English is the mother tongue cannot name all of the 12 tenses, but still know how to use them. This is all the more remarkable because many of us rarely, if ever, use some of these tenses. Sometimes months, even years, go by before we use the future perfect progressive (The dancing will have been going on for a long time before you have to choose a winner). When we do use it, we do so unconsciously. Grammar, as we have said repeatedly in this book, is largely a built-in skill as natural and automatic as walking. Seeing all the tenses listed here should also make us appreciate the effort that ESL students must put in to master English as a second language.

Present Tense Endings

In standard English, you must use the correct endings with verbs. You cannot use a plural ending with a singular subject, or a singular ending with a plural subject. Here are the correct endings for regular verbs in the present tense:

PRESENT TENSE—SINGULAR

INCORRECT	CORRECT
I walks	I walk
you walks	you walk
he / she / it } walks	he / she / it } walks

PRESENT TENSE—PLURAL

INCORRECT	CORRECT
we walks	we walk
you walks	you walk
they walks	they walk

Present Tense Problems

There are two kinds of problems that commonly occur with verbs in the present tense.

1. Dropped *-s*/*-es* endings for *he*, *she*, and *it*.

Incorrect: She walk home the long way.

Correct: She walks home the long way.

Incorrect: Bob play the piano for relaxation.

Correct: Bob plays the piano for relaxation.

Incorrect: He wash the kitchen floor once a week.

Correct: He washes the kitchen floor once a week.

2. Unnecessary *-s/-es* endings for *we, you,* and *they.*

Incorrect: We plays hard every day.

Correct: We play hard every day.

Incorrect: You checks out everything.

Correct: You check out everything.

Incorrect: They watches out for everybody.

Correct: They watch out for everybody.

EAR ALERT

Problems with dropped and added endings occur, as we said, because we are less precise in our speech than we must be in our writing. If you regularly make such errors in your speech, your ear may not be particularly helpful in catching them. In that case, you should simply memorize the correct endings.

PRACTICE 1

Underline the correct verb.

Example: The bus (<u>stops</u>, stop) in front of Mary's house.

1. The waiters (wears, wear) purple suspenders.
2. A big white dog (sit, sits) on the porch swing.
3. All the girls (wants, want) to pierce their ears.
4. The lemons (need, needs) to be grated.
5. Two fleecy clouds (drifts, drift) across the sky.
6. Suzy and I (prefers, prefer) to eat later.
7. We (believe, believes) that country life is better than city life.
8. The schools (deserve, deserves) the most modern libraries.
9. Greg and Karin (promises, promise) to make the punch.
10. Several movie stars (lead, leads) troubled lives.

PRACTICE 2

In the blank provided, mark *S* if the noun is singular and *P* if it is plural. Correct the verb if it does not agree with the noun.

Example: <u>S</u> He always whistle in the dark. ***<u>whistles</u>***

1. ____ Jim and I live on Broadway. ________
2. ____ We love baseball. ________
3. ____ This restaurant need remodeling. ________
4. ____ Franny own two cats. ________
5. ____ She finish her report early. ________
6. ____ Women wants good careers nowadays. ________
7. ____ I hope Harry washes his car. ________
8. ____ My computer save me lots of time. ________

9. ____ Aunt Elsie walks two miles every day. ________

10. ____ Jake and Marvin spends too much time watching television. ________

PRACTICE 3

In the passage that follows, strike out any incorrect verb and write the correct form above it.

1. Mrs. Farrow, our next-door neighbor, hate dogs. 2. Anytime she hear our dog bark, she yell at him, "Shut up, you ugly mutt." 3. I suppose people like this neighbor dislikes pets because they never had a pet of their own. 4. I feel sorry for Mrs. Farrow because she believe that dogs exists just to be yelled at and never to be treated as friends. 5. Mrs. Farrow live alone, and it seem to me that a dog could be excellent company for her if she would just change her attitude.

PRACTICE 4

In the blanks provided, write the present tense of a verb that would fit the sentence.

1. My dad ____ a tall, athletic man. 2. He ____ no guff from anyone. 3. My sister and I ____ my dad and try to please him. 4. Whenever he comes home from work, we ____ him read the paper in peace without disturbing him with questions. 5. Some of my friends wonder if my dad and I ____ good friends, and I always insist that we ____ . 6. I ____ that my dad is stern and strict, but I ____ also convinced that he basically ____ me. 7. The most fun I ____ with my dad is when we ____ together. 8. Then we ____ good heart-to-heart talks. 9. Dad ____ always honest and he ____ that developing integrity is important. 10. Can you blame me if I ____ my dad a lot?

Past Tense Endings

Here are the correct endings for regular singular verbs in the past tense:

PAST TENSE—SINGULAR

INCORRECT	CORRECT
I walk	I walked
you walk	you walked
he / she / it } walk	he / she / it } walked

Here are the correct endings for regular plural verbs in the past tense:

PAST TENSE—PLURAL

INCORRECT	CORRECT
we walk	we walked
you walk	you walked
they walk	they walked

With both singular and plural verbs, we sometimes are careless in our speech and drop the *-ed* ending. But in writing, you must always use the *-ed* ending with regular verbs in the past tense.

Incorrect: I hike there yesterday.
Correct: I hiked there yesterday.

Incorrect: She bake a pie last week.
Correct: She baked a pie last week.

PRACTICE 5

Write the past tense of the italicized verb in the blank.

Example: Only his nose *remain* uncovered. ***remained***

1. The giggling clown *twist* his nose. ______
2. We *decide* to match him dollar for dollar. ______
3. To my deep sorrow, John *believe* a stranger, not me. ______
4. She barely *manage* to wheel her bicycle into the garage. ______
5. They *last* much longer than expected. ______
6. They *deliver* the paper two days late. ______
7. Fred and Marv *order* two big pizzas. ______
8. I *decide* to spare myself much grief by breaking up with Sally. ______
9. Two or three days ago the weather *change* abruptly. ______
10. Disregarding the sign, he *park* in a Disabled parking spot. ______

PRACTICE 6

In each of the following sentences, change the verb to the past tense if it is in the present tense or to the present tense if it is in the past tense.

Example: I loved my new car. (verb in past tense) I love my new car. (verb now in present tense)

1. She was speaking dreamily of the good old days.
2. The old man remembers his youth in Brooklyn.
3. You give me no choice.
4. Some observers doubted that the tribes were really cannibals.
5. On my visit to the zoo, I see a giant panda.
6. Why didn't we try again?
7. She asked what the pacing meant.
8. They hired a 27-year-old consultant.
9. Some bank robbers are incredibly stupid and leave fingerprints.
10. Be it ever so humble, there was no place like home.

Problems with *-ing* Verbs

Verbs ending in *-ing* describe an action that is either happening now or has happened in the past but is still ongoing. As you learned in Unit 7, all *-ing* verbs need a helping verb.

She is studying in the library.

She was studying in the library.

She has been studying in the library.

She had been studying in the library, but now she studies in her dorm.

Two kinds of problems can occur with *-ing* verbs:

1. *Be* or *been* is used instead of the correct helping verb:

Incorrect: She be studying in the library.

Correct: She is studying in the library.

or

She has been studying in the library.

Incorrect: She been studying in the library.

Correct: She was studying in the library.

or

She has been studying in the library.

2. The helping verb is completely omitted:

Incorrect: They pretending not to know.

Correct: They are pretending not to know.

They were pretending not to know.

or

They have been pretending not to know.

They had been pretending not to know.

Both kinds of errors can confuse and mislead a reader. *She has been studying in the library* is more precise than *She be studying in the library.* With the helping verb missing, we can't tell whether an action is ongoing, or has already gone on but is now over. *They pretending not to know* is therefore fuzzier than *They have been pretending not to know.* Be alert to the possibility of both errors.

PRACTICE 7

Rewrite the following sentences to correct the misuse of *be* or *been* or to insert the missing helping verb.

Example: The children be screaming in the room.

The children are screaming in the room.

Example: Macy's having a sale.

Macy's is having a sale.

1. My family be wanting to move to Baltimore.

2. She telling her daughter not to marry Bud.

3. Amy putting up with her roommate's messy ways.

4. How she be doing at her job?

5. Frank wishing he were class president.

6. They be listening to the professor's lecture.

7. Mr. Goldman watching the movie *Working Girls* when the storm hit.

8. Every generation be creating its own music.

9. Mitch pushing the idea of creating a band.

____

10. We be expecting too much from that motor.

____

PRACTICE 8

Underline the correct form of the verb.

1. She (be, has been) studying without proper lighting.
2. Our art class (hoping, is hoping) to go on a museum field trip.
3. The mechanic at the gas station (had been working, working) on Pete's jeep when suddenly lightning struck.
4. Most of the children (be, are) asking for hot dogs.
5. Raquel (has been, be) trying out for the swim team.
6. Whenever the teacher (be, was) reading from his notes, we fell asleep.
7. I (was expecting, expecting) to have to show my ID.
8. Lindsay (be, has been) feeling much better today.
9. We constantly (be, are) hearing that the family is in trouble.
10. Actually, Dad (trying, was trying) to reach you by phone.

Difficult Verbs: *Be, Have, Do*

Verbs can be hard to master. Few, though, are harder to master than the three verbs we probably use more than any others in the language: *be, have,* and *do.* Not only are these verbs in their own right, but they are also commonly used as helping verbs. (Try saying a few sentences without *be*, *have*, and *do* and see how much you miss them.) We'll treat each one separately.

To Be

To be is commonly used both as a verb on its own and as a helping verb. Here is a list of the forms of the verb *to be*:

PRESENT TENSE—SINGULAR: TO BE

INCORRECT	CORRECT
I be, I ain't	I am, I am not
you be, you ain't	you are, you are not
he / she / it } be/ain't	he / she / it } is/is not

PRESENT TENSE—PLURAL: TO BE

INCORRECT	CORRECT
we be, we ain't	we are, we are not
you be, you ain't	you are, you are not
they be, they ain't	they are, they are not

PAST TENSE—SINGULAR: TO BE

INCORRECT	CORRECT
I were	I was
you was	you were
he / she / it } were	he / she / it } was

PAST TENSE—PLURAL: TO BE

INCORRECT	CORRECT
we was	we were
you was	you were
they was	they were

As you can see—indeed, as you already know from repeated use—*to be* is an irregular verb. As both a verb and a helping verb, it is often incorrectly spoken. All of the following sentences, for example, are wrong, even if your ear tells you otherwise:

INCORRECT	CORRECT
I ain't going to do it.	I am not going to do it.
Absence be the reason he gets poor grades.	Absence is the reason he gets poor grades.
You was right about her.	You were right about her.

If you commonly use the incorrect forms in your daily speech, be especially careful not to trust your ear with *to be*. Instead, memorize its correct forms.

PRACTICE 9

The following passage contains several errors in the use of the verb *to be*. Cross out any incorrect use of the verb *to be* and, in the space between the lines, write the correct form of the verb. *(Hint: You should find 10 errors.)*

My car be a 10-year-old Chevy. I bought it for $300 and I ain't going to sell it because it be a great car. Hank, my buddy, and I worked all last summer to improve the car and make it run. We be proud of our work because the car be the best in our school. The paint job be bright red. The other kids are jealous of us because they ain't smart enough to fix up a car the way we fixed up ours. Hank be the kind of friend who helps me with keeping up this car. It be good to have such a loyal buddy, ain't that so?

To Have

To have, like *to be*, is commonly used both as a verb and as a helping verb. Like *to be*, it is also an irregular verb. Here are its main forms:

PRESENT TENSE—SINGULAR: TO HAVE

INCORRECT	CORRECT
I has	I have
you has	you have
he, she, it have	he, she, it has

PRESENT TENSE—PLURAL: TO HAVE

INCORRECT	CORRECT
we has	we have
you has	you have
they has	they have

PAST TENSE—SINGULAR: TO HAVE

INCORRECT	CORRECT
I has	I had
you has	you had
he, she, it have	he, she, it had

PAST TENSE—PLURAL: TO HAVE

INCORRECT	CORRECT
we has	we had
you has	you had
they has	they had

Like *to be*, *to have* is so often misused in daily speech that you should be cautious about trusting your ear to judge its correctness. The sentences below, for example, are all incorrect:

She have a problem.

He have on a new coat.

They has a quarrel yesterday.

Here are the correct forms:

She has a problem.

He has on a new coat.

They had a quarrel yesterday.

PRACTICE 10

In the following sentences, fill in the correct form of the verb *to have.*

Example: She ***has*** to go.

1. Mary _____ a pet collie.
2. You _____ to stop saying that.
3. Mr. Ward _____ the only blue house on the street.
4. You _____ my only copy, and I must _____ it back.
5. I _____ got to let go of her, and she _____ to understand why.
6. _____ he said anything to you about it?
7. Where _____ you been?
8. He _____ borrowed my car for the last time.
9. No one _____ a right to say that.
10. I _____ many friends, but she _____ only one.

PRACTICE 11

The following passage contains several errors in the use of the verb *to have*. Cross out the incorrect uses of the verb *to have,* and write the correct form of the verb above each error. *(Hint: You should find six errors.)*

Jimmy have decided to register for English 120 with me. Both of us has trouble with English because, in the past, no one have made us feel that writing is important. We are both football players, and for us, the game means everything, while writing correct English have never seemed to be important. But now we are both motivated because we want to get good jobs when we finish college. Jimmy said to me the other day, "OK, Buddy, we has to prove that we can change our bad English habits, right?" I slapped him on the back and said, "Right on, I agree with you." Now we has a new attitude.

To Do

The verb *to do*, like *to be* and *to have*, is used both as a main verb and as a helping verb. It is so common in both writing and speech that it is found nearly everywhere. Here are its correct forms:

PRESENT TENSE—SINGULAR: TO DO

INCORRECT	CORRECT
I does	I do
you does	you do
he	he
she } do	she } does
it	it

PRESENT TENSE—PLURAL: TO DO

INCORRECT	CORRECT
we does	we do
you does	you do
they does	they do

PAST TENSE—SINGULAR: TO DO

INCORRECT	CORRECT
I done	I did
you done	you did
he	he
she } done	she } did
it	it

PAST TENSE—PLURAL: TO DO

INCORRECT	CORRECT
we done	we did
you done	you did
they done	they did

The main problem with *to do* is that it is frequently used incorrectly in informal speech. This common use makes it difficult to judge the correctness of *to do* by ear. All of the sentences below, for example, are incorrect:

He don't know what he's saying.

I does what I have to.

She done with him.

Here are the correct forms:

> He doesn't know what he's saying.
>
> I do what I have to.
>
> She is done with him.

If you are used to speaking the incorrect forms, don't trust your ear; instead, memorize the correct forms.

PRACTICE 12

Use the correct form of *to do* in the following sentences.

1. He _____ understand the subject.
2. She _____ carry on, _____ she?
3. _____ you know what the meeting is about?
4. How you change the sparkplugs?
5. Tiffany always _____ badly on the tennis court when she plays a match.
6. I _____ feel a sense of pride.
7. _____ she know about the sale?
8. Where _____ you find such good people?
9. _____ not speak to me that way!
10. It _____ not matter what you are talking about.
11. We _____ the best individuals to pull her out of the car.
12. When _____ the night custodian come on duty?
13. You always _____ what your teachers expect of you.
14. _____ you agree that I did slam on the brakes to avoid him?
15. Oh, how he _____ stick his nose into our business.

PRACTICE 13

The following conversation was overheard in a campus coffee shop. The topic was worrisome problems. Each sentence contains at least one error in the verbs *be, have,* or *do*. Write the sentence correctly on the lines provided.

1. I be worried about Sue lately.

   ____

   ____

2. Why? It don't make sense to worry.

   ____

   ____

3. She have a car that's always giving her trouble.

____

____

4. Why that be your worry?

____

____

5. She have a habit of getting in a bad mood when it don't work properly.

____

____

6. Why ain't you fixed it for her?

____

____

7. I be spending all my time trying to fix it, and Sue just be getting madder and madder at me.

____

____

8. Well, you has your problems and I has mine.

____

____

9. I guess we be of a different opinion about our problems.

____

____

10. Right. You be in one corner, and I be in the other.

____

____

Helping Verbs

Helping verbs, as the name implies, are verbs that are combined with the regular verb forms of the present, present participle, and past participle to express additional tenses. Here is a list of common helping verbs:

is	was	does	have
am	were	did	had
are	do	has	

Helping verbs often change their form, depending on their subject. Here are some examples:

Jim *is* fighting with his brother.

We *are* fighting with his brother.

I *am* fighting with his brother.

Fixed-form Helping Verbs

Some helping verbs never change form and are thus called "fixed-form helping verbs." Here is a list of fixed-form helping verbs:

can	will	may	shall	must
could	would	might	should	

Notice that in the following sentences, the helping verb does not change with the subject:

Mary *can* swim.

I can swim.

The boys *can* swim

We *can* swim.

Mary *might* swim. We *might* swim. They *might* swim

I *should* swim. Mrs. Jorge *should* swim. Dozens of people *should* swim.

The boys *must* swim. Bibi and Buba *must* swim. You, of all people, *must* swim.

Here are some other facts you need to know about certain helping verbs:

Can always indicates the present tense: Now (today) Pete *can* pay his bills.

Could is tricky because it can indicate the past tense, but also a possibility or a wish:

Past: Two weeks ago, his mother *could* drive to work.

Possibility: His mother *could* drive if she had a driver's license.

Wish: He wishes his mother *could* drive.

Will indicates the future as viewed from the present:

Dan doubts (present) that he *will* (future) pass the test.

Would is tricky because in addition to indicating the future as viewed from the past, it can also indicate a possibility or a wish:

Future from the past: We thought (past) for sure we *would* (future) make it.

Possibility: We *would* learn to dance if we had a good teacher.

Wish: We wish we *would* make a big profit this quarter.

PRACTICE 14

Underline the helping verb. In the blank provided, indicate "FF" if the helping verb is a fixed-form helping verb and "R" if the helping verb is a regular helping verb.

Example: FF The firefighters might quit.

1. _____ Since you're tall, you can reach the top shelf.
2. _____ It does matter that he hates hot weather.
3. _____ She has questioned the test results.
4. _____ All football players must meet the coach today.
5. _____ His sister is calling the ticket booth.
6. _____ Jennifer and Maria should volunteer today.
7. _____ You were asked to leave immediately.
8. _____ John wishes he could comfort them.
9. _____ Last March she did complain to the police.
10. _____ They have dialed the phone all day.
11. _____ Tomorrow it may rain for the next two days.
12. _____ Jerry could barely walk because he had a broken toe.
13. _____ Every blogger has given his or her opinion on global warming.
14. _____ Do those campers ever stop singing so loudly?
15. _____ Jack played basketball at Farmington High, so he might know Phil.

Unit Test

Fill in the blank with the correct form of the verb in parentheses.

1. Yesterday Julie (walk) _____ all the way to Jan's house.
2. My brother (be) _____ the best athlete in his class until he sprained his ankle.
3. We are both guitarists, but he (be) _____ better than I (be) _____.
4. Felix (do) _____ take his good looks too seriously.
5. Beverly still (smoke) _____ like a chimney.
6. Last year, Stan (fish) _____ for an entire month in Montana.
7. She (hide) _____ every time I try to find her.
8. If you (be) _____ happy, that's all that matters.
9. The room (have) _____ a bad smell.

10. (Do) _____ she always do the best she can?

11. Doris and Jim (have) _____ many financial problems.

12. The city (have) _____ to protect its citizens from fire hazards.

13. If she (do) _____ most of the work herself, it won't be expensive.

14. The winner (take) _____ the entire purse.

15. The furniture (have) _____ to be waxed and polished.

Unit Talk–Write Assignment

In the Talk column below, a student chatting with a friend expresses his opinion on when teenagers should get their drivers' licenses. His comments are casual, using somewhat lax grammar. Turn them into appropriate written sentences, paying special attention to the correct use of verbs.

TALK	WRITE
1. My brother's driving scares the living daylights out of me.	
2. Yesterday, he pile eight kids into my parents' van and burn rubber all the way down our hill to Main Street.	
3. My eyes bug out when I seen him.	
4. Then I remember how I use to drive just like him.	

5. Wrapping cars around posts or whamming them into garage doors be almost a badge of honor for us idiots.

6. Now I see that we was total jerks.

7. So what? Well, I don't think kids should get their licenses until they turns 18. My parents agrees with me.

8. I also think teenagers should be on probation for a year before their licenses be permanent.

9. Kids who shoplifts or paints graffiti should get their probation extended, too.

10. Probies should have their probation extended if they be driving recklessly or with piles of other kids in the car.

11. And if a guy is busted driving under the influence, that kid loses his proby license and can't get another one until he be twenty-one.

12. In other words, permanent driver's licenses should be given only to drivers who has good overall records.

13. These be sounding like tough rules, but I bet they'd save lives.

Unit Collaborative Assignment

Do this assignment with a classmate. The sentences that follow have singular subjects. Your classmate should read sentences 1–5 aloud. You will then write each sentence in the plural form, making sure that the subject and verb agree. Reread the changed sentences and discuss them with your partner.

Then reverse your roles for sentences 6–10. Finally, with your partner, check all of your written sentences to make sure that the subjects and verbs agree. (Note: Sometimes there is more than one verb in the sentence.)

1. Every student needs a healthy breakfast.
2. The train arrived from Philadelphia.
3. He doesn't care about wealth.
4. The woman pants because the hill is steep.
5. A child forgets quickly.
6. She goes to a movie every weekend.
7. Does he live in town?
8. I walk until I drop.

9. That book has a torn cover.

____

10. My wool sweater has no sleeves.

____

Unit Writing Assignment

Write a description of your childhood. Was it carefree? Happy? Lonely? Using brainstorming and freewriting, find a discussible point and support it with well-chosen details. When you have completed your writing, go over it to make sure that all of your verbs are correct.

Photo Writing Assignment

Study the following picture. Then brainstorm, freewrite, or cluster until you find a discussible point on the advantages of having a big brother, big sister, or another older relative. Think about such benefits as feeling protected; having someone to teach you to play sports, music, or some other skills; and having someone to look up to. Pay particular attention to using verbs correctly.

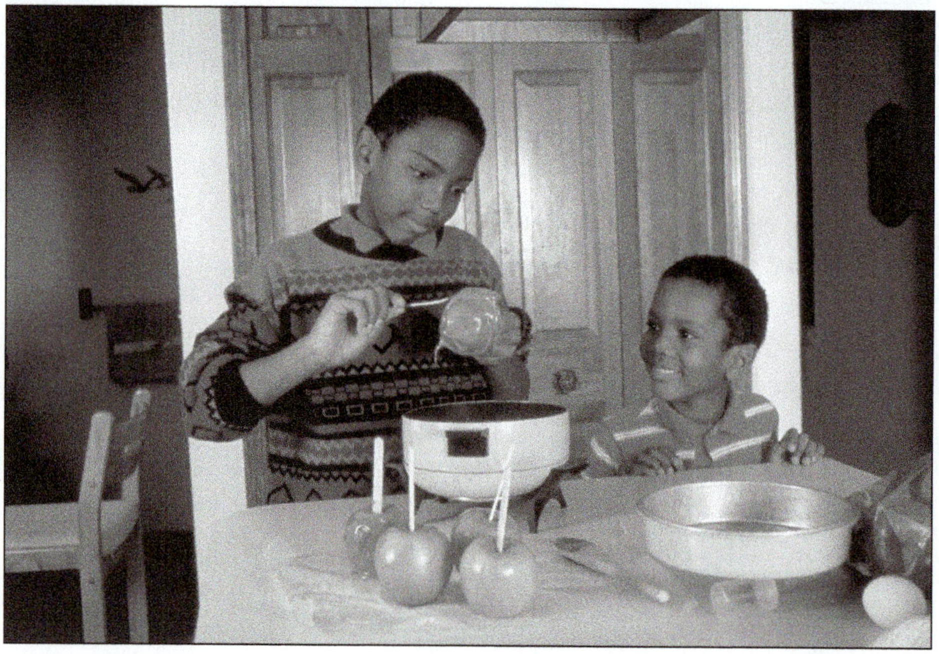

8 Regular and Irregular Verbs

"The cat snuck into my bed."
"He brung the book to school."

In Unit 7, we learned that nearly every day we all use complex verb forms correctly without knowing their formal names. Most of this use is governed by the user's ear. Being a native speaker allows you to use, say, the present perfect progressive tense—"My uncle has been playing baseball lately"—without knowing its academic name. Responsible for this skill is an internal sense of time that tells us what tense to use to describe an action that happened in the past.

ESL students, on the other hand, are not that lucky, and in the beginning they may have to rely on the book rule and formal name of the tense to use it accurately. But eventually, the foreign speaker will acccumulate enough experience with using various tenses to gradually acquire the ear of the native for tenses.

Regular Verbs

Very early in life, our ear tells us that the past tense of a verb is usually signaled by *-ed* at the end. At first, we stubbornly apply this rule to every verb. It is not unusual to hear toddlers say, "I sitted on my chair," or "David hitted me with his cup." Later, we learn that the rule applies only to regular verbs, not to verbs that are irregular.

Verbs are either regular or irregular. Regular verbs form the past tense by adding *-d* or *-ed*. They also form the past participle by adding *-d* or *-ed*. Combined with the helping verb *have* or *has,* the past particle can be used to indicate the present perfect tense. Adding the helping verb *had* to the past participle forms the past perfect. Here are some examples of common regular verbs:

PRESENT	PAST	PRESENT OR PAST PERFECT
charge	charged	have/has/had charged
cook	cooked	have/has/had cooked
pack	packed	have/has/had packed

Here are some examples of these words in sentences:

Past: She charged $7 per hour for painting the porch.
Present perfect: She has charged less for simpler jobs.
Past perfect: She had charged Mr. Jones overtime.
Past: They packed the books yesterday.
Present perfect: They have packed nearly everything now.
Past perfect: They had packed until nearly midnight.

Don't let your ear fool you into dropping the *-d* or *-ed* endings of past tense verbs. Although this is a common mistake that we all occasionally make in everyday speech, you must not make it in your writing.

EAR ALERT

Dropped ending: We were suppose to meet her at the theater.
We were use to doing it that way.

Correct: We were supposed to meet her at the theater.
We were used to doing it that way.

Here's an easy rule to remember about the past tense: If a verb ends in "e," just add a "d." If it ends in "y," change the "y" to an "i" and add "ed." Examples: *chase* becomes "chased"; *carry* becomes "carried." Use your ear to decide whether you should double the consonant to form the past tense of certain verbs, such as *butted, clubbed, fanned, manned, pitted, popped, ripped, rigged, wrapped,* and others. Read the word aloud. For instance, you would not write, "I riped off his shirt" because "riped" is pronounced with a long "i," whereas "ripped" is pronounced with a short "i." Your ear will give you the right spelling.

IN A NUTSHELL

- Regular verbs form the past tense by adding *-d* or *-ed.*
- Regular verbs form the past participle with the helping verb *to have* by adding *-d* or *-ed.*
- Don't be fooled by your ear into dropping the *-d* or *-ed.*

PRACTICE 1

The following sentences are adapted from a Southern woman's Civil War diary. Change the verb in parentheses to its simple past tense.

1. Sherman's troops (march) past my window.

____

2. Of course, we (expect) to sleep through the noise.

____

3. They (surround) the campus with their sentries.

____

4. The southern horizon (reflects) the glare of fire.

____

5. I (imagine) night being turned into day by the blaze.

____

6. The men (carry) buckets of water.

____

7. The wounded from the hospital (help) as much as possible.

____

8. The heat (forces) us away from the burning building.

____

9. The flames (approach) from all sides.

____

10. Snipers (fire) at the firefighters.

____

11. The cannon (roar) with unspeakable might.

____

12. The fire (wraps) the campus in the brightness of daylight.

____

13. One soldier (apologizes) for the destruction.

____

14. We (walk) away from him without speaking.

____

15. We all (remember) that dreadful night.

____

Using the Present Perfect Tense

The present perfect tense is made up of the present tense of *to have* plus a past participle. This tense is used when an action has started in the past but is continuing in the present:

Past tense:	Eric played the guitar for five years.
Present perfect tense:	Eric has played the guitar for five years.

In the first example, Eric played the guitar for five years, but is no longer playing it. In the second example, Eric played the guitar for five years and is still playing it.

PRACTICE 2

Cross out the italicized regular verb in each sentence, change it to the present perfect tense, and write the new verb above the old one. Remember to use *have* or *has*.

Example: Fred ~~pumps~~ **has pumped** gas at an Arco station.

1. I *part* my hair on the left side.
2. Jamie's father *looked* under the bed.
3. My favorite writer *appeared* on campus.
4. The private *salutes* the general.
5. We *vacation* in Santa Fe.
6. They *delivered* the furniture.
7. The Zunis *live* in pueblos.
8. Aunt Susan *talks* about getting a new job.
9. The boys *move* lawn for a fee.
10. You *helped* yourself.

PRACTICE 3

After reading each sentence below carefully and studying its meaning, underline the correct verb—either the past tense or the present perfect tense.

1. Uncle Harry (used, has used) our vacation cabin since he was a young boy.
2. I opened the door and (looked, have looked) inside.
3. Most of us (traveled, have traveled) to Mexico until we were eight years old.
4. Last Tuesday, she (behaved, has behaved) like a wild woman.
5. Our alarm is so loud that it (awakened, has awakened) me many times.
6. Ever since I was twelve, I (believed, have believed) that travel expands the mind.
7. We (discussed, have discussed) the terrible heat for one hour. Now let's turn on the air conditioning.
8. While my aunt was in the Galapagos Islands, she (photographed, has photographed) many strange-looking creatures.

9. To this day, green, sour apples (never appealed, have never appealed) to me.
10. My mom and dad both (worked, have worked) until we graduated from college.

Using the Past Perfect Tense

The past perfect tense is made up of the past tense of *to have* plus the past participle. It describes the earlier of two actions done in the past. (The later action usually is expressed in the simple past tense.)

Past tense: Juan *wandered* down the street to meet his dad.

Past perfect tense: Juan *had wandered* way down the street before his dad appeared.

In the first sentence, *wandered* is in the simple past tense. In the second sentence, *had wandered* is in the past perfect tense because it happened before the arrival of his dad.

PRACTICE 4

After reading each sentence carefully and studying its meaning, underline the correct verb in parentheses—either the simple past or the past perfect.

1. The newspapers revealed that the victim was found dead; I (believed, had believed) that the victim was simply hiding.
2. In response to the announcement, Crystal (slammed, had slammed) her books on the desk.
3. While the rain continued to fall, we (picked up, had picked up) our picnic basket and left the park.
4. I (finished, had finished) high school two years before my brother started elementary school.
5. Jeff (worked, had worked) on his boat for two years by the time he actually launched it.
6. My parents (announced, had announced) that they were moving to Savannah this winter.
7. Much to my surprise, my best friend purchased the motorcycle that he (wanted, had wanted) ever since he had learned to ride motorcycles.
8. Peter suddenly (checked, had checked) his watch and started to run.
9. Many of us (learned, had learned) Arabic several years before we enlisted in the army.
10. As I (rented, had rented) the snowboard, I wondered if I was wasting my money.

11. The dog (escaped, had escaped) just a few seconds before I ran to get his food.
12. At Mel's birthday party, we (kept, had kept) silent while Ginny sang off key.
13. While Big Al (smoked, had smoked) his pipe without apologizing to the people in the bus, he kept watching out the window for pretty scenery.
14. My father wondered if Mother (took, had taken) her medicine before breakfast as the doctor had ordered.
15. Every Christmas, year in and year out, Felicia (flew, had flown) home to Mexico to visit her mother.

EAR ALERT

Omitting the Helping Verb of a Past Participle

In informal speech, it is common to drop the helping verb of a past participle—an act your ear might even excuse. But dropping the helping verb, whether your ear approves or not, is always wrong in writing. Here are some examples:

Dropped verb: I been a team player.
Correct form: I have been a team player.

Dropped verb: I drawn the picture.
Correct form: I have drawn the picture.

Dropped verb: We driven around for ten minutes.
Correct form: We had driven around for ten minutes.

Dropped verb: Why Fred bought a white Honda?
Correct form: Why has Fred bought a white Honda?

IN A NUTSHELL

In writing, you must always include the helping verb of a tense that uses the past participle.

PRACTICE 5

Insert the omitted helping verb where it belongs, writing it in the space above the sentence.

had
Example: Before noon, she spoken to her staff twice.

Before noon, she had spoken to her staff twice.

1. Most of the children written their parents letters from camp.
2. Before getting a job, I been pretty poor all my life.
3. Many people seen cruelty and violence in their families.

4. Farmers in Fresno grown beautiful tomatoes.
5. He said that he frozen the bananas before they had a chance to rot.
6. Why you broken your promise?
7. Where you been when they found your wallet?
8. He hidden the candy in the bottom drawer.
9. Lupe missed the bus because no one given her the new schedule.
10. The snow fallen early this winter.
11. Before playing their first game, the polo players practiced all summer.
12. We given them all of the tools they need to become successful.
13. She tossed her Social Security card into the garbage can when the office nurse asked for her number.
14. My eyesight caused me serious problems when I drive at night.
15. Before the jury reached a verdict, the TV pundits declared the defendant guilty.

PRACTICE 6

The paragraph that follows contains errors in the use of past participles. First, underline each error; second, correct the error.

What is a real American? Some people have claim that a real American is a person who is loyal, patriotic, and proud to live in the United States. Other people have suppose that a real American is someone who watches football on Monday nights and eats hot dogs. The definition of a real American changes constantly because different generations have experience different problems, such as war or depression. For instance, during the 1950s, when Senator Joseph McCarthy had made everyone paranoid about Communism, a "real American" was someone who was against Communism. Later, in the 1970s, a "real American" was someone who had battle the Vietnamese even though he might have believe that the war was illogical and immoral.

During the late 1970s, a "real American" might have been someone who had purchase an American gas-guzzling car instead of a foreign economical car, just to show that he supported the American economy. Today, the term "real American" is still not easy to define even though on September 11, 2001, we experienced a real war and crisis to pull us together. But this is what I think the term means: "A person who wants to change America for the better and will work to do so."

Irregular Verbs

Verbs are *irregular* if their past tense is not formed by adding *-d* or *-ed*. For example, if the rule for changing tenses were applied to *bring*, its past tense should be *bringed*, which it isn't—it's *brought*. *Bring* is therefore an irregular verb.

There is no single rule for forming the past tense of irregular verbs. Whether a native speaker or an ESL student, you simply have to memorize the forms of those verbs that are irregular. In the past, students memorized these forms by chanting them. It is an old technique, but it works.

A list of irregular verbs follows that many of us use practically every day. Remember, the past participle always requires the use of the helping verb *to have*.

PRESENT	PAST	PAST PARTICIPLE
arise	arose	arisen
be	was	been
bear	bore	borne (not *born*)
become	became	become
begin	began	begun
break	broke	broken
bring	brought (not *brung*)	brought
build	built	built
burst	burst (not *busted*)	burst
buy	bought	bought
catch	caught	caught
choose	chose	chosen
cling	clung	clung
come	came	come
dive	dove	dived
do	did (not *done*)	done
drag	dragged (not *drug*)	dragged
draw	drew	drawn
drink	drank	drunk
drive	drove	driven
eat	ate	eaten
fall	fell	fallen
feed	fed	fed
feel	felt	felt
fight	fought	fought
fly	flew	flown
forgive	forgave	forgiven
freeze	froze	frozen

get	got	gotten
go	went	gone
grow	grew	grown
hang (*clothes*)	hung	hung
hang (*execute*)	hanged	hanged (is a regular verb)
have	had	had
hold	held	held
hurt	hurt (not *hurted*)	hurt
know	knew	known
lead	led	led
lay (*place*)	laid	laid
lie (*rest, recline*)	lay	lain
lose	lost	lost
make	made	made
mean	meant	meant
meet	met	met
pay	paid	paid
put	put	put
read	read (pronounced like *red*)	read (pronounced like *red*)
ride	rode	ridden
ring	rang	rung
rise	rose	risen
run	ran	run
say	said	said
see	saw (not *seen*)	seen
seek	sought (not *seeked*)	sought
sell	sold	sold
set	set	set
shake	shook	shaken
shine	shone	shone
shrink	shrank	shrunk
sing	sang	sung
sink	sank	sunk
sleep	slept	slept
sneak	sneaked (not *snuck*)	sneaked
speak	spoke	spoken
spend	spent	spent
spin	spun	spun
spit	spat	spat
spring	sprang (not *sprung*)	sprung

stand	stood	stood
steal	stole	stolen
sting	stung	stung
stink	stank (not *stunk*)	stunk
strike	struck	struck
strive	strove	striven
swear	swore	sworn
swim	swam (not *swum*)	swum
swing	swung	swung
take	took	taken
teach	taught	taught
tear	tore	torn
tell	told	told
think	thought	thought
throw	threw	thrown
understand	understood	understood
wake	woke	woken
wear	wore	worn
weave	wove	woven
win	won	won
wring	wrung	wrung
write	wrote	written

If you don't know the past tense of an irregular verb, you can always look it up in a dictionary. For example, if you looked up the verb *give*, you would find its past tense listed as *gave* and its past participle listed as *given*. If the verb is regular, the dictionary will not give its past tense, which means that to form the past tense or past participle you simply add *-d* or *-ed*.

IN A NUTSHELL

- Irregular verbs do not form the past tense by adding *-d* or *-ed*.
- Irregular verbs must be memorized.

PRACTICE 7

Complete the following sentences using the form of the verb indicated.

Example: Present: I drag my suitcase all over Europe.

Past: I ***dragged*** my suitcase all over Europe.

Present perfect: I ***have dragged*** my suitcase all over Europe.

1. **Present:** I tell the truth.
   Past: I ____ the truth.
   Past perfect: I ____ the truth.
2. **Present:** I hurt.
   Past: I ____.
   Past perfect: I ____.
3. **Present:** They swim.
   Past: They ____.
   Present perfect: They ____.
4. **Present:** The cats spring.
   Past: The cats ____.
   Present perfect: The cats ____.
5. **Present:** Rains bring hope.
   Past: Rains ____ hope.
   Present perfect: Rains ____ hope.
6. **Present:** The children see.
   Past: The children ____.
   Past perfect: The children ____.
7. **Present:** They freeze.
   Past: They ____.
   Present perfect: They ____.
8. **Present:** The bells ring.
   Past: The bells ____.
   Past perfect: The bells ____.
9. **Present:** The dogs stink.
   Past: The dogs ____.
   Present perfect: The dogs ____.
10. **Present:** You choose.
    Past: You ____.
    Present perfect: You ____.
11. **Present:** They spit.
    Past: They ____.
    Past perfect: They ____.
12. **Present:** Poets write.
    Past: Poets ____.
    Present perfect: Poets ____.

13. **Present:** They shrink.

    Past: They ____.

    Past perfect: They ____.

14. **Present:** The rabbits sleep.

    Past: The rabbits ____.

    Past perfect: The rabbits ____.

15. **Present:** The people speak.

    Past: The people ____.

    Present perfect: The people ____.

PRACTICE 8

In the following sentences, the past tense of the italicized verb is used incorrectly. Write the correct form of the verb in the space provided.

1. My friend *brung* me to school yesterday. **brought**
2. I *seen* him playing ball in the gym. ____
3. The cat *sprung* at the bird. ____
4. You know fully well what you *done.* ____
5. He *drug* the garbage can down the driveway. ____
6. I *drawed* a picture of the forest. ____
7. The pipe *busted* in the freezing weather. ____
8. You *stunk* after working in the garage. ____
9. Yesterday, we *swum* in the city pool. ____
10. I *freezed* in the chilly water. ____
11. My father *teached* me how to drive a car. ____
12. At our last meet, Cheryl *swum* faster than any other student. ____
13. When he *spit* on the floor, we all looked at him in horror. ____
14. Who *stealed* the alarm clock? ____
15. My sister *woken* me up at 6:00 A.M. ____

PRACTICE 9

Fill in the blank with the past tense of the verb in parentheses. Then, on the line below, write a sentence using the same subject and either the present perfect or the past perfect tense of the verb. If you are in doubt, check the list of irregular verbs.

Example: She (swim) ____ swam in the lake.

She had swum there often during her childhood.

1. She (hang) ____ her wet bathing suit in a tree nearby.

2. The man (rise) ____ to allow the lady to be seated.

3. He (take) ____ down the kite from the tree.

4. Who (blow) ____ the whistle in the middle of the night?

5. Was it you who (drag) ____ the sack of potatoes into the living room?

6. She (swear) ____ eternal love to him.

7. The pigpens (stink) ____ really bad yesterday.

8. Today the birds fly; yesterday the birds (fly) ____.

9. Fred (tear) ____ a big hole in his pants.

10. Who (lead) ____ the opposition last year?

11. When Jack heard a loud bang, he (hide) ____ under his bed.

12. Fred (draw) ____ a line in the sand to make his point.

____

____

13. Each day I think of how much those people (mean) ____ to me.

____

____

14. In a cruel gesture, Manfred (spit) ____ in the beggar's face.

____

____

15. He lifted his shirt from the stream and (hang) ____ it on a tree to dry.

____

____

Problems with Irregular Verbs

Two kinds of problems commonly occur with irregular verbs:

1. We use the simple past instead of the correct past participle.

Incorrect: He has ran in two marathons.
Correct: He has run in two marathons.

Incorrect: She has just wrote him a letter.
Correct: She has just written him a letter.

Incorrect: We had never wore those clothes before.
Correct: We had never worn those clothes before.

2. We use an incorrect form of the past tense or past participle.

Incorrect: She drug him along.
Correct: She dragged him along.

Incorrect: He has never wore that before.
Correct: He has never worn that before.

Beware of these two common errors.

PRACTICE 10

Some of the underlined past participles that follow are correct; others are incorrect. If the participle is correct, write *C* in the blank; if it is incorrect, write the corrected participle in the blank. If in doubt, check the list of irregular verbs.

Example: Most of the students should have <u>spoke</u> English. <u>spoken</u>

If you had <u>*gone*</u> to the store, we would have enough milk for dinner. <u>*C*</u>

1. I have <u>ran</u> the Boston Marathon. ____
2. She has <u>swore</u> to bring up her grades. ____
3. One of the rugs she has <u>woven</u> is in the living room. ____
4. The soldiers had <u>dragged</u> the flag through mud and filth. ____
5. Before the party was over, all of the balloons had <u>bursted</u>. ____
6. Had I <u>knowed</u> then what I know now, I would be rich. ____
7. I have <u>swum</u> from here to the islands with no trouble. ____
8. I have <u>lead</u> in that competition all semester. ____
9. She had <u>took</u> much trouble to write a perfect essay. ____
10. Someone had <u>stole</u> his wallet from the car. ____
11. She has not yet <u>paid</u> the rent for this month. ____
12. The taxi drivers <u>striked</u> the city at four this afternoon. ____
13. We <u>swinged</u> from the tree in the moonlight. ____
14. They had not <u>understanded</u> the problem. ____
15. She has <u>tore</u> a leaf from that book. ____

PRACTICE 11

Underline the correct form of the verb. Some sentences require the simple past tense, while others require the present perfect or past perfect.

Example: They (fighted, <u>fought</u>) valiantly at the Battle of Bull Run.

1. We were surprised that the tomato vines had (grew, grown) so tall.
2. If the people had (forgiven, forgave) him, he probably would have survived.
3. Was it you who (brought, brung) the huge dog to church?
4. When was the last time you (driven, drove) Sara's station wagon?
5. The chemistry professor (rode, ridden) in all the way from Manchester.
6. Before he could stop her, she (spit, spat) on the floor.
7. For what reason had the townspeople (rang, rung) the bell?
8. Most of the sweaters had (shrunk, shrank) two sizes.
9. The little rowboat (sank, sunk) into the sea.
10. A large "B" had been (woven, wove) into the rug.
11. The vegetables were rotten and (stank, stunk).
12. If the soldiers had (worn, wore) their helmets, they might have lived.

13. Who would have (thinked, thought) that the woman was only fifty?
14. They (struck, striked) the chair three times.
15. I wish you had (wrote, written) me a note to inform me.

Problem Verbs: *Lie/Lay, Sit/Set, Rise/Raise*

A few verbs seem to give the entire English-speaking world trouble. They are *lie/lay, sit/set,* and *rise/raise.*

Lie/Lay

To lie means to rest in a horizontal position like a sleeping person. *To lay* means to put or set down something as you might a book. To confuse matters further, the past tense of *lie* is *lay.*

Here are the principal parts of these two verbs:

PRESENT	PAST	PAST PARTICIPLE
lie	lay	lain = to rest in a horizontal position like a sleeping person
lay	laid	laid = to set down something, as you might do a book

Lie is always done *by* someone or something; *lay* is always done *to* someone or something. You *lie* down to take a nap, but you *lay* your glasses on the table. You *lie* in your bed, but you are *laid* to rest in your grave. Here are more examples:

TO LIE	TO LAY
I often lie on the floor to watch TV.	He lay the doll on the floor.
She is lying on the floor.	She is laying the doll on the floor.
Yesterday, I lay on the floor.	Yesterday, she laid the doll on the floor.
I have lain on the floor.	I have laid the doll on the floor.

PRACTICE 12

Underline the correct verb.

1. "(Lie, Lay) down!" I shouted to my stubborn dog.
2. Tara had been (lying, laying) in bed daydreaming when the phone rang.
3. Within a month, the contractor had (lain, laid) all the tile.
4. Yesterday, Maxine (laid, lay) in bed with a cold.
5. All she does is (lie, lay) on the living room sofa, watching soap operas.

6. Before they had (lain, laid) two miles of track, the mine exploded.
7. She had (lain, laid) her beach towel next to mine.
8. Just to (lie, lay) on the cool, green grass and look at the clouds is heaven.
9. For two weeks, Mary conscientiously (lay, laid) napkins on the table for every meal.
10. Yesterday, Maxine (lay, laid) a blanket on her bed.

Sit/Set

To sit means to rest on your bottom as you might do in a chair. *To set* means to place something somewhere. *To set* always requires an object, except when it refers to the sun, which always *sets* but never *sits*.

Here are the principal parts of *sit* and *set*:

PRESENT	PAST	PAST PARTICIPLE
sit	sat	sat = to rest on one's bottom
set	set	set = to place something somewhere

The basic difference is this: Someone or something *sits*; someone or something is *set*. So you *sit* on the floor, but you *set* the glass on the floor.

TO SIT	TO SET
The old man sits by the fire.	The man sets flowers on the table.
He is sitting by the fire.	He is setting the table.
All of us sat in stony silence.	Last year, they set a record.
She has always sat in the back row.	Have you set your books down?

PRACTICE 13

Underline the correct verb.

1. I had (sat, set) the books on top of the piano.
2. For two hours, Marie (sat, set) on the bench and waited.
3. It felt to her as if she had (set, sat) there for two days.
4. Who is (setting, sitting) to his right?
5. (Sit, Set) that box down this very moment!
6. We have (sat, set) around twiddling our thumbs long enough.
7. Had they told the truth instead of (setting, sitting) on it, they would have been better off.

8. (Sit, Set) down and listen!
9. He (sat, set) the groceries on the sink.
10. Come and (sit, set) down next to me.

Rise/Raise

To rise means to get up or move up on your own; *to raise* is to lift up someone or something or to cultivate or rear something.

Here are the principal parts of *rise* and *raise*:

PRESENT	PAST	PAST PARTICIPLE
rise	rose	risen = to get up or move up on your own
raise	raised	raised = to lift up someone or something

You *rise* from a sitting position or *rise* to the top of your profession. You *raise* your arms or your voice; sometimes, you even *raise* Cain. You always *rise* to the occasion and doing so might get you a *raise* in pay.

Here are some other examples:

TO RISE	TO RAISE
Let us rise and salute the flag.	Let us raise the flag on the pole.
She is rising to greet the man.	I am raising cattle.
The farmers have risen early.	The farmers have raised tons of corn.
The old men rose from the bench.	The old men raised their hands.

PRACTICE 14

Change the italicized word(s) by filling in *rise* or *raise* in the blanks provided. Do not change the tense of any other verb.

1. India *breeds* beautiful tigers. ____
2. What a thrill to see the sun *come up* over the hilltops! ____
3. The entire audience had *stood up* to applaud the rock band. ____
4. I *pulled up* the shades to see the tulips in the back yard. ____
5. The manager *has increased* Ellen's pay. ____
6. Lazarus is supposed to *have returned* from his grave. ____
7. He *increased* his grade point average this year. ____
8. She will *be equal* to the challenge of chemistry. ____
9. When she walks in, let's *get up* and applaud her. ____
10. When taxes *become higher*, people demand a new president. ____

IN A NUTSHELL

- *To lie* means to rest in a horizontal position; to lay means to put something down.
- *To sit* means to rest on your bottom; to set means to place something somewhere.
- *To rise* means to get up; to raise means to lift up something.

ESL Advice!

These differences in meaning between *lie/lay, sit/set, rise/raise* must be memorized

Lie/Lay, Sit/Set, Rise/Raise: Does It Really Matter?

Even if students don't ask the question, "Does it really matter if I say *lie* or *lay?*" they often think it. The answer is, yes, it does matter.

True, if you commanded *Lay down!* instead of *Lie down!* your dog would probably obey just as quickly. Many students might then wonder, "If I'm understood when I incorrectly say *lay* instead of *lie* or *lie* instead of *lay,* what does using the correct form matter?"

However, being understood is no substitute for being correct. Often, being correct is what makes you understandable.

Language does change, and as the years go by, we predict that one day *lie* and *lay* will have the same meaning in grammar books. Until that day comes, though, these differences do matter.

For example, you might scribble this memo to your boss: "Dear Boss, I lay the contract on your desk before I left." Upon reading it, your boss might mutter, "No, you didn't. You laid it there. If you can't get that right, how can I trust you with this important contract? I'm giving the account to Nancy." In other words, these little differences are important because they matter to people.

Of course, they don't matter if you work for a dog.

Unit Test

Fill in the blanks with the correct past and past participle of the verb in the left column. Some of the verbs are regular; others are irregular.

PRESENT	PAST	PAST PARTICIPLE
1. bring	_____	_____
2. drink	_____	_____
3. hunt	_____	_____

4. sing ______ ______
5. speak ______ ______
6. choose ______ ______
7. lie ______ ______
8. decide ______ ______
9. ride ______ ______
10. throw ______ ______
11. swim ______ ______
12. wear ______ ______
13. fear ______ ______
14. raise ______ ______
15. go ______ ______
16. write ______ ______
17. demand ______ ______
18. study ______ ______
19. forgive ______ ______
20. eat ______ ______

Unit Talk–Write Assignment

Many college students worry about being overweight. One student expresses her fears in the *Talk* column below. She makes a clear point, but in the slangy, informal English typically used in everyday talk. Your assignment is to use the *Write* column to turn her informal remarks into sentences in standard English that support a discussible point. Correct any errors in verb use.

TALK	WRITE
1. I have a beef with magazines that write about healthy living.	______
2. When they claim "healthy living," they really mean "stay Twiggy thin."	______

3. DAMN! Look who they have chose to warn us about anorexia and bulimia.

4. Glamour girls like Bridget Hall or pop stars like Paula Abdul or famous film stars like Halle Berry.

5. Give me a break!

6. And whose bodies are projected as super cool?

7. Not Rosie O'Donnell's, Oprah Winfrey's, or even Elizabeth Taylor's.

8. No, it's the bodies of skeletons like Demi Moore, Kate Winslet, and Sharon Stone.

9. I'm telling you, kids who already have relationship problems, self-worth problems, or any other psychological baggage get really depressed when they look in the mirror and find that they don't look like Helen Hunt.

10. They'll feel like laying down and dying—for sure.

11. My mom says that when she was young, the stars that were considered glamorous were sorta round, like Marilyn Monroe and Sophia Loren.

12. Boy, do I wish the round look would come back and women could eat like normal people. Now that would be healthy living.

Unit Collaborative Assignment

The following paragraph about the human desire for peace contains errors in the past participles of irregular verbs. First, correct the errors. Then team up with a partner, exchange books, and check (correcting, if necessary) each other's work. Discuss any mistakes, referring to the list of irregular verbs on pages 150–152 to settle any disagreements.

The other day, while I drived along the freeway, I noticed a bumper sticker. It red, "Aim for peace." I thinked to myself, "Isn't peace what human beings all over the world want?" How many lives of every generation are drawed into the struggle for peace? Will peace be achieved only when millions of additional bodies are lain in unmarked graves? Martin Luther King, who lays buried in a Southern cemetery, killed by an assassin's bullet, tried to rise our consciousness for peace. His idea of peace didn't set well with the power structure of his day. Mohandas Gandhi also seeked peace for India. He, too, perished at the hand of an assassin who laid in wait for him. The wish for peace has obviously not just springed up. Human beings have always craved peace. Getting it, however, has not prove to be easy.

Unit Writing Assignment

Below is a list of commonly seen bumper stickers. Choose one from the list and write about it. Or, choose a bumper sticker that you have on your own car or have seen and write about that. Pay particular attention to verb forms. Use the Revising Checklist inside the front cover of this book to help you revise.

1. If you want peace, work for justice.
2. Treat me no differently than you would the queen.

3. The worst day fishing is better than the best day working.
4. I love N.Y. (*or some other city or state*)
5. Give a damn.
6. I brake for animals.
7. Hand over the chocolate and no one will get hurt.
8. Children are such a great way to start people.
9. Basketball (*or football, baseball, hockey, golf, tennis*) is life. All the rest is details.
10. Challenge authority.

Photo Writing Assignment

The following picture shows an overturned car and rescue workers trying to free trapped passengers in it. Using your imagination to put yourself in the position of an eyewitness, write a paragraph in which you describe the accident that resulted in this wreck. As your topic sentence, use your first impressions of the car as it approached—whether it was speeding, weaving, etc. Then, as support for the topic sentence, describe the accident as you saw it in your imagination. Pay special attention to using both regular and irregular verbs correctly. Use the Revising Checklist to help you revise.

9 Subject–Verb Agreement

"Fifi and Rex is well-trained dogs."

Subjects and verbs must agree in number: That is the one rule of subject–verb agreement. A singular subject always takes a singular verb; a plural subject always takes a plural verb. Most of the time, this rule is plain and easy to follow, as shown in the following sentences:

Jane loves John.

The women love John.

Jane, a singular subject, takes the singular verb *loves. Women*, a plural subject, takes the plural verb *love.*

We are also likely to come across sentences like these:

She don't watch much television.

There is four reasons why I bought a Jeep.

EAR ALERT

She, a singular subject, is incorrectly paired with the plural verb *don't. Reasons*, a plural subject, is incorrectly paired with the singular verb *is.*

Although such errors are common in daily speech, writing demands a greater exactness. Subjects and verbs may disagree as they tumble out of the mouth, but on the page they must agree.

Subject–verb agreement errors are typically caused by some common grammatical situations. They are, in no particular order:

1. Certain forms of the verbs *to do* and *to be: Do, does, doesn't, don't; was, wasn't, were, weren't:*

Incorrect:	He don't care about me.
Correct:	He doesn't care about me.

Incorrect: You was at the party.
Correct: You were at the party.

2. Indefinite pronouns (see complete list on p. 169):

Incorrect: Neither of us are going home.
Correct: Neither of us is going home.

Incorrect: Anybody taking advanced courses try to study hard.
Correct: Anybody taking advanced courses tries to study hard.

Incorrect: Everyone in our sociology class like the textbook.
Correct: Everyone in our sociology class likes the textbook.

Incorrect: Somebody have mispronounced her name.
Correct: Somebody has mispronounced her name.

3. Prepositional phrase between a subject and a verb:

Incorrect: One of the three cousins are very smart.
Correct: One of the three cousins is very smart.

4. Sentences beginning with *there/here*:

Incorrect: There is a lot of chores to do.
Correct: There are a lot of chores to do.

Incorrect: Here is the correct answers.
Correct: Here are the correct answers.

5. Questions:

Incorrect: Where is the books?
Correct: Where are the books?

6. Compound subjects joined by *and, or, either/or*, or *neither/nor*:

Incorrect: The man and his son was smiling.
Correct: The man and his son were smiling.

Incorrect: The man or his son were smiling.
Correct: The man or his son was smiling.

7. *Who, which,* and *that*:

Incorrect: Richard is one of those students who works hard.
Correct: Richard is one of those students who work hard.

We'll take up these situations one by one.

Do, Does, Doesn't, Don't/Was, Were, Wasn't, Weren't

Subject–verb agreement errors are often caused by the words *do, does, doesn't, don't, was, were, wasn't, weren't.* Here are the correct forms of *to do*:

SINGULAR	PLURAL
I do, don't	We do, don't
You do, don't	You do, don't
He / She / It } does, doesn't	They do, don't

Among the most common subject–verb agreement errors is the use of *he* or *she* with *do* instead of the correct *does*:

Incorrect: He do his job quite well.
Correct: He does his job quite well.

This error occurs second in frequency only to the incorrect use of *don't* with a singular subject:

Incorrect: She don't know what she's talking about.
Correct: She doesn't know what she's talking about.

Was, wasn't, were, and *weren't* are also often involved in many subject–verb agreement errors. Here are the correct forms:

SINGULAR	PLURAL
I was, wasn't	We were, weren't
You were, weren't	You were, weren't
He / She / It } was, wasn't	They were, weren't

Here are some examples of errors commonly made with this verb:

Incorrect: You was at the party.
Correct: You were at the party.

Incorrect: We was ready to leave.
Correct: We were ready to leave.

IN A NUTSHELL

Do, does, doesn't, don't, was, were, wasn't, and *weren't* often cause subject–verb agreement errors. Always check to be sure that you've used them correctly.

PRACTICE 1

Underline the subject in each of the following sentences and mark *S* in the space to the left if the subject is singular or *P* if the subject is plural. Then underline the form of the verb in parentheses that agrees with the subject.

Example: ***P*** Many of us (was, were) happy when it rained.

1. ____ That green chair (doesn't, don't) match the blue table.
2. ____ (Wasn't, Weren't) you at home when he arrived?
3. ____ The end (doesn't, don't) always justify the means.
4. ____ Jimmy and Frank (was, were) both great swimmers.
5. ____ She (don't, doesn't) ever deliver what she promises.
6. ____ (Was, Were) those the only letters you wrote?
7. ____ (Doesn't, Don't) it matter to you that you hurt her feelings?
8. ____ Many of the cows (were, was) hungry and diseased.
9. ____ We (was, were) happy to attend the wedding.
10. ____ Both the sergeant and the corporal (was, were) nice people.
11. ____ Where (was, were) you when the daffodils blossomed?
12. ____ It (wasn't, weren't) many days ago that he left for good.
13. ____ Why (doesn't, don't) the stockholders complain?
14. ____ Most of the time, we (wasn't, weren't) paying attention.
15. ____ Eating cookies between meals (was, were) what made her fat.

Indefinite Pronouns

The following pronouns, called "indefinite pronouns," always take a singular verb:

one	somebody	each
anyone	everybody	either (either/or), neither (neither/nor)
someone	nothing	
everyone	anything	
nobody	something	
anybody	everything	

Memorize these pronouns correctly, and remember that they always require singular verbs. Bear in mind, too, that the grammar check function on your computer will do only a so-so job of catching such subject–verb agreement errors.

See Chapters 11 and 12, pp. 207–222 for more instruction on the correct use of indefinite pronouns, including some exceptions.

> **ESL Advice!**
>
> Notice that indefinite pronouns often end in *one, body,* or *thing.* Since these words are singular, they can help you remember to use the singular verb form.

Here are some examples of how indefinite pronouns should be used:

Each pen, pencil, and ruler was (not <u>were</u>) assigned a number.

Every piano and violin is (not <u>are</u>) being used for the performance.

Neither of the students works (not <u>work</u>) very hard.

Either of the cars is (not <u>are</u>) a bargain.

Everyone in the class makes (not <u>make</u>) an effort to participate.

Anybody, including the elderly, is (not <u>are</u>) invited to sign up.

Someone among all of these men surely remembers (not <u>remember</u>) that day.

Don't be confused by the prepositional phrase—for example, *of the cars*—that usually follows *each, every, either,* or *neither.* Cross it out, as we suggested in Unit 7, and the verb choice will be clear. If *each* confuses you, and you can't remember whether it's singular or plural, add *one* after it. The *one* is already implied. A *one* is similarly implied in *either* and *neither* used alone. Adding the *one*—whether on the page or in the privacy of your mind—will help you remember that *each, either*, and *neither* are always singular.

Each [one] of the men wore a coat.

Each [one] of the cats had on a pretty collar.

Either [one] is as good as the other.

Neither [one] speaks English.

Either/or and *neither/nor* are also troublesome. Here are some examples:

Incorrect: Neither the principal nor the guidance counselor know me by name.

Correct: Neither the principal nor the guidance counselor knows me by name.

Incorrect: Neither the secretary nor the president were to blame.

Correct: Neither the secretary nor the president was to blame.

If one subject joined by either/or or neither/nor is singular and one is plural, the verb should agree with the nearer subject. Here are some examples:

Incorrect: Either the rats or the raccoon were here.

Correct: Either the rats or the raccoon was here.

Incorrect: Either the raccoon or the rats was here.

Correct: Either the raccoon or the rats were here.

IN A NUTSHELL

Indefinite pronouns usually take a singular verb. *Each, every, either/or,* and *neither/nor* take singular verbs except when they join two subjects, one singular and one plural, in which case the verb agrees with the nearer subject.

PRACTICE 2

In the following sentences, underline the correct form of the verb in parentheses.

Example: Neither of the boats (are, <u>is</u>) sinking.

1. Each of the girls (has, have) a purple hat.
2. Neither of the books (is, are) written in fine print.
3. Neither Bill nor the two girls (have, has) offered to collect the tickets.
4. Every house within two blocks (is, are) rented.
5. Each hat and umbrella (was, were) assigned a number.
6. Every car and truck (are, is) available for leasing.
7. Each of the thousand applicants (take, takes) a number.
8. Neither of the boys (understands, understand) the explanation.
9. Either coat (is, are) warm enough for now.
10. Either all of the ducks or one swan (is, are) playing in the pond whenever I walk by.
11. Everybody in my cooking class (wears, wear) a large apron.
12. Nobody with an interest in nature (want, wants) to miss the hike tomorrow.
13. Nothing in the whole world (compare, compares) with a rainbow.
14. Everything on my bed and in my drawers (needs, need) to be reorganized.
15. Something in the bushes or behind the trees (keeps, keep) moving.

PRACTICE 3

Underline the correct form of the verb in parentheses.

1. Everyone (has, have) an opinion.
2. None of the clouds (is, are) below the mountain range.

3. Everybody (loves, love) a beautiful sunset.
4. No one (refuses, refuse) to be in the parade.
5. None of the chocolate (is, are) melted.
6. Anybody who is somebody (knows, know) the mayor personally.
7. One of the actors (wears, wear) a false nose.
8. Somebody (know, knows) who ate my porridge.
9. Everything you say (is, are) a lie.
10. Nobody (knows, know) my name.
11. Here (is, are) everybody from our campus.
12. You can count on the fact that neither of the boys (are, is) going to smile.
13. Either one iPhone or two iPods (is, are) his choice.
14. Neither the renters nor the landlord (have, has) offered to back down.
15. Either Professor Stern or Professor Allred (are, is) giving a lecture on DNA this morning.

Phrases Between a Subject and Its Verb

A prepositional phrase that comes between a subject and a verb can cause an agreement error. Here is a list of common prepositions:

about	beside	inside	through
above	besides	into	throughout
across	between	like	to
after	beyond	near	toward
against	by	of	under
along	despite	off	underneath
among	down	on	until
around	during	out	up
at	except	outside	upon
before	for	over	with
behind	from	past	within
below	in	since	without
beneath			

Here is a typical agreement error caused by a prepositional phrase coming between a subject and a verb:

One of the blue cars were out of gas.

The prepositional phrase *of the blue cars* comes between the subject *one* and the verb *were.* The subject, though, is still *one,* and *one* is always singular. Cross out the prepositional phrase and the subject is immediately clear:

One ~~of the blue~~ cars was out of gas.

IN A NUTSHELL

An agreement error can be caused by a prepositional phrase that comes between a subject and its verb.

PRACTICE 4

In the sentences that follow, cross out all prepositional phrases. Then circle the subject and underline the correct verb in parentheses.

Example: The sloop ~~under the lights~~ (is, are) mine.

1. The houses at the end of our block (is, are) old.
2. The stairs behind the library (is, are) very steep.
3. That box of clothes and books (go, goes) to the garage sale.
4. An analysis of the tissues (indicates, indicate) that disease is present.
5. Five stores in the old alley (shows, show) signs of damage.
6. An army of ants (is, are) forming behind the cabinet.
7. This comment about The Rolling Stones (explains, explain) their songs.
8. At Ralph's, a package of dried bananas (sells, sell) for less.
9. A quilt of little blue patches (hangs, hang) on the wall.
10. The diamonds scattered on the counter (looks, look) unreal.

Sentences Beginning with *There/Here*

Subject–verb agreement errors can easily occur in sentences that begin with *there is, there are, here is,* and *here are.* Here are some examples:

Incorrect: There was two strangers dressed in black.
Correct: There were two strangers dressed in black.

Incorrect: Here is the pencils you asked me to buy.
Correct: Here are the pencils you asked me to buy.

EAR ALERT

In these examples, the writer is confused by *there* or *here*, which strikes the ear as singular. However, neither *here* nor *there* is the subject of the sentence. If you're confused by such sentences, reword them to make the subject come before the verb, and the error will quickly become apparent:

> Two strangers dressed in black were there.
>
> The pencils you asked me to buy are here.

Indeed, many sentences beginning with *there* or *here* can be made crisper if they are reworded to avoid such dead openings. Here is an example:

Original: There are many children who go to bed hungry.
Rewrite: Many children go to bed hungry.

The *there is* or *there are* is often unnecessary.

IN A NUTSHELL

Watch out for subject–verb agreement errors in sentences that begin with *there* or *here.* To check the agreement of such a sentence, reword it to place the subject first.

PRACTICE 5

Circle the subject in each sentence. Then underline the correct form of the verb in parentheses.

1. There (is, are) the snowcapped mountains.
2. There (was, were) three papers about cats.
3. Here (is, are) a map of India, Pakistan, and Bangladesh.
4. There (is, are) moments in my life when I would like to be a hermit.
5. Here (is, are) the towels you borrowed.
6. There (is, are) three dresses hanging in the closet.
7. There (was, were) two shacks between the house and the mansion.
8. There (was, were) many Italian songs sung that night.
9. There (was, were) big iron pots boiling and bubbling on the stove.
10. Here (is, are) the autographs you wanted.

PRACTICE 6

Rewrite each sentence below to avoid starting with *there* or *here* and to make the writing crisper.

1. There is a mountain of laundry to be washed.

   ____

2. Here are the two diaries for you to read and enjoy.

   ____

3. There are certain band members who would prefer to play golf rather than perform.

   ____

4. Here is the computer expert who promised to install your hardware.

   ____

5. There are details that need to be added to the paragraph.

   ____

6. There are many American citizens who never bother to vote.

   ____

7. Here are some chocolate bunnies and jelly beans to put in the basket.

   ____

8. There are so many kinds of ballpoint pens that I don't know which one to choose.

   ____

9. Here is a map that will tell you how to get to the center of town.

   ____

10. There is an entire family story contained in that old stone wall.

    ____

Questions

Most sentences that we write or speak are statements, such as these:

> The newspaper is here.
>
> The toast is brown.
>
> The coffee is burned.

In these, and in most statements, because the subject comes before the verb, it is easy to spot an agreement error. However, when we ask a question, the verb typically comes before the subject:

> Where is the newspaper?
>
> What color is the toast?
>
> What happened to the coffee?

With the subject now following the verb, it is easy to make an agreement error:

> Where is John and Mary sitting?

To use the plural verb *are* correctly requires a speaker or writer to know that a plural subject—*John and Mary*—lies ahead. If you're in doubt about the agreement between subject and verb in a question, simply reword it as a statement. For example:

> John and Mary (is/are) sitting here.

It is now evident that the plural *are* is the correct verb since *John and Mary* refer to two people.

IN A NUTSHELL

To check subject–verb agreement in a question, simply reword it as a statement.

PRACTICE 7

Circle the subject in each question. Then underline the correct form of the verb in parentheses.

1. What (is, are) the names of the players?
2. Where on earth (do, does) such people live?
3. Where (is, are) Daddy's gloves?
4. How many attorneys (do, does) the defendant have?
6. What (has, have) the people done about it?
6. What (is, are) Donna's favorite subjects?
7. Who (is, are) those strangers coming up the walkway?
8. (Have, Has) the tenants complained to the landlord?
9. What (has, have) they said about me?
10. After all, what (do, does) they know?

Compound Subjects Joined by *And, Or, Either/Or, Neither/Nor*

The sentence that occasionally gives writers trouble is one that looks like this:

singular noun + *and* + singular noun

Here are some examples:

The man and the woman was there.

The house and the car is mine.

Time and energy makes a difference.

In all these sentences, the writer was fooled by what seemed to be a singular subject. However, just as one plus one makes two, one singular subject plus another singular subject joined by *and* always makes a subject plural. The sentences should therefore read:

The man and the woman <u>were</u> there.

The house and the car <u>are</u> mine.

Time and energy <u>make</u> a difference.

Just remember that one plus one makes two, and two is plural.

> **ESL Advice!**
>
> ESL students should commit this rule to memory:
>
> subject + *and* + subject = plural verb

Another test is to substitute a suitable pronoun for the double subject. For example, the sentence

The man and the woman was there.

becomes

They was there.

which should strike your ear as wrong. The correct sentence is therefore

They were there.

or

The man and the woman were there.

Although two singular subjects joined by *and* always take a plural verb, two singular subjects joined by *or* require a singular verb:

Burt and Tom are on the team.

but

Burt or Tom is on the team.

Joan and Linda are coming.

but

Joan or Linda is coming.

Of course, two plural nouns joined by *or* take a plural verb:

Usually, captains or co-captains are elected.

What happens when a sentence has two subjects, one singular and one plural, joined by *or*? In that case, the verb agrees with the nearer subject:

The co-captains or the coach <u>is</u> calling a meeting.

but

The coach or the co-captains <u>are</u> calling a meeting.

As we saw earlier in the chapter, the same rule applies with two subjects joined by *either/or* and *neither/nor*: The verb agrees with the nearer subject:

Either the co-captains or the coach <u>is</u> calling a meeting.

but

Either the coach or the co-captains <u>are</u> calling a meeting.

IN A NUTSHELL

- Two singular subjects joined by *and* are plural.
- Two singular subjects joined by *or, either/or,* or *neither/nor* are singular.
- If a singular and a plural subject are joined by *or, either/or,* or *neither/nor,* the verb agrees with the nearer subject.

PRACTICE 8

In the following sentences, underline the correct form of the verb in parentheses.

1. His bristling eyebrows and large frown (scare, scares) children.
2. Either you or Gus (water, waters) the plants while we're gone.
3. A fool and his money (is, are) soon parted.

4. Neither money nor power (motivate, motivates) him.
5. *Newsweek* and *Time* (is, are) not light reading.
6. Avocado or papaya (is, are) in the salad.
7. London and Paris (attract, attracts) many tourists.
8. Either the president or the sales manager (is, are) going to speak.
9. My mother and father (inspires, inspire) me to achieve.
10. Neither the waiters nor the manager (take, takes) responsibility for the accident.

PRACTICE 9

Complete the following sentences using a correct singular or plural verb form.

Example: Juan or Frederico always ***takes out the garbage***. ________

1. Neither the teacher nor the students ________________
2. Love and marriage ________________
3. Fighting or screaming ________________
4. Either the chef or the owner ________________
5. Neither Pat nor I ________________
6. Arthritis and other pains of old age ________________
7. Two apples or one orange ________________
8. The gorilla and the chimpanzee ________________
9. Neither that bowl nor those plates ________________
10. His favorite books and CDs ________________

Who, Which, and *That*

Who, which, and *that* are often used to replace nouns in dependent clauses. In such cases, the verb should agree with the nearest noun before the *who, which*, or *that.* Consider this example:

Incorrect: John is among the men who thinks that we have a problem.

Correct: John is among the men who think that we have a problem.

Who stands for the nearest preceding noun, which is *men,* not *John.* Therefore, it is *men* that determines the form of the verb. In fact, the sentence is a blend of two shorter sentences:

John is among the men. The men think that we have a problem.

If you have trouble with this rule, split the sentence into two shorter sentences, and the subject will become clear.

Here are other examples:

> Jeff or Joe is one of those who are going to Tibet.

Split: Jeff or Joe is one of those. Those are going to Tibet.

Those, not *Jeff* or *Joe*, is the nearest noun before *who*. Since *those* takes a plural verb, the *who* that stands for it must also take a plural verb.

> Among our daily plagues and troubles is a fly that bites.

Fly, not *plagues* or *troubles*, is the nearest noun before *that*, so the verb must be singular.

Note: Do not be confused by a prepositional phrase that may intervene between the pronouns *who, that*, or *which* and their antecedents. Here is an example:

> I admire John because he is the only worker in our offices who cares about other workers.

The antecedent of *who* is not *offices,* which is plural, but *worker,* which is singular. The verb must therefore likewise be singular. Simply disregard the prepositional phrase.

IN A NUTSHELL

Who, which, and *that* used in dependent clauses must agree with the nearest preceding noun.

PRACTICE 10

Circle the nearest noun preceding *who, which*, or *that* in the following sentences. Then underline the correct form of the verb in parentheses.

1. A coach who (allow, allows) personal attacks on an opposing player teaches bad sportsmanship.
2. Bob is one of the players who (score, scores) regularly.
3. Peter is the only student who (qualify, qualifies) for advanced math.
4. Marie is one of the dancers who (hopes, hope) to go to New York.
5. These two movies, which (contains, contain) pointless violence, should not win Oscars.
6. Betty is among the students who (is, are) dissatisfied.

7. His questions, which (has, have) to do with cost and color, must be answered before we can select the paint.
8. These herbal tablets, which (look, looks) harmless, can cause an upset stomach.
9. The big, billowy clouds that (fill, fills) the sky make me feel like singing.
10. He is one of those who (object, objects) to the proposal.

Changed Word Order

Most sentences place the subject before the verb as in this typical example:

> The cow jumped over the moon.

But not all sentences follow this pattern. Questions and sentences beginning with words such as *there*, and *here*, as we have seen, are exceptions to the rule. Other sentences also change the typical word order. In such cases, you need to be on your toes to avoid a subject–verb agreement error. Here are some examples of changed word order with the subject marked "S" and the verb marked "V":

```
      V       S
Where is the tablecloth?
```

```
                        V       S
Under the old bridge grew a sturdy pine tree.
```

```
      V       S
There is a new director in charge.
```

To avoid a subject–verb agreement error, don't depend solely on your ear. Use the technique you've been taught to correctly identify the subject and the verb in a sentence.

PRACTICE 11

In each of the following sentences, underline the subject and the correct verb form in parentheses.

Example: Where (have, has) all the flowers gone?

1. Above the clouds (is, are) the firmament.
2. Deep inside his heart, a desire (were, was) blossoming.
3. Among the many visitors (was, were) a tiny Asian girl.
4. There (are, is) one dozen paintings hidden away in the shed.
5. When (is, are) Jamil and Mary joining you?

6. Down the road (roars, roar) three Harley–Davidson motorcycles.
7. Behind every successful man (is, are) at least two strong women.
8. With so many jobs in his past, he (seems, seem) unstable.
9. At the merging of the roads (stands, stand) a white cross.
10. There (are, is) a torn belt and a brown sweater in the drawer.

Unit Test

Use your imagination to complete the following sentences, making verb and subject agree.

1. One of the dogs that ____________________
2. Either of the desks ____________________
3. There is ____________________
4. The amount of work ____________________
5. Nobody in this town ever____________________
6. Stinginess, among other faults, ____________________
7. At the edge of town was____________________
8. Not only the assistants but the manager ____________________
9. Talent and hard work ____________________
10. The paper and the ribbon on this gift package ____________________
11. Neither his beloved cat nor all four dogs ____________________
12. Pete, by himself, or the committee members ____________________
13. Both the gorgeous pink roses and the silver ribbon ____________________
14. There are ____________________
15. Here is ____________________
16. A sidewalk filled with spring flowers ____________________
17. Everyone who loves sea animals ____________________
18. Neither of the two colors ____________________
19. Every man and woman ____________________
20. The feathers inside the pillow ____________________

____

Unit Talk–Write Assignment

In this exercise, a student expresses his opinion on animal cruelty. In the process, he makes several errors in subject–verb agreement. You have two assignments: First, correct all subject–verb agreement errors found in the *Talk* column. Second, using the sentences in the *Talk* column as your starting point, create a standard English paragraph in the *Write* column, beginning with a discussible point and proving it with sufficient details.

TALK	WRITE
1. I know a man who don't care about animals and always treat them cruelly.	
2. Each of his dogs are dying for affection. Maybe you don't think that's important, but I promise you it is.	
3. There is lots of violent criminals who starts out being mean to cats and dogs in the neighborhood. I saw a television program that said criminals was often animal abusers as children.	
4. One of my cousins are that way, too, always being mean to her pets.	
5. Where is the reward in being mean to an animal who haven't a chance to complain about bad treatment?	
6. Nobody make these mean people stop mistreating animals because they don't want to interfere. Well, interfere!	

7. Often, neither the mother nor the father seem to care if their child tease an animal.

8. Some people say, "Aw, animal abuse—that's not a real crime." But the TV show said it is a crime in many states. Moreover, both a scientist and a doctor on the show says it is a proven fact that abusing animals lead to abusing humans.

9. One of those guys who just get a tongue lashing for being mean to a pet might be the next serial rapist or killer.

10. The bottom line is this: Every one of us need to do our best to stop cruelty to all living creatures if we want to be moral people.

Unit Collaborative Assignment

A. The following paragraph contains errors in subject–verb agreement. Working with a partner, make all the required corrections. Then exchange papers with your partner and discuss your answers.

Old age and youth is different. Whereas children move from childhood to adulthood, to what role does senior citizens progress? In this country, there are only two generations: parents and their children. A grandmother often do not play an essential role in our society. Instead, she spend her life feeling unnecessary. No wonder so few of my friends' parents wants to retire, but keep on working past the age of sixty-five. They feel that if they gives up working, they will be ignored and forgotten. Both our young people and the state has a responsibility to help the aged, whose taxes keeps our economy stable. That does not mean that we should spoil senior citizens by letting them vegetate in comfort. Helping them and caring for them means finding creative jobs that appeals to the elderly. Old people needs solid roles that makes them feel important. To feel useful and to engage in some significant activity gives older people a sense of self-worth.

B. Choose a partner and create a paragraph about a person you admire. This person might be one of the following:

1. A relative, family friend, neighbor, teacher, or coach
2. A political figure

3. A sports personality
4. An entertainer
5. Someone you've read about

Encourage your partner to ask you questions about the person you chose. Your answers should help you give a well-rounded, vivid picture of the person.

Unit Writing Assignment

Write about the person you described in the Unit Collaborative Assignment above. Begin by giving a general impression of this person, which you should then support with appropriate details taken from the conversation between you and your partner. Pay special attention to subject–verb agreement. Use the Revising Checklist inside the front cover of this book to help you revise.

Photo Writing Assignment

Are Hip-Hop and Rap music responsible for the violence among youth in some poor urban neighborhoods? Or are the critics who praise the creativity of both musical movements as astonishing correct in their judgment. What do you think? Express your opinions, either pro or con, in a paragraph of either praise or scorn that correctly uses both plural and singular verbs. Cite lyrics with which you are familiar or listen to some of the most popular Hip-Hop and Rap artists to gather examples. Use the Revising Checklist to help you revise.

10 Problems with Verbs

"Mom fed me an egg and then just ignores me."
"I would of gone if invited."

If English is a car, then the verb is its engine. Like the engine of an actual car, the verb is the part of speech that is most likely to cause problems. In this unit, we will cover some common problems with verbs. Specifically, we'll deal with the following:

- Shifts in tense.
- The use of *would have, could have, should have,* and *must have* instead of *would of, could of, should of,* and *must of.*
- The avoidance of double negatives.
- Active and passive voice.

Shifts in Tense

If you begin a sentence in the present tense, you must end it in the present tense. If you begin in the past tense, you must end in the past tense. For example, look at this sentence:

Mom fed me an egg and then just ignores me.

The problem with the sentence is that it begins with a verb in the past tense and ends with a verb in the present tense. Mom is made into a time-traveler—hopping from the past to the present in one breath. To be correct, the sentence must read:

Mom fed me an egg and then just ignored me. **(all past tense)** or

Mom feeds me an egg and then just ignores me. **(all present tense)**

Your use of tenses must be consistent. If there is no logical reason for doing so, you must not jump from present to past tense or from past to present tense in a single sentence. Yet, because we mix up our verb tenses all the time in everyday speech, your ear might mislead you into making the same mistake in writing. Be alert to this possible error. Make sure that your verbs in a written sentence all use the same tense.

IN A NUTSHELL

Verbs in the same sentence must all be in the same tense.

PRACTICE 1

Underline the verbs in the following sentences. Then, correct the shifts in verb tense by making both verbs past tense.

1. The thief stole all four wheels and leaves the body of the car on the sidewalk.

   ____

2. When I told her that the package had arrived, she simply shrugs.

   ____

3. The doctor asks me lots of questions and then gave me a shot of penicillin.

   ____

4. When they demanded to see the manager, a secretary tells them to wait.

   ____

5. I had just surfed a wave when an unexpected wave hits me from the back.

   ____

6. The grizzly leaned over and scoops a salmon from the stream.

   ____

7. On his birthday, Bernie bought a lottery ticket and wins.

   ____

8. My heart races when I saw the police cruiser behind the billboard.

   ____

9. My mother recites the poem "Bobby Shaftoe," and we broke up with laughter.

____

10. She ran past me and yells, "Hurry up!"

____

____

PRACTICE 2

Correct the shift in verb tense in the following sentences by making both verbs present tense.

1. When the bell rings, all the children assembled in the auditorium.

____

2. She sees the cereal and shouted, "I want that, Mommy!"

____

3. His friends tried to change his mind, but he still believes he was right.

____

4. He unfurled the sail and starts up the motor.

____

5. My boy loved our rowboat and wants to take it out on the lake.

____

6. The bass were biting well, so we do not stop fishing.

____

7. The landlord is pretending that he wasn't going to raise our rent.

____

8. The deer jumps to its hoofs when it saw the stalking hunters.

____

9. He takes a joke with good humor and often cracked a smile when something funny happened.

____

10. When she was pregnant, her husband is very supportive.

____

____

PRACTICE 3

Complete the sentences below, using the correct verb tense.

Example: Her mother scolded her and ***made her realize her mistake.***

1. I came, I saw, and I ______________________________

2. The diver checks his oxygen and then ______________________________

3. Once the emergency team had her on her back, they ______________________________

4. When Dad had his coffee, ______________________________

5. The violins tune up, the singers hum, and the conductor ______________________________

6. You think you're so smart, but you ______________________________

7. When he warned them about the road, they ______________________________

8. Little Red Riding Hood takes her basket of food and ______________________________

9. The coyotes howled and ______________________________

10. The car sputtered, stuttered, and ______________________________

Would Have, Could Have, Should Have, and *Must Have*

Because *have* and *of* sound so much alike in speech, it's easy to begin saying *would of* instead of *would have.* But *would of, could of, should of,* and *must of* are mispronunciations. You should never use them in your writing. Instead, always use *would have, could have, should have,* and *must have.*

PRACTICE 4

Correct the use of *would of, could of, should of,* or *must of* in the sentences that follow.

1. I would of come if you had told me.

   ____

2. Should we of accompanied her to the bridge?

   ____

3. For the right price, she could of bought the car.

   ____

4. He must of left his keys in the car again.

   ____

5. If he would of reported the crime, the police would of come.

   ____

6. She never should of promised to move to Connecticut.

   ____

7. She must of been very angry with me that day.

   ____

8. You would of liked Joe, my best friend.

   ____

9. Everyone should of shared in the expense.

   ____

10. If she would of been more patient, Mary wouldn't of broken the zipper.

    ____

Double Negatives

Use only one negative for each idea. Do not use a negative qualifier (*no, not,* or *never*) with a negative verb or with the adverbs *hardly* or *scarcely.*

Incorrect:	She didn't buy no onions.
Correct:	She didn't buy any onions.
Incorrect:	I can't hardly wait for Spring Break.
Correct:	I can hardly wait for Spring Break.

Incorrect:	John wouldn't scarcely give her the time of day.
Correct:	John would scarcely give her the time of day.
Incorrect:	The boys hadn't found no apples.
Correct:	The boys hadn't found any apples.

PRACTICE 5

Rewrite each sentence to correct the double negative.

1. Nobody knew nothing about the theft.

____

2. We never play no card games.

____

3. Tom can't hardly wait for the peaches to ripen.

____

4. She never ordered no donuts.

____

5. All of us couldn't scarcely remember that picnic.

____

6. The storage area didn't contain no usable bicycles.

____

7. Didn't the police ask you no questions?

____

8. In second grade, I hardly spoke no English.

____

9. Although they looked at us, they didn't give us no trouble.

____

10. The Olympic judges don't give no scores aloud.

____

Active and Passive Voice

English has two voices: the active and the passive voice. The **active voice** stresses who did an act. The **passive voice** stresses to whom or to what an act was done. Most of us usually speak in the active voice because it is simpler and more direct.

Active voice: The students greeted the professor.

Passive voice: The professor was greeted by the students.

Because it hides the doer, the passive voice is often preferred by writers who wish to avoid pointing fingers. Here is a case in point:

> The oak trees were ordered to be bulldozed to make room for a high-rise office complex.

Who gave this order? The active voice would have told us:

> Commissioner Smith ordered the oak trees to be bulldozed to make room for a high-rise office complex.

In writing, you should mainly use the active voice. It is livelier, stronger, and more like everyday talk than the passive voice. The passive voice is occasionally used in scientific reporting, where what was done is more important than which researcher did it:

> The bacteria were isolated for further study. (Rather than "Dr. Farwell's research team isolated the bacteria for further study.")

The passive voice is also occasionally used in instances where an act is more important than its cause:

> The village was destroyed by a terrible flood. (Rather than "A terrible flood destroyed the village.")

The important fact here is the destruction of the village. That it was destroyed by a flood is secondary.

IN A NUTSHELL

Write mainly in the active voice, which is livelier and stronger than the passive voice.

PRACTICE 6

Read the paired sentences aloud and underline the verbs. Write an *A* in the blank beside the sentence if it is in the active voice and a *P* if it is in the passive voice.

Example _A_ (a) The children <u>opened</u> the door.

_P_ (b) The door <u>was opened</u> by the children.

1. ____ (a) The vacation was announced by the teacher.

   ____ (b) The teacher announced the vacation.

2. ____ (a) Students are hurt by the battle for grades.

   ____ (b) The battle for grades hurts students.

3. ____ (a) Some months, Fred owes more money than he earns.
____ (b) Some months, more money is owed by Fred than is earned by him.

4. ____ (a) The president of the club deceived its members.
____ (b) The members of the club were deceived by its president.

5. ____ (a) The tenants were told to evacuate the building.
____ (b) The police told the tenants to evacuate the building.

6. ____ (a) We found few faults with the house.
____ (b) Few faults were found with the house.

7. ____ (a) Never let a fool kiss you.
____ (b) Never be kissed by a fool.

8. ____ (a) Three flies were swallowed by the frog.
____ (b) The frog swallowed three flies.

9. ____ (a) The miracle must be accepted on faith.
____ (b) We must accept the miracle on faith.

10. ____ (a) The Ecological Society chopped down the fir trees.
____ (b) The fir trees were chopped down by the Ecological Society.

PRACTICE 7

Rewrite the sentences below in order to change them from the passive to the active voice.

Example: The chili was burned by the cook.

The cook burned the chili.

1. The point was made by the field-goal kicker.

____

2. The plane was struck by lightening.

____

3. The stamps were bought by Ricardo, and the letters were mailed by Luisa.

____

4. The pictures were taken by my sister.

____

5. The contract was signed last week by Mr. Wong.

____

6. The idea was opposed by a vocal minority of students.

7. Weightlifting is done by many athletes.

8. The popcorn was popped by Joel.

9. The roof was blown off by the explosion.

10. A deal was struck with management by the truck drivers.

11. A diet was begun by the gymnast.

12. Those lopsided houses were built by the contractor.

13. The sandwiches were fixed by Keisha, and the potato salad was brought by Rujendra.

14. The beanstalk was cut down by Jack.

15. Tasteless jokes were made by the unfunny comedian.

Unit Test

Underline any errors in each sentence. Then, rewrite each sentence, correcting any errors.

1. She could of slept all day.

2. They don't have no time for us.

3. She scrambled to her feet and looks him in the eye.

4. All of us should of thanked our guide.

5. A bone was given to the dog by Mark.

6. I never promised you nothing whatsoever.

7. We don't never have no fun.

8. My dad don't never play with me.

9. Don't feed me no garbage today.

10. Fran stopped studying at nine o'clock and goes for ice cream.

11. At the beginning of the movie, the audience laughed, but suddenly they become silent.

12. We would of all visited her in the hospital if we would of known she was sick.

13. My neighbors can't hardly wait to find out who won the $120 million lotto.

14. Don't you have no manners at all?

15. "Stand by Your Man" was made famous by Tammy Wynette.

Unit Talk–Write Assignment

In a brainstorming session for an English composition class, several college students expressed their opinions on telephone answering machine greetings. The students' unedited comments are expressed in the *Talk* column. First, identify the error, if there is one, in each sentence. Second, correct the error in the *Write* column. Third, using the students' comments as background, write a polished paragraph in the space provided at the end of this section about telephone answering machine greetings. Make sure that you avoid shifts in tense, "would of, could of, should of, and must of" errors, and double negatives. Do not use the passive voice where it isn't needed. Be sure to use standard English.

TALK	WRITE
1. My friend bought an answering machine and then puts a really stupid message on it.	
2. It infuriated me that he puts on this long message filled with useless details like "speak slowly and clearly," and "Your call is important to me, so do please leave your name, number, and the date you called1/4."	
3. I know what you mean. A long message is left by my French teacher about how she would of answered the phone, but please leave a message, have a nice life, and eat your vegetables. Then the same long message is repeated by her in French. She must have been drinking. And all I want to tell her was that I'd be absent from the next class.	
4. Personally, I don't think no little kids should ever be allowed to leave a message.	
5. Yeah, that's a mess, but I think it's just as bad to have some professional voice you can't never recognize. Then you're not sure you have the right number.	
6. Worse even is some digital voice that sounds like it could of come from the grave.	
7. What about funny messages? I get sick of those. The other day I called someone, and the message said, "This is Mary's refrigerator answering. Please leave a message."	

8. That reminds me of my uncle's message, which was him singing, "Come be my love" or something. Weird!

9. What about messages that wait so long for the beep to sound that you think there's no beep, so you start leaving a message. Then the beep sounds, and you had to start all over again.

10. People should of realized by now that you don't have to leave no cute messages on answering machines. All you should say was, "Hi, this is Shirley. Please leave a message."

Unit Collaborative Assignment

A. Working with a partner, read aloud the following paragraph, which contains shifts in verb tense, double negatives, and incorrect use of *would have, could have, should have,* and *must have.* Also, the passive voice is used when the active voice would be more effective. Take turns reading each sentence while the other partner rewrites it, as necessary, to correct the errors. When you are through, discuss your rewrites with your partner, referring any points of disagreement to the instructor.

I arrived in Paris and quickly settle into a decent youth hostel. I realize that I was running out of money. "If only I would of spent less money in England," I thought regretfully. My next thought was, "I'd better get a job." The problem was that I didn't have no work permit. No one wanted to hire me since work could not be performed by me legally. Also, French wasn't spoken by me very well. I must of looked terrible because worry was definitely felt by me. My concern would of turned into desperation if I had not met another American at the post office who suggests that I try the American Center situated along the Seine River. Several ads were posted by people who wanted English-speaking nannies. Before long, I found a job, but the hours are long and the kids don't have no respect for adults. I thought I must of been crazy to take such a job. I could of put up with these hardships if I would of received some decent meals. However, the French family I work for ate French bread, cheese, and cabbage day in and day out. So I quit. A few days later, a nanny job was found by me for a four-year-old girl who lived near Versailles. The job was great because the little girl has such a sweet temperament. My six months in Paris helped me become independent both emotionally and financially. It is a great experience and taught me a second language.

B. Discuss with your partner a job you have or once had. Talk out a paragraph on this topic.

Unit Writing Assignment

Write about a job you have or once had, based on your discussion in the Unit Collaborative Assignment above. Avoid the wrong use of problem verbs.

Photo Writing Assignment

Study the two photos below with an eye toward comparing and contrasting the two scenes as a place to call home. You might make a list of pros and cons for living in a bustling city, and another such list for living in a quiet small town. After thinking about the matter, write a paragraph in which you state your preference. Begin with a discussible point, such as, "Living in a huge city is exciting and makes me feel important." Or, by contrast, "Nothing can rival the comfort of living in small town, where you feel safe and comfortable." Write in the active voice; avoid shifts in verb tense; do not use double negatives; do not use *of* for *have,* as in "I *would of* died of boredom if I *would of* continued living in Lone Pine."

11 USING PRONOUNS CORRECTLY

"Maggie's sister encouraged her to wear her miniskirt."

If writing were baseball, the pronoun would be a relief pitcher whose job is temporarily to relieve nouns, who are the starters. In both speech and writing, the pronoun is a word used in place of a noun.

Here is a paragraph that might be written in a world without pronouns:

> My favorite aunt is my Aunt Ida. Aunt Ida is my mother's sister. Aunt Ida loves to read. Aunt Ida reads everything, especially romance novels. Aunt Ida's house is crammed full of books. One room, which Aunt Ida calls Aunt Ida's library, is filled to the brim with books Aunt Ida has read. Aunt Ida not only reads many books, but Aunt Ida also saves every book Aunt Ida has read. Why? Because, Aunt Ida says, Aunt Ida loves rereading old books Aunt Ida has already read.

This paragraph is repetitious and stiff because it uses no pronouns. Adding a few pronouns makes the writing livelier and more natural:

> My favorite aunt is my Aunt Ida. She is my mother's sister. Aunt Ida loves to read. She reads everything, especially romance novels. Her house is crammed full of books. One room, which she calls her library, is filled to the brim with books she has read. Aunt Ida not only reads many books, but she also saves every book she has read. Why? Because, Aunt Ida says, she loves rereading old books she has already read.

EAR ALERT

All speakers use pronouns by ear, often without even thinking. Although our ear gets them right for the most part, because pronoun use in speech is more informal than in writing, we can't rely on our ear alone. We also need to learn the formal rules of pronoun use. That is what this unit covers.

Here are some common problems associated with pronouns in both speaking and writing:

- Antecedent problems
- Agreement problems
- Shifting point of view

We'll take up these problems in order.

Antecedent Problems

The **antecedent** of a pronoun (also called the *referent*) is the noun it replaces. Consider this sentence:

> John may be shy, but he loves to go to parties.

The pronoun is *he*; its antecedent—the word it refers to—is *John*.

Most of the time, the antecedent of a pronoun is perfectly clear from the context of the sentence. Sometimes, however, it isn't. Sometimes an antecedent is either unclear or altogether missing.

Unclear Antecedent

Here are some examples of unclear antecedents:

> Sheila drove Sylvia and her mother to the airport.
>
> Harriett asked Janet if she needed an umbrella.

In the above sentences, the antecedents of the pronouns are unclear. We do not know whether Sheila drove her own mother or Sylvia's mother to the airport, or whether it is Harriet or Janet who needs an umbrella. Here are the same sentences rewritten to avoid the unclear antecedent:

> Sheila drove Sylvia and Sylvia's mother to the airport.
>
> Harriett asked Janet if Janet needed an umbrella.

Sometimes the unclear antecedent is not a person, but an action, feeling, or episode.

Unclear: Not only was the fish old, but Sally paid too much, which really made her angry.

Was Sally angry because the fish was old, or because she overpaid, or both?

Clear: Not only was the fish old, but Sally paid too much, both of which made her angry.

Unclear: Vera told Melanie that she was taking her dog for a walk.

But whose dog is it? Rewriting the sentence should clarify the antecedent:

Clear: Vera told Melanie that she was taking Melanie's dog for a walk.

Unclear: Back in Boston, they told me that I should buy a heavy coat.

Who is this unidentified *they* that is often used in talking, as well as in writing?

Clear: Back in Boston, my aunt and uncle told me that I should buy a heavy coat.

In the back-and-forth of daily talk, fuzzy antecedents are cleared up easily. The listener blurts out, "Who?" and gets a clarifying answer. However, in writing, we get no chance to ask the writer *Who?* If a pronoun does not have a clear antecedent, you risk confusing your reader.

IN A NUTSHELL

Every pronoun must have a clear antecedent.

PRACTICE 1

Rewrite the following sentences so that the pronouns clearly refer to only one antecedent (the word the pronoun stands for).

1. Matilda was planning to share the meat with her dog, but she was so hungry that she ate it.

___

___

2. Betty gave Caroline homemade cookies, which she thought was a nice gift.

___

___

3. We took the curtains off the windows and cleaned them.

___

___

4. Bob and Harry started a business that went bankrupt because he always spent money before it was made.

___

___

5. Mary should help Joan, but she should help herself first.

6. My brother was a close friend of our neighbor's son until he left for college.

7. Maggie's sister encouraged her to wear her miniskirt.

8. Professor Jones implied to Jack that he was far too liberal for his own good.

9. Charlie told Julio that he had been rude.

10. John had the courage to tell his friend that he owed him money.

11. Mr. Chan told his neighbor that his car looked old and junky.

12. Ferdinando asked Brett if he was allowed to see the baby.

13. Two of my buddies love being waiters, but I'm not interested in it.

14. At the hospital, they gave me a prescription for antibiotics.

15. Ivan was tickled pink to tell Frank that he had finally kicked a successful field goal.

Missing Antecedents

In both speech and writing, we often use pronouns that have no antecedents. This is especially true of the pronouns *which*, *this*, *that*, *they*, and *it*. Here is an example:

Even though my mother is a marathon runner, I have no interest in it.

What is the *it*? We have a fuzzy idea that by *it*, the writer means running, but the word *running* does not appear in the sentence.

Usually, the best way to rewrite such a sentence is to omit the pronoun and provide the missing noun.

Even though my mother is a marathon runner, I have no interest in running.

Here are some other examples:

Missing: At the Emergency Room, they said that Mara had broken her ankle.

Clear: At the Emergency Room, the doctors said that Mara had broken her ankle.

Incorrect: It says to print your name under your signature.

Correct: The directions say to print your name under your signature.

Now we know the identity of the unnamed *it*.

Unclear: The Coast Guard located the missing boat within an hour and rescued the boys, who said that they were not frightened by the experience. This amazed their parents.

What does *this* refer to? We do not know. It could refer either to the boy's rescue, their supposed lack of fear, or both.

Clear: The Coast Guard located the missing boat within an hour and rescued the boys, who said that they were not frightened by the experience. The parents were amazed by the Coast Guard's quick response.

Now we know exactly what the writer means. Note that to get around an unclear antecedent, you may need to rewrite the sentence.

Here is yet another example of a pronoun with an unclear antecedent:

Unclear: Sharon arrived late and quietly took a seat in the back row. That was very unlike her.

What is the antecedent for *that*? The antecedent could be that *she arrived late*, or that *she quietly took a seat in the back row*, or *both*.

Clear: Sharon arrived late, which was very unlike her, and quietly took a seat in the back row.

The requirement that every pronoun have a specific and clear antecedent is not simply a picky rule. In everyday talk, we do not observe such exactness in pronoun use because we can always ask "What?" and get an answer. In writing, though, you have no second chance. Every pronoun must therefore have a specific antecedent.

IN A NUTSHELL

Be alert to the possibility of a missing antecedent when using the pronouns *which, this, that, they,* and *it.*

PRACTICE 2

Rewrite the following sentences to clarify the pronoun reference.

1. We were standing in line when they informed us that the show was sold out.

   ____

   ____

2. In the directions, it says to add one cup of flour.

   ____

   ____

3. My sister refused to go to college because she felt that they required too much math for graduation.

   ____

   ____

4. My mother's friend and her aunt drove to the airport.

   ____

   ____

5. It says to change the oil every three months or 3,000 miles.

   ____

   ____

6. Most of my classmates write poems, but I have no talent for it.

   ____

   ____

7. I deposited the money in my bank, but they haven't posted the correct balance.

   ____

   ____

8. Mary bragged about her dancing ability although she had never been one.

____

____

9. We ordered a large pizza, but they delivered a medium.

____

____

10. Claire said that they advised her to have a perm.

____

____

Agreement Problems

A pronoun and its antecedent must agree in number. Singular nouns require singular pronouns. Plural nouns require plural pronouns. Some examples follow.

> The widow wanted *her* land back.
>
> The farmers wanted *their* land back.

In the first sentence, the singular noun *widow* requires the singular pronoun *her.* In the second sentence, the plural noun *farmers* requires the plural pronoun *their.*

Indefinite Pronouns

Most of the time, pronoun agreement is not a problem, but it can be troublesome when we try to find a pronoun to replace an indefinite pronoun.

An **indefinite pronoun** is a pronoun that refers to no one in particular. Here is a list of common indefinite pronouns that are always singular:

INDEFINITE PRONOUNS

another	either	nobody	somebody
anybody	everybody	no one	someone
anyone	everyone	none	something
anything	everything	nothing	
each	neither	one	

Study these sentences:

Incorrect: Each of the boys has their cap on backward.

Correct: Each of the boys has his cap on backward.

(*Each* requires a singular pronoun. Remember to cross out the prepositional phrase if you are confused about the subject.)

Incorrect: Either Tammy or Tina will give me their ticket.

Correct: Either Tammy or Tina will give me her ticket.

(*Either* requires a singular pronoun.)

In both speech and writing, to avoid being sexist, we often use the plural *their* to refer to many indefinite pronouns that are singular. We say, for example, and it sounds perfectly fine to our ear:

Someone left their coat on the desk.

Technically, this is wrong. *Their* is plural; *someone* is singular. On the other hand, *his*, the singular pronoun, is *sexist*:

Someone left his coat on the desk.

It is sexist because *someone* could be a female, a possibility that is ignored by the use of the pronoun.

Rewriting that sentence is the best way to correct an agreement problem. You can tiptoe around the sexist passage by changing it to either singular or plural. Both are correct. Here is an example:

Incorrect: Would everyone who ordered chicken raise their hands?

Correct: If you ordered chicken, raise your hand.

Correct: Would all the people who ordered chicken raise their hands?

Here is another example:

Incorrect: Did everyone in class get their seat assignments?

Correct: Did you get your seat assignment?

Correct: Did all students get their seat assignments?

PRACTICE 3

Correct the agreement errors in the following sentences, using both ways that you've learned—by changing to the singular and changing to the plural.

1. Does everyone in the class have their notebooks?

   Correct singular: ______________________________

   Correct plural: ______________________________

2. If anyone needs a ride, they should let me know.

   Correct singular: ______________________________

   Correct plural: ______________________________

3. Is anybody taking their camera to the party?

   Correct singular: ______________________________

   Correct plural: ______________________________

4. Did somebody offer their seat to Mr. Kimble?

   Correct singular: ______________________________

   Correct plural: ______________________________

5. No one will be seated if they arrive after the show starts.

   Correct singular: ______________________________

   Correct plural: ______________________________

6. Would everyone please introduce themselves?

   Correct singular: ______________________________

   Correct plural: ______________________________

7. If someone has a good barbecue sauce recipe, they should be required by law to share it.

   Correct singular: ______________________________

   Correct plural: ______________________________

8. Is anyone going to bring their partners to the reunion?

   Correct singular: ______________________________

   Correct plural: ______________________________

9. Everyone should hang their coats in the front closet.

   Correct singular: ______________________________

   Correct plural: ______________________________

10. Nobody should take themselves too seriously.

    Correct singular: ______________________________

    Correct plural: ______________________________

Note: The indefinite pronouns *all*, *any*, *some*, *none*, *half*, and *most* can be either singular or plural, depending on how they are used in a sentence. Study these examples:

Plural: Jeremy loves horses. Some *are* prize-winning Tennessee Walkers. (This is the same as writing "Some Tennessee Walkers are prize-winning horses.")

Singular: He had lots of money. Some *was* used for hungry children. (This is the same as writing "Some money *was* used . . ."

Plural: Some walls are made of brick. (*Walls* is plural and requires a plural verb.)

Singular: Some butter *requires* water to preserve it. (*Butter* is singular and requires a singular verb. In both of these cases, the pronoun *some* acts like an adjective.)

EAR ALERT

Neither native students nor ESL students should depend on their ears to use these pronouns correctly. Study the sentence to see whether the antecedent of the pronoun is plural and requires a plural verb or is singular and requires a singular verb. Check whether the pronoun acts like an adjective.

PRACTICE 4

Complete the following sentences with a verb used correctly.

1. Most of the loan ________________________
2. Most of the flags ________________________
3. Any cats with fleas in their fur ________________
4. Any girl wearing huge tattoos on her arms and legs ________
5. Half of the football field ____________________
6. Half the contestants ______________________
7. None of my friends ______________________
8. None ______________________________
9. All of the castle ________________________
10. The men assembled. All ____________________

Pronouns as Direct and Indirect Objects

A pronoun can be the *direct object* of a verb as in this sentence:

> Thomas Jefferson chose *him* as Secretary of State.

Or, a pronoun can also be the *indirect object* of a verb as in this sentence:

> The quarterback decided to pass *him* the ball.

In the first sentence, the pronoun receives the action directly from the verb. (Whom did Thomas Jefferson choose? He chose *him.*) In the second case, the indirect object *him* comes between the verb and the direct object. (*Ball* is the direct object because it receives the direct action from the verb. *Him* is the indirect object.)

PRACTICE 5

In the blank provided, write a *D* if the underlined pronoun is the direct object; write an *I* if the pronoun is the indirect object.

1. _____ The coach reached <u>him</u> by phone.
2. _____ Harry Potter gave <u>her</u> a piercing look.

3. ____ His grandfather bought them warm raincoats.
4. ____ The commander ordered him to get a military haircut.
5. ____ When did you first notice us?
6. ____ Dodge him if you possibly can!
7. ____ As a gesture of gratitude, they left them three baskets full of roses.
8. ____ Melissa hugged him with all her might.
9. ____ The Devil tempted us to do that.
10. ____ "You idiots, leave him the bag; there's nothing in it!" he shouted.

Collective Nouns

A collective noun is a noun that refers to more than one person or thing. Here are some commonly used collective nouns:

audience	family
class	government
committee	group
company	jury
council	numbers (1,000, 500, etc.)
crowd	tribe

Usually, collective nouns are singular and therefore take singular pronouns.

The audience **was** very restless.

The jury **was** out for only five minutes.

He spent $10,000, which **is** a lot of money.

Collective nouns are *count nouns*, which means that they themselves have plurals. *Mass nouns,* on the other hand, have no plurals: *ice*, *electricity*, *dancing*. A collective noun will be plural only when its members are acting as individuals. Notice the difference:

Acting as a single unit:	The Committee gave its report as requested.
Acting individually:	The Committee gave their individual answers to the report.
Acting as a unit:	The crowd abandoned its place on the hill.
Acting individually:	The crowd left their posters on the ground.
Acting an a unit:	The jury took its time.
Acting individually:	The jury took their seats.

PRACTICE 6

Underline the correct pronoun in each of the following sentences.

1. The Nominating Committee will notify you of (its, their) first choice.
2. When the family saw each other again, (it, they) had each aged by ten years.
3. The U.S. Government stands by (its, their) democratic principles.
4. The audience ran out the door with (its, their) hands held high.
5. The council lost all credibility when (its, their) chairwoman never appeared.
6. Every major corporation must be concerned about (its, their) employees.
7. Our senior class requested (its, their) class portraits before graduation.
8. The basketball team wanted to beat (its, their) opposition in the worst way.
9. The Pacific Gas and Electric Company is proud of not gouging (its, their) customers.
10. This time, several wives in the group gave (its, their) own private account in writing.

Sexist Use of Pronouns

You have just learned how to avoid sexism with indefinite pronouns. But sexism is even worse when a singular pronoun automatically assigns the male sex to professionals:

> Every doctor should listen to his patients.

The use of *his* in the above sentence suggests that every doctor is a man, which is both sexist and untrue. On the other hand, using *his or her* is correct, but clumsy. One solution is to make the whole sentence plural, using the neutral pronoun *their.* Here are the possible nonsexist choices:

Sexist: Every doctor should listen to his patients.

Nonsexist: Every doctor should listen to his or her patients.

Nonsexist: Doctors should listen to their patients.

Their includes both men and women, and it is not as clumsy as *his or her.*

If you are facing a pronoun agreement problem that you simply cannot rewrite in the plural, then use *his or her.* If the choice is between being sexist or being clumsy, it is better to be clumsy.

IN A NUTSHELL

- Pronouns and their antecedents must agree in number.
- Avoid the sexist use of pronouns.

PRACTICE 7

Rewrite the following sentences to correct the pronoun agreement problem or the sexist bias.

1. No student on the social committee was willing to give up their vacation.

____

____

2. A newspaper reporter often uses his cell phone.

____

____

3. A defense attorney can lose his case even if his client is innocent.

____

____

4. As soon as a person realizes that they have been insulted, they leave.

____

____

5. A good neighbor mows their lawn regularly.

____

____

6. You may borrow either of these blouses if you promise to iron them.

____

____

7. One or the other of these girls must admit that they stole the cake.

____

____

8. Each of the nurses will buy their own ticket for the hospital's banquet.

____

____

9. Before someone learns to drive, they have to walk or take a bus.

____

____

10. Anyone who does not pay their health fee will not be given a flu shot.

____

____

PRACTICE 8

Complete the following sentences with the correct pronoun.

Example: Anyone who plans to donate blood must show his or her driver's license or another form of photo identification to the nurse.

1. Another of the women stood up to express ____ personal opinions.
2. All that was required of either man was ____ personal assurance to be good.
3. Somebody has left ____ purse in the kitchen.
4. Everybody thinks ____ is right on this issue.
5. An antiquarian is a person who prefers to spend ____ life in the past.
6. Each of the gunmen came to court with ____ personal attorney.
7. Anyone can become better at sports if ____ works hard.
8. Each of the women felt that ____ idea was the better one.
9. Anyone who thinks ____ has a better way should share it with me.
10. Neither of the students knew ____ way around the campus.

Shifting Point of View

Writing is easier to read if it uses the same point of view throughout. You may choose a first person, second person, or third person point of view:

FIRST PERSON	SECOND PERSON	THIRD PERSON
I	you	he, she, it, one
we	you	they

Here are some examples:

Incorrect: If a person finds a wallet with identification, you should return it to the owner.

Correct: When you find a wallet with identification, you should return it to the rightful owner.

or

When one finds a wallet with identification, one should return it to the rightful owner.

Here is another example containing many shifts:

If you're unhappy, try taking a good hard look at your priorities. When we do that honestly, we can often see imbalances. You can be spending all your time working and not paying attention to the important people in your life. Is one's job really more important than your family? We say no, but then we accept the promotion that means working longer hours and on weekends. Think again about your priorities.

Here is the correction using *you*. *You*, *we*, or *one* would all be correct as long as the same point of view is used throughout, with no shifts from one pronoun point of view to another.

If you're unhappy, try taking a good hard look at your priorities. When you do that honestly, you can often see imbalances. You can be spending all your time working and not paying attention to the important people in your life. Is your job really more important than your family? You say no, but then you accept the promotion that means working longer hours and on weekends. Think again about your priorities.

IN A NUTSHELL

Avoid shifts in pronoun point of view. In other words, be consistent in your use of pronouns.

PRACTICE 9

Correct the pronoun shifts in the following sentences by crossing out the incorrect word or words and writing the correction above them.

1. When I first visited the Louvre, you could see all the tourists heading toward the Mona Lisa.
2. Despite the fact that we are loyal and honest, you can't count on others being that way.
3. One should learn a little tact if they are a mother-in-law.
4. At our college, students have to study hard if you want top grades.

5. As you enter the building, the personnel office is on one's left.
6. If person is going to graduate from college, they must practice good study habits.
7. You have to step back and take an objective look at yourself if a person wants to get over some bad habit.
8. If one is traveling to an unfamiliar state, you should buy a map.
9. If someone were to invent a cream that would dissolve body fat, you could become a millionaire.
10. We always look forward to the Fourth of July because you can cook out during the day and see fireworks at night.

Unit Test

Rewrite the following sentences to correct the pronoun errors.

1. Tanya told Mary she had to study hard.

   ____

   ____

2. They spread the rumor that Murray was suffering from flesh-eating bacteria.

   ____

   ____

3. Everyone who wants your picture in the yearbook should sign up today.

   ____

   ____

4. A surgeon should always reassure his patients.

   ____

   ____

5. In the counseling office, they said that I needed a cultural diversity course.

   ____

   ____

6. At the edge of the park, it says, "Don't litter."

   ____

   ____

7. One of the people in line dropped their checkbook.

   ____

   ____

8. Each of my neighbors put their flags out on the Fourth of July.

9. Does anyone care about their car getting wet?

10. Bert paid for Ben and his dad to attend the game.

11. I love beautiful flowers that also have a fragrance, making you appreciate them.

12. All of us loved to hang out with Peter and Jim, but then he suddenly left town.

13. Although my father is an excellent preacher, my brother has no interest in it.

14. Neither of the boys care one hoot about sports.

15. Everybody thinks their country is the best.

Unit Talk–Write Assignment

Students in a social problems class were asked to discuss their greatest fears about society today. Some students mentioned high divorce rates; others talked about crime and drugs. Several students mentioned terrorism—which became the focus of the discussion. Here are some of their comments, written down more or less the way they were spoken. First, correct the pronoun errors in the sentences. Then, write a paragraph about your worst fear about society. When you have finished your paragraph, check it for the correct use of pronouns.

TALK	WRITE
1. Terrorism is everywhere, it seems. You never know when you get on a plane whether they might highjack it.	
2. A person just doesn't feel as safe as you used to. When my friend and her mother flew to Europe last spring, she felt very threatened.	
3. Anyone in their right mind should be afraid. Terrorists have killed hundreds of innocent people all over the world.	
4. My mother says that since the September 11, 2001, New York and Washington, D.C., terrorist attacks, you don't even feel safe in the United States. It's scary.	
5. Yeah. And there was other terrorist acts, too. Remember the Unabomber and the bombs found at the Olympic Games in Atlanta in 1996?	
6. My chemistry teacher says that anyone with a little know-how can build a bomb. They don't even need a college degree!	
7. We have to find a way to stop sickos from committing terrorist acts. It has to stop, or they will just get worse and worse.	

8. But you can't just let the FBI do electronic surveillance on everyone. Pretty soon everyone becomes a suspected terrorist and their home is bugged.

9. But at least we'd be safe. You wouldn't get blown up just walking along the street.

10. Yeah, it would be a very safe police state. Terrorism is a real problem.

Unit Collaborative Assignment

A. Read the following sentences aloud to a classmate, whose job is to catch the pronoun errors and tell you how to correct them. Try to reach agreement on all sentences.

1. Mary told Felice that her boss was too strict.
2. At the Career Center, they said that Judy should be an architect.
3. Anybody who gets up will lose their seat.
4. If you have your health, one has everything.
5. Not only was the coat much too tight, it was also made of cheap material, which made Irene angry.
6. Merlin walked with a hot dog in one hand and a piece of carrot cake in the other, munching on it as he headed down the steps.
7. It clearly states that you must have a parent's signature.
8. As we walked into the movie, they told us that only the two front rows were unoccupied.
9. Nancy intended to tell her teacher that she had been rude.
10. Everyone wanted his ticket back.

B. Now reverse your roles. Again, try to reach agreement on all sentences.

1. Jane told Marguerite that her cousin would be at the meeting.
2. At the market, they said that the peaches were ripe.

3. Neither of the girls want to attend the wedding.
4. Every nurse should be gentle with her patients.
5. As one enters the restaurant, it says, “No checks, please.”
6. Neither of the grocery checkers ever smile.
7. They have a lot of freeway traffic in Los Angeles.
8. Each of the volunteers takes pride in their service to others.
9. Everyone scored at least 80 on their algebra test.
10. If we are aware of a problem, you should try to help.

Unit Writing Assignment

Write a brief essay about the best or worst job you’ve ever had. Tell your reader exactly what the job required and what make it so good or so bad, using vivid details to back up your points. Check that you have used all pronouns correctly. Use the Revising Checklist inside the front cover of this book to help you revise.

Photo Writing Assignment

The photo below shows a soldier receiving a medal of honor for bravery during combat. Write a paragraph on the military practice of awarding medals and citations for acts of heroism. Think about the civilian equivalent of these awards and ponder the usefulness served by both kinds of recognition. Ask yourself which award you would prefer to get—a military or a civilian one—and why. Begin with a discussible topic sentence and use the appropriate details to support your point. Focus on using pronouns correctly.

12 PRONOUN PROBLEMS

"Him and I are good buddies."

English has three cases: subjective, objective, and possessive. Nouns do not change form when they are used as subjects or objects. They change form only in the possessive case:

Larry kissed Nancy.	**(Larry is the subject.)**
Nancy kissed Larry.	**(Larry is the object.)**
Larry 's kisses were sweet.	**(The's added to the noun *Larry* indicates that they are his kisses. He "possesses" them.)**

If we replace *Larry* with a pronoun, the pronoun is different in all three cases, the subjective, objective, and possessive:

He kissed Nancy.

Nancy kissed *him.*

His kisses were sweet.

If pronouns, like nouns, would only stay the same whether used as subjects or objects, English would be a far easier language to write and speak. Unfortunately, only the pronouns *it* and *you* take the same case and spelling whether they are used as subject or object.

Here are the pronouns in all three cases:

SUBJECT PRONOUNS	OBJECT PRONOUNS	POSSESSIVE PRONOUNS
I	me	my, mine
you	you	your, yours
he	him	his

she	her	her, hers
it	it	its
we	us	our, ours
you	you	your, yours
they	them	their, theirs

Case Problems

Because pronouns change case depending on how they are used, many of us often make case errors. Typically, we use a subject pronoun for an object pronoun, or the other way around. In the following sections, we will discuss the correct use of subject pronouns, object pronouns, possessive pronouns, and reflexive pronouns.

Subject Pronouns

Subject pronouns replace nouns used as subjects. Here are the rules for using subject pronouns correctly:

1. **Use a subject pronoun as the subject of a verb.** We usually use subject pronouns correctly, saying *I work at McDonald's,* not *Me work at McDonald's.* But we can run into problems with pronouns used in compound subjects.

Incorrect: Buddy and me made a pact.

Correct: Buddy and I made a pact.

> **ESL Advice!**
>
> We recommend that ESL students commit the list of pronouns to memory rather than trusting their ears. Also, remember that in English the pronoun must always be stated, except when using a command, such as "Stop that complaining," where the "you" is understood.

Buddy and *I* form the compound subject of the verb *made.*

To test whether you are using the correct pronoun in a compound subject, try the two possible pronouns separately. Your ear will tell you which is right. For example:

Buddy and (I, me) made a pact.

Test: I made a pact.

Me made a pact.

EAR ALERT

This test might not work for you if you don't have a good ear for English. In that case, you should memorize the rule. Clearly, Me made a pact sounds wrong. The correct pronoun is therefore I. Try the test with another sentence:

Incorrect:	We and them can't get along.
Test:	They can't get along.
	Them can't get along.

Your ear tells you which pronoun is correct—*they.*

PRACTICE 1

Underline the correct subject pronoun in parentheses in the following sentences: If you have trouble deciding which pronoun is incorrect, try letting your ear tell you. Read the sentence aloud using first one pronoun and then the other.

1. Chaney and (me/I) had a class together.
2. She and (he/him) don't get along too well.
3. Howard and (they/them) are always arguing.
4. (She/her) and (he/him) went out to dinner.
5. (She/her) and (I/me) have always been good friends.
6. We and (her/she) went for a long hike together.
7. (She/her) and (he/him) have dated for a long time.
8. You know that (she/her) and (I/me) grew up in the same neighborhood.
9. In December, (she/her) and (I/me) will take a trip to California.
10. (She/her) and (he/him) used to study in the library together.

2. **Use a subject pronoun in comparisons.** In sentences using *than* or *as* to make a comparison, the second verb is usually omitted because we know what is meant. For example, in the sentence *Mary is more patient than I,* we really mean,

   Mary is more patient than I am patient.

To test whether you're using the correct pronoun in a *than* or *as* sentence, simply complete the comparison. Here is another example:

They are as tough as (we, us).

Test:	They are as tough as us are tough.
	They are as tough as we are tough.

Your ear tells you that *we* is correct.

PRACTICE 2

Underline the correct pronoun in the following comparison.

1. Jane is taller than (me/I).
2. Peter is smarter than (him/he).
3. Martha is as tall as (I/me).
4. They are better in English than (we/us).
5. Do you really think that they can play soccer better than (we/us)?
6. I have never felt that I was a better athlete than (him/he).
7. John is nicer than (him/he).
8. No matter what you think, I know that Hubert can play tennis better than (her/she).
9. Come to think of it, I believe that I am a better chess player than (he/him).
10. They are as determined as (we/us).

EAR ALERT

3. **Use a subject pronoun after the verb *to be*.** If you rely on your ear to get the pronoun right after the verb to be, you will probably get it wrong. Here are some examples:

Incorrect: It is her speaking.
Correct: It is she speaking.

Incorrect: Was it them who swam to the island?
Correct: Was it they who swam to the island?

The correct sentences probably sound bizarre to your inner grammar ear. After all, most people say *it's me* rather than the grammatically correct *it's I.* In spoken language, that usage is fine, but as we have often said in this book, written standard English requires grammatical correctness.

If you think that the grammatically correct sentences don't sound right, you can always rewrite them to avoid the *it* + *to be* + *pronoun* construction. For instance:

Original: It is she speaking.
Rewrite: She is speaking.

Original: Was it they who swam to the island?
Rewrite: Did they swim to the island?

One good thing about talking or writing in English: You always have a choice.

IN A NUTSHELL

- Use a subject pronoun as the subject of a verb.
- Use a subject pronoun in comparisons.
- Use a subject pronoun after the verb *to be.*

PRACTICE 3

In the blank provided, write *C* if the italicized pronoun is correct and *NC* if it is not correct. Cross out each incorrect pronoun and write the correct pronoun above it.

Example: **NC** It is ~~us~~ (we) who will win in the end.

1. ____ Was that *her* making the decision?
2. ____ Yes, it was *I* who baked the cake.
3. ____ If I were *them*, I would pay the fine.
4. ____ It was supposed to be *them* who sat at the corner table.
5. ____ Would you like to be *she*?
6. ____ Who sent the e-mail? It was *he.*
7. ____ To be *him* would mean living in a fish bowl.
8. ____ If it had to be *they,* it had to be—that's fate for you.
9. ____ Yes, it was *her* who wrote the letter.
10. ____ Is that your mother over there? Yes, it is *she.*

Object Pronouns

Object pronouns take the place of nouns used as objects. The object of a verb is the word that receives its action. For example, in the sentence:

I kissed Mary.

the object of *kissed* is *Mary*, who received the kiss. If you used a pronoun in place of *Mary*, it would have to be in the objective case.

Correct: I kissed her.

Incorrect: I kissed she.

Although your ear is generally a good guide to the correct use of object pronouns, one trouble spot is the pronoun after a preposition.

4. **Use an object pronoun after a preposition.** A pronoun that follows a preposition becomes its object and must be in the objective case.

Incorrect: I mentioned the problem to she and the landlady.

Correct: I mentioned the problem to her and the landlady.

Incorrect: Between you and I, she didn't mean to put you down.

Correct: Between you and me, she didn't mean to put you down.

> **ESL Advice!**
>
> Be very careful with pronouns used after prepositions. This particular usage gives even native speakers trouble.

If you do not know which pronoun to use in a sentence, simply try the pronoun by itself in a sentence. Your ear will tell you if you've used the correct form. For example:

I mentioned the problem to the landlady and (she, her).

Test: I mentioned the problem to the landlady.

I mentioned the problem to her.

Your ear will tell you that *her* is correct.

The preposition that probably gives people the most trouble with pronoun use is *between*. How many times in everyday speech have you heard these incorrect forms?

INCORRECT	CORRECT
between you and I	between you and me
between John and he	between John and him
between Mary and she	between Mary and her
between you and he	between you and him
between they and the police	between them and the police
between he and she	between him and her

Because the incorrect form is so common in everyday speech, this is one usage where you simply cannot trust your ear. Just remember that *between* is a preposition, and an object pronoun must be used after a preposition. You must observe this ironclad rule of grammar in your writing and should learn to use it in speaking.

> **ESL Advice!**
>
> The use of *between* confuses almost everyone. You should memorize the rule about its use.

IN A NUTSHELL

- Use *me, you, him, her, it, us,* or *them* when the pronoun is an object.
- Use an object pronoun after a preposition.

PRACTICE 4

Underline the correct pronoun in parentheses.

1. Legislation now protects (we, us) disabled students.
2. The picture was painted by three of us—Pete, Mabel, and (I, me).
3. For (we, us) nature lovers, the Sierras are like a temple.
4. If it weren't for (he, him) and (I, me), you'd be in trouble.
5. Sitting between (he, him) and Mary, I couldn't move an inch.
6. The volleyball team chose Terry and (she, her).
7. We stood right behind my dad and (they, them).
8. The wealthy aunt gave money to Laura and (he, him).
9. You can't stop us from voting for (they, them).
10. Between Gus and (I, me), we have all the bases covered.

PRACTICE 5

In the sentences that follow, cross out any italicized pronoun used incorrectly, writing the correct form above it. If the sentence is correct, make no changes, but write a *C* in the blank.

1. ____ Kira spoke of the trust between *she* and Ricardo.
2. ____ Between you and *me*, the weather is turning ugly.
3. ____ The minister spoke to the couple and *he* at great length.
4. ____ Watch out! Stand behind Ernesto and *they*.
5. ____ That is a matter for *her* to discuss.
6. ____ I told Mr. Faber that I had seen Raoul's letter to the class and *me*.
7. ____ The love between his grandmother and he was obvious to everyone.
8. ____ She lives right next door to *I*.
9. ____ The person with *they* arrived from Iran yesterday.
10. ____ Let's all vote for *she*.

PRACTICE 6

The sentences that follow contain both subjective and objective pronouns, some of which are in the wrong case. If the pronouns used in the sentence are correct, write a *C* in the blank. If the pronouns are incorrect, draw a line through the incorrect form and write the correct form above the sentence.

1. ____ Oprah and him gave the books to she.
2. ____ Without my uncle and he as guides, Cheney and me are likely to get lost.
3. ____ Willard and me have not spoken to they for over a year.
4. ____ The group invested for she a year before him knew.
5. ____ Candy and her told Mother that nothing will ever come between you and I.
6. ____ "Pretend not to notice," he said, "and Joshua and she will go away."
7. ____ After the storm, Martin and her repaired the damage her did.
8. ____ Without she, the house us lived in then would never have been painted.
9. ____ The basketball game that we played was won by us.
10. ____ The foreman agreed with me that my workers and I needed a vacation.

To review direct and indirect object pronouns, go back to Chapter 12, pages 222–23.

Possessive Pronouns

Possessive pronouns are pronouns that show ownership or possession. A list of the possessive pronouns follows.

my, mine	its
your, yours	our, ours
his	your, yours
hers	their, theirs

There are three common possessive pronoun errors:

- *It's/its:* The contraction *it's* (short for *it is*) is sometimes incorrectly used instead of *its* (meaning, belonging to *it*).

Incorrect: The dog wagged it's tail.

Correct: The dog wagged its tail.

You can test the correctness of such a sentence by using the long, rather than the contracted, form of *it's* in a sentence.

Test: The dog wagged it is tail.
The mistake is now plainly visible.

- *Hers, his, and theirs:* These words do not need an apostrophe. They are already possessive.

Incorrect: That's hers'.
Correct: That's hers.

Incorrect: The tweed coat is his'.
Correct: The tweed coat is his.

Incorrect: The red sports car is theirs'.
Correct: The red sports car is theirs.

- *Yourn/hisn:* These words are ungrammatical. They are not standard English. The correct forms are *yours* and *his.*

Incorrect: That cup of coffee is yourn.
Correct: That cup of coffee is yours.

Incorrect: That algebra book is hisn.
Correct: That algebra book is his.

IN A NUTSHELL

- *Its* is a possessive pronoun; *it's* is short for *it is.*
- Do not use an apostrophe with *hers, his,* and *theirs.*
- *Yourn* and *hisn* are not standard English.

PRACTICE 7

In the blank, write either *its* or *it's,* whichever is correct. If you have trouble deciding on the correct answer, try the "it is" test.

1. _____ disgusting to see teenagers smoking.
2. The ramshackle house, with _____ broken chimney, makes an excellent postcard.
3. I dialed the restaurant, but _____ line was busy.
4. What kind of music is it? _____ jazz.
5. _____ very selfish of her not to visit her grandmother in the hospital.
6. Why did you say, " _____ going to rain"?
7. From the day of _____ first clang, the bell became a symbol.
8. _____ smooth and powerful engine makes it an expensive car.

9. When _____ time to go, we'll let you know.
10. Don't worry; _____ only the first draft.

PRACTICE 8

Correct the following sentences by rewriting them correctly in the space provided. If the sentence is correct, leave it as is.

1. The cat licked it's fur.

____

2. Its your turn to drive, not mine.

____

3. The hat sitting on the table in the front hall is hers'.

____

4. That beautiful motorcycle is theirs'.

____

5. I thought that new laptop computer was yourn.

____

6. Your sister didn't agree with that story of yours.

____

7. Isn't that black leather jacket his'?

____

8. Nobody's car is bigger than his.

____

9. Its a pity that its such a rainy day.

____

10. On a long golf fairway, there is no more beautiful swing than his.

____

____

Reflexive Pronouns

A **reflexive pronoun** refers back to the subject in the sentence. It clarifies meaning or adds emphasis.

I bought myself a pair of cowboy boots.	**(I bought the boots not for *him*, but for *me*.)**
He made himself an omelet.	**(He made the omelet for no one else.)**

The architect himself checked the staircase.	**(The architect didn't send his assistant—he did it *himself*.)**

The reflexive pronouns are listed below:

myself	itself
yourself	ourselves
himself	yourselves
herself	themselves

There are two common problems with reflexive pronouns. First, *hisself* is often used for *himself* and *theirself* for *themselves.* These nonstandard words, like *ain't*, exist only in slang.

Incorrect: He drives hisself to work.
Correct: He drives himself to work.

Incorrect: They surprised theirself.
Correct: They surprised themselves.

The second common problem with reflexive pronouns is the use of *me* (an objective pronoun) instead of *myself* (the reflexive pronoun).

Incorrect: I bought me a new pair of boots.
Correct: I bought myself a new pair of boots.

Another problem is inappropriate use of *myself* instead of *me.*

Incorrect: If you don't know what to do, be sure to ask Diego or myself for help.
Correct: If you don't know what to do, be sure to ask Diego or me for help.

Incorrect: You can send your complaint to myself.
Correct: You can send your complaint to me.

IN A NUTSHELL

- *Hisself* and *theirself* are not standard English words.
- Do not use *me* in place of *myself.*
- Do not use *myself* in place of *me.*

PRACTICE 9

Underline the correct reflexive pronoun in parentheses for each sentence.

1. They blamed (theirselves, themselves) for the dismal outcome.
2. They congratulated (theirself, themselves) on a job well done.

3. I bought (me, myself) a new mattress for my bed.
4. Benny spilled grape juice on (himself, hisself).
5. They (theirselves, themselves) speak highly of the coach.
6. They bought (theirselves, themselves) steak dinners to celebrate.
7. John pulled (himself, hisself) out of the pool.
8. Bring any problems to (me, myself), I told her.
9. Why can't they carve the pumpkin (theirselves, themselves)?
10. He should be thoroughly ashamed of (himself, hisself).

Pesky Pronouns

Some pronouns are pesky—they give everyone trouble. Among the peskiest pronouns are *who/whom*, *who's/whose*, *who/which/that*. (For a discussion of *this*, *that*, *these*, and *those*, see Unit 13, pages 257–58.)

1. Who/Whom

Two of the peskiest pronouns are *who* and *whom*. In fact, we sometimes get the impression that they are so pesky that some writers simply use only *who*, never *whom*. Eventually, the two forms may merge into one. Until that day arrives, however, we must observe the distinction between *who* and *whom*.

Use who as a subject pronoun.

Who may be used in place of the following pronouns:

SUBJECT PRONOUNS		
I	he	we
you	she	they

Who is in class? *She* is in class.

Who is going to speak? *He* is going to speak.

Use whom as an object pronoun.

Whom may be used in place of the following pronouns:

OBJECT PRONOUNS		
me	him	us
you	her	them

Whom do you love? I love him.

To whom do I owe an apology? I owe an apology to *them*.

If you don't know whether to use *who* or *whom* in a question, try answering the question using *he*, *she*, *they*, *him*, *her*, or *them*. For example:

(Who, whom) do you know?

Test: I know him.

I know he.

Because *him* is correct, you know that the objective form—*whom*—is therefore correct.

To apply the test to a statement, you have to turn the sentence around:

I know the detective to (who, whom) he confessed.

Test: He confessed to she.

He confessed to her.

Again, because *her* is correct, you know that the objective form—*whom*—is correct.

IN A NUTSHELL

Who is always used as a subject; *whom* is always used as an object.

PRACTICE 10

Fill in the blanks below with either *who* or *whom*.

1. _____ are you referring to?
2. I spoke to a loan officer _____ was very helpful.
3. Many of the writers _____ my teacher adores are dead.
4. The game of life is best played by the person _____ has the best sense of humor.
5. They knew no one _____ matched that description.
6. As to _____ she meant, we could not say for the life of us.
7. Know _____ you are dealing with.
8. I saw a man _____ danced with his wife in Chicago.
9. Ask not for _____ the bell tolls.
10. He says that he knows many people _____ are very stubborn.
11. _____, may I ask, is calling?
12. To _____ do you wish to speak?

13. _____ do you trust?
14. _____ do you consider more trustworthy?
15. I don't know; _____ do you think is more trustworthy?

2. Who's/Whose

Who's is short for *who is*; *whose* shows possession. Here are some examples:

Incorrect: They wondered who's car this was.
Correct: They wondered whose car this was.

Incorrect: I know whose to blame.
Correct: I know who's to blame.

To test *who's/whose*, simply write out *who's* as *who is*:

They wondered who's car this was.

Test: They wondered who is car this was.
They wondered whose car this was

Whose is obviously correct.

IN A NUTSHELL

Whose shows possession; *who's* is short for *who is.*

PRACTICE 11

Fill in the blanks with either *who's* or *whose*.

1. _____ ball is this?
2. He's the man at _____ house we had dinner and _____ responsible for the neighborhood's block party.
3. You may well wonder _____ life this is and destiny is at stake here.
4. _____ at the door?
5. He asked for the name of the person _____ the boss.
6. _____ paying for the birthday cake?
7. _____ locker is this?
8. The student in _____ wallet the money was found never appeared.
9. Our neighbor, in _____ garage we stored our lawn mower, is moving.
10. I haven't a clue _____ tennis shoes these are.

Who, Which, and That

Knowing when to use *who*, *which*, and *that* is easy if you remember the following rules:

- Use *who* to refer to people. Do not use *which*. Use *that* to refer to a group of people considered to be a single unit (like a committee, class, audience, crowd, family).

  Lot's wife was the woman who looked back. (not *which*)

  The people who live across the street have a St. Bernard. (not *which*)

  The jury that convicted him was fair.

  Bob played on the team that won the championship.

- Use *who* with animals that are named. Use *which* or *that* for animals that are unnamed.

  Burt, who is a black lab, loves the water.

  Black labs, which love the water, are my favorite dog.

  If you want a dog that loves water, get a black lab.

- Use *which* or *that* to refer to ideas or things. Use a comma before *which*; do not use a comma before *that*. (See Unit 19, page 353.)

  She has patience, which is important in teaching.

  Get the towels that are on the dryer.

IN A NUTSHELL

- Use *who* to refer to people; use *that* to refer to a group of people considered to be a single unit (like a team or jury).
- Use *who* to refer to animals that are named and *which* or *that* to refer to unnamed animals.
- Use *which* or *that* to refer to ideas or things.

PRACTICE 12

Underline the appropriate relative pronoun (*who, which,* or *that*) in the sentences that follow.

1. The man (which/who) spoke at the meeting was quite convincing.
2. (Whom/Who) among you will cast the first stone?
3. Jumping to conclusions (that/which) are wrong won't help.
4. The people (who/whom) helped the most spoke the least.
5. I am the monarch of all (which/that) I survey.

6. The chairs, (that/which) both have broken legs, are in the kitchen.
7. My cat, Millie, (that/who) is 14, is starting to show her age.
8. It was an audience (which/that) every performer would love.
9. Treman Park, (that/which) is part of the state park system, has several waterfalls.
10. The committee (which/that) I am on is meeting tonight.

PRACTICE 13

Insert the pronoun *who*, *which*, or *that* in the blanks according to the rules that you have just learned.

1. I don't know _____ is right, the speaker or her challenger.
2. The panel _____ advised the governor was chaired by a woman.
3. My cat, Pookie, _____ is sitting on the car, loves to purr.
4. The man spoke next was the most convincing.
5. The author, _____ is an elderly gentleman, read his work beautifully.
6. Dumbo is an elephant _____ is beloved by children.
7. The family _____ I liked moved to Atlanta.
8. Most of these houses, _____ were built in the 1920s, need to be remodeled.
9. Mr. Smith, _____ is my father-in-law, takes an interest in my career.
10. The house you see perched atop the hill was once owned by a rich lady.

Unit Test

In the blank provided, write *C* if the sentence is correct and *NC* if there is a pronoun error. Cross out the incorrect pronouns and write the correct form above them.

1. _____ Narbeh and me decided to climb Mt. Whitney.
2. _____ For whom did she work last year?
3. _____ Who did you kiss at the prom?
4. _____ A long time ago, we mentioned the letter to Mom and she.
5. _____ He is the clerk which waited on me.
6. _____ Between Bob and him, the choice is easy.
7. _____ I wonder to whom she told that story.

8. ______ Who's idea was that?
9. ______ Juan and him are going to the movies.
10. ______ Why did you let him paint the door all by hisself?
11. ______ Just between you and me, the Dodgers will lose.
12. ______ I brought me some new shoes.
13. ______ He asked Alonzo and myself out to dinner.
14. ______ They are every bit as disgusted as we.
15. ______ I want that lovely vase, but it's side is cracked.
16. ______ My best buddy and she went out together behind my back.
17. ______ My sister has a huge black and white cat who hates me.
18. ______ With my dark glasses, I can't see who's at bat.
19. ______ Don't throw out those shoes; they're hers'.
20. ______ Oh yes, it was them for sure.

Unit Talk–Write Assignment

Would you rather live a short life in good health or a long life with some of it in bad health? This age-old question lies at the heart of the euthanasia ("mercy killing") debate. Students were asked to research this topic and present their views to each other in preparation for a writing assignment. One student had really done his homework and held strong opinions. His views are given in the *Talk* column pretty much as he spoke them. Turn his sentences into standard English in the *Write* column, correcting all errors in pronoun reference. Then write a paragraph giving your own views on euthanasia.

TALK	WRITE
1. It's a bad idea to push euthanasia.	
2. My buddy and me have discussed it often. Him and me just can't agree. Come on, let's face it, for most old people, quantity of life is more important than quality.	

3. The *Journal of the American Medical Association* published an interesting study in February of 1998. By far the majority of patients between 80 and 98—which are old duffers—said that they would not trade living one year in their current condition for living a shorter time without pain.

4. Remember that Dr. Kevorkian? He's the one who finally got sent to jail for a mercy killing he did right on TV. I wonder whether he thinks it's such a good idea now?

5. Between you and I, helping someone die is pure rubbish. Life is the most precious thing we have, and nobody wants to give it up, not even people which are in a lot of pain.

6. A team of researchers at the University of Cincinnati asked 300 people what they thought a relative which was in the hospital would want.

7. Twenty percent of them said the person would prefer a shorter but pain-free life to a longer life with pain. But it was them, the relatives, which guessed wrong—completely wrong!

8. Even victims of advanced AIDS, didn't want to trade time for better health.

9. My roommate and my girlfriend didn't believe myself. I showed the study to him and she, and were they surprised!

10. I remember my 89-year-old grandfather saying to my mother and myself, "I don't know why—but I'm curious about tomorrow."

11. People which are sick get used to crummy health, and they theirselves don't want to give up life.

12. I know a woman whom at 103 got leukemia. She kept asking, "Who's idea is it that I don't want to live longer?"

13. Euthanasia for who?

14. Listen, you guys, no matter who you ask, people want to live.

15. Don't sell life so cheap. Its all we got.

Unit Collaborative Assignment

Get together with a classmate. One of you should read aloud part A, while the other follows along making corrections. Discuss any points of disagreement. To settle differences of opinion, apply any test you have learned for determining the correct form of a pronoun (substituting *it is* for *it's*, *who is* for *who's*, and so on). Exchange places with your partner and do the same for part B.

Part A

One of my favorite activities is biking because I learn from nature, and also its good exercise. Last summer, I bought me a new mountain bike and took several trips to Colorado. When my friend Fred and me first biked to the mountains, I felt as if I had entered a whole new world. The mountains and canyons seemed to tell a very ancient story. For instance, Snow Bird Peak, rising majestically out of the earth, seemed to say that human beings like Fred and I are insignificant compared to the power of nature.

Part B

At the same time that we were seeing so much beauty, we were also getting good aerobic exercise. Its quite challenging to pedal up a steep grade. Between you and I, I can't think of another sport that would have allowed Fred and I to experience so much beauty and get such good exercise while costing so little money. All college students should take a biking trip and find out for theirself what a great experience and good exercise it is.

Unit Writing Assignment

Write a note to your economics professor, asking him for an extension on the written assignment due April 12. Tell him or her that the due date conflicts with an important event in your life. Try to be persuasive, yet fair. Pay special attention to the correct use of pronouns.

Photo Writing Assignment

The following photo shows teenagers smoking. Write a paragraph in which you offer your opinion on why teenagers continue to smoke despite all the public warnings about cancer, heart disease, emphysema, wrinkles, and tooth decay or gum disease. Begin with a topic sentence that expresses your main point. Support that point with the appropriate evidence. Use the Revising Checklist inside the front cover of this book to help you to revise. Paragraphs will vary.

13 Using Adjectives and Adverbs

"Gertie dances real good."

If you are a native speaker, using your ear for grammar to help you write is, for the most part, a good strategy. When it comes to the correct use of adjectives and adverbs, however, your ear is likely to be too infected with street talk to be trusted.

Indeed, adjectives and adverbs are often misused in casual speech. The following are some typical sentences you might overhear in public:

Gertie dances real good.

The Olympic contestants swam terrific.

The guards told us to walk slow.

That remark bothered me considerable.

All of us were real tired.

She felt sadly about her mother's illness.

That guitar sounded oddly.

If these sentences sound right to you, your ear is leading you astray. Here are the sentences correctly written:

EAR ALERT

Gertie dances really well.

The Olympic contestants swam terrifically.

The guards told us to walk slowly.

That remark bothered me considerably.

All of us were really tired.

She felt sad about her mother's illness.

That guitar sounded odd.

No matter what your ear tells you, these sentences are grammatically correct. This unit will help you to use adjectives and adverbs correctly in your writing.

Adjectives and Adverbs

Adjectives and adverbs are **modifiers**—words that describe and explain. **Adjectives** describe a noun or a pronoun by narrowing it down to a specific one, such as in the following cases:

I adore that purple hat.	**(Which hat? The *purple* one.)**
She certainly seems happy.	**(What kind of person does she seem to be? A *happy* one.)**
The milk smells sour.	**(How does the milk smell? It smells *sour.*)**

Adverbs describe verbs, adjectives, and other adverbs in the following ways:

- How
- When
- Where
- To what extent

Here are some examples:

She spoke excitedly.	**(*Excitedly* tells how she spoke.)**
I'm going now.	**(*Now* tells when I'm going—describes the verb *going.*)**
I put the book there.	**(*There* tells where the book was put—describes the verb *put.*)**
Orson Welles became excessively fat.	**(*Excessively* tells to what extent Welles became fat—describes the adjective *fat.*)**

Many—but not all—adverbs end in *-ly.* Indeed, many adjectives can be turned into adverbs simply by adding *-ly.* Some typical examples follow.

ADJECTIVE	ADVERB
careful	carefully
real	really
most	mostly
forceful	forcefully

However, some of the most commonly used adverbs do not end in *-ly*. Here are a few examples:

Walk *fast*.

He is *very* patient.

The lemonade is *too* sweet.

They are *always* late.

She is leaving *tomorrow*.

A common error committed by both native and non-native students is to follow a linking verb with an adverb instead of an adjective. If you are unsure about the definition of a linking verb, refer back to Unit 4, page 57. Here are some examples of typical linking verb errors:

Incorrect: That cheese smells horribly.
Correct: That cheese smells horrible.

Incorrect: Mary feels confidently about the exam.
Correct: Mary feels confident about the exam.

In every case above, the linking verb should be followed by an adjective that describes the subject rather than an adverb that describes the verb.

IN A NUTSHELL

- Adjectives describe nouns and pronouns.
- Adverbs describe verbs, adjectives, and other adverbs.
- Many—but not all—adverbs end in *-ly*.
- Follow linking verbs with adjectives, not adverbs.

PRACTICE 1

Underline the correct modifier in parentheses—adjective or adverb—in each sentence below.

1. The old man crossed the railroad tracks (slow, slowly).
2. His fingernails looked (real, really) dirty.
3. He (nimble, nimbly) climbed down the mine shaft.
4. The birds flew away, chirping (angry, angrily).
5. He (most, mostly) ignored the letters.
6. He had a bad cold and was feeling (miserable, miserably).
7. John examined the roof (careful, carefully).
8. My friend felt (complete, completely) alone in his poverty.

9. He flies (frequent, frequently) on business.
10. The engine hummed (smooth, smoothly).
11. He called (loud, loudly) to the people on the bench.
12. Why does the woman feel so (disgusted, disgustedly) with her son?
13. He never appears (calm, calmly) before an oral exam.
14. The girl looked (youthful, youthfully) in her miniskirt.
15. We walk most (energetic, energetically) before eating a big meal.

PRACTICE 2

Complete the sentences below with an appropriate modifier—either an adjective or an adverb—from the following list. Each word should be used only once.

sadly	immediately
popular	slowly
silently	dreadful
terribly	hot
playful	most

In the parentheses at the end of each sentence, identify the modifier as an adjective or adverb.

1. The telephone company hired Byron ________ . (____)
2. My bath water was ________ . (____)
3. It was a call ________ . (____)
4. Soccer is a sport ________ . (____)
5. The next mile of the road was ________ rough. (____)
6. We approached the intersection ______ . (____)
7. The waitress looked _______ at the rain. (____)
8. The _______ puppies romped in the grass. (____)
9. She _____ picked up her suitcase and walked away. (____)
10. Tom complained _____ often. (____)

PRACTICE 3

Change the italicized adjective to an adverb; you will need to rewrite the sentence.

Example: Have you noticed her *elegant* walk?

Answer: Have you noticed how *elegantly* she walks?

1. Mark is *happy* to work.

____

2. Dogs can be *noisy* barkers.

____

3. His performance was *admirable.*

____

4. What a *tight* jacket!

____

5. He's a *slow* walker.

____

6. He wrote a *poor* essay.

____

7. The man was a *glib* talker.

____

8. Her arrival was *unexpected.*

____

9. He gave her an *intimate* hug.

____

10. It was a *quiet* moan.

____

Past Participles Used as Adjectives

The past participles of verbs may also be used as adjectives. Consider the verb *mash*:

Please mash the potatoes.	**(*mash* = present)**
I mashed the potatoes yesterday.	**(*mashed* = past)**
I have mashed the potatoes every day.	**(*have mashed* = present perfect, which includes a past participle)**
These mashed potatoes are good.	**(*mashed* = past participle as an adjective)**

Here are other examples of past participles used as adjectives:

broken bones

forgotten key

rented car

frozen food

torn jacket

lost wallet

distracted policeman

In each case, the past participle is an adjective because it describes a noun.

EAR ALERT

A common problem with using past participles as adjectives is dropping the *-d*/*-ed* or *-n*/*-en* ending. We do this so often, especially in rapid speech, that the error usually goes unnoticed. A dropped ending in writing, however, is always obvious. Look at these examples:

Dropped ending: We ate mash potatoes with butter.
Correct: We ate mashed potatoes with butter.

Dropped ending: I was sad to see those broke toys.
Correct: I was sad to see those broken toys.

IN A NUTSHELL

Don't let your ear trick you into dropping the *-d/-ed* or *n/-en* ending when you write a past participle.

PRACTICE 4

Correct the misused past participles in the sentences that follow.

1. He wept about his dash hopes. ______
2. Watch out for the broke glass! ______
3. His pants were tore. ______
4. The potatoes are all peel. ______
5. The eraser of the pencil looked chew. ______
6. He was a practice liar. ______
7. That's not an excuse absence. ______
8. He seemed confuse by all the noise. ______
9. He said that the fish was fresh-froze. ______
10. I'll have two hard-boil eggs, please. ______
11. Dad wore a borrow tie. ______
12. They quarreled over some spoke words. ______
13. Our neighborhood promotes recycle bottles. ______
14. What a wonderful home-bake cake! ______
15. His pain was merely imagine. ______

Comparisons

Adjectives and adverbs are often used to make comparisons between two things. The rules for making comparisons are straightforward:

- For an adjective or adverb of one syllable, add *-er*.

  My uncle Bob is *rich*.
  Uncle John is *richer*. **(one-syllable adjective)**
  He spoke *fast*.
  She spoke *faster*. **(one-syllable adverb)**

- For an adjective or adverb of more than one syllable that does not end in *y*, add *more*.

  This is an *affordable* car.

  This is a *more affordable* car. **(adjective of more than one syllable)**

Comparative adverbs are usually formed by placing *more* before them, but sometimes by adding *-er* to the positive form:

When my sister graduated from college with honors, my mother praised her *more enthusiastically* than she had praised me years earlier.

The man snored *loudly*. His wife, however, snored *louder*.

- For an adjective or adverb that ends in *y*, drop the *y* and add *-ier* in the comparative.

  The road to the farm was *icy*.
  The road to the mountains was *icier*.

PRACTICE 5

Write the comparative form of each word listed below. In the space provided, use the comparative form in a sentence.

Example: feverish ***more feverish***

The sick child was more feverish in the morning.

Example: fresh ***fresher***

The fish at Jake's Gormet Fish Shop is fresher than the fish at the supermarket.

1. ugly ______

____

2. hateful ______

____

3. junky ______________________________

____

4. marvelous ______________________________

____

5. hot ______________________________

____

6. silly ______________________________

____

7. silent ______________________________

____

8. lucky ______________________________

____

9. spicy ______________________________

____

10. thorough ______________________________

____

Double Comparisons

A common error often heard in everyday speech is the **double comparison,** using both *-er* and *more.*

Incorrect:	Janet's writing is more neater than Mary's.
Correct:	Janet's writing is neater than Mary's.
Incorrect:	I spoke more louder than you.
Correct:	I spoke louder than you.

Incompleteness, which fails to make clear what is being compared with what, is a common error in comparisons.

Incorrect:	Our streets are much wider today.
Correct:	Our streets are much wider today than they were twenty years ago.
Incorrect:	His car is much faster.
Correct:	His car is much faster than her car.

Be sure that your own comparisons are not incomplete.

PRACTICE 6

Rewrite the following sentences, correcting the comparisons.

1. You carry the more heavier suitcase.

____

2. If I study hard, I should do more better in math.

____

3. She was more angrier than I've ever seen her.

____

4. Who was the more nicer of the two?

____

5. The wind was terrifyinger than the rain.

____

6. The cheese is more fresher than the salami.

____

7. My brother was more badlier hurt than my sister.

____

8. When can you give me a more better answer?

____

9. Working at three jobs was difficulter than I thought.

____

10. The cut was more deeper than the doctor expected.

____

Using Superlatives

The comparative form of adjectives and adverbs is used to express a difference between two things:

The brown suitcase is strong.
The black suitcase is stronger. **(comparative)**

To express differences among *three or more things,* you must use the superlative form of an adjective or adverb:

The brown suitcase is strong.
The black suitcase is stronger. **(comparative)**
The blue suitcase is strongest. **(superlative)**

ESL Advice!

To use the correct forms of the comparative and superlative, memorize the rules.

The rules for changing adjectives and adverbs into the superlative form follow:

- For an adverb or adjective of one syllable, add *-est.*

  wild → wilder → wildest

  glad → gladder → gladdest **(Note that the "d" is doubled.)**

  tall → taller → tallest

She was the saddest of all the relatives there.

- For an adverb or adjective that ends in *y,* drop the *y* and add *-iest.*

  silly → sillier → silliest

  tiny → tinier → tiniest

  pretty → prettier → prettiest

  He was the luckiest of them all.

- For an adjective or adverb of two or more syllables that does not end in *y,* add the word *most.*

  dreadful → more dreadful → most dreadful

  cheerful → more cheerful → most cheerful

  interesting → more interesting → most interesting

  She is the most cheerful person in the morning.

PRACTICE 7

In the blanks provided, write the correct superlative forms of the words below. Use each superlative form in a sentence.

Example: lucky ***luckiest***

When she played blackjack, she was the *luckiest* person alive.

1. funny ______________________________

   ____

2. disappointed ______________________________

   ____

3. meek ______________________________

   ____

4. rich ______________________________

____

5. pushy ______________________________

____

6. snappy ______________________________

____

7. regretful ______________________________

____

8. ripe ______________________________

____

9. short ______________________________

____

10. slick ______________________________

____

Problems with Superlatives

When you use superlatives, watch out for these two common errors of everyday speech:

- Use the superlative only when you are speaking of *more than two* things.

Incorrect:	She is the most beautiful of the two sisters.
Correct:	She is the more beautiful of the two sisters.
Incorrect:	This is the riskiest of the two choices.
Correct:	This is the riskier of the two choices.

- Do not use both an *-est* or an *-iest* ending and *most.*

Incorrect:	She is the most unkindest person.
Correct:	She is the most unkind person.
Incorrect:	He is the most trendiest dresser.
Correct:	He is the trendiest dresser.

IN A NUTSHELL

- Use a comparative adjective or adverb to compare two things.
- Form most comparatives by adding *-er, -ier,* or *more.*
- Use a superlative adjective or adverb to compare three or more things.
- Form most superlatives by adding *-est, -iest,* or *most.*

PRACTICE 8

Rewrite the following sentences to correct the problems with the superlatives.

1. This is the beautifulest rose I have ever seen.

2. That movie is the fascinatingest one I've seen this year.

3. Give the piece of pie to the most biggest football player.

4. Brianna was the smartest of the two sisters.

5. Just because she is the most oldest, my sister gets more spending money.

6. Have you chosen the most fastest runner yet?

7. Maggie is definitely the interestingest of the three girls.

8. Jake is the most stingiest roommate he ever had.

9. Of the two choices, that is the wisest.

10. Go down Maxwell Street, and you'll find the most poorest people you have ever seen.

PRACTICE 9

For the following sentences, first decide whether a comparative or superlative form is needed. In the blank to the left of the sentence, write a *C* if the comparative form is needed, an *S* if the superlative form is needed. Then write the correct form in the blank following the sentence.

Example: __C__ All of us wanted to climb the (tall) *taller* of the two towers.

1. _____ It was the (frightening) _____ story I have ever heard.
2. _____ Of the two deans, Smith was the (reasonable) _____.
3. _____ My high school graduation was the (long) _____ day of my life.
4. _____ Ann's wedding was (expensive) _____ than Mary's.
5. _____ The desert is much (dry) _____ than the beach.
6. _____ Of the two wrestlers, Moe was the (big) _____.
7. _____ Aunt Ethel is the (generous) _____ person in our family.
8. _____ Get the (large) _____ cake they have.
9. _____ What was the (nice) _____ experience you had in elementary school?
10. _____ Sardines are (oily) _____ than salmon.

Using Good/Well and *Bad/Badly*

Most adjectives and adverbs follow the basic rules for forming comparatives and superlatives that we have just described. A few, however, have irregular forms. The most troublesome are *good/well* and *bad/badly.*

	COMPARATIVE	SUPERLATIVE
good	better	best
well	better	best
bad	worse	worst
badly	worse	worst

Good is an adjective; *well* is an adverb (unless you are talking about someone's health). Here are some examples.

Correct: This is a good bicycle. (***Good* is an adjective describing *bicycle*.**)

Incorrect: She rides good.

Correct: She rides well. (***Well* is an adverb telling how she *rides*.**)

Incorrect:	I don't feel good.	
Correct:	I don't feel well.	(**Use *well* to describe someone's health.**)

Bad is an adjective; *badly* is an adverb. A common error made in everyday speech is to use *badly* to describe emotions when *bad* should be used.

Incorrect:	I feel badly that we were late.
Correct:	I feel bad that we were late.

To say *I feel badly* is to mean that your sense of touch is bad—perhaps your fingers are numb.

There are no such words as *bestest* and *worsest.* The correct form is either *best* or *worst.*

IN A NUTSHELL

- *Good* is an adjective; *well* is used as an adverb unless you're talking about someone's health.
- *Bad* is an adjective; *badly* is an adverb.
- To say *I feel badly* means that something is wrong with your sense of touch.

PRACTICE 10

Write either *good* or *well* in the blanks provided.

1. All the sophomores on the team swam _____.
2. Even the honor students did not do _____ on the final test.
3. His coat was made of _____ leather.
4. It was obvious that she was not feeling _____.
5. This cream is _____ for your complexion.
6. I have been _____ to you lately.
7. You must try to do _____ on your final exam.
8. He spoke _____, and he gave us _____ advice.
9. You know very _____ what I mean!
10. You will do _____ if you try your best.

PRACTICE 11

In the blanks below, insert either *bad* or *badly.*

1. He felt _____ about eating the last piece of pie.
2. She felt _____ for her father.

3. I felt _____ that we lost the game.
4. His manners are very _____.
5. The crew sailed the first leg of the race _____.
6. I'm _____ sick with the flu.
7. The flu shot made me feel _____.
8. They hoisted the flag very _____.
9. No matter how _____ you feel, you must go.
10. My heart was _____ broken.

This/That and *These/Those*

The four demonstratives—*this/that* (singular) and *these/those* (plural)—are generally used to point to or single out something.

I just love *this* book.	(**A particular book is singled out.**)
Don't you dare eat *those* cookies.	(**Particular cookies are singled out.**)

This and *these* refer to something nearby, whereas *that* and *those* refer to something farther away.

I love petting *this* cat.

but

Would you mind walking across the room to bring me *that* blanket?

> **ESL Advice!**
>
> Memorize the rules for using *this, that, these,* and *those.* Native speakers usually know them from frequent use.

Note that when a demonstrative is paired with a noun, it becomes an adjective:

I won't buy *those* plums.

These books are mine.

On the other hand, a demonstrative that stands alone functions as a pronoun:

Those are green tomatoes.

The books to be shelved are *these.*

Two kinds of problems can occur in the use of *this/that* and *these/those.* The first is putting *here* or *there* after *this* or *that.*

Incorrect: This here boat belongs to my neighbor.
Correct: This boat belongs to my neighbor.

Incorrect: That there house belongs to my uncle.
Correct: That house belongs to my uncle.

The second problem is using *them* in place of *these* or *those.* Unlike *these* and *those,* which can function as an adjective or a pronoun, *them* is always a pronoun, never an adjective. It is incorrect to use a pronoun in place of an adjective:

Incorrect: Them doughnuts are fattening.
Correct: Those doughnuts are fattening.

or

These doughnuts are fattening.

Incorrect: Them weeds are hard to kill.
Correct: These weeds are hard to kill.

or

Those weeds are hard to kill.

IN A NUTSHELL

- Never use *them* in place of *these* or *those.*
- Never use *here* or *there* after *this* or *that.*

PRACTICE 12

Underline the correct word in parentheses.

1. (Those, them) ducks are quacking nonstop.
2. Please take (this, that there) package to Mrs. Jones.
3. (This, this here) suitcase is too heavy to carry.
4. Did Peter borrow (them, those) roller skates?
5. Marcos, would you please take (that, this here) painting across the street to (this, that) house?
6. (That, that there) piano needs tuning.
7. Take (this here, that) one, right next to me.
8. If (that there, this) current weather continues, you should buy a raincoat.
9. Be polite to (these, those) women standing over there.
10. (That, that there) rug was woven in India.

Conjunctive Adverbs

Some adverbs play two roles: They act as adverbs; but they also act as conjunctions. Study this sentence:

> He drove off with the car; *meanwhile*, his mother stood in the rain.

The word *meanwhile* is an adverb modifying *stood*. (It answers the question, "When did his mother stand in the rain?" The answer is "She stood in the rain *meanwhile*.") But *meanwhile* also connects the two clauses "He drove off with the car" and "His mother stood in the rain." The conjunctive adverb enables a writer to express ideas in one strong emphatic sentence in place of two weaker sentences.

Note that when a conjunctive adverb connects two independent clauses, it must be preceded by a semicolon and followed by a comma, unless the conjunctive adverb consists only of one syllable; then the comma may be omitted. Study these examples:

> Ali should give up performing jumping twists on his skate board; otherwise, he might end up with a broken limb.
>
> (A semicolon and a comma are needed.)
>
> Marguerite had expected to graduate in June; instead, she must wait until next year.
>
> (A semicolon and a comma are needed).
>
> I paid my traffic fine; then I attended traffic school.
>
> (The comma is not needed because the conjunctive adverb consists of one syllable only.)

Here is a list of commonly used conjunctive adverbs:

also	furthermore	next
anyhow	however	otherwise
	instead	similarly
besides	likewise	then
consequently	meanwhile	therefore
finally	nevertheless	still

PRACTICE 13

Complete the sentences below by adding an idea following the conjunctive adverb. Make sure that the idea you add makes sense when you read the entire sentence.

1. My dad's truck is a big improvement over his old one; however,
____
2. Let's take the fast train; otherwise,
____
3. He took a blue handkerchief out of his pocket; next
____

4. Mary's boots were filled with snow and ice; still

____

5. His parents told him to fill the car with gas; instead,

____

6. Use your cell phone to call your dad; meanwhile,

____

7. India is far away from where we now live; nevertheless,

____

8. At first, the cut could hardly be seen; then

____

9. My great grandfather never attended school beyond the fourth grade; consequently,

____

10. Some college students find anti-establishment comedians admirable; similarly,

____

IN A NUTSHELL

- A conjunctive adverb plays two roles: it modifies a verb and it also joins two simple sentences, pointing out or clarifying the relationship between the sentences.
- Writers use conjunctive adverbs in order to make their writing more emphatic.
- When a conjunctive adverb is used to connect two independent sentences, use a semicolon before the conjunctive adverb and a comma following it. Omit the comma if the conjunctive adverb consists of one syllable only.

Unit Test

Correct the following sentences.

1. Mary's essay is the bestest in the class.

____

____

2. She scribbled her signature quick.

3. The beggar looked envious at the mountain of food.

4. John was the most patient of the two men.

5. The fish was froze.

6. Billy folded his blanket most carefulliest.

7. It is best for you to walk home rather than ride.

8. Feeling badly that she had lost the ring, Fran wept.

9. Them there carrots taste too salty.

10. Mark said, "Them apples are too sour to eat."

11. Jamie feels badly about what happened last night.

12. It was the most fastest race he had ever run.

13. Those hands were the most dirtiest you could imagine.

14. My uncle tells the amazingest stories.

15. She is much more fussier about her room than I am.

16. Every day they asked for mash potatoes at breakfast time.

17. Why is she limping so bad?

18. Let's stay home because the sky looks horrible dark.

19. The mechanic said that the fan belt was wore out.

20. It's real stupid to bite the hand that feeds you.

Unit Talk–Write Assignment

This unit's *Talk* column is a dialogue between two students, Lisa and Frank, who have opposing points of view on being famous. Your assignment is to rewrite their comments as complete sentences and in standard English. Be sure to correct all adjective and adverb errors. Then, decide how you feel about what it means to be famous, and express your thoughts in a polished paragraph. Check carefully for errors in adjective–adverb use. Paragraphs will vary.

TALK	WRITE
L: You couldn't pay me enough to be rich and famous, it would be like living in a fishbowl.	
F: Are you serious? I can't think of anything more better.	
L: Oh, sure. Hound by the paparazzi, maybe stalk by some nut, and constantly crush by crowds of people trying to touch you. Crap!	
F: You're missing the point. Fame gives you the mostest money and money is power. Power to do anything you want.	
L: Yeah, and fame brings tragedy, too, what about Princess Diana, who was killed in a car chase by the paparazzi?	
F: No way. She died because of a drunk chauffeur who was driving reckless.	
L: What about John Lennon, who was murdered by an obsess fan?	
F: You just have to take precautions. It's a small price to pay for living good and having hot cars and mansions.	

L: Think of poor Madonna, having to hide her baby girl for fear she will be kidnap.

F: Sure, poor Madonna with her millions. Don't cry too loud for her, Argentina.

L: Arnold Schwarzenegger had to sue some pushier photographer to stop him from badgering the Schwarzenegger kids. Them kids don't know how lucky they are.

F: Yeah, yeah—the Terminator/governor has the most pitifullest life. Tell that to some hungry and froze homeless person. That there man isn't suffering, lemme tell you.

L: Well, I definitely would feel badly if I became famous and lost my privacy. I don't care what you say.

F: And I'd sure give up some privacy in return for a closetful of the most beautifullest clothes and a Cadillac in my driveway.

Unit Collaborative Assignment

The following paragraph is about leasing versus buying a car. Work with a partner to fill in the blanks with the appropriate adverbs or adjectives from the list of words below. Talk through, and agree on, the possible choices.

also	strongly	cheaper
definitely	smart	better
thriftiest	smarter	more economical
busiest	major	constantly

1. Because cars are so expensive, leasing is often ______ than buying.
2. In a number of states, it is actually ______ to lease a car than to own one.
3. Leasing a car is ______ because the lessee does not have to worry ______ about trade-in values or maintenance costs.
4. Leasing appeals to some of the ______ and ______ people I know. They want their money's worth, and they don't want to spend a lot of time taking care of a car.
5. Many people are ______ leasing other goods besides cars.
6. For instance, they're leasing such ______ appliances as freezers, dishwashers, washers, dryers, and air-conditioners.
7. These people see "temporary use" rather than "permanent ownership" as the ______ choice.
8. Next year, the lease on my car will be up, and I ______ plan to lease a brand new car.
9. I ______ like driving a new car rather than an ______ car, and it's ______ to lease than buy.
10. Furthermore, I ______ believe that leasing helps a person get rid of the curse of possessions.

Unit Writing Assignment

Beginning with one of the topic sentences listed below, develop a paragraph that is vivid and clear. Pay special attention to your use of adjectives and adverbs. Use the Internet to find specific details that might enrich your paragraph. Pay attention to the correct use of adjectives and adverbs as explained in this chapter.

1. Our love for machines lessens our love for human beings.
2. Preserving the wilderness is our hope for planet Earth.
3. People who don't have pets are missing a lot.

4. I have found that failure teaches me more than success.
5. I have learned that it is not wise to burn one's bridges.

Photo Writing Assignment

The people in the photo below are relaxing at the beach. Brainstorm with a friend or classmate about the importance of leisure time. Ask yourself what could happen if people buried themselves in their work without taking time to reflect or relax. Discuss other leisure activities, such as listening to music, having a latte, observing nature, or sitting on a park bench to read. Follow the rules explained in this unit.

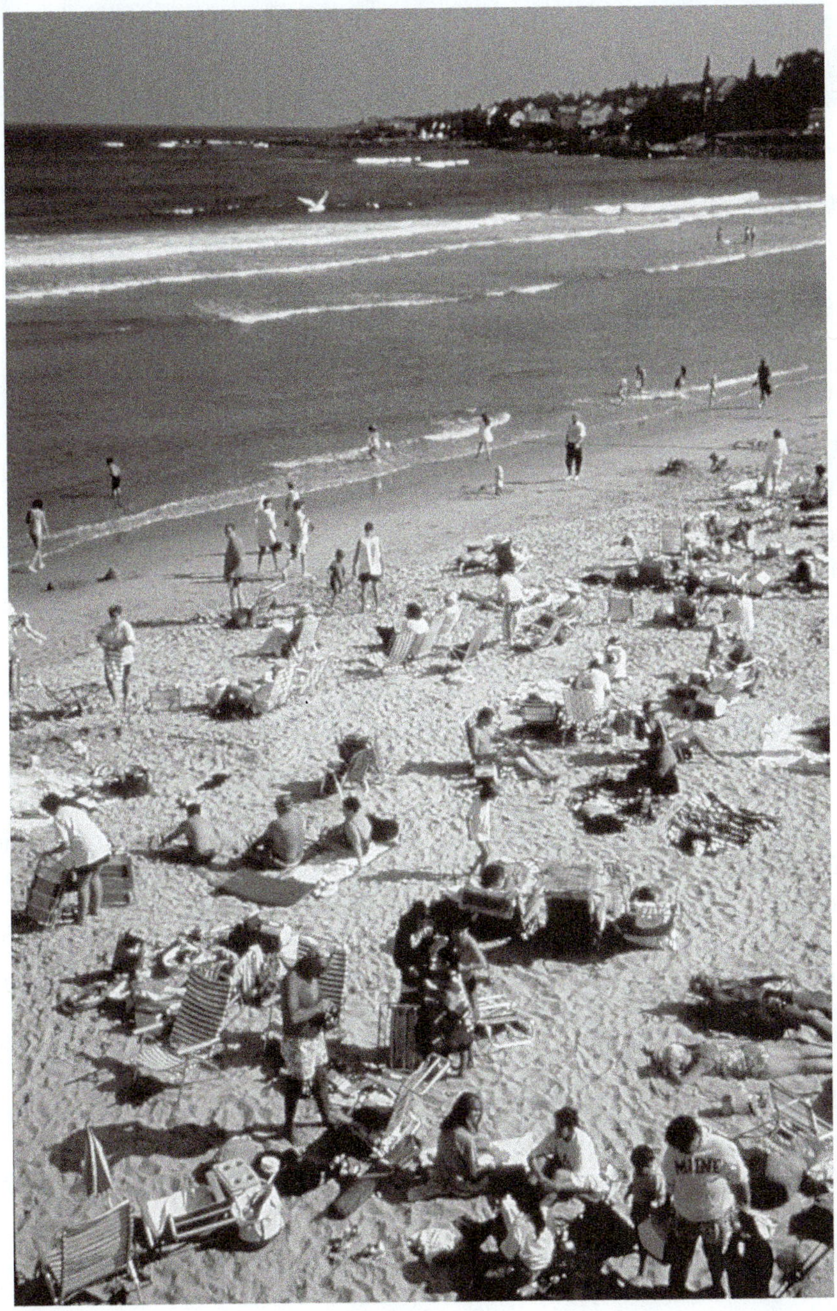

14 Dangling and Misplaced Modifiers

"After watching the movie, the sky turned black and it began to rain."

A modifier is a word or phrase that describes another word or phrase. Modifiers are either adjectives or adverbs, or words or phrases that function as adjectives or adverbs. What a modifier describes in a sentence depends not only on what it says, but also on where it is located.

Dangling Modifiers

Panting, the bus that Mary boarded pulled away.

Here, the word *panting*, because it is misplaced in the sentence, modifies *bus* rather than *Mary*. Such a modifier is said to *dangle*. **Dangling modifiers** consist of a word or phrase that illogically modifies the wrong word in a sentence. In this particular sentence, the dangling modifier makes the bus pant as it pulls away. What the writer intended to say was, "Panting, Mary boarded the bus that pulled away." Here are some other examples:

Dangling:	Walking home that day, the sun seemed unusually warm.
Dangling:	Having reached the age of six, my grandfather marched me off to grade school.
Dangling:	Sitting on the veranda and eating ice cream every day, the summer passed too quickly.

Because of its misplacement, the modifier in each of these sentences refers to the wrong word, making a ridiculous sentence. In the first sentence, the sun is walking home. In the second sentence, the grandfather is 6 years old, and in the third, the summer eats ice cream on the veranda.

There are two ways to correct these sentences. Either you can place the word being modified *immediately* after the modifier, or you can rewrite the sentence.

Correct: Walking home that day, I thought that the sun seemed unusually warm.

or

As I walked home that day, the sun seemed unusually warm.

Correct: Having reached the age of six, I was marched off to school by my grandfather.

or

My grandfather marched me off to school when I reached the age of six.

Correct: Sitting on the veranda and eating ice cream every day, I regretted the summer passing so quickly.

or

As I sat on the veranda eating ice cream every day, I regretted the summer passing so quickly.

IN A NUTSHELL

Correct dangling modifiers by rearranging or adding words until the modifier clearly modifies the right word.

PRACTICE 1

Rewrite these sentences, each of which contains a dangling modifier.

1. Having no time to waste, the article was left unread.

____

____

2. Having finished all the chores, the baseball game was turned on.

____

____

3. Worn out from hiking, the alarm clock didn't wake me up.

4. Being newly painted, $4,000 was not bad for the car.

5. As a mother of twins, my washing machine is always running.

6. After taking our seats, the Ice Capades started off with a waltz.

7. Jumping through fiery hoops, everyone in the audience went wild.

8. When shredded and salted, you will enjoy the taste of Russian cabbage.

9. The test was not taken, having not studied enough.

10. Flying to New York, the Empire State Building gleamed below.

Misplaced Modifiers

A modifier whose place in a sentence causes it to modify the wrong word is said to be **misplaced.** Misplaced modifiers, like dangling modifiers, do not communicate what the writer intended. Unlike dangling modifiers, which are always found at the beginning of a sentence, a misplaced modifier occurs later in the sentence. For example, notice how the meaning of the following sentence changes as we move the modifier *only.*

She went into the pool wearing her only bikini.	**(She owned only one *bikini.* *Only* is modifying *bikini.*)**

She went into the pool wearing only her bikini.	**(She wore nothing else but a bikini. *Only* is modifying *wearing*.)**

Sometimes a modifier is misplaced because it is too far from the word it is meant to modify. In this case, the result is often an unintended, humorous meaning. Here are some examples:

Misplaced: We could watch the stars sitting on the balcony.

Misplaced: My grandmother showed us how to sew a quilt with an encouraging smile.

Misplaced: I stood in the cold stream and caught a fish without waders.

Because of a misplaced modifier, we have *stars sitting on the balcony, quilts with an encouraging smile*, and *a fish without waders*. A misplaced modifier can be corrected in only one way: by rewriting the sentence. You must reword the modifier or move it closer to the word it modifies. Here are some possible corrections:

Correct: Sitting on the balcony, we could watch the stars.

Correct: With an encouraging smile, my grandmother showed us how to sew a quilt.

Correct: I stood without waders in the cold stream and caught a fish.

or

Without waders, I stood in the cold stream and caught a fish.

To avoid the confusion of misplaced modifiers, always place a modifier immediately *before* the word it is intended to modify. This is especially true of one-word modifiers such as *only*, *just*, *almost*, *even*, *hardly*, *nearly*, and *often*. Because these words limit what follows, where they occur in a sentence is important. Keep in mind the bikini example discussed earlier.

IN A NUTSHELL

Here are three steps you can take to make sure that modifiers are placed correctly:

1. Find the modifier.
2. Ask yourself, "Does the modifier have something to modify?"
3. Ask yourself, "Is the modifier in the right place?"

If the answer to question 2 or 3 is "No," rewrite the sentence.

PRACTICE 2

For each of the following pairs of sentences, tell how the meaning of the sentence changes when the modifier is moved.

Example: He just washed the dishes.

He did it a moment ago.

have

He washed just the dishes.

He didn't do the pots.

1. Francine did only 20 sit-ups.

   ____

   Only Francine did 20 sit-ups.

   ____

2. Rico was just eating dinner when the phone rang.

   ____

   Just Rico was eating dinner when the phone rang.

   ____

3. She even drinks Coke for breakfast.

   ____

   Even she drinks Coke for breakfast.

   ____

4. He just said that he would be late.

   ____

   He said that just he would be late.

   ____

5. The mechanic said that only the front brakes need to be adjusted.

   ____

   The mechanic said that the front brakes only need to be adjusted.

   ____

PRACTICE 3

Underline the misplaced modifier in each sentence below, then rewrite the sentence so that the modifier is correctly placed.

Example: I borrowed a ballpoint pen to write a letter that didn't work.

Answer: ***To write a letter, I borrowed a ballpoint pen that didn't work.***

____

1. Mimi fed her dog on the porch she had received for Christmas.

____

____

2. A World War II pilot since 1945, he received an award for his many years of service.

____

____

3. The waiters served French pastries to customers on expensive bone china.

____

____

4. Caroline could not attend the dance in her lovely new off-the-shoulder gown with a broken foot.

____

____

5. He nearly exercised every morning.

____

____

6. John Henry School needs volunteers to read to their students badly.

____

____

7. Peter is canvassing the neighborhood for voters dressed in an Uncle Sam costume.

____

____

8. We saw many deer driving to the country.

____

____

9. We drank 10 gallons of cranberry juice with enjoyment.

____

____

10. At 10:00 A.M. the students heard that an earthquake had hit on television.

____

____

PRACTICE 4

A. Underline the dangling and misplaced modifiers in the following paragraph. Then rewrite those sentences correctly in the spaces below. You should find four errors.

An Afternoon by the Lake

It was July, and we were out of school. Having finished our chores and having changed into our bathing suits, the lake seemed to invite us to come down and feel its coolness. My mind was only fixed on two things—swimming and what fun we would have. We ran to the lake and plunged into the cool water. We stayed until past dinnertime. But after explaining how much fun we had had, my mother didn't punish me. To this day, I connect beautiful vacations with a lake in my mind.

1. ____________________

____

2. ____________________

____

3. ____________________

____

4. ____________________

____

B. Underline the dangling and misplaced modifiers in the following paragraph. Then rewrite those sentences correctly in the spaces below. You should find four errors.

The Gift of Music

Like a beautiful butterfly or a rainbow, a person who loves music finds it healing. Our neighbor, who has constant back pain, almost listens to an entire Beethoven symphony every day. He says that the music keeps him alive. My closest friend listens to the radio driving to a job 20 miles from his home. He tells me that because of the music, he actually looks forward to the drive. I can't imagine my life without music. With my lifetime ahead of me, music will be my trusted companion and gracious friend.

1. ____________________

____

2. ____________________

____

3. ____________________

____

4. ____________________

____

Unit Test

The following sentences contain either a dangling or a misplaced modifier. Correct the sentences by rewriting them.

1. Having already waited an hour for the traffic to die down, our car wouldn't start.

2. After sticking my key card into the slot, the gate opened automatically.

3. Purring, I stroked the cat on the table.

4. Driving down the country road after the rain, a lovely rainbow arched across the sky.

5. We finally found her ring during our lunch break in the desk.

6. Rolling on wheels, I steered the suitcase down the hill.

7. Thinking about this poem, the meaning was unclear.

8. Drifting off to sleep, my plaid sheets felt clean and cool.

9. Mr. Smith took the broken pipes to the dump in his truck.

10. Do not eat the brownie until completely baked.

Unit Talk–Write Assignment

Students were asked to discuss the problems of their age group. Older students talked about combining school and a job and sometimes even a family, too. Some younger students talked about their parents' lack of understanding; others described problems with relationships or said that college made them feel isolated. But one student saw her worst problem as acne. Rewrite her comments in complete sentences and standard English. You should also find four dangling and four misplaced modifiers. Then write a paragraph on what you consider the most difficult problem for your age group. Use the Revising Checklist inside the front cover of this book to help you improve your paragraph.

TALK	WRITE
1. Have you ever had acne? Well, looking in the mirror, my acne is really awful.	
2. Having no patience, the job seems impossible to do.	
3. Desperately wanting to look decent, your skin suddenly explodes into a field of zits.	
4. Going to a party last week, my face looked terrible—like I had measles!	

5. My date could see all those red spots sitting next to me on the couch.

6. I kept wondering whether even he heard anything I was saying or whether he was fixating on my face.

7. My doctor prescribed a drug, but then I was told it can cause severe depression and that even some kids had committed suicide.

8. Nice choice. Depressed from the zits or depressed from the medication.

9. Experiencing some form of acne, pimples can be really painful as well as embarrassing.

10. Please, can we find just a medication that will put an end to our pain and embarrassment without having us committing suicide?

Unit Collaborative Assignment

Pair up with a partner. Each of you should alternate reading a sentence while the other corrects it, if necessary, in the space below. Decide what kind of error you have found. You should find four dangling or misplaced modifiers.

Children should live free from fear. Fear in a child's life has no redeeming qualities; it does not make a child stronger, nor does it teach the child how to be more independent. One of a child's worst fears comes from watching parents fight. Arriving home from work, little Freddy is afraid that Dad will start a fight with Mom. So Freddy whispers a silent prayer that his parents will be peaceful under his breath. Children not only fear quarrels between their parents, they also fear snakes and spiders. For instance, if little Suzy is in bed, ready for sleep, but sees a black spider crawling out of the corner of her eye, she may panic and have terrible nightmares the rest of the night. Again, fear of this kind is not good for the child's development. Perhaps a child's worst fear is the fear of abandonment. To feel safe, secure, and protected by one's parents is crucial to a child. Some children only feel secure when they finally grow up and have children of their own. When bringing up children, fear must be removed by parents.

1. __________

2. __________

3. __________

4. __________

Unit Writing Assignment

Write a paragraph agreeing or disagreeing with the idea that "College is not for everyone." Begin with a discussible topic sentence and support it with the appropriate facts and examples. Check your writing for misplaced or dangling modifiers. Use the Revising Checklist to help you revise.

Photo Writing Assignment

After studying the following picture, use brainstorming, freewriting, clustering, or any other method of gathering ideas to write a paragraph answering the question, "What services should a good modern library offer?" Consider such conveniences as a reference librarian, online research capability, the availability of a computer, copy machines, a reading room, magazines, and books. Avoid dangling or misplaced modifiers.

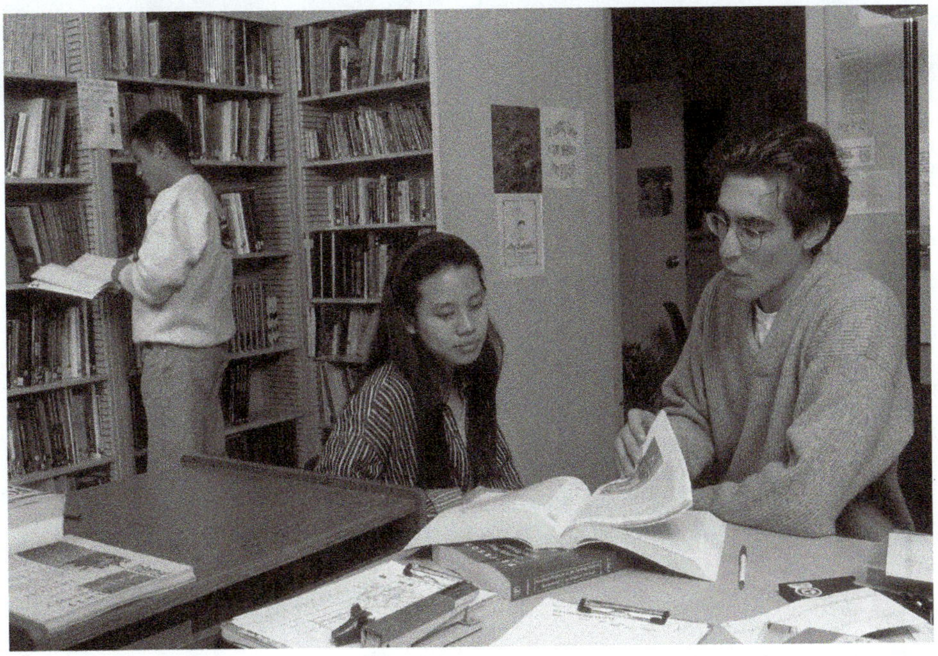

15 Using Prepositions

"The plane flew above the cloud, behind the cloud, around the cloud, below the cloud, beneath the cloud, beside the cloud, beyond the cloud, into the cloud, near the cloud, outside the cloud, over the cloud, past the cloud, through the cloud, toward the cloud, under the cloud, and finally dived underneath the cloud."

A **preposition** is a word that shows the relationship between two things. In the example above, the prepositions show the relationships between a plane and a cloud. Indeed, one informal definition of the preposition is anything an airplane can do to a cloud. This, however, is not a complete definition, as our list of common prepositions makes clear:

about	beneath	in	since
above	beside	inside	through
across	besides	into	throughout
after	between	like	to
against	beyond	near	toward
along	by	of	under
among	despite	off	underneath
around	down	on	until
at	during	out	up
before	except	outside	with
behind	for	over	within
below	from	past	without

Multiword Prepositions

Some prepositions consist of more than one word. Here is a list of the most common multiword prepositions:

along with	in place of
because of	in spite of
due to	instead of
except for	on account of
in addition to	out of
in case of	up to
in front of	with the exception of

PRACTICE 1

Without consulting the above lists, place a check mark next to each preposition. (If you're uncertain about a word, try the plane–cloud test.) Leave the other kinds of words unchecked.

1. ____ behind
2. ____ house
3. ____ for
4. ____ too
5. ____ singing
6. ____ certainly
7. ____ in
8. ____ underneath
9. ____ a
10. ____ below
11. ____ lightly
12. ____ however
13. ____ beyond
14. ____ occasionally
15. ____ inside
16. ____ crying
17. ____ speak
18. ____ upon
19. ____ outside
20. ____ bitterly

PRACTICE 2

In the blank provided, write an appropriate preposition.

1. My grandmother used to tell me stories ____ life in Japan.
2. ____ the semester, I have received A's and B's in my course work.
3. I fell in love ____ last summer.
4. We spoke about it ____ over an hour.
5. ____ her stubbornness, she never made up with her brother.
6. As they say, "Too much water has run ____ the bridge."
7. You know very well that he slashed the tire ____ pure spite.
8. A big brown bear kept coming ____ our tent.
9. I am tired ____ his constant lying.
10. ____ the rain, the dance was great fun.

Prepositional Phrases

A preposition is always followed by a noun or pronoun, called its **object.** Together, the preposition and its object form a **prepositional phrase,** as illustrated below.

PREPOSITION	+	OBJECT	=	PREPOSITIONAL PHRASE
beyond		the stars		beyond the stars
inside		the NFL		inside the NFL
except for		them		except for them
with		his help		with his help
into		the room		into the room

PRACTICE 3

Underline the prepositional phrase in each sentence. Some sentences may contain more than one prepositional phrase.

Example: I would hate to fall into the lake.

1. Don't be in a hurry to go up the stairs.
2. The scissors are on the table right before your eyes.
3. Because of his drinking, he lost the job.
4. She's sitting in the first row between Bert and Harriett.

5. Bob left for school at 9:00 A.M.
6. A large part of his salary is used for rent.
7. The burglar hid behind the door in the attic.
8. Put glass in this recycling bin and paper in that one.
9. Margie stood in the cold and yelled, "Hello!"
10. We immediately headed down the street and through the alley.

Prepositions in Commonly Used Expressions

Prepositions are often combined with other words to create certain set expressions. Here are some examples of these combinations:

acquainted with	He was acquainted with grief.
addicted to	Teddy is addicted to cigarettes.
agree to	I shall never agree to that rule.
apply for	Pedro did not apply for the job.
approve of	Does her mother approve of that?
consist of	The pile consists of three types of rocks.
deal with	We refuse to deal with such nonsense.
depend on	Can the team depend on him?
differ from (a thing)	Computers differ from fax machines.
differ with (a person)	I differ with my neighbor.
fond of	Are you fond of cheese?
grateful for (something)	Americans are grateful for their freedoms.
grateful to (someone)	I am grateful to Toni for the oranges.
interested in	Why are you so interested in cats?
object to	The Smiths object to all the noise.
protect against	Let's protect our land against terrorists.
reason with	We try to reason with him.
reply to	In reply to your question, I say, "No."
responsible for	Who's responsible for the umbrellas?
specialize in	The company specializes in alarm clocks.
succeed in	She'll help him succeed in his studies.
take advantage of	It's wrong to take advantage of the poor.
worry about	Our entire class worries about grades.

ESL Advice!

If you find these combinations tricky, memorize them.

Most native speakers are familiar with these combinations and have little difficulty with them. ESL students, however, because of their lack of experience with them, may find some of these combinations tricky. If necessary, you should memorize as many of them as you can until you gradually get used to hearing them. One particular preposition that may puzzle many ESL students is the word *up*. Because *up* is used idiomatically—sometimes as a preposition, sometimes as another part of speech—some ESL students find *up,* well, a bit upsetting. Consider these expressions: "Paul always *stirs up* trouble." "Why don't you just *shut up*?" "We need to *wake up* and smell the coffee." "*Look* it *up* in the dictionary." "Don't *give up* until the work is done." "*Divide up* the peaches now." In these examples, the preposition *up* has many functions as part of a verb. The only way to catch up with *up* is through repeated exposure to its use in idiomatic English.

PRACTICE 4

If the combination of prepositions and other words is correct, write a *C* in the blank. If it is incorrect, write it correctly in the space after the sentence.

1. ____ Most of us are acquainted about ghost stories. ______
2. ____ The piano differs from the organ. ______
3. ____ How many members approved of the poster? ______
4. ____ We could rarely depend with her for payment. ______
5. ____ He was told to apply about the title of treasurer. ______
6. ____ There is no point in getting angry with mosquitoes. ______
7. ____ Uncle Luigi is terribly fond about pasta. ______
8. ____ My bicycle is identical of Julia's. ______
9. ____ The strong should never take advantage of the weak. ______
10. ____ President Lincoln succeeded at freeing the slaves. ______

Frequently Misused Prepositions

Although your speaker's ear is a fairly accurate guide to using prepositions, your ear may mislead you occasionally because of slang and the general informality of speech. Here are some frequently misused prepositions.

ESL Advice!

These rules need to be memorized:

- **beside, besides.** *Beside* means *next to,* whereas *besides* means *in addition.*

  The comb is beside the brush.

  Besides planning the trip, she is also getting the tickets.

- **between, among.** Generally, *between* is used when two items are involved; with three or more, *among* is preferred.

  Between you and me, he is among friends.

- **due to.** *Due to* should not be used as a preposition meaning *because of.*

  Because of (not due to) his speeding, we were all ticketed.

- **inside of, outside of, off of.** The *of* is always unnecessary.

  Stay inside (not *inside of*) the house.

  The man stayed outside (not *outside of*) the post office.

  Take your foot off (not *off of*) the table.

- **like/as/as if.** *Like* is a preposition and should always be followed by a noun (the object of the preposition).

  He eats like a bear

  She walks like a cat.

  As is a conjunction and should be followed by a clause.

  He eats as a hungry bear might.

  She walks as if she were a cat.

  Note that this distinction is often overlooked in informal speech and writing (they tell it like it is), but it is expected in formal writing.

- **regarding, with respect to, in regard to.** All of these expressions sound pompous. Use *about.*

  I want to speak to you about (not *regarding, with respect to,* or *in regard to*) your essay.

- **through, throughout.** *Through* means *by way of*; *throughout* means *in every part.*

  You drive through Bog Walk to get to Linstead.

  People are the same throughout the world.

- **toward, towards.** Both are correct.

  He walked toward (towards) me.

PRACTICE 5

In the blank provided, write a *C* if the preposition is used correctly or an *NC* if it is not correct. Cross out the errors and write the correct form of the preposition above each error.

1. ____ Slowly, slowly, the bear moved towards the cabin.
2. ____ We have remained best friends throughout a decade.

3. ____ Brand X tastes good like a cigarette should.
4. ____ I am writing this letter in regard to your vacation.
5. ____ Because of his height, he decided not to play basketball.
6. ____ The money was divided between Marge, Alice, and Bob.
7. ____ She whines and complains; beside, she is always late.
8. ____ When you turn off Highway 5, go two miles.
9. ____ Get off of my property!
10. ____ I wish I looked like you.

Frequently Misused Prepositional Expressions

The expressions with prepositions listed below are also frequently misused.

- **agree on, agree to.** *Agree on* is to be of one opinion, whereas *agree to* requires an action.

  They agreed on the terms of the contract.

  They agreed to get a divorce.

- **angry about, angry with.** *Angry about* is used for anger about a thing; *angry with* is used with people.

  Everyone was angry about the detour.

  If you are angry with Sue, tell her so.

- **Differ with, differ from.** *Differ with* means to disagree, whereas *differ from* is to be unlike or dissimilar.

  I differ with you on the death penalty.

  Houses in Boston differ from the ones in Santa Fe.

- **grateful to, grateful for.** You are *grateful to* a person, but *grateful for* something.

  We are grateful to Mrs. Smith.

  We are grateful for the sunshine.

- **independent of, independent from.** *Independent of* is the preferred usage.

  He is independent of any political party.

IN A NUTSHELL

- A preposition shows the relationship between two things.
- Look out for some commonly misused expressions involving prepositions.

PRACTICE 6

In each pair of sentences, check the preferred version in the blank provided.

1. ____ (a) Morrison was always independent of other rock bands.
   ____ (b) Morrison was always independent from other rock bands.
2. ____ (a) Joey differs from his father on the subject of taxes.
   ____ (b) Joey differs with his father on the subject of taxes.
3. ____ (a) Why should I be grateful to my good health?
   ____ (b) Why should I be grateful for my good health?
4. ____ (a) Indeed, we agreed to keep the doors open.
   ____ (b) Indeed, we agreed on keeping the doors open.
5. ____ (a) I was shocked at how angry he was with me.
   ____ (b) I was shocked at how angry he was about me.
6. ____ (a) People can differ from each other on how to vote.
   ____ (b) People can differ with each other on how to vote.
7. ____ (a) Scottie and Maria agreed on seeing a marriage counselor.
   ____ (b) Scottie and Maria agreed to see a marriage counselor.
8. ____ (a) We are grateful for getting into the championship finals.
   ____ (b) We are grateful to get into the championship finals.
9. ____ (a) Max was angry about the long delay at the airport.
   ____ (b) Max was angry with the long delay at the airport.
10. ____ (a) We agree to several issues, including gun control.
    ____ (b) We agree on several issues, including gun control.

PRACTICE 7

Cross out the incorrect preposition in each sentence.

Example: My dreams differ (~~with~~, from) my hopes.

1. We could not agree (on, to) the rental contract.
2. The Civic Association was angry (about, with) the builder for cutting down the oak tree.
3. I am grateful (for, to) my student loan.
4. I am grateful (to, for) my landlord for extending the grace period for paying the rent.

5. If you're angry (about, with) the new dorm rules, speak up.
6. They agreed (on, to) the wedding date.
7. We were angry (about, with) having to wait in line.
8. My brother differs (from, with) my father in looks.
9. But when it comes to politics, my brother differs (with, from) my father on many issues.
10. I am independent (of, from) her.

Unit Test

In the blank provided, write a *C* if the italicized preposition or prepositional phrase is used correctly; write an *NC* if it is not correct. Cross out the errors and write the correct form above each error.

1. _____ Put the book *besides* my bookbag.
2. _____ Can't we agree *to* a single issue?
3. _____ Why is he so *angry with* his grandfather?
4. _____ Let's share the rent *between us* four buddies.
5. _____ Get *off of* that ladder right now!
6. _____ The dean wants to see Mike *in regard to* his grades.
7. _____ All children must someday become *independent from* their parents.
8. _____ Senator Smith *differs with* Senator Brown on how to pay for child care.
9. _____ I worked *throughout* the semester to learn more about astronomy.
10. _____ *Due to* her red hair, we called her "Red Beauty."
11. _____ We parked *outside of* the stadium and walked.
12. _____ Put the bread basket *beside* the butter.
13. _____ We walked *through* the parking lot to get to the mall.
14. _____ She slowly walked *towards* me.
15. _____ I slowly walked *toward* her.
16. _____ Matt is *grateful for* the chance to repay the favor.
17. _____ First put the groceries *inside of* the house.
18. _____ She told funny stories *throughout* the evening.
19. _____ *Between* you and me, I'm glad he won.
20. _____ We got a ticket *due to* parking illegally.

Unit Talk–Write Assignment

The sentences below, on the topic of televised sports, are typical of everyday conversation. Some of the sentences are unsuitable, however, because they use idioms, slang, fragments, and other informalities. A few contain preposition errors. Rewrite each sentence to make it suitable for formal writing, correcting all the preposition errors in the process. Then write a paragraph on your opinion of sports on television.

TALK	WRITE
1. Man, can you believe all the sports on TV nowadays? Cool!	
2. Yeah, man, there's a bunch. Beside, there's more getting on everyday.	
3. Take a sport like football, for instance. During the season, there's games on almost every day of the week.	
4. Sometimes I can't study with the number of games that are on.	
5. I know what you mean, man. Instead of going outside and enjoying the day, I stay inside of the house all Sunday watching football on TV.	
6. What about basketball? If you watch all the college games and pro games through the week, your eyes start to bug out.	

7. Yeah, and that's not even the playoffs. Sometimes five or six of my friends will come over, and we'll split the cost of pizza between us and sit there and pig out on basketball.

8. I don't think anybody else watches as much TV through the world as Americans. Especially sports. Not by half.

9. Sometimes my old man gets angry about me for watching so much sports. I tell him I can't help it. I'm hooked.

10. Me, too. What'd we do without it? It's nothing to be angry with if you're a sports fan.

Unit Collaborative Assignment

A. Form a group. Write 10 sentences supporting the following topic. Each sentence should contain at least one prepositional phrase.

Example: Computers exert a growing influence on our lives.

1. ______________________________

2. ______________________________

3. ______________________________

4. ______________________________

5. ______________________________

6. ______________________________

7. ______________________________

8. ______________________________

9. ______________________________

10. ______________________________

B. Now go back over the sentences and underline all the prepositional phrases.

Unit Writing Assignment

Write about the influence of computers on our lives. Use ideas from the Unit Collaborative Assignment above and new ideas of your own. Use the Revising Checklist inside the front cover of this book to help you revise.

Photo Writing Assignment

After studying the following photo, write about the joy of escaping into daydreams. Think of some examples from your own life, or from the life of someone you know, when you derived pleasure from a daydream or an escapist fantasy. Be as specific as you can. Give at least one example from your own or someone else's experience. Pay special attention to using prepositions, prepositional phrases, and expressions correctly. Use the Revising Checklist to help you revise.

16 Moving from Sentences to Paragraphs

"What kinds of supporting details do paragraph writers most often use? That depends on the topic sentence."

A typical paragraph consists of two main parts: a topic sentence and supporting details. The topic sentence is the sentence—usually the opening one—that states the main point of the paragraph. Supporting details are sentences that back up this main point with specifics.

Here is a typical paragraph, with the topic sentence underlined:

> <u>The Greek Orthodox Church celebrates seven sacraments.</u> They are Baptism, Chrismation, Confession, Holy Communion, Marriage, Holy Orders, and Holy Unction. Baptism is the sacrament that cleanses Greek Orthodox Christians of guilt from personal and original sin. Chrismation safeguards the baptized against future temptations. In Confession, done in the church before a priest, the sinner begs for God's forgiveness for sin. Holy Communion is the physical intake of the body and blood of Christ. Marriage unites a man and a woman under the grace of God. Holy Orders inducts a man into the priesthood, and Holy Unction is given to the sick and dying. Baptism, Chrismation, Confession, and Holy Communion are required of all Greek Orthodox Christians; Marriage, Holy Orders, and Holy Unction, however, are optional.

How important is the topic sentence? Try reading this same paragraph without it.

Without the topic sentence, the paragraph is merely a collection of facts. Without the supporting details, on the other hand, we have merely an unproved sentence:

> The Greek Orthodox Church celebrates seven sacraments.

The topic sentence and supporting details, then, go hand-in-hand. In the previous unit, we talked about the topic sentence. In this one, we will discuss supporting details.

Supporting Details

What kinds of supporting details do paragraph writers most often use? That depends on the topic sentence. A good topic sentence suggests the kinds of details needed for its support. Basically, there are five kinds of supporting details:

1. Examples
2. Facts
3. Testimony
4. Reasoning
5. Personal observation

We'll cover each type of supporting detail separately.

Examples

An **example** is a part used to represent the whole. You say that working at Joe's Diner is hard. Someone asks, "What do you mean by 'hard'?" You say, "Employees must work 12-hour shifts without a break." Working long hours without a break is one example that supports your point.

The example is an effective supporting detail that is used as often by writers as by speakers. Here is an example from a student paragraph on hazing in fraternities:

> Hazing is a dangerous and humiliating ritual. For example, a friend at another university told me about a pledge who was hospitalized with broken ribs after being beaten during hazing. In my own case, I was commanded to drink excessively, appear in boxer shorts at an alumni function, and run stupid late-night errands for brothers. This hazing made me feel so humiliated that I withdrew my pledgeship.

To use examples, simply introduce them with a suitable phrase, such as *for example, for instance,* or *take the case of,* and then spell out the example you have in mind.

Naturally, any example you use should support your point. For instance, Joe's Diner may have a wonderful employee training program, but mentioning that won't support your point that working at Joe's Diner is hard.

PRACTICE 1

Write two appropriate examples that support the following topic sentences.

1. **Topic sentence:** Blue jeans have become our culture's fashion statement.

   First example: ______________________________

   ____

   Second example: ______________________________

   ____

2. **Topic sentence:** The pressures to conform are as strong in college as they are in high school.

   First example: ______________________________

   ____

   Second example: ______________________________

   ____

3. **Topic sentence:** Sometimes it hurts to tell the truth.

   First example: ______________________________

   ____

   Second example: ______________________________

   ____

4. **Topic sentence:** (Fill in the blank) is the busiest person I know.

   First example: ______________________________

   ____

   Second example: ______________________________

   ____

5. **Topic sentence:** Autumn is a beautiful time of year.

   First example: ______________________________

   ____

   Second example: ______________________________

   ____

6. **Topic sentence:** Children need to learn to control their tempers.

   First example: ______________________________

   ____

   Second example: ______________________________

   ____

7. **Topic sentence:** In recent years, sports idols have won fame by cheating.

First example: ______________________________

____

Second example: ______________________________

____

8. **Topic sentence:** Going to the zoo is a great afternoon adventure.

First example: ______________________________

____

Second example: ______________________________

____

9. **Topic sentence:** Mothers often make many sacrifices for their children.

First example: ______________________________

____

Second example: ______________________________

____

10. **Topic sentence:** Our laws tell much about our history.

First example: ______________________________

____

Second example: ______________________________

____

Facts

A **fact** is a statement that is true or can be verified. Anyone who is curious can look up the statement in a proper source and confirm its truth. For instance, the fact that George Washington was born on February 22, 1732, can be confirmed by checking an encyclopedia or any biography of our first president. Some facts are simply accepted by everyone because they have never been proven untrue. That sooner or later all humans die is one such fact.

The opposite of a fact is an **opinion.** Unlike a fact, an opinion is a personal belief, often accompanied by emotion, that cannot be proven either true or false. Here are some examples of facts and opinions:

Accepted Fact:	The sun will always rise in the east.
Verifiable Fact:	John Steinbeck wrote *Of Mice and Men.*
Opinion:	Steinbeck's best book is *Of Mice and Men.*

That the sun rises in the east is a universally accepted fact, and every morning nature again confirms its truth. Anyone can look up who wrote *Of Mice and Men,* and every book consulted will give the same answer: John Steinbeck wrote it. It is not universally accepted that *Of Mice and Men* is Steinbeck's best book. Some readers will argue that *East of Eden* is his best book, whereas others will just as strongly make that claim for *Grapes of Wrath*. The third statement is therefore an opinion because it is not universally accepted like the first nor verifiable like the second.

Here is a paragraph that supports its topic sentence with facts:

> Textbooks at Becky's Bookstore are cheaper than they are at the Student Union. My sociology text at the Student Union store was $65. I found the same text at Becky's Bookstore for $30. The text required for my public speaking class was $49.95 at the Student Union, but $27.50 at Becky's. Likewise, I paid $15 less for my Psychology 101 text at Becky's than I would have at the Student Union. These cheaper prices are why I buy my books at Becky's.

Properly cited, facts add believability to a paragraph. Of course, you must always be sure that your facts are indeed facts and not opinions. Ask yourself, can a reader look up this statement and confirm its truth? If not, the statement is an opinion, not a fact.

Unfortunately, writers seldom have at their fingertips all the facts that they need to write about a particular topic. Most of the time, writers have to dig up facts before they can begin writing. Digging up facts may involve interviewing specific people or even conducting a minisurvey. Some of your assignments may require you to interview certain professors or your fellow students. When you have access to a computer, the Internet is another rich source of facts. It is probably the most popular tool used by students in writing papers.

But overall, the best place for finding facts is the library. Reference books found there, such as encyclopedias or biographical yearbooks, are literally brimming with **accurate** facts on nearly every topic. Moreover, many libraries are staffed by friendly librarians who can help you find facts on almost anything. All you have to do is ask.

PRACTICE 2

From the pairs of sentences that follow, indicate the sentence that is a fact, not an opinion.

Example: ✓ **(a)** My grandmother, who lives with us, was diagnosed as having Alzheimer's, a disease that affects some four million Americans.

____ **(b)** Alzheimer's disease is just the most horrendous, awful curse because it places an unbearable burden on everyone in the family.

1. ____ **(a)** A more enticing place to see than the town market of Ciudad Rodrigo, with its heavenly fresh vegetables, can't be imagined.

____ **(b)** Ciudad Rodrigo sponsors a market every Tuesday in the town square, where the farmers sell baskets of vegetables with the dark, damp soil still clinging to their roots.

2. ____ (a) To be called a cathedral, a church must contain a bishop's see and his official throne.

____ (b) Cathedrals are boringly alike all over the world, always smelling musky and filled with ugly old crypts.

3. ____ (a) Izzy's hamburgers are mouthwateringly delicious and should win a prize for being the best hamburgers in the city.

____ (b) Izzy's menu offers four different kinds of hamburgers: mushroom, ground turkey, vegetarian, and pineapple.

4. ____ (a) Let's face it, people today don't seem to care at all whether or not they can support themselves once they have retired from work.

____ (b) According to the 2007 Employee Benefits Research Institute survey, only 15 percent of 1,000 adults had $100,000 or more in savings despite a decade-long bull market.

5. ____ (a) The Duncan Clark Company is manufacturing and distributing an invisible fence that conditions dogs to stay within a marked area by giving them a light shock when they stray.

____ (b) A company that sells some kind of contraption to shock dogs in order to keep them from bothering freshly planted flower beds should be hauled into court.

6. ____ (a) How exciting it is to realize that it is only a matter of time before a pill is discovered that will keep human beings from aging.

____ (b) While no one has yet discovered the Fountain of Youth, biologists like Bruce Ames and Judith Campisi are studying ways to keep our body cells from aging.

7. ____ (a) According to psychologist Richard J. Davison and colleagues at the University of Wisconsin, meditation is a kind of medication because it helps you clear your mind and boost your spirits.

____ (b) I'm convinced that meditation is a spiritual healer because my day always proceeds with so much more clarity and assurance after I have meditated.

8. ____ (a) Country music is still as popular as ever, as can be seen by the prominence of new performers like Faith Hill, Kenny Chesney, Lonestar, Keith Urban, and Rascal Flatts.

____ (b) The days of honky-tonk have been replaced by some whiz-bang new country music performers who simply make your hips sway, your feet dance, and your back feel goose pimply.

9. ____ (a) According to Dr. Neil Nedley's book *Proof Positive,* approximately 16 million Americans are diabetic, costing the health industry between $90 billion and $130 billion per year.

____ (b) Millions of Americans suffer from diabetes, which I consider a monstrous disease that causes blindness and death, and can run victims of the disease into bankruptcy.

10. ____ (a) Southwest Airlines saves on expenses by serving bags of peanuts or pretzels to customers instead of full meals.

____ (b) Airlines are becoming more and more stingy with the kinds of services that make a trip pleasant.

PRACTICE 3

Support the following topic sentences with at least three facts. You may need to interview or survey classmates, visit your library, or go on the Internet.

1. **Topic sentence:** The students in my English class come from many different backgrounds (or, The students in my English class come mainly from the same background).

   First fact: ____

   ____

   Second fact: ____

   ____

   Third fact: ____

   ____

2. **Topic sentence:** The college library has an adequate book collection and excellent facilities (or, The college library has an inadequate book collection and poor facilities).

   First fact: ____

   ____

   Second fact: ____

   ____

   Third fact: ____

   ____

3. **Topic sentence:** An automobile is expensive to run and maintain.

   First fact: ____

   ____

Second fact: ____________________

____

Third fact: ____________________

____

4. **Topic sentence:** Body piercing is an attempt to make a cultural statement.

First fact: ____________________

____

Second fact: ____________________

____

Third fact: ____________________

____

5. **Topic sentence:** Autism is a disease that affects the emotions and muscles of children.

First fact: ____________________

____

Second fact: ____________________

____

Third fact: ____________________

____

6. **Topic sentence:** New York has spent considerable effort and money on plans for a September 11, 2001, memorial.

First fact: ____________________

____

Second fact: ____________________

____

Third fact: ____________________

____

7. **Topic sentence:** In the last five years, several celebrities have been on trial for criminal acts.

First fact: ____________________

____

Second fact: ____________________

____

Third fact: ____________________

____

8. **Topic sentence:** Major bridges in many of our cities are dangerously flawed.

First fact: ______________________________

____

Second fact: ______________________________

____

Third fact: ______________________________

____

9. **Topic sentence:** Springtime is lovely, but it has its downside.

First fact: ______________________________

____

Second fact: ______________________________

____

Third fact: ______________________________

____

10. **Topic sentence:** Having to give a speech in front of a large audience causes stage fright, which has certain physical effects.

First fact: ______________________________

____

Second fact: ______________________________

____

Third fact: ______________________________

____

Testimony

Testimony is expert opinion that backs up your topic sentence. The expert may be someone who is recognized in the field or who has had personal experience with your topic. Getting the testimony you need may require you to check a newspaper or to interview the right people. Here is a paragraph that has both kinds of testimony—personal experience and expert opinion.

> If you are stopped by the police for a traffic violation, there are some things you should not do. You should not get out of your car unless the officer asks you to. My friend Joe was pulled over by the police late one night on a lonely city street and he got out of the car, thinking that it would make him seem friendly. It had the opposite effect on the officer. Joe says that she put her hand on her gun and ordered him to get back into the car. He said he was afraid she would shoot him. Officer Yankers of the campus police

> says that a motorist who gets out of the car without being told is considered a threat. Says Officer Yankers, "I'm always cautious when a motorist gets out of the car and walks toward me. I think he's being aggressive."

As testimony, the writer quotes his friend's personal experience, as well as the expert opinion of Officer Yankers.

PRACTICE 4

Cite at least two opinions as testimony, supporting the following topic sentences. Use either expert opinion or personal experience.

1. **Topic sentence:** When you're in college, parents should treat you like an adult, not a child.

   First opinion: ______________________________

   ____

   Second opinion: ______________________________

   ____

2. **Topic sentence:** The Environmental Protection Agency (EPA) tries to catch farms and industries that threaten local water supplies by polluting them.

   First opinion: ______________________________

   ____

   Second opinion: ______________________________

   ____

3. **Topic sentence:** Working your way through college can be a stressful experience.

   First opinion: ______________________________

   ____

   Second opinion: ______________________________

   ____

4. **Topic sentence:** Children who are not loved are at risk of becoming social misfits.

   First opinion: ______________________________

   ____

   Second opinion: ______________________________

   ____

5. **Topic sentence:** Genuine religion and patriotism should be quietly felt, not trumpeted with words or special clothing (or,

Genuine Religion and patriotism should be broadcast to the world in word and appearance)

First opinion: ____________________

____

Second opinion: ____________________

____

6. **Topic sentence:** When they are out with friends, kids are often subject to peer pressure that can ultimately ruin their health if they succumb to it—like smoking cigarettes.

   First opinion: ____________________

   ____

   Second opinion: ____________________

   ____

7. **Topic sentence:** The Vietnamese are hard-working, family-oriented immigrants who have established some useful businesses wherever they have settled.

   First opinion: ____________________

   ____

   Second opinion: ____________________

   ____

8. **Topic sentence:** Playing simple card games—like Hearts, Canasta, or Gin Rummy—can help sharpen your memory.

   First opinion: ____________________

   ____

   Second opinion: ____________________

   ____

9. **Topic sentence:** Synthetic fabrics have helped reduce housework for many men, as well as women.

   First opinion: ____________________

   ____

   Second opinion: ____________________

   ____

10. **Topic sentence:** People handle rumors in different ways.

    First opinion: ____________________

    ____

    Second opinion: ____________________

    ____

Reasoning

Some topic sentences are best supported by **reasoning**—explanations based on common sense, good judgment, clear thinking, and logic. This kind of support is most commonly used when a writer is trying to persuade the reader to change an opinion.

In the following paragraph, reasoning is used to support the writer's argument that cafeteria food should be prepared on campus and not by off-campus caterers.

> <u>Cafeteria food should be prepared in campus kitchens, not trucked in by off-campus caterers.</u> Common sense tells us that a sandwich made to order and served immediately is going to taste fresher and better than one made miles away and trucked to the campus for sale. Even if the sandwich is prepared elsewhere on the same day, it's going to lose some of its taste from being refrigerated and transported. Fresh food tastes better because it's fresh, not half-fresh. If we want better cafeteria food, we should insist that it be prepared on campus, where it is eaten.

Not every topic sentence can be supported by reasoning. However, for those topic sentences that can be supported in this way—and your common sense should be the judge—reasoning can be highly effective.

PRACTICE 5

Use reasoning to support one of the following topic sentences.

1. **Topic sentence:** In cases of murder, capital punishment makes sense.

____

____

____

____

____

____

____

____

2. **Topic sentence:** Capital punishment does not stop murder.

____

____

____

____

____

Personal Observation

Some topics are strictly personal and must be supported mainly by your own personal observation. That old standby topic, "Write about how you spent your summer vacation," is a classic example of a personal topic. Unless he or she vacationed with you, no librarian can help you find support for it. You must draw entirely on your own personal observations for support.

Personal observation includes descriptive details and examples. Here is an example of both in a paragraph:

> Last summer I spent a week hiking and discovered that I hate it. To begin with, we got caught in a 2-day rain on the Appalachian Trail. The tent turned out not to be waterproof, and for one whole night I tried to sleep with water dripping on my nose. When I moved, it dripped on my belly. I turned over, and it dripped on my butt. I also found out that aside from weather problems, hiking is unhealthy for you. For example, I ate so poorly for the week that I was starving and pigged out afterward on hamburgers and French fries for a month. So I ended up gaining weight. Next time I go camping, it'll be in a Winnebago.

The details this writer uses are not available in any library, but come only from memory. Paragraphs written on such topics as a favorite place, a special friend, the first day on a new job, or a personal experience that sheds light on a problem must be similarly supported by personal observations.

IN A NUTSHELL

The supporting details of a paragraph typically consist of examples, facts, testimony, reasoning, and personal observation.

PRACTICE 6

Develop a topic sentence on one of the following subjects and write a paragraph about it, supporting the topic sentence with personal observations.

1. A favorite time of the year for my family
2. My best vacation
3. An incident that changed me in some way

4. My first broken heart
5. A beautiful (or ugly) scene I shall always remember
6. An experience I had with ignorance
7. An injustice I witnessed
8. The financial difficulties I have experienced while going to college
9. Loneliness and discouragement can lead to maturity and understanding
10. Why I love (or hate) potlucks

____

____

____

____

____

____

____

____

____

____

Unit Test

In the blank provided, place a check mark in front of the phrase that most accurately completes the sentence.

Example: A typical paragraph consists of

_____ (a) a title and an opening sentence.
__✓__ (b) a topic sentence and details.
_____ (c) adjectives and nouns.
_____ (d) details and questions.

1. Supporting details are sentences that

_____ (a) should rarely be used.
_____ (b) confuse the reader.
_____ (c) create a verbal picture.
_____ (d) back up the main point.

2. The kinds of details to be used depend on

_____ (a) what kind of topic sentence you wrote.

_____ (b) how you feel about your subject.

_____ (c) the reader's level of education.

_____ (d) the length of your paragraph.

3. Which of the following is NOT suggested as a kind of supporting detail:

_____ (a) example

_____ (b) fact

_____ (c) hint

_____ (d) personal observation

4. Which of the following examples DOES NOT support the topic sentence "Climbing a ladder can be dangerous"?

_____ (a) One of the rungs in the ladder could break, causing you to fall.

_____ (b) Today most ladders are made of metal.

_____ (c) The ladder could be placed on wet ground, causing it to slip.

_____ (d) The ladder may be old and rickety.

5. Which of the following statements is a verifiable fact:

_____ (a) Mrs. Smith is a delightful woman.

_____ (b) My teacher doesn't know beans about what he's teaching.

_____ (c) James Garfield served as president of the United States in 1881.

_____ (d) *Beauty and the Beast* is the best cartoon ever made.

6. Expert testimony is a good way to back up a topic sentence because

_____ (a) courts like to use it in medical cases.

_____ (b) the expert must swear to tell the truth.

_____ (c) this kind of testimony is rare and therefore valuable.

_____ (d) it comes from someone who is recognized in the field.

7. Which of the following is NOT a reason that could be used in support of the topic sentence "Aspirin has long been recognized as having both good and dangerous effects"?

_____ (a) The history of the aspirin goes back to the year 200 B.C.

_____ (b) Aspirin is actually salicylic acid, which, in its pure form, is capable of burning a hole in the stomach.

_____ (c) I take aspirin because it helps me when I get a headache.

_____ (d) Many pediatricians advise against baby aspirin for their patients because it has been linked to a rare, but dangerous, condition in children called Reye's syndrome.

8. The topic sentence "My boss is a hard-nosed business man" can probably best be supported by

_____ (a) personal observation.

_____ (b) logic.

_____ (c) good judgment.

_____ (d) reasoning.

9. Which method of support does this topic sentence call for? "No one should complain about giving welfare to people who are handicapped or down on their luck."

_____ (a) Personal observation

_____ (b) Facts

_____ (c) Reasoning

_____ (d) All of the above

10. How important is the topic sentence to students who must write?

_____ (a) Not important except when you use a computer

_____ (b) Important only to English majors

_____ (c) Important because it makes a point the writer can then support

_____ (d) As important as having a readable handwriting

Unit Talk–Write Assignment

On the lines provided under the *Write* column, rewrite the *Talk* column sentences to remove any nonstandard expressions and to include only details that support the topic sentence. Omit any sentence that does not support the topic.

Topic sentence: More and more adults are going back to college in the United States.

TALK	WRITE
1. I've got to quit goofing off and get this assignment done.	______________________________
2. According to what I read in the *L.A. Times* last Sunday, the number of students 25 or older has gone up by 10 percent since 1984.	______________________________

3. After rapping with several older students on campus, I figured out the three main reasons for returning to college later in life: to make more bucks, to make up for losing a job as a result of quick company changes, or just to learn.

4. Well, I have to say that my gut feeling is that these older students generally make the classes more competitive for people like me.

5. For instance, a 31-year-old guy in my econ class, who works full-time in a bank, told me that he starts his homework around eight every night and hits the books until midnight.

6. Wow! That kind of motivation frosts me because he's going to mess up my A or B by screwing up the grade curve.

7. Dr. Brenda Fillmore, who is the head honcho of the Foreign Language Department, swears she loves having the older students in her class because they're so gung ho about studying.

8. What else can I say?

9. Well, I guess I gotta admit I really admire these old dudes—and lady dudes—who return to college.

10. I sure hope these guys will give me a push—I could use it.

Unit Collaborative Assignment

Get together with two or three students in the class and talk out a paragraph on each of the topic sentences listed below. Discuss what types of supporting details the topic sentence requires and suggest some specific details that could be used. Make note of what kinds of supporting statements—examples, facts, testimony, reasoning, or observation—were suggested in your discussion.

1. Today's new cars incorporate many useful safety features.
2. Students must often write under great pressure.
3. Everyone should play a sport.
4. Doctors are too quick to give people drugs.
5. Pets are a comfort to many people.
6. Some television commercials border on bad taste.
7. Housecleaning should be a unisex chore.
8. American-made cars are not better than foreign models.
9. Good health depends on taking responsibility for yourself.
10. Couples should not marry until they are 25.

Unit Writing Assignment

Write about one of the topics that follow. Come up with a discussible topic sentence and support it with appropriate examples, facts, testimony, reasoning, or personal observation. Follow these steps:

1. Choose the topic.
2. Warm up by freewriting.
3. Gather ideas by brainstorming.
4. Refer to an appropriate journal entry, if you have one.
5. Narrow the subject to a manageable topic by clustering.

If you aren't happy with your topic at this point, put away what you've done, choose another topic, and repeat the listed steps; then write your topic sentence. Check it by asking these questions:

(a) Is it discussible or is it too dry and narrow?

(b) What kinds of supporting details does it need?

Now write about one of these topics:

1. An exciting place
2. Student jobs

3. The importance of high school GPAs
4. Being a teenager *or* living with a teenager
5. A major league sport
6. My career goals
7. Managing loneliness or fear
8. The importance of learning geography or a foreign language
9. The effect of money on politics
10. Movies

This is how one student completed the assignment:

During my recovery from mononucleosis in junior high, I discovered the power of fantasy to help me handle loneliness. I had to spend lots of time in bed. I felt so weak that I could hardly even walk. Every day I got out an atlas and looked up a map of a foreign country. Then I would lie back and imagine myself in that country. Using my imagination, I went on a tiger hunt in India. I went surfing in Australia (even wiping out once). I saw the steppes of Russia during a blizzard, and I went swimming on the beaches of Barbados. My mother used to come in the room, see me lying there staring at the ceiling, and ask me if I felt all right. One day I said to her, "Mom, watch out for the cobra," and she looked worried and asked me if she should call the doctor. That was a long time ago. Nowadays I hardly have time for fantasy. But I know that if I ever have time on my hands again, it'll pass quickly if I just settle back and let my imagination roam.

Photo Writing Assignment

The following photo shows a politician campaigning for office. Write about why you think political campaigns are (or are not) effective showcases for giving voters a glimpse of a candidate's position and basic character. What do you think is the most effective technique or mechanism for exposing candidates to voters? How much attention do you pay to campaigning politicians? Sum up your feelings about the political process in a well constructed paragraph. Use any of the techniques discussed in this unit. Write a discussible topic sentence, and then prove it with appropriate details.

17 WRITING A SOLID PARAGRAPH

"The sentences of a true paragraph always function to make a common point. They are like horses linked together to pull a cart in the same direction."

We write in paragraphs—everyone knows that. What is less well known is that we tend to talk in paragraphs, too. For example, here is a "paragraph" we overheard:

> The Redskins outplayed the Cowboys by a mile in yesterday's game. For one thing, the Redskins' defense was great. The vaunted running attack of the Cowboys didn't even gain 50 yards. Every time a back had the ball, he was swarmed by the Redskins' linebackers. Then there was the Redskins' offense. Their running back gained over a hundred yards, and their special team returned two punts to the Cowboys' 20-yard line. I just think that Dallas is overrated.

This could be called a spoken paragraph because it does everything a good written paragraph does. First, it announces its topic—the Dallas versus Washington football game—and makes a point about it. Second, it sticks to that point. Third, it tries to prove the point with reasoning and examples. Finally, all of its sentences are linked together so that it is easy to follow the speaker's train of thought.

To write a solid paragraph, therefore, you should do the following:

- Begin with a discussible point.
- Stick to the point.
- Prove the point; don't merely repeat it. (Use enough details to prove the point.)
- Link your sentences to make your ideas easy to follow.

Begin with a Discussible Point

Some clever writers can write a paragraph about anything, even a safety pin. Most of us, though, need a discussible topic sentence before we can write a good paragraph. Here is an example of a paragraph without a discussible topic sentence:

> The clock in the kitchen is broken. It broke last year. It stopped at 10:25 A.M. My father tried to repair it but couldn't. My mother hit it with a broom. Before it broke, it ran fast. Now it doesn't run at all.

This paragraph is meaningless because the writer has no topic sentence and consequently no point. A discussible point is a statement that immediately calls for further explanation. Here is the rewritten paragraph with a topic sentence added:

> My father and mother react differently to household problems. For example, when the clock in the kitchen broke, my father tried to repair it. He sat down at the kitchen table and took it apart. He worked on it for nearly an hour but couldn't get it to run. So he put it together again and put it back on the wall. My mother, on the other hand, got mad and hit the clock with a broom. Another time, she threw her purse at it. Finally, she broke it open with her shoe. Then the two of them went out and bought another clock.

PRACTICE 1

Write a plus (+) beside the sentences that would be good discussible topic sentences and a minus (–) beside those that lead nowhere.

1. _____ Autumn leaves are often multicolored.
2. _____ As a child, I always had fun on Sundays.
3. _____ A grade of F means failure.
4. _____ A travel iron is used to iron clothes while traveling.
5. _____ My CD player is one of my most valuable possessions.
6. _____ To *memorize* means to commit facts to memory.
7. _____ I have discovered three ways to manage my time.
8. _____ Extracurricular activities enrich college life.
9. _____ Bunk beds save space.
10. _____ The single life has many drawbacks.

PRACTICE 2

Turn each sentence in Practice 1 that you marked with a minus (–) into a discussible topic sentence.

____

____

Stick to the Point

A block of print on the page is not necessarily a paragraph just because it looks like one. Consider this example:

> Basketball Coach Burns is the exact opposite of what a good coach should be. The Type A personality is always nervous about something. Sailing is my favorite hobby. My mother saves anything—money, string, even rubber bands. This winter was unusually cold.

This block of print only looks like a paragraph because its first sentence is indented. But it isn't really one. Its sentences do not function like the sentences of a paragraph; they are not linked to make a common point. Rather, each sentence is like a horse galloping in a different direction. The sentences of a true paragraph, on the other hand, always function to make a common point. They are like horses pulling a cart in the same direction.

If you begin to write a paragraph about bass fishing, stick only to bass fishing. Save all your other thoughts for another paragraph. Here is an example of a paragraph that drifts from the point:

> <u>Bass fishing is a popular sport in the South.</u> Fishermen have their own boats and tackle. Some of these boats are very expensive and are bought with prize money. Most have electric trolling motors in addition to a powerful outboard. Personally, I prefer backpacking. My brother, Bob, likes kite building and flying. My sister likes to play chess with her computer. I guess you could say that we all have our own way of enjoying ourselves. Bass boats are not cheap and can cost up to $20,000. The electronics that help the fishermen locate bass holes include depth finders and sonar bottom scanners.

It is easy to spot the annoying drift in the above paragraph. Here is the paragraph without it:

> <u>Bass fishing is a popular sport in the South.</u> Fishermen have their own boats and tackle. Some of these boats are very expensive and are bought with prize money. Most have electric trolling motors in addition to a powerful outboard. Bass boats are not cheap, and can cost up to $20,000. The electronics that help the fishermen locate bass holes include depth finders and sonar bottom scanners.

With the writer now sticking to the point, the paragraph is sharper, crisper, and easier to read.

PRACTICE 3

Cross out the sentences that stray from the point in the paragraph that follows. The topic sentence is underlined.

<u>Passive smoking is a public health menace.</u> Studies by the Environmental Protection Agency show that people exposed to second-hand smoke are as much as 150 percent more likely to get lung cancer than those who are not exposed. Spouses of inconsiderate smokers have a 30 percent greater risk of getting lung cancer during their lifetimes. Smoking is a bad habit, but drinking alcoholic beverages is also a terrible habit. In my family, my Uncle Irving is a heavy smoker and drinker. I don't know which of his vices is worse—the smoking or drinking. Not only does he smoke, but he is also an inconsiderate smoker and is always puffing around my Aunt Elizabeth, who frequently comes down with colds. Because the evidence is so conclusive, several states have passed laws to restrict workplace smoking. More needs to be done to protect people from the bad habits of a few.

Prove the Point; Don't Merely Repeat It

Proving a point is not the same as repeating it. When you prove a point, you add something new to it—an example, a fact, a reason, or an expert's opinion. Look at this paragraph, for example:

<u>The tradition of exchanging gifts at Christmas is practiced differently in different families.</u> Many people practice it differently. Some families do one thing, others do something different. Some families exchange gifts, others don't. In some families, fewer gifts are exchanged. Others go all out. This tradition is a good, wholesome tradition. My family has been practicing this tradition forever.

The paragraph adds nothing to the underlined topic sentence, but merely repeats it in different words. Here, on the other hand, is a paragraph that uses examples to support the same topic sentence:

<u>The tradition of exchanging gifts at Christmas is practiced differently in different families.</u> In my family, for example, we exchange wrapped presents on Christmas Eve after dinner. On Christmas Day, there are gifts from Santa Claus under the tree for me and my sister. Santa Claus has been bringing such gifts to our house since I was a child, and my sister and I like the tradition so much that, even though we're now grown, we've asked him never to stop. In my husband's family, on the other hand, the gifts are not opened on Christmas Eve, but on Christmas Day. Santa Claus stopped coming by their house once the children became teenagers. Their gifts to each other, however, are not identified by a tag, so you never know who gave what to whom. Nevertheless, one thing stays the same: Both families enjoy the spirit of Christmas equally, although in their own way.

The writer moves quickly from the tradition of exchanging gifts at Christmas to examples of how it is practiced in the two families.

PRACTICE 4

Each of the two topic sentences below is followed by 10 related sentences. Write a plus (+) beside the statements that you think add something specific to the topic sentence and a minus (−) beside those that merely repeat it.

1. **Topic sentence:** Toy manufacturing is a stupendous business.

____ (a) Manufacturers are in an enormous enterprise.

____ (b) The toy market is an $18 billion market.

____ (c) Huge numbers of manufacturers are involved.

____ (d) In 1994, toy manufacturers spent $800 million to advertise their products.

____ (e) Toy makers in America produce 12,000 different toys every year.

____ (f) Over time, the number of toy manufacturers has increased tremendously.

____ (g) Between 5,000 and 6,000 new toys are introduced each year.

____ (h) The toy business is really something monumental.

____ (i) Few people realize how big the toy business really is.

____ (j) Since my dad is in toy sales, I know that the business is bigger than people realize.

2. **Topic sentence:** People who pretend to be what they are not, don't usually enjoy the respect of their peers.

____ (a) You simply can't respect someone who is always putting on a show.

____ (b) For instance, some of the students on campus go around bragging about their money.

____ (c) They love to invite me to ride in their new Honda Civics, just so my mouth will water at their luck.

____ (d) You can't look up to someone who you know is hiding behind a fake existence.

____ (e) I don't even know what the social backgrounds of my best friends are because I don't find them important to our friendship.

____ (f) The worst social pretenders, though, are students who brag about their grades even though some are close to flunking.

____ (g) Intellectual pretense really turns people off.

____ **(h)** How can you respect someone who lies about his intelligence?

____ **(i)** One student in my sociology class insisted that he got an A on a paper; yet, a grade of C was clearly written on the first page.

____ **(j)** I believe in modesty and honesty.

Use Enough Details to Prove the Point

Your paragraph should say enough about your point to prove it. You have to use your common sense in deciding when you have said enough. If you pack your paragraph with too many details, you could bore your reader. But if you don't use enough details, as is common with most students, your paragraph will be too skimpy to sound convincing.

Here is an example of a paragraph that lacks enough details to be convincing:

> I think that it would be exciting to live in a skyscraper as my aunt does. Think of the view you would have if you lived on the 80th floor. Every day, you could take an elevator to your apartment. Whenever you looked down at the street below, people would seem like ants crawling along.

This is to the point as far as it goes. But it doesn't go far enough. The second time around, after some criticism from his group, the student improved the paragraph by adding more details:

> I think that it would be exciting to live in a New York skyscraper. I have an aunt who lives on the 35th floor of one of those modern apartment buildings on Lexington Avenue that seem to stretch into the clouds. When I visit her, I have to use a code at the front door and wait until she rings me in. Then I cross the lobby, enter the elevator, and push the button marked "35." I zip up, up, up, until the elevator door opens, and I am facing my aunt's apartment. The first time I stood on her little balcony and looked down at the street below, I became slightly dizzy and could see how some people might feel as if they were magnetically drawn to the ground from such a vast height. But once I felt comfortable, I watched the traffic jams and the crowds of people winding along the sidewalk as if they were performing a dance. Everything looked so tiny from so far up that I couldn't take my eyes off the scene. I'm sure that, in time, I might get tired of living so far away from trees, lawns, and flower beds, but I like to dream about having the chance to live in a New York skyscraper, high off the ground level.

The difference between the first and second version is a matter of extra details. Notice that in the second version the writer tries his best to show us what it must be like to view the world every day from so far up. Most well-developed paragraphs run between 6 and 12 sentences long. To decide whether you have done enough, try to see your paragraph from a reader's point of view. If you have a nagging feeling that you have not said enough, add some details. As a rule of thumb, the topic sentence or major point of a paragraph should have at least three meaty details to back it up.

PRACTICE 5

Add three or four details to each of the following topic sentences.

1. **Topic sentence:** My favorite part of any supermarket is the racks next to the cash register.

   1. ______________________________
   2. ______________________________
   3. ______________________________
   4. ______________________________

2. **Topic sentence:** Because of their unusual qualities, Dalmatians have always been the mascots for fire stations.

   1. ______________________________
   2. ______________________________
   3. ______________________________
   4. ______________________________

3. **Topic sentence.** Bendy, short for Belinda, is one of the loveliest persons I know.

   1. ______________________________
   2. ______________________________
   3. ______________________________
   4. ______________________________

4. **Topic sentence:** A bowl of fresh peaches makes a mouthwatering, healthy dessert.

1. ______________________________

____

2. ______________________________

____

3. ______________________________

____

4. ______________________________

____

5. **Topic Sentence:** To many seasoned travelers, Jamaica is one of the most beautiful islands in the entire West Indies.

1. ______________________________

____

2. ______________________________

____

3. ______________________________

____

4. ______________________________

____

PRACTICE 6

Using one of the lists from Practice 5, turn it into a complete paragraph that proves the topic sentence. You do not have to use the same order of details as in the list you chose.

IN A NUTSHELL

To write a solid paragraph, you should do the following:

- Begin with a discussible point.
- Stick to the point.
- Prove the point; don't merely repeat it. (Use enough details to prove the point.)

Link the Sentences

A paragraph is a block of print with all of its sentences **linked** and on the same topic. Consider this example:

> <u>Coach Burns is the exact opposite of what a coach should be.</u> He runs the same old simple plays over and over again so that the other team can easily figure out our game plan. He does not motivate. All he ever does is make his players feel as if they are losers. He points out our weaknesses, game after game, without a single word of encouragement. He makes the team depressed and angry. He lacks basic kindness. If you play for Coach Burns and have a personal problem, you can't go to him. One day, after a game, I found that someone had stolen the wheels off my car. I went to Coach Burns's office and, practically in tears, said, "Coach, someone stole the wheels off my car." "So," he sarcastically replied, "what do you want me to do about it?"

By our definition, the above text is definitely a paragraph. But it is not a good one. The writing is choppy, and the writer's train of thought is hard to follow. Helpful links between its sentences are missing. A paragraph with missing links between its sentences is said to lack **coherence.** Here is the same paragraph rewritten to add sentence links.

> <u>Basketball Coach Burns is the exact opposite of what a coach should be.</u> First, he does not even know the game of basketball. He runs the same old simple plays over and over again so that the other team can easily figure out our game plan. Second, he does not motivate. All he ever does is make his players feel as if they are losers. He points out our weaknesses, game after game, without a single word of encouragement. He makes the team depressed and angry. Finally, he lacks basic kindness. If you play for Coach Burns and have a personal problem, you can't go to him. For example, one day, after a game, I found that someone had stolen the wheels off my car. I went to Coach Burns's office and, practically in tears, said, "Coach, someone stole the wheels off my car." "So," he sarcastically replied, "what do you want me to do about it?" If you ask me, Coach Burns hurts the basketball team more than he helps it.

Now we can easily follow the writer's thinking. The words, *first, second*, and *finally* set off the reasons why Coach Burns is a bad coach, and the phrase *for example* introduces the example. Because of these **added links,** the writing is smooth, not choppy.

To link the sentences of a paragraph, writers use the following techniques:

- Transitional words and phrases
- Repeated key words and pronouns
- Similar sentence patterns

Transitional Words and Phrases

A *transition* is a word or phrase that links the sentences of a paragraph. In the following paragraphs, the transitions are in bold, and the topic sentence is underlined:

> <u>No main dish is simpler to prepare than roast chicken.</u> **Moreover,** there is no more elegant dish for company. To serve two to four people, buy about a 3-pound roaster or fryer. Buy a fresh bird, not frozen, and look for a plump bird with light-gold-colored skin. **When** you get home, take out the giblets that are packaged inside, wash the bird, and pat it dry. Put a couple cloves of garlic and a few slices of lemon inside. **Next,** sprinkle paprika on top; this adds a nice color to the finished chicken. Place the bird breast-down in a shallow pan and cook in a 300 degree oven for 30 minutes per pound. Baste often. The juices add flavor and keep the bird moist. During the last 20 minutes, turn the bird over so it browns evenly. **Then,** all you have to do is present your chicken on a pretty platter and stand back for the compliments.

The writer makes it easy to follow the directions by linking the sentences with transitional words—*moreover*, *when*, *next*, and *then*. Here are some other common words and phrases used to link sentences:

after all	finally	in addition	moreover	plus
also	first, second	in contrast	moreover	so
and	for example	in fact	nevertheless	therefore
as a consequence	for instance	in particular	next	then
but	however	in spite of	once	what's more

PRACTICE 7

Link the following sentences to make it easy for the reader to follow the train of thought.

Example: His problem was to make his way to the back of the auditorium without seeming in a hurry. He slowly picked up his jacket and shuffled up the aisle.

Rewritten: His problem was to make his way to the back of the auditorium without seeming to be in a hurry. **Consequently,** he slowly picked up his jacket and shuffled up the aisle.

1. My brother can really annoy me sometimes. He keeps pinching me every time he passes by me.

____

____

2. My math teacher keeps complaining about living in town. He refuses to move.

____

____

3. Terry had to run errands during lunch. He would not be able to meet Meg for a sandwich.

____

____

4. Ann slept through her morning dental appointment. She slept through basketball practice.

____

____

5. The story was filled with violent scenes. The teacher decided not to assign it as reading.

____

____

6. First, we went swimming in the lake. We lay on the grass and rested.

____

____

7. Three of his habits annoy me. He leaves dirty dishes on his desk, he leaves wet towels hanging in the bathroom. He never locks the door when he leaves the apartment.

____

____

8. The heavy box was about to fall on Jim's head. Bob held it back just in time.

____

____

9. He weighed 200 pounds. He was extremely fast.

____

____

10. I couldn't help feeling lonely. I was in a new neighborhood where I didn't know a soul.

____

____

Repeated Key Words and Pronouns

Another way to link the sentences of a paragraph is to repeat key words and pronouns. Pronouns are words that take the place of nouns, such as *he* for *Mr. Jones* or *it* for *the book*. Here is an example:

> Uncle Dan is a good example of a perfectionist. Whenever he sets out to do anything, he always does it right. Once when he was

making me a Halloween costume, he stayed up all night sewing until it fit perfectly. If he hangs a picture, he uses a carpenter's level. When Uncle Dan rakes the leaves in the driveway, it looks scrubbed when he is finished. Not a single leaf is left behind. Uncle Dan is such a perfectionist that sometimes he drives my Aunt Ida, who is somewhat of a slob, crazy.

The sentences in this paragraph are tightly linked by the repetition of the key words *Uncle Dan* and *perfectionist*, which are used in the topic sentence, and the pronoun *he*.

PRACTICE 8

In the paragraph that follows, underline any noun, pronoun, or key word that is repeated as a link between the sentences.

During the past several years, my home state, Nevada, has been bothered by a band of invading crickets. These horrid little creatures are big; they stink; they're ugly; and they're all over the place. The area most bothered by these bugs is Reno, where entire flower beds and agricultural crops are being chewed up. In fact, entomologists for the Nevada Department of Agriculture are concerned and have called the infestation one of the worst since the 1970s. These crickets tend to multiply fast and are voracious eaters of wheat, barley, alfalfa, garden vegetables, and flowers. Additionally, when they band together, they emit an unpleasant odor. Although their movement is restricted to crawling and hopping, they migrate in groups that can cover as much as a mile a day and up to 50 miles in a summer. How dreadful to think that an army of crickets could ruin the economy of an entire state.

Similar Sentence Patterns

This linking technique simply means that similar ideas are expressed in similar words. For example, you could use the same sentence patterns to compare places, things, ideas, or people as the writer does below:

My brother Joe and my brother John are completely different when it comes to being neat. My brother Joe is messy, whereas my brother John is neat. Joe comes home and tosses his clothes on the floor. John comes home and neatly folds and puts away his clothes. Joe cooks breakfast and leaves the dirty dishes in the sink. John cooks breakfast and washes every dish afterwards. Joe brushes his teeth and splatters water all over the bathroom mirror. John brushes his teeth and leaves everything bone dry, even his teeth. I love both of my brothers, but I prefer living with John.

Notice the definite pattern used in this paragraph to compare Joe's habits with John's. For each point, the writer first talks about Joe's messiness and then John's neatness, using the same sentence pattern. This technique makes it easy to follow the writer's thoughts.

IN A NUTSHELL

Help your reader follow your train of thought by

- Using transitions.
- Repeating key words and pronouns.
- Using similar sentence patterns.

PRACTICE 9

In the following passages, underline the repeated sentence patterns.

Example: Happy is the person who believes in the dignity offered by labor and in the opportunity offered by freedom.

1. We are what we eat, as well as what we think.
2. I had no time whatsoever to enjoy good music or to watch good films.
3. This computer is killing me. Whenever I stare at it, my eyes hurt; whenever I type, my hands ache.
4. Here's some good advice: Think before you speak, and read before you think.
5. Money means having power; it means having status; and it means having freedom. Money isn't such a bad thing.
6. Why is she always here today and gone tomorrow? Please give me the answer to that question.
7. Rick's life has been bumpy: He has known what it is to be hungry, and he has known what it is to eat at the best restaurants.
8. If we don't reward good teachers, teaching will become a lost art and a lost tradition.
9. Most of us prefer to believe what we like, not what we fear.
10. We never became strong friends, but we never became strong enemies, either.

☑ Unit Test

In the blank provided, place a check mark in front of the answer that best completes the idea of the sentence.

Example: The sentences of a true paragraph are like

_____ (a) oxen carrying a heavy burden.

__✓__ (b) horses pulling a carriage together.

_____ **(c)** chickens laying eggs.

_____ **(d)** snakes crawling through the grass.

1. You will write better paragraphs, if you begin with a

_____ **(a)** nice computer font.

_____ **(b)** simple sentence.

_____ **(c)** discussible point.

_____ **(d)** shocking idea.

2. A discussible point is one that

_____ **(a)** is complex.

_____ **(b)** calls for further explanation.

_____ **(c)** is controversial.

_____ **(d)** is one found in your textbook.

3. The way that you indicate that you have written a paragraph is to

_____ **(a)** indent the first line of the paragraph five spaces.

_____ **(b)** link your sentences so that they make a common point.

_____ **(c)** compose short, crisp sentences.

_____ **(d)** make more than one point.

4. You prove your point by

_____ **(a)** repeating it several times in different words.

_____ **(b)** making statements with which most people agree.

_____ **(c)** quoting a famous person, such as a president or a movie star.

_____ **(d)** using an example, a fact, a reason, or an expert's opinion to support your point.

5. Which of the following techniques is NOT a way of linking sentences?

_____ **(a)** Placing a period between sentences

_____ **(b)** Repeating key words and pronouns

_____ **(c)** Using transitional words and phrases

_____ **(d)** Using similar sentence patterns

6. Insert an appropriate transitional word to link the sentences that follow.

_____ **(a)** Xavier owns a stack of good videos. His friends like to visit him.

_____ **(b)** The audience laughed continuously in the first act. Many walked out during the second act.

7. Place a check mark in the blank by the sentences that use a pronoun as a transition between them.

_____ **(a)** Lynn Dale is a fast runner. Michelle Jaeger is even faster.

_____ **(b)** Some pop stars shine brighter in the darkness of death than in the daylight of life. Athletes, however, don't seem to get more popular after death.

_____ **(c)** When Aaron was a kid, I was already in college. By the time he reached college age, I had kids of my own.

_____ **(d)** More and more stores are getting Web sites to make shopping easier. Many direct mail retailers are getting Web sites, too.

8. Place a check mark by the sentences that use the repetition of key words to link them.

_____ **(a)** Our school is helping Nelly to win a medal in basketball. The coach gives her personal attention.

_____ **(b)** Twenty-five people come to our house for dinner every Thanksgiving. We have to borrow chairs from our neighbor to be able to seat all of our guests.

_____ **(c)** Nature probably has a cure for every disease if we could just discover it. Medical scientists are our explorers.

_____ **(d)** Cheap labor is what many employers seek. However, cheap labor is not always the most skilled and trainable labor.

9. Place a check mark by the sentences that use similar sentence patterns to link them.

_____ **(a)** We agree that most drug abusers are losers. We agree that most drug users are troubled. But we do not agree on whether they should be jailed or hospitalized.

_____ **(b)** A fabulously preserved fossil from China all but proves that dinosaurs and birds are closely related. I read a recent newspaper article that explains the connection to those of us who aren't scientists.

_____ **(c)** The tests that elementary school students often have to take at the end of the school year are causing youngsters terrible stress. This anxiety keeps them from succeeding in school.

_____ **(d)** Having been bullied at school is no excuse for shooting other students and teachers. However, parents and teachers should certainly foster self-esteem in children.

10. Use whichever of the three linking techniques you think best—transitional words or phrases, repeated key terms, or similar sentence patterns—to rewrite the passage that follows to better link the sentences.

Many myths exist about the founding fathers. They were believers in democracy. They were not. They thought that unchecked democracy would lead to mob rule that would threaten the social order. Distrust of democracy was common. They merely reflected the thinking of their age.

Unit Talk–Write Assignment

On the lines provided under the *Write* column, rewrite the *Talk* column sentences in standard English, linking the sentences smoothly. Delete any material that does not stick to the topic sentence.

Discussible topic sentence: Solving crossword puzzles keeps your mind alert and flexible.

TALK	WRITE
1. Solving crossword puzzles keeps your mind alert and flexible.	
2. One Alzheime's specialist indicates that doing a crossword puzzle daily keeps your memory from going down the tubes.	
3. The challenge of trying to think of a synonym for "nimble" forces you to concentrate like crazy until finally you come up with the word *quick*.	
4. The word you come up with may not fit into the grid; then you have to come up with another word.	
5. It's that heavy-duty concentration that stretches your head and keeps it OK.	
6. The trickier the puzzle, the more your head busts itself and the more it remains young.	

7. Making friends is important for staying young, too.

8. Most of my friends have a fit when I tell them how much I like crossword puzzles.

9. The beauty of exercise is that you can do it alone and at home, unlike tennis or mountain climbing, which are cool exercises mostly for your physical body and must be done with another person or away from home.

10. If you have never tried doing a crossword puzzle, start now; you'll have a ball while stimulating your brain.

Unit Collaborative Assignment

Pair up with a classmate. One person should read the following paragraph aloud. Discuss how the paragraph can be improved according to what you have learned in this unit. Check the following:

- Does it have a discussible topic sentence?
- Does it stick to the point?
- Does it prove the point or merely repeat it? (Does it include enough details to prove the point?)
- Are all of the sentences linked so that the reader can easily follow the train of thought?

Then, you and your partner should work together to rewrite the paragraph, making sure that its sentences stick to the point, prove the point, and are smoothly linked.

When I was about five years old, my dream was to be an astronaut and explore unknown paths in space. I can remember, as a little boy, climbing onto the roof of my house to stare at the stars, wishing that I might touch these gleaming lights and hold them in my hands. I wondered what it would be like to travel past the stars.

My sights began to turn to new subjects, and this childish dream faded away. Then I have devoted much time to my studies. I always wanted to make my parents happy with my good grades; it was the reason that I looked forward to report card day. I thought that if it was my parents' wish that I go to college, then so be it; I would go. My boyhood dream took on purpose on December 7, 1995, when the *Galileo* space probe plunged into Jupiter's atmosphere. As I watched this historic event on television, I decided to study space science and become an engineer or computer specialist. My boyhood dream would become a reality.

Unit Writing Assignment

Choose one of the topics listed below. In your journal, gather ideas about your chosen topic by freewriting, brainstorming, or clustering. On a separate sheet of paper, develop a strong paragraph, observing the guidelines that follow the list of topics.

1. A memorable outdoor experience
2. What you would like to know about your ancestors (in addition to what you already know)
3. A significant conflict you had with your parents
4. How luck can be as important as hard work in being successful
5. A time when you felt totally alone and abandoned
6. An experience with racism or prejudice
7. The importance of recycling
8. Your reaction to a recent newspaper headline story
9. The sports figure you most admire
10. A Fourth of July (or another holiday) you remember

Guidelines for Writing

- Begin with a discussible topic sentence.
- Support the topic sentence with appropriate examples, testimony, reasons, or personal observations.
- Stick to your topic sentence.
- Link your sentences smoothly.

This is what one student wrote about topic #3:

Where fashion is concerned, my mother and I live in two different worlds. Mom still lives in the Victorian Age, when women who didn't wear long sleeves and long dresses were considered vulgar. The other day I was leaving our house in a hurry, on my way to geography class, when my mother yelled, "Jessica, your dress barely hides your bottom. Can't you wear something more discreet?" The fact is that my outfit consisted of a pale blue silk skirt, topped by a white cotton tee shirt. The majority of attractive girls in college were wearing outfits just like mine, and these girls aren't sluts. Most of them study hard to get on the honor roll and they avoid lewd behavior with the males on campus. But style is style, and you're either "with it" or you're not. On a hot day, we female students don't want to wear black gabardine pants, which is what Mom loves for me to wear. I told her, "Mom, it's a hot day, and I want to feel cool and comfortable, especially while I'm studying on the campus patio." But Mom has no use for fashion. All that matters to her is that I look "decent." That means looking like the frumpiest, dowdiest person on campus. The really popular girls wear miniskirts that end about 10 inches above the knee. But they make sure that they sit with their knees together and they avoid bending over in public; observing these rules is part of the protocol of wearing miniskirts. When Mom kept getting more and more vehement about how "awful" I looked and how I was a "disgrace to the family," I finally roared out of the house and found refuge in my car on the way to school, where my girlfriends would understand my fashion statement.

Photo Writing Assignment

The person in the following picture is obviously trying to achieve a unique look. Ask yourself these questions: How far are you willing to go make a fashion statement about your uniqueness? How do you know when you've gone over the top? What is your reaction to the person whose taste is extravagant? What is likely to be the backlash of a style that is too revealing? Make sure that your writing has a discussible topic sentence, is supported by appropriate evidence, sticks to the point, and contains smoothly linked sentences.

18 Revising Paragraphs

"First drafts are nothing more than a crude beginning. They're not supposed to satisfy."

Do writers generally turn out flawless text on the first try? The answer is a loud and clear "No!" Over the years, many writers have left behind much testimony about their working habits. We know from this record that nearly all writers repeatedly rewrite their work.

One of our favorite quotations about the importance of rewriting comes from the French writer Antoine de Saint-Exupéry, author of *The Little Prince*:

> Whenever I hear an echo, years later, from an article of mine in . . . a newspaper, it is always, always an article that I rewrote thirty times. When I read a quotation of my own somewhere, it is always, always, always a phrase I rewrote twenty-five times.

The lesson here is simple: If your first draft doesn't satisfy you, don't be disappointed. First drafts are nothing more than a crude beginning. They're not supposed to satisfy. Indeed, if you are totally pleased with your first draft, you're most likely being too easy on yourself. Of course, you could have gotten lucky. It is possible to write a good paragraph on the first try, just as it is possible to be hit on the head by a meteorite. However, neither event is very likely.

What Is Revision?

Imagine you're cleaning your room. How would you logically proceed? First, you'd probably pick up clothes, trash, and dishes coated with dried-up food. Then you'd make your bed and vacuum. The last thing you would do is dust and polish the furniture. In other words, you would do the biggest jobs first and the smallest ones last.

The same logic applies to rewriting. First comes the big step: checking that you have developed your topic sentence with enough good details, deleting sentences that don't stick to the point, and inserting links between sentences. Smaller changes—called *editing*—involve correcting errors in grammar, punctuation, and spelling, and are made throughout the writing process. Inside the front cover of this book are the revising and editing checklists that you should consult before submitting your paper. Both tasks fall under the broad heading of *rewriting*. The third draft aims at editing the language for grammar, punctuation, spelling, and capitalization errors—as covered in Units 4–15 and in Units 19–24. To edit, use the Editing Checklist inside the front cover of this book, next to the Revising Checklist. For now we shall concentrate on revising.

Of course, few student writers can afford to rewrite their work 25 or 30 times as Saint-Exupéry did. A more practical goal is three drafts. The first draft is the original composition. The second draft concentrates on revising—doing the big job. The third draft aims at editing the language for grammar, punctuation, spelling, and capitalization errors.

To help you revise your paragraphs, use the Revising Checklist inside the front cover of this book. Note that the checklist tells you the unit that you will need to review if you're unsure of how to answer a particular question. Don't be reluctant to go back and review an earlier unit. Indeed, the practical advice in those units is more likely to sink in only after you actually try to apply it to your own writing. To learn is to do; to do is to learn.

Using Talk Skills to Revise Your Work

If you are a native speaker, talking can help with revision. Start by reading the work **aloud** to a partner or friend. Reading aloud forces you to pay attention to every word and not skip any sentence or passage. It also helps you to hear how your writing might sound to someone else.

To use talk skills to revise your written work, take the following steps:

1. Read your first draft aloud to yourself or to a friend.
2. Ask your friend what you can do to improve it.
3. Apply every question on the Revising Checklist to your first draft.
4. Make changes to the draft as you or your friend thinks of them.
5. If you don't understand a question on the checklist, review the appropriate unit until you do.

Naturally, if you're working with someone in your class, you will have to take turns going over each other's material. Be patient with each other. The mutual give-and-take will help you both learn how to revise.

If you must work alone, follow the same steps given above. If you feel funny about reading your work aloud, do it in private. Reading your work aloud lets you use your speaker's ear to help judge the writing.

Finally, don't be afraid to scribble mercilessly over your first draft. Scratch out and rewrite sentences to your heart's content. First drafts are supposed to look as if they'd been beaten up. If yours is clean and nice, ask yourself honestly, "Have I suddenly struck gold or am I being too easy on myself?"

Here is an example of a paragraph that needs to be revised:

> Petulia is a pet iguana that perches on my shoulder whenever I go out. I keep her in my apartment. People who see us together stare at me as if I were crazy. Unfortunately, many people are repulsed at the idea that I actually have a reptile as a pet. Even my roommate screams at me, "Get that horrid critter out of our place." He is especially angry when he sees Petulia climbing the wall of our shower stall just when he wants to take a shower. Most people have this illogical fear of snakes and lizards, probably because they think that most of them are poisonous. If you give an iguana the affection and attention it wants, it will respond by entertaining you and being wonderful company. Petulia is so tame that she waddles alongside me on a leash. My roommate, along with many other people, needs to broaden his mind about what makes a good pet. I wouldn't trade Petulia for any cat or dog I know. Not that I don't like dogs and cats. I do. I used to have a beautiful little Yorkshire terrier who was so smart that at dinnertime he would hop onto the chair next to me, hoping for a treat.

The student writer applied the Revising Checklist, going over the paragraph point by point. She found major problems with this paragraph. First, it has no discussible topic sentence. Second, it lacks unity; some sentences are off the topic. To revise, the student made four changes: (1) She added a discussible topic sentence. (2) She moved up the sentence on why people fear reptiles to where it fits better and takes on more importance. (3) She added transitional words to link her ideas to the rest of the paragraph. (4) She deleted the material about the Yorkshire terrier because it was off the topic.

Here is the paragraph after these revisions were made:

> In spite of how people feel about reptiles, I have found that iguanas make great pets. I keep a pet iguana in my apartment. Her name is Petulia, and she perches on my shoulder whenever I go out. Of course, people who see us together stare at me as if I were crazy. Most people have this illogical fear of snakes and lizards, probably because they think that most of them are poisonous. But if you give an iguana the affection and attention it wants, it will respond by entertaining you and being wonderful company. In fact, Petulia is so tame that she waddles alongside me on a leash. Unfortunately, many people are repulsed at the idea that I actually have a reptile as a pet. Even my roommate screams at me, "Get that horrid critter out of our place." He is especially angry when he sees Petulia climbing the wall of our shower stall just when he wants to take a shower. My roommate, along with many other people, needs to broaden his mind about what makes a good pet. Despite the negative comments made about her, I wouldn't trade Petulia for any cat or dog I know.

PRACTICE 1

Here are four passages that need to be revised. Work on them either alone or, if your teacher approves, with a classmate. In either case, read the paragraph aloud and use the Revising Checklist to help you revise it.

(1)

"Damn Jap!" Did I hear right? From the scowl on his face, I must have. But I could not understand what I had done to deserve this ugly label. It was incomprehensible to me that someone who did not know me could make such a demeaning comment when I had done nothing. I was stunned. People should not hurt others by using racial slurs. This incident revealed the sheer power that two words can have and their ability to hurt. This was my first experience with racism, and it changed my perception of the world. I grew up in a diverse neighborhood in North Hollywood among African Americans, Caucasians, Latinos, and Asians. I knew that a generation before I was born in the United States, my native country had been at war with Japan, the faraway land from which my mother's parents had come. He might have some lingering prejudices from World War II. But I was just as American as anyone in this melting pot of a country, the U.S.A. I thought of myself as a patriotic American, but obviously this man did not see me that way. It was not the last time that I was to hear a racial slur. The point, though, is that I decided to make sure that I myself would not succumb to stereotyping others. I would work hard at appreciating every individual, separate from his or her stereotype. By the way, I have included ethnic studies in my curriculum so that I can better understand the different cultures that compose our nation. I also work in a Thai restaurant that employs Thai-Americans and LatinoAmericans, whom I have come to regard as my second family.

(2)

Different people learn lessons about life differently. Many people learn from other people's mistakes, but in my opinion, the majority of people learn lessons about their lives from their own mistakes, and some learn from their personal experiences. Every person knows that life is a long journey, and it is filled with experiences that help people to understand more about the meaning of life. I believe that everybody in this world has had an incident or an experience that taught him or her an important lesson about life, and I am one who has had a memorable experience, which I shall never forget. It happened while I was babysitting the Geyer family's four-year-old child, Wally. While eating, he choked on a green bean. His face turned red, then blue, and he kept gasping for air. In my first aid class, I had learned the Heimlich maneuver, and I used it on Wally—grabbing him from behind and vigorously squeezing below his diaphragm, with the result that he spit up the green bean and started to breathe normally. It felt really good to have learned something so useful in class.

(3)

I have a cousin who loves using our family gatherings to discuss the latest family scandals. She gets a kick out of blabbing about anything bad that has happened to the family. She makes me so mad. At one Thanksgiving dinner, she went on and on about how terrible it was that Uncle Mark was leaving Aunt Gertrude for another woman. I was furious with her. We already felt bad enough about the situation without hearing about the secret phone calls he had been caught making and the expensive gifts that showed up on credit card bills. This cousin uses our family reunions as a pulpit to expose any family wrongdoings. She makes me so angry. I think that when a member of the family has a personal problem, it should stay that way—personal—not broadcast to everyone. Let the people involved work it out themselves or get professional help. Gossiping about the matter only makes it worse. Gossiping is such a bad habit.

(4)

It is difficult to look up to a leader who lies and cheats. George Washington was the founding father of our nation, and Abraham Lincoln liberated the slaves. Richard Nixon never received the full admiration of American citizens after his Watergate affair. If he had just told the truth about breaking into the Watergate apartments to find out what his enemies were up to, he might have recovered his reputation. The television evangelist Jim Bakker lost all credibility with his audiences once they found out that he had had an affair with a church secretary. How could a religious person preach morality and have an affair? For that matter, how can religious leaders be seen with drug peddlers, drunks, and convicted murderers? Even a charismatic leader like John F. Kennedy lost some of his popularity once the newspapers revealed how he had had affairs with various women, including Marilyn Monroe, who happens to be one of my favorite actresses. The public will forgive a popular leader's character faults, but the leader must admit them and show some repentance. Personally, I am not that forgiving.

Getting Rid of Wordiness

Wordiness means the overuse of words to make a point. Usually it has one of two causes. The first is editorial carelessness. The writer has simply not read and edited the material closely enough to catch the wordy passage. A more likely cause is the desire to pad the paragraph because the writer is aware that it is too skimpy. Revision is the answer in both cases. If your material is too brief, the answer is to learn and include more details on your topic. Merely adding words without adding substance won't help. Writing is a more concise kind of communication than talking. Rambling in writing generally stands out more than rambling in speech.

ESL Advice!

Many cultures associate a flowery style with politeness. It is not so with English. Do not make the mistake of thinking that you are being impolite if you write in a plain, direct style.

Here are some examples of wordiness:

Wordy: Because of the fact that Mona loved jewelry that is white in color, she begged and pleaded for a pearl necklace.

Revised: Because Mona loved white jewelry, she begged for a pearl necklace.

Wordy: If you promise to tell me the true facts and relevant details about yourself, I'll be grateful.

Revised: If you promise to tell me the truth about yourself, I'll be grateful.

Wordy: According to my opinion, a house that is square in shape lacks charm.

Revised: A square house lacks charm.

Wordy: Christmas is a tradition that people all over the world of every class and creed and color celebrate everywhere you go for as long as anyone can remember.

Revised: Christmas is a worldwide tradition.

There are some word combinations that are simply unnecessary. Here are some examples:

Young [in age]

Oval [in shape]

Red [in color]

At 5:00 A.M. [in the early morning]

A sour[-tasting] lemonade

There are also some well-known phrases that can be replaced by single words:

In this day and age	Today
Forever and always	Forever
With a serious attitude	Seriously
Involving a lot of money	Expensive

Some words should be avoided because they are meaningless. You may use these words unconsciously, like clearing your throat. Here are some examples:

kind of	really	basically	actually
generally	practically	various	

Check out this sentence:

> Professor Block *kind of* knows his subject, but *basically* I wish he would lighten up his lectures to *really* keep my attention.

Get rid of the italicized words, and the sentence is now short and snappy:

> Professor Block knows his subject, but I wish he would lighten up his lectures to keep my attention.

Your effort to avoid wordiness should always be based on an attempt to substitute substance for fluff. Say what you have to say, but say it crisply.

PRACTICE 2

Rewrite the following sentences to make them less wordy.

1. If only she had listened to me and worn a dress bright red in color.

   ____

2. In our opinion, we think that gas is getting too expensive in price.

   ____

3. My boss gave me a watch for the purpose of celebrating my birthday.

   ____

4. At the age of five years old, Michael Jackson already sang and danced like a dream.

   ____

5. When I get married, I would like to buy a house located in the vicinity of my parents' home.

   ____

6. My youngest sister came as an unexpected surprise to our family.

   ____

7. Dear Sir: Enclosed herewith in this letter you will find my check for $20.

   ____

8. The September 11, 2001, attack on the World Trade Center was a serious and terrible crisis for our country.

   ____

9. Some people never learn; they just repeat again the same mistake.

   ____

10. The computer is our century's greatest new innovation.

____

11. Actually, I'm sure that I can name practically everyone on our swim team.

____

12. It's a true fact that sugar causes tooth decay.

____

13. Generally, Liam speaks English without an accent.

____

14. Poor Elissa kept running all over campus in a confused state.

____

15. In this day and age, everyone should know how to use e-mail.

____

Unit Test

In the blank provided, fill in the word that best completes the sentence.

Example: First drafts are nothing more than a crude beginning.

1. Most writers do not turn out ________ copy on first try.
2. Does my topic sentence make a ________ point? (from the Revising Checklist)
3. Do I support my topic sentence with strong ________? (from the Revising Checklist)
4. Do I ________ to my point? (from the Revising Checklist)
5. Do I ________ my point or merely repeat it? (from the Revising Checklist)
6. Do I link the ________ of my paragraph? (from the Revising Checklist)
7. Do I use ________ English throughout? (from the Revising Checklist)
8. Talking can help with revision. Start by reading the work aloud to ________.
9. To cut wordiness from your writing requires ________.
10. Don't be afraid to mess up your first draft by ________ on it.

Unit Talk–Write Assignment

The *Talk* column reflects a conversation between two college women—J and M. Using what you learn from their discussion and ideas of your own on the subject of dieting and diet drugs, draft a paragraph in the *Write* column. Then, using the Revising Checklist, turn the draft into a polished paragraph on a separate sheet of paper.

TALK	WRITE
J: Can you believe they've come out with another diet drug?	
M: You mean like fen-phen?	
J: You got it! What a drag! Now we can expect some more heart disease or cancer or heaven knows what awful side effects.	
M: I have to say, kiddo, I'd love to take a pill that would just burn off the fat. I love to eat and I get so ticked off with my weight!	
J: Oh, get off it; you're thin, bordering on sickly looking.	
M: Oh yeah? In your dreams. Anyway, what's the new stuff called?	

J: Meridia. And I read that instead of boosting the production of seratonin—the way fen-phen did—it slows down the loss of seratonin.

M: I don't understand all the scientific gobbledy-gook. All I want to know is that it works. Is it expensive?

J: $3 a day.

M: Did you read about any side effects?

J: Yeah, the FDA says that it can increase blood pressure.

M: Hmmm, I'd love to try it, but I'm scared. Thin and dead wouldn't be much fun.

J: People oughta just eat moderately and take a 20-minute brisk walk every day and forget about these so-called miracle weight loss pills.

M: At least, I hope that the pharmaceutical company that makes Meridia will educate doctors to use it with only patients whose weight is life threatening.

Unit Collaborative Assignment

Join with two or three classmates to write a paragraph. First, choose one of the topic sentences from the list below.

1. Attending college is a privilege.
2. People love to watch the Academy Awards because they are fascinated by celebrities.
3. Conforming to high school dress styles is the rule for students.
4. It's OK for men to cry.
5. Every person should pay a flat 10 percent federal income tax to avoid so much chaos at tax filing time.
6. Suicide bombers seem to be in love with death.
7. Unless the downtown areas of cities are kept up, they will deteriorate quickly.
8. I would love to observe our world from a distant planet.
9. I find TV advertising a nuisance when it interrupts the football game I'm watching.
10. Most of us consider independence a virtue, but it has its faults.

Now, do a little brainstorming for details to support the topic sentence. Have one participant write down everyone's ideas. Discuss the ideas and choose the ones that best support the topic sentence. Expand the ideas into complete sentences. Make sure that each sentence supports the topic sentence without being repetitious. Finally, link your sentences with transitions. After you have developed a written paragraph, read it aloud and apply the Revising Checklist. Revise the paragraph further.

Unit Writing Assignment

Write about the importance of the family, whether it consists of one parent, of grandparents and other relatives, or of a mother and a father. You might want to explore the following questions:

1. Was the concept of family important in your upbringing?
2. What are some of your special family memories?
3. What values (e.g., honesty, hard work, tolerance) should a family teach children?
4. What impact has the day care center had on the modern family?
5. According to the 2000 U.S. census, the traditional family, in which children live with both their mother and father, is now a

minority of households. How does this change affect the way you think about the family?

Use the Revising Checklist to make sure that your writing sticks to the point, proves the point, and progresses smoothly, without unnecessary repetition.

Photo Writing Assignment

This photo won a prize for being among the best in the 2003 World Press Photo contest. Observe the photo carefully and write a paragraph in which you answer the following questions: What is the overall impression of the photo (your topic sentence)? How would you describe the father and son featured here? What thoughts are going through their minds? What do you imagine the surroundings to look like in Najaf, Iraq, where the photo was shot? Read your paragraph aloud, and then review your work against the Revising Checklist.

19 Punctuation You Can Hear

"Charlie, will you please close the door?"

Punctuation marks are the traffic signs of writing. They tell the reader when to slow down, when to speed up, and when to stop. In writing, punctuation marks direct eye movement across the page. In spoken sentences, punctuation is heard as pauses, upbeats, and downbeats.

Indeed, you can definitely hear some punctuation marks. For example, say the following sentences out loud:

> You are going home.
>
> You are going home?
>
> You are going home!

If you listen carefully to yourself, you will notice that you ended the first sentence on a flat note, the second on an upbeat, and the third on a downbeat. These spoken cues help us tell the difference between a statement, a question, and a command.

In this unit, we will discuss punctuation marks you can hear. These marks include end punctuation (periods, question marks, exclamation points), commas, and apostrophes. You can trust your speaker's ear to help you use these punctuation marks correctly.

ESL Advice!

If you can't hear these punctuation marks, you should memorize the rules.

End Punctuation

All sentences end with a period, a question mark, or an exclamation point. There are no exceptions to this rule.

Period (.)

Use a period after a sentence that makes a statement:

My mother lost her wallet.

Her car is in the garage.

Question Mark (?)

Use a question mark after direct questions:

Where did the sunshine go?

Have you seen my pen?

The question mark is not used after an indirect question:

Mary asked where the sunshine had gone.

John wondered if we had seen his pen.

Exclamation Point (!)

Use an exclamation point to show intense emotion, such as happiness, surprise, anger, or disgust, or to give a strong command:

What a fabulous day!

Get out of my house!

IN A NUTSHELL

- Use a period at the end of a statement or indirect question.
- Use a question mark with direct questions.
- Use an exclamation point to indicate strong emotion or to give a command.

PRACTICE 1

Place the proper punctuation mark at the end of each sentence.

Example: What would you do without me**?**

1. Is long hair on men attractive to women
2. I was very happy to hear about his grades

3. Save the whales
4. Is she as calm as she seems
5. They asked whether we would be at home
6. Watch out
7. We waited in line for 40 minutes
8. Are you driving or flying
9. Using your imagination, describe your ideal vacation
10. What an incredible bargain

Comma (,)

You hear the comma as a half-pause. Sometimes the comma just makes listening or reading easier, but sometimes it is crucial to meaning, as shown in these examples:

Trying to escape, Alexander Gordon ran out the door.

Trying to escape Alexander, Gordon ran out the door.

As we watched, Patsy Sue dived off the tallest board.

As we watched Patsy, Sue dived off the tallest board.

The huge difference in the meanings of these sentences depends on where the comma is placed. In the first sentence, *Alexander Gordon* is trying to escape an unknown someone or something. In the second, *Gordon* is trying to escape *Alexander*. In the third sentence, *Patsy Sue* dived off the board, whereas in the fourth, *Sue* did the diving.

We shall cover the hard-and-fast rules of comma usage.

Place a comma in front of coordinating conjunctions (and, but, or, for, nor, so, yet) that link independent clauses (see pp. 000–000).

He dodged the cold germs, but he caught pneumonia.

My mother is an accountant, and my father is her assistant.

He spoke with authority, so I believed him.

Do not use a comma before *and* if it is not followed by an independent clause.

Incorrect:	He did the laundry, and made dinner.
Correct:	He did the laundry and made dinner.
Correct:	He did the laundry, and he made dinner.

PRACTICE 2

Finish the following sentences by adding another independent clause and a coordinating conjunction. Remember to use a comma.

Example: The house she lived in was small, ***but it was wonderfully cozy.***

1. Be kind to all animals ______________________
2. I drive by that house daily ______________________
3. On Christmas we always stay home ______________________
4. I sat in the barber's chair ______________________
5. I believe life exists on other planets ______________________
6. My mother baked bread every Tuesday ______________________
7. The book was filled with pictures ______________________
8. Most repair people are honest ______________________
9. The embers glowed in the fireplace ______________________
10. She will probably break down and cry ______________________

Use a comma after introductory words, phrases, and dependent clauses at the beginning of a sentence.

Words: Furthermore, he received a big bonus.

Well, why don't you move out?

Louise, I did it.

Phrases: From the point of view of health, he was perfect.

Having lost everything, I really did not care what happened.

By the way, your mother called.

Clauses: Because it was raining, we stayed home.

(Use a comma after a dependent clause only if it comes at the beginning, but not the end, of a sentence.)

but

We stayed home because it was raining.

If I win the lottery, I will buy you the car.

but

I will buy you the car if I win the lottery.

IN A NUTSHELL

Use commas after introductory words, phrases, and dependent clauses at the beginning of a sentence.

PRACTICE 3

Insert commas, if necessary, in the following sentences.

1. Yes they can use the camping site.
2. As far as I am concerned everyone is invited.
3. Though feeling awkward John continued to dance.
4. Okay I'll work Saturday.
5. Elizabeth when are you leaving?
6. Moreover you owe me an apology for being late.
7. From behind the curtain he could not see his brother.
8. If you study the history of Russia you will understand why the peasants rebelled.
9. First of all none of us knows the future.
10. Scoring 15 points he led the team.
11. We decided to return home since it was getting late.
12. Furthermore he will land in the hospital by tomorrow.
13. As we watched the TV screen we saw the missile explode in the air.
14. No you did not offend me with your remark.
15. Because you are a Latina you can translate the Spanish for us.

PRACTICE 4

Insert commas where needed. In the space provided, state the rule that makes the comma necessary.

Correction: Mike, we were truly disappointed in your performance.

Rule: ***A comma follows an introductory word.***

1. When students succeed in their studies they bring joy to their teachers.

   Rule: ______________________________

   ____

2. From the street we could see the flag at half mast.

   Rule: ______________________________

   ____

3. We went to the movies and then we stopped for coffee.

   Rule: ______________________________

   ____

4. If they had given us the right directions we would not have gotten lost.

   Rule: ____

   ____

5. Furthermore he had no right to open her mail.

   Rule: ____

   ____

6. Well why did you lend him the money if you knew that he wouldn't repay you?

   Rule: ____

   ____

7. Yes, she is my cousin. No she does not speak English.

   Rule: ____

   ____

8. He earns a good salary yet he doesn't have any savings.

   Rule: ____

   ____

9. Are you stopping at the mall or are you going straight home?

   Rule: ____

   ____

10. While we were watching the waves come in we saw a whale.

    Rule: ____

    ____

Use commas to separate items in a series.

We ate steak, baked potatoes, and sweet corn.

The thick, juicy steak hit the spot.

You can read a book, watch television, or go to bed.

Up the road, through the woods, and along the river they trudged.

Do not, however, use commas unnecessarily with words in a series.

Do not use a comma before *and* if only two items are mentioned.

Incorrect: He plays the piano, and the trumpet.

Correct: He plays the piano and the trumpet.

Do not use a comma between modifiers unless you can insert the word *and* between them.

Incorrect: The old, red rowboat finally sank.

Correct: The old red rowboat finally sank.

You wouldn't say *The old and red rowboat finally sank,* so you shouldn't use a comma.

You would, however, use a comma between the modifiers of this sentence:

A cold, bitter wind blew off the lake.

You could insert the word *and* between the modifiers, and the sentence would still sound right.

A cold and bitter wind blew off the lake.

Do not use a comma before the first item in a series or after the last.

Incorrect: Other reasons not to smoke include, the smell, the expense, and the inconvenience.

Correct: Other reasons not to smoke include the smell, the expense, and the inconvenience.

Incorrect: You can add chocolate chips, raisins, or nuts, to the cookie batter.

Correct: You can add chocolate chips, raisins, or nuts to the cookie batter.

PRACTICE 5

Insert commas as necessary to separate items in a series.

1. They complain morning noon and night.
2. Give me some rollers a hairbrush and a blow dryer to make her look stylish.
3. I will climb the highest mountain swim the deepest ocean and struggle through the darkest jungle for a raise.
4. I need a hammer a saw and some nails.
5. The punch has 7-Up lemonade and sliced oranges in it.
6. Not everyone thought that the dinner was tasty well priced and nutritious.
7. Pick one from column A one from column B and one from column C.
8. Would you like potatoes rice or beans?

9. The professor entered the room piled his books on the desk and began to hand out our papers.
10. I never watch anything on television except the news the movie reviews and the weather.

PRACTICE 6

In the following sentences, strike through the unnecessary commas.

Example: The elderly gentleman took off his hat, and sat down.

1. All of us need love, challenging work, and a sense of purpose, to be happy.
2. Give me some loyal, and amusing friends.
3. The kinds of textbooks that I can't stand include, economics, finance, and math.
4. My first, real bicycle still sits in the attic.
5. Go ahead and serve the hors d'oeuvres, the salad, and the lemonade, before the guest of honor arrives.
6. Don't you enjoy listening to Elvis Presley, and the Beatles?
7. Other factors that make for pleasant camping include, smooth ground, leafy trees, and a running stream.
8. The old, Ford convertible sat in the garage.
9. My whole family plays tennis, and basketball.
10. For the picnic, we need, paper plates, napkins, and ants.

Place commas around parenthetical elements that interrupt the flow of a sentence.

In speaking, it is natural to pause before and after words that interrupt the flow of thought. In writing, this pause is signaled by a comma. These interruptions—called parenthetical elements because they can be included in parentheses without affecting the meaning of the sentence—include any expression, phrase, aside, or other remark not essential to your meaning. The commas, in effect, take the place of parentheses. Here are some examples:

Expression:	She is, of course, a very thoughtful person.
	Registration for the class is, unfortunately, closed.
	You understand, by the way, that I have no other choice.
Descriptive phrases:	We struggled, cold and wet, to climb the mountain.

	I'll ask Milo, our neighbor, if he wants the tickets.
	The governor, running for re-election, shook hands with everyone.
Nonessential clauses that begin with *who, whose, which, when,* or *where.*	Mr. Jones, who wore a striped suit, caught a fly ball at the baseball game.

Here are other examples:

My Aunt Matilda, whose pickled beets won first prize, waved at me.

The Hope Botanical Gardens, where flowers bloom all year long, is open to the public.

My days off, when I get such breaks, are cluttered with chores.

The report, which took two weeks to write, earned Henry a promotion.

All the above clauses contain nonessential information—that is, information that can be deleted without changing the meaning of the sentence—and are therefore punctuated as parenthetical elements by commas.

On the other hand, a clause introduced by *who, whose, which, when, where*, or *that* containing information that is *essential* to understanding the sentence is not punctuated by commas:

The man who wore the striped suit got hit by a baseball.

Now the information in the clause is essential to identify who got hit by the baseball—the man in the striped suit, not the man in the gray suit.

Here are some other examples of essential *who, whose, which, when, where* clauses:

The aunt whose pickled beets won first prize is Aunt Matilda.	**(It wasn't Aunt Minnie's beets that won.)**
The Hope Botanical Gardens are where flowers bloom all year long; they are open to the public.	**(The Brooklyn Botanical Gardens do not have flowers that bloom all year long.)**
The rains began the week when I was away.	**(The rains did not fall during the weeks when the writer was home.)**
The report that took two weeks to write earned Henry a promotion.	**(It was the report that took two weeks to write, not some other report.)**

Notice in this last sentence that *which* changed to *that.* Nonessential clauses referring to things are introduced with the relative pronoun *which*, while essential clauses referring to things are introduced with the relative pronoun *that*. Use commas with nonessential *which* clauses; do not use commas with essential *that* clauses. Here are some more examples:

Commas needed:	The band repeatedly played "One Love," which I'd never heard before.
Commas not needed:	The band repeatedly played a song that I'd never heard before.

In the first sentence, that the band repeatedly played "One Love" is the main point. The fact that the writer had never heard that song before is not important, so the information is set off with *which* and commas. In the second sentence, the main idea is that the song the band was playing was one the writer had never heard before, so *that* is used and the information is not punctuated with commas.

Commas needed:	My Chevy convertible, which I usually drive to work, is in the garage.
Commas not needed:	The car that I drive to work is in the garage.

The first sentence says that the writer's Chevy convertible is in the garage; that he drives this car to work is not information that is essential to identifying it, so the phrase is set off with *which* and commas. The second sentence specifies that the car in the garage is the one the writer drives to work—not the one his wife drives. Since this is essential information, *that* is used and the information is not punctuated by commas.

You can usually "hear" the interruption in a parenthetical element. When you can't, context will tell you whether a clause is essential or nonessential. Consider this sentence:

> The job fair, which was held in Sanders Hall, was very successful.

This sentence is fine if only one job fair was held. But if there were two job fairs, one held in Sanders Hall and the other in Prentiss Hall, then the above sentence would be written and punctuated this way:

> The job fair that (not *which*) was held in Sanders Hall was very successful. (But the one that was held in Prentiss Hall was a flop.)

IN A NUTSHELL

- Use commas to set off expressions and phrases that interrupt a sentence.
- Use commas to set off clauses that contain information that is not essential to understanding the sentence.

PRACTICE 7

Use commas to set off the nonessential interruptions in these sentences. If the sentence is correct, leave it alone.

Example: My uncle Albert, who is my favorite relative, is here tonight.

1. Mr. Clark of course is running for mayor.
2. Professor Robinson whom we really admire won the Best Teacher Award.
3. The incision which left a large scar needed plastic surgery.
4. Any official who takes a bribe should be ashamed.
5. The sky filled with billowy white clouds made me want to write a poem.
6. Our next-door neighbor who was a nice man often chatted with me over the fence.
7. My uncle who served in two major wars still has his uniforms.
8. The old family home where my brother now lives needs remodeling.
9. Who owns the Honda Civic that is blocking the driveway?
10. Give this ticket to the man who is standing at the gate and to no one else.
11. Get out of the shack that is going up in flames!
12. Mrs. Gomez who is the assistant manager of the local Bank of America explained my bounced check to me.
13. We each carried a pack that weighed over 100 pounds.
14. My pack which weighed over a hundred pounds made the hike tiring.
15. Roses with their wonderful fragrance are a fit symbol for love.

PRACTICE 8

Underline the words that interrupt the flow of the sentence, then place commas around them.

Example: My brother, who always hated suits, wants a tuxedo for his birthday.

1. His father loved and respected by all members of the family just turned 85.
2. Her wedding expected for so many years took place last month.
3. Peter Dunkin who is very graceful and coordinated will be the lead dancer.
4. It is not by a long shot my first choice.

5. Old people often neglected by their families need community help to remain independent.

6. All the children in our neighborhood considered Harry the local bakery owner a great hero.

7. Dr. Jensen who gave the commencement address kept her audience entertained.

8. Pizza King especially on Friday nights is very busy.

9. All cultures you realize are becoming more and more technological.

10. She is by the way my aunt.

PRACTICE 9

Using context as your guide, cross out either *that* or *which* in the following clauses and punctuate them appropriately.

I own two sailboats, both sloops. One I race, the other I cruise. The sloop (that, which) I race is blue and old. The other sloop (that, which) I don't race but cruise is red with green trim. Both sloops are lovely. A sailor once offered to buy the sloop (that, which) I cruise for $10,000. I told him that he could have the old, blue sloop (that, which) I race for that price, but the sloop (that, which) I cruise is not for sale at any price.

Use commas for dates and addresses and in the openings and closings of letters.

Commas for separating items in a date:	My twentieth birthday party took place on Tuesday, March 14, 1999. On July 9, 2004, the entire balance on the car will be due.
Commas for separating items in an address:	Max lived at 15 Mangrove Avenue in Dallas, Texas, before he moved to Colorado. Alicia lives at 30 Munson Drive, Detroit, Michigan 40202. Mail the card to 1500 North Verdugo Road, Glendale, California 34525.
Commas in the openings and closings of letters:	Dearest Caroline, Dear Sir (or Madam), Yours truly, Sincerely,

Note: A comma follows the year in the date and the state in an address when the date or address is used within a sentence. No comma is needed to separate the state from the zip code.

IN A NUTSHELL

Use commas for dates and addresses and in the openings and closings of letters.

PRACTICE 10

Insert commas where needed below. Some of the entries may require no commas.

1. On Monday September 4 we celebrated Labor Day.
2. My dear Mrs. Wong I was delighted to receive your note.
3. We will stay at the campgrounds from Monday August 27 to Friday September 1 2005.
4. We moved from Huntington Beach to La Mirada.
5. Pasquale's Hair Salon has moved to 420 Camden Drive.
6. Her complete address is 489 Rock Road Apartment 3 Tampa Florida 34555.
7. Sincerely yours
8. They used to live at 6201 Main Street.
9. She's leaving for Lincoln Nebraska on Tuesday January 17.
10. Now she lives at 2322 Chevy Chase Drive Lansing Michigan.
11. He was born on Saturday May 7 1982 in Tucson Arizona.
12. Send Peter's mail to 933 Andover Street Worthington Ohio 43085.
13. We drove from Jackson Hole to Aspen.
14. Mary was born on August 12 1978 and Kevin was born on February 5 1983.
15. Is she from Miami Ohio or Miami Florida?

Use commas to set off direct quotations from the rest of the sentence.

A quotation may be either direct—exactly what someone said—or indirect—a report of what someone said.

Direct quotation:	"Forget you ever saw me," he whispered.
Indirect quotation:	He said that she should forget she had ever seen him.

Direct quotations can be reported in three ways, each requiring commas.

"Forget you ever saw me," he whispered.

"Forget," he whispered, "you ever saw me."

He whispered, "Forget you ever saw me."

Commas and periods always go inside the quotation marks.

PRACTICE 11

First turn the following indirect quotations into direct quotations. Then punctuate the direct quotations in the three ways taught in this section.

Example: She said that she was not going.

"I am," she said, "not going."

"I am not going," she said.

She said, "I am not going."

1. He said that you should try the dip with the banana chips.

____

____

____

2. Mary said that was not what she thought would happen.

____

____

____

3. Howard remarked that's how the game should be played.

____

____

____

4. Jennifer added that's what she was taught about the procedure.

____

____

____

5. Catherine snapped that she thought the movie was boring.

____

____

____

PRACTICE 12

Add commas to set off the quoted material from the rest of the sentence.

1. "Steve has a new job" he announced.
2. "The results" he announced "speak for themselves."
3. "I have never drunk anything stronger than Coca Cola" he replied.
4. Frederico insisted "It's a perfect day for the picnic."
5. The clerk said "Shoes and shirts are required."
6. "I ordered one deluxe pizza" she answered.
7. "I certainly didn't mean any harm" indicated Barry "but I had to tell the truth."
8. "Let's go downstairs and do the laundry" Linda suggested.
9. "Stacking the books on the shelf" he told Rhonda "is very time-consuming."
10. "They do not resemble each other one bit" he noted.

The Apostrophe (')

The apostrophe has two uses: to show possession and to indicate a contraction.

Use the apostrophe to show possession.

The chart below shows how apostrophes are used to show possession or ownership. For a singular noun, always add *'s*. However, to form the possessive of a plural noun ending in *s*, add only the apostrophe. If the plural does not end in *s*, add *'s*.

SINGULAR (ALWAYS ADD 'S)	PLURAL
the girl's notebook	the girls' notebooks
the bus's driver	the buses' drivers
the child's toy	the children's toys
Carl Keith's house	the Keiths' house
Ross's car	the Rosses' car
Mrs. Jones's house	the Joneses' house

PRACTICE 13

Turn the phrases below into possessives.

Example: the book of Jack

Answer: Jack**'s** book

1. the umbrella of Lucy

____

2. the fence of the garden

____

3. the victory of Luis

____

4. the anniversary of the Davises

____

5. the seat of the driver

____

6. the house of Mel

____

7. the meager food of the people

____

8. the car of James

____

9. the treatment of the doctor

____

10. the complaints of most guests

____

PRACTICE 14

Make the following italicized nouns possessive. First decide whether the noun is singular or plural. Then decide whether you need only an apostrophe or *'s*. Finally, change the singular possessive nouns to plural and the plural possessive nouns to singular.

Example: Max and Sara *Marcus* daughter

Answer: Max and Sara *Marcus***'s** daughter, the Marcuses' daughter

1. the *Smiths* law
2. the *lion* mane
3. the *firefighters* trucks
4. the *grass* color
5. the *men* hats
6. the *bus* horn
7. the *churches* bells

8. the *tulips* petals
9. the police *officers* promotions
10. *Louis* suspenders

PRACTICE 15

Rewrite each of the following pairs of sentences as one sentence by using a possessive.

Example: Fritz has a roommate. The roommate's name is Ivan.

The name of Fritz's roommate is Ivan.

1. Bert just bought a car. His car already has 150,000 miles on it.

____

2. Sanjay broke his shoulder. The shoulder causes him severe pain.

____

3. Moses wrote the Ten Commandments. These commandments should be obeyed by all people.

____

4. The Baumbachs have a huge garden. It requires daily work.

____

5. The geese left tracks in the mud. The tracks were clearly visible.

____

Use the apostrophe to show an omission in a contraction.

Apostrophes are used to show omitted letters in contractions, such as *don't* (do not) and *isn't* (is not). Contractions are commonly used in informal writing. Here are some common contractions:

can not	can't
could have	could've
could not	couldn't
did not	didn't
do not	don't
has not	hasn't
have not	haven't
he is	he's
I am	I'm
I would	I'd

it is	it's
she is	she's
should have	should've
should not	shouldn't
they are	they're
they are not	they aren't
who is	who's
will not	won't
would have	would've
would not	wouldn't
let us	let's

Don't trust your ear in punctuating contractions. Learn the rules.

In speech, we can hear these contractions. What we cannot hear is exactly where the apostrophe goes—where the letter was actually omitted.

couldn't (not could'nt)	**(the apostrophe marks the omission of the o)**
they're (not theyr'e)	**(the apostrophe marks the omission of the a)**

Remember to put the apostrophe exactly where the letter is missing.

It is, of course, important to learn the formal rules of contractions. But knowing when to use contractions and knowing when not to them are equally important. As a general rule, contractions are used in informal writing and hardly ever in academic writing. If you have a doubt about the appropriateness of contractions in your writing for a particular class, ask your instructor.

PRACTICE 16

Insert contractions in the following sentences whenever possible. Cross out the words being turned into contractions, and write the contraction in the space above the crossed-out word.

couldn't
Example: We ~~could not~~ remember their names.

1. Why in the world would you not want to help out?
2. We could not have studied harder.
3. Ten years from now it will not matter in the least.
4. They were not the least bit excited about being on television.
5. If Manny had not eaten, he would have offended the hostess.
6. Surely you could have been more tactful.

7. Why are they not meeting us at the movie?
8. If Felice had been polite, we would have included her.
9. She should not have said that.
10. Who is this funny man?

Do not use apostrophes unnecessarily.

1. Use an apostrophe only with a possessive.

Incorrect: Apple's are on sale this week.
Correct: Apples are on sale this week.

To test whether a noun is possessive or not, turn it into an *of* phrase.

The <u>book's cover</u> is red.	**(book's cover = cover of the book = possessive)**
The library <u>books' are</u> due.	**(books' are = the are of the books = not possessive)**

2. Do not use apostrophes with the pronouns *his*, *hers*, *its*, *ours*, *yours*, or *theirs*.

Incorrect: The sweater is hers'.
Correct: The sweater is hers.

Incorrect: The cat washed it's face.
Correct: The cat washed its face.

It's is a contraction—short for *it is*. If you unravel the contraction, you get:

The cat washed *it is* face.

This sentence makes no sense.

PRACTICE 17

Correct the following unnecessary apostrophes and insert the missing apostrophes in the following sentences.

1. My father always seems to buy cars' that are lemons.
2. It's hers' to lose and ours' to win.
3. She made three batches' of cookies.
4. She gave us our due and asked us to give them their's.
5. Its' not what you say, its what you do that counts'.
6. Johns' in a bad mood today.
7. My cats' very affectionate.

8. How you think about your future can be the key's to success.
9. The job of asking why is not yours'.
10. Cathys pet projects' all involve her garden.

IN A NUTSHELL

- Use the apostrophe to show possession.
- Use the apostrophe to mark omitted letters in a contraction.
- Do not use unnecessary apostrophes.

PRACTICE 18

Every sentence below has one apostrophe error. It may be missing an apostrophe (or *'s*) in a possessive or in a contraction. Sometimes the error is an unnecessary apostrophe. Add missing apostrophes (or *'s*), and strike out all unnecessary apostrophes.

1. You should add potatoes and bean's to the stew.
2. Werent you surprised to see Jenny's boyfriend there?
3. I think that the red convertible is Johns.
4. The mountain bike is her's.
5. I get two weeks of vacation this year.
6. That shirt is missing two button's.
7. Its not clear whether the party is at Jane's or Bill's house.
8. The job is your's if you want it.
9. Hanging by it's tail, the monkey chattered.
10. The volleyball players uniforms are purple and white.

PRACTICE 19

Insert an apostrophe where needed. In the line after each sentence, explain why the apostrophe is needed by writing a *P* for possessive or a *C* for contraction. Some sentences require more than one apostrophe.

1. Many peoples attitudes toward taxes have changed. ____
2. Theyre sick of having to clean up everyone elses mess. ____
3. Mothers worry is needless. ____
4. Which girl hasnt hung up her coat? ____

5. Doesnt it matter to you that they think you lied? ____
6. New Yorks tall buildings amaze visitors. ____
7. Her essays titles werent very imaginative. ____
8. His fathers fishing rod was in the garage. ____
9. The companys profits were at an all-time low. ____
10. Jeffs uncle is a nice person. ____

Unit Test

In the blank provided, write a *C* if the sentence is correctly punctuated or an *NC* if it is not correct. Correct the incorrect sentences.

Example: _***NC***_ When did they leave town.

1. _____ What could you possibly want from me!
2. _____ She asked when the wedding would take place?
3. _____ We bought all kinds of green vegetables but they rotted.
4. _____ You could of course, do the dishes.
5. _____ Since you prefer carrot cake I baked one for you.
6. _____ Birds fly, dogs bark, and bees buzz.
7. _____ Your need to bring, a flashlight, a sleeping bag, and some dried food.
8. _____ She was however unable to follow the directions.
9. _____ John whose last name is Abbott went first.
10. _____ We arrived worn out but happy at the summit of the mountain.
11. _____ Any mother, who loves her child, will be concerned with the child's diet.
12. _____ Dwight D. Eisenhower a general in World War II was also president of the United States.
13. _____ We graduated on Saturday, May 16 1999.
14. _____ The letter was sent to 926 Mayfair Lane, Columbus, Ohio.
15. _____ "Let's pledge allegiance to the flag," he said.
16. _____ "None of this would've happened" he said "if you'd swept the floor."
17. _____ That coat is not hers'; it's his.
18. _____ Its about time for you to grow up and quit whimpering.
19. _____ If you aren't sure, don't volunteer the answer.
20. _____ Its the Millers' back yard.

Unit Talk–Write Assignment

This assignment is about the current fad of body tattooing. The *Talk* column reflects one student's (Merrilee's) spirited defense of her own tattoos. We have deliberately scrambled the punctuation. Rewrite her sentences in the *Write* column, correcting all the punctuation errors, incomplete sentences, and nonstandard English. Then write a paragraph giving your views on the popularity of tattoos today.

TALK	WRITE
1. So I have three tattoos. So big deal.	
2. You can see the one on my shoulder. Its a springing tiger. The others—well theyre off-limits to everyone except my boyfriend.	
3. OK you guys grow up. Quit your stupid giggling. No Im not a druggie.	
4. Im just a modern girl. Thats it. Why do I get tattoos? Its my way of being me Merrilee a special person an individual not just another sheep in a big herd of sheep.	
5. My tattoos which are a form of expressing myself can be compared to the way some people always wear a certain perfume to be recognized by.	
6. The tiger, thats on my shoulder, lets the world know that somewhere on the inside Im ready to leap at my enemies and tear them apart.	

7. Maybe I sound mean or something but tigers are gorgeous animals.

8. And I think of myself as having a tigers courage.

9. Dont laugh everybody likes to be special.

10. In this robot world we need to establish our individuality.

Unit Collaborative Assignment

A. Dictate the following sentences to a partner, using pauses, upbeats, and downbeats to indicate the necessary punctuation. The goal of this exercise is for your partner to insert the appropriate punctuation mainly by ear, based on your reading.

1. Call me again you lovely man
2. Were you startled to see her
3. She took his advice so she drove to see her mother
4. I'll have scrambled eggs fried potatoes and toast
5. He told his soldiers This is your time to achieve glory
6. Sit down and then give the answer
7. Did you really see an eagle
8. Mrs. Gooch our student advisor said This should be (y)our goal
9. Lees car is a really sleek machine
10. Mr. Nelsons dog, which now weighs more than I do almost knocked me over

B. Punctuate the following sentences, using the same approach as in Exercise A, with your partner now doing the dictating.

1. Run for your life
2. How can you help our neighborhood
3. My fathers stamp collection however will go to my sister
4. Benjamin Franklin made his fortune as a printer editor inventor and a statesman
5. When did you move to South Dakota
6. Adams home is his castle
7. Theyre so much alike
8. I'm leaving at noon said Millie
9. Where are you going she asked and why cant I go with you
10. Shouldn't you be getting ready to leave

Unit Writing Assignment

Write a paragraph about what your best friend means to you. Include a conversation that is typical of your relationship. Be specific and focus particularly on the rules of punctuation that we have just covered. Use the Revising Checklist inside the front cover of this book to help you revise.

Photo Writing Assignment

This photo comes from the television show "American Idol," one of the so-called reality programs that some people find irresistibly addictive. The show features the judging of talent by a panel of experts and by millions of television viewers who are given an opportunity to vote on their favorite contestant by telephone. Write a paragraph giving your opinion on these new shows and saying what you like or dislike about them. You might bear in mind these questions: Why are talent shows so popular? How do they affect ordinary watchers? What, if any, yearnings in people can they fulfill or destroy? Begin the paragraph by stating your opinion in a topic sentence. (If you don't watch "American Idol" or prefer to write about another reality television program, do so.) Check your punctuation, and use the Revising Checklist to help you revise.

20 Punctuation You Can't Hear

"I drank tea for breakfast; then I ate a muffin."

Your ear may often tell you when a pause means a comma or an upbeat means a question mark. To detect other punctuation marks, such as the colon or the dash, however, your ear is an unreliable judge. For certain kinds of punctuation, you simply must learn the rules. In this unit, you will learn how to detect and use the punctuation marks that we can't accurately hear:

- semicolon
- colon
- dash
- quotation marks
- parentheses

Semicolon (;)

The semicolon has a beat somewhere between a period and a comma—too fine for most of us to hear. It is a punctuation mark more commonly associated with writing than with speaking. In writing, the semicolon has two main uses:

Use a semicolon to join two closely related, complete thoughts not connected by a conjunction, such as and, but, or, for, or nor.

The winds were as high as 50 mph; tiles flew off our roof.

Bats were roosting in the attic; the renters still stayed.

Notice the close relationship between the thoughts expressed in both sentences. In the first sentence, the tiles flew off the roof because there were high winds. In the second, the renters stayed in spite of the bats. So closely related are these thoughts that both sentences could have been written with a coordinating conjunction.

The winds were as high as 50 mph, so tiles flew off our roof.

Bats were roosting in the attic, yet the renters stayed.

PRACTICE 1

Place a semicolon between the two thoughts in each of the following sentences.

1. This is the worst food I ever tasted we shall never eat here again.
2. A camel can go for weeks without water it stores water in its hump.
3. Last year Ben was a high school dropout now he manages Target's toy division.
4. Bertha had to leave the movie all the bloodshed made her sick.
5. I dislike shopping during the holidays people are so rude and in such a hurry.
6. You have a good attitude you will do well on your new job.
7. Don't blame him for being silent he was scared out of his wits.
8. I find most poems hard to understand they don't make sense.
9. Sit quietly in the room you will hear mysterious whispers.
10. He loves movies he probably rents three or four videos each week.

Use a semicolon between two complete thoughts joined by the following transitions (also called conjunctive adverbs).

also	indeed	otherwise
anyway	instead	similarly
besides	likewise	still
consequently	meanwhile	then
finally	moreover	now
furthermore	nevertheless	therefore
however	next	thus
incidentally	now	

Place a comma after the transition if it is longer than one syllable.

Comma needed after a long transition:	I informed the agent; however, he never called back.

No comma needed after a short transition:	I informed the agent; then I went to sleep.

IN A NUTSHELL

- Use a semicolon to connect two complete thoughts not separated by *and, but, or, for,* or *nor.*
- Use a semicolon between two sentences joined by certain transitions, called *conjunctive adverbs.* Use a colon after the transition *if it is longer than one syllable.*

PRACTICE 2

Insert a semicolon after each of the following incomplete statements. Then, using a transition word from the preceding list, finish the statement so that it represents a complete idea and reflects the grammatical use of a semicolon. Be sure to place a semicolon before the transition word and a comma after it if it is more than one syllable.

Example: He said he was hungry ______________________

He said he was hungry; however, we had no food to give him.

____

1. Annie was bogged down with homework ______________________

____

2. He was told to turn left at the gas station ______________________

____

3. He received a scholarship ______________________

____

4. He had to get some rest ______________________

____

5. They could find only red balloons ______________________

____

6. Please lend me your book ______________________

____

7. There were five children in my family ______________________

____

8. The waiter was young ______________________

____

9. They did not lead an exciting life ______________________

____

10. It occurred to him that he should join a church ______________________

____

11. First he hosed down the driveway ______________________

____

12. Ten years went by ______________________

____

13. The guards abused the prisoners ______________________

____

14. They were instructed to rest only one half hour ______________________

____

15. Clarice loved to buy clothes ______________________

____

PRACTICE 3

Place semicolons where needed. Use commas after transitional words of more than one syllable.

1. Poverty means being tired moreover it means being tired day after day.
2. Yesterday my battery went dead consequently I am walking to work today.
3. Educated people tend to be open-minded and curious uneducated people tend to be closed-minded and set in their ways.
4. They climbed 150 steps to the top of the tower then they took pictures of the town square.
5. I like her a lot however I love you.
6. Betty loves her neighborhood nevertheless she wishes it were safer.
7. People who walk two miles every day feel better they can also eat a dessert now and then.
8. Stand tall be proud.
9. Large, leafy trees provide shade they also need much water.
10. He was utterly generous he gave money to everyone in town.
11. The future will contain many service jobs however a college education will be required.
12. Elise missed her stop she had fallen asleep on the bus.
13. So much of our manufacturing is outsourced to China consequently the U.S. labor market is complaining.

14. Reading good novels will improve your reading skills furthermore it will teach you much about people and places.

15. State Highway 5 is long and boring I hate to drive it.

Colon (:)

The colon has several uses. One of the most common is to introduce a list. A colon used in that way always follows an independent clause.

> These are the people who will sit at the head table: the mayor, all City Council members, the trustees of the college, and the master of ceremonies.

If the list is not introduced by an independent clause, do not use a colon.

Incorrect: The chief ingredients are: parsley, sage, rosemary, and thyme.

Correct: The chief ingredients are parsley, sage, rosemary, and thyme.

PRACTICE 4

Mark each of the following sentences *C* for correct or *NC* for incorrect. Correct the errors by inserting a colon if it is missing or crossing it out if it is used incorrectly.

1. ______ On my soccer team are: Mark, Billy, Theodore, and Juan.
2. ______ Flying a kite requires these elements: a kite, string, and a stiff breeze.
3. ______ You are: a monster, a leech, and a worm.
4. ______ But you are many people to me: my lover, my confidante, my best friend.
5. ______ These difficult words are: lie, lay, sit, set, rise, and raise.
6. ______ There are three kinds of people in this world: workers, dreamers, and doers.
7. ______ I need to find: a needle, a spool of thread, and a thimble.
8. ______ For our camping trip, we took: a pup tent, two sleeping bags, and a compass.
9. ______ I have accessorized my car with these items: a funny bumper sticker, a convex rearview mirror, and a psychedelic paint job.
10. ______ She wore: a headband, cutoff jeans, and dirty tennis shoes.

A colon can also be used to introduce a quotation or to add further explanation.

Quotation:	This is what S. J. Lee had to say about heaven: "What a pity that the only way to heaven is in a hearse!"
Further explanation:	When police violate the law, they encourage contempt for the law: People simply will not obey laws that the people in authority do not obey.

If the material after the colon is a complete sentence, capitalize the first letter. If the material after the colon is not a complete sentence, do not use a capital letter, as in the following example.

Further explanation:	Soccer teaches players at least one useful skill: a sense of balance.

Here, the material following the colon is not a complete sentence, so its first word does not begin with a capital letter.

Further explanation:	Soccer teaches players at least one useful skill: It trains them to work as a team.

Here, the material that follows the colon is a complete sentence, so its first word is capitalized.

Use a colon after the salutation in a formal letter, to set off the subtitle of a book, between chapter and verse of the Bible, and to separate hours from minutes in time.

Here are some examples:

In a formal letter:	Dear Mrs. Jones:
Title and subtitle:	The Mother Tongue: English and How It Got That Way
Chapter and verse of the Bible:	Proverbs 6:34
Hours from minutes:	5:30 P.M.

IN A NUTSHELL

- Use a colon after an independent clause to introduce material that follows, such as a list, a quotation, or a further explanation.
- If the material after the colon is a complete sentence, it should begin with a capital letter.
- Use a colon after the salutation in a formal letter, to set off the subtitle of a book, between chapter and verse of the Bible, and to separate hours from minutes in time.

PRACTICE 5

Add colons where they belong. Capitalize after the colon if necessary.

1. This is what John F. Kennedy said about poverty "if a free society cannot help the many who are poor, it cannot save the few who are rich."
2. Here is the author's name David Halberstam.
3. Today's typical home office contains several necessary machines a computer, a duplicator, a fax, and a telephone.
4. Recently I read *Have a Word on Me A Celebration of Language*.
5. There is one positive result from having a migraine headache the next day you feel better than ever.
6. It was 1130 P.M. before I finally got to bed.
7. Dear Prof. Gonzalez
8. There is one thing stronger than all the armies in the world it is an idea whose time has come.
9. These are the items I would like you to bring to the picnic ketchup, mustard, potato chips, hot dog buns, and pickles.
10. Who said the following "whoever named it necking was a poor judge of anatomy"?
11. Ever since elementary school, Marcie had dreamed of owning a particular kind of dog a Dalmatian.
12. Don't forget the most important qualities compassion, loyalty, and diligence.
13. I'll never forget her advice "paint as birds sing."
14. She said that the quotation came from Psalm 236.
15. Fighting boredom is not easy it requires patience, understanding, and endurance.

The Dash (–)

The dash (—) may also be typed as two hyphens (--). It is spoken as a short pause, like a comma. A dash is used in writing to signal a sudden break in thought or to emphasize a side comment or an afterthought. Here are some examples:

Sudden break in thought:	He would like to be polite—just as we would—but he interrupts constantly.
	I spoke at length to the class—at least, it seemed long to me—but they listened attentively.
Side thought:	Democracy is based on sharing the good things in life—especially power.

I would hate myself—and so should all children who have had good mothers—if I neglected my mother now that she is old.

Afterthought: Stay away from Ben—unless you're looking for trouble.

If you want to be imaginative, you have to be willing to tolerate criticism—even ridicule.

Don't overuse the dash, or your style will seem breathless.

IN A NUTSHELL

- Use the dash to emphasize a sudden break in thought or to add a side comment or afterthought.
- Do not overuse the dash.

PRACTICE 6

Use dashes to set off sudden breaks in thought, side thoughts, and afterthoughts in the sentences that follow.

1. You owe me $10.00. Oh, I'm sorry I thought you were someone else.
2. I asked her I begged her to pay the bills on time.
3. Do you blame others especially society for the way your marriage turned out?
4. I need a new computer or at least a few more memory chips.
5. She's not my biological mother not that that makes any difference.
6. We rounded the curve a whole carload of us.
7. We would all sit in the living room Uncle Charlie, Auntie Mae, and Big Ned listening to the radio.
8. Bring me a needle and no, just sit down and read to me.
9. I can now see what he was trying to tell me that it would not be easy.
10. Looking at me or through me I couldn't exactly tell which he seemed like a ghost.

Quotation Marks (" ")

One of the two main written uses for quotation marks is to indicate a person's exact words—called a **direct quotation.**

Use quotation marks to indicate a person's exact words.

Direct quotations can be reported in a number of different ways, all requiring quotation marks.

> She said, "You know I love you."
>
> "You know I love you," she said.
>
> "You know," she said, "I love you."
>
> "You know I love you," she said. "I miss you."

Begin every quotation with a capital letter. Do not, however, use a capital letter for the second part of a divided quotation that is *not* a full sentence.

> "I became a librarian," he explained, "because I love books."

Here, the second part of the divided quotation is not a full sentence, so a comma is used after *explained,* but there is no capital letter.

> "Put the book on the table," the librarian said. "I'll shelve it later."

Here, the second part of the divided quotation is a full sentence. A period follows *said* and a capital letter is used.

Do not use quotation marks in indirect quotations. An indirect quotation—rewording what someone has said—does not require quotation marks. Often an indirect quotation is announced by the word *that.* Here are some examples:

Direct quotation:	Jane said, "Dad will be down in 10 minutes."
Indirect quotation:	Jane told us that Dad will be down in ten minutes.
Direct quotation:	Mom warned us, "Stay away from the poison ivy."
Indirect quotation:	Mom warned us to stay away from the poison ivy.

IN A NUTSHELL

- Use quotation marks to indicate a person's exact words.
- Begin every quotation with a capital letter.
- Do not use a capital letter for the second part of a divided quotation that is not a complete sentence.
- Do not use quotation marks in indirect quotations.

PRACTICE 7

Add the required quotation marks.

Example: "I'm calling you," said the salesman, "because you filled out our form."

1. Try to look at it my way, through the corner of your eye, said Audrey.
2. You know I love ice cream, said David. Chocolate is my favorite.
3. When have I ever asked you to make dinner? she asked.
4. Watch out, she murmured. I'm going to tickle you.
5. Jenny asked, Has the mailman arrived yet?
6. You can't remember the sermon, interrupted Mr. Smith, because you were not in church when it was delivered.
7. It's not a bad feeling to be kissed, she laughed. It's actually a good feeling.
8. Letting his arms droop, he answered, Oh, I'm just tired.
9. If I don't get a bath soon, Agnes declared, I'll start itching all over.
10. He said, I like coming here because the place makes me happy.

PRACTICE 8

Place quotation marks only around the exact words of the speaker; leave the sentence unchanged if the quotation is indirect.

1. We asked ourselves, How long will they be gone?
2. Rachel asked him if he would return before sunset.
3. Aaron asked his mother if her boss had been rude again.
4. Marge promised that she would make a special effort to speak loudly enough for Grandma to hear.
5. Tell us about the accident, we said.
6. She insisted that she didn't care a bit.
7. Don't use that snippy tone with me, she warned.
8. If you can't afford to travel, read books, he said.
9. I've tried desperately to keep the truth from you, she cried.
10. She told him that the sunsets in Hawaii were spectacular.

PRACTICE 9

Change each of the following indirect quotations into a direct quotation in three ways: with the speaker indicated before the quoted words, after the quoted words, and interrupting the quoted words. Check your punctuation.

Example: He explained that Celia was his aunt and Stephen was his cousin.

He explained, "Celia is my aunt, and Stephen is my cousin."

"Celia is my aunt, and Stephen is my cousin," he explained.

"Celia is my aunt," he explained, "and Stephen is my cousin."

1. She insisted that it was the funniest bumper sticker she'd ever seen.

____

____

____

2. My landlady told us we'd have to move.

____

____

____

3. He said that he hated Godzilla movies.

____

____

____

4. My aunt said that she lost all her money in the savings and loan crisis.

____

____

____

5. She told us bluntly that nothing we said or did would change her mind.

____

____

____

Other punctuation is also used with quotation marks.

- Commas and periods always go inside quotation marks.

  He said, "I am not going."

He said, "I am not going," and then added, "at least, not today."

ESL Advice!

If you learned English either in Great Britain or in a British colony, you were taught an entirely different way of using quotation marks. In that case, you'll have to learn the American rules and practice observing them.

- Question marks and exclamation marks go either inside or outside the quotation marks, depending on the sentence.

Inside: "Is he just making a wild guess?" Larry asked.

Outside: Who just said, "He's making a wild guess"?

Inside: Why do they keep asking, "What's for dinner?" (In the case of a question within a question, place the question mark inside the quotation marks.)

In the first example, the spoken words make up a separate question; in the second example, the spoken words are part of the question. In the third example, a question is asked within a question.

"Watch out!" Karen cried.

Karen, stop saying, "Watch out"!

In the first example, the spoken words make up a separate command; in the second example, the spoken words are part of the command.

IN A NUTSHELL

- Always put periods and commas inside quotation marks.
- Question marks and exclamation points go either inside or outside quotation marks, depending on the sentence.

PRACTICE 10

The sentences that follow use other punctuation marks in conjunction with quotation marks. In the blank provided, write a *C* if the sentence is punctuated correctly or an *NC* if the sentence is not correct. Correct the incorrect sentences.

Example: <u>**NC**</u> "Are you happy"? she asked.

Correction: <u>***"Are you happy?" she asked.***</u>

1. _____ The teacher said to Leo, "Explain your answer."
____

2. _____ Was it Snoopy who asked, "Do you like dog?"
____

3. _____ She screamed, "I love that story!"
____

4. _____ Who said, "I think; therefore, I am"?
____

5. ______ "Get off my lawn!" she screamed.

____

6. ______ What is the meaning of "Blessed are the poor"?

____

7. ______ Stop telling me to "shut up"!

____

8. ______ She loudly cried, "Give me some air, please!"

____

9. ______ "No, never!" she insisted.

____

10. ______ He asked, "Have you actually read that book?"

____

Use quotation marks to indicate the titles of shorter works. Italicize (or underline) the titles of longer works.

Use quotation marks to indicate the titles of shorter works, such as magazine articles and short stories. Italicize (or underline) the titles of longer works.

SHORTER WORKS	LONGER WORKS
magazine article—"Easy Desserts"	magazine—*Healthy Eating*
newspaper article—"Hurry Up and Relax"	newspaper—*The Atlanta Journal*
song—"Summer Wind"	book—*David Copperfield*
poem—"Mary Had a Little Lamb"	poetry collection—*Leaves of Grass*
book chapter—"The Darkness Appears"	movie—*The Truman Show*
editorial—"Education at the Crossroads"	television show—*60 Minutes*

IN A NUTSHELL

- Use quotation marks to indicate the titles of shorter works.
- Italicize (or underline) the titles of longer works.

PRACTICE 11

Add quotation marks and underline as required.

Example: "Rules for Aging" is an essay that appears in an anthology titled <u>Readings for Writers</u>.

1. Chapter 1 is titled Mattie Michael.
2. My sister was going to read the book The Littlest Angel.
3. Troy was a good movie.

4. One of my favorite songs is Gimme Shelter by the Rolling Stones.
5. She searched through the book Great Italian Recipes.
6. People magazine is filled with juicy gossip.
7. The San Francisco Chronicle is a fine newspaper.
8. Did you see the movie A Perfect Murder?
9. The Taming of the Shrew is my favorite Shakespeare play.
10. My wife likes to watch reruns of Seinfeld on television.

Parentheses [( )]

Use parentheses for side comments that illustrate a point or add information. They are also used to enclose numbers when you list items.

To illustrate a point: Curiosity (the kind exemplified by Edison and Newton) is one mark of intelligence.

My brother and his friend (the best man at his wedding, actually) were both rushed to the emergency ward.

To add information: Ritz–Carlton hotels train their managers in Total Quality Management (TQM).

The average person (the so-called reasonable man) used to be defined as a male in the English language.

Brad Anderson (b. 1924) is my favorite cartoonist.

The author explains precisely how the team works (see p. 213). **(Place the period *after* the parentheses in references.)**

With numbers: Here are the rules: (1) Keep your room clean, (2) be on time, and (3) don't complain about the food.

IN A NUTSHELL

- Use parentheses to add information or a side remark to a sentence.
- Use parentheses with numbers.

PRACTICE 12

Add parentheses where needed.

1. Edward M. Kennedy b. 1932 is the only surviving brother of President John F. Kennedy.
2. Read the chapter on civil rights pp. 85–98.

3. The chapter on moving westward pp. 25–36 will be on the test.
4. It was freezing weather 13 degrees Fahrenheit.
5. The National Endowment for the Arts NEA may have its budget severely slashed.
6. Make a list of goals and divide them into three categories: 1 immediate goals, 2 short-term goals, and 3 long-term goals.
7. Maya Angelou b. 1928 writes about the black experience in America.
8. Define "cajole" and "ascendancy" see paragraph 5.
9. There are five types of microorganisms: 1 bacteria, 2 algae, 3 fungi, 4 protozoa, and 5 viruses.
10. By noon, twelve of us sat there the number required for jury.

Unit Test

Use what you learned in this unit to correctly punctuate the following passage.

> Russell Baker 1925–present began his career in journalism in 1947 as a staff member of the Baltimore Sun. Today, his newspaper articles have been collected in book form for two reasons they are simple and they reveal life as many of us have experienced it. The other day, I asked my classmate Deanna, Do you ever read Russell Baker? She answered, Of course not. I hate reading in my spare time. I pointed out to her that she would enjoy Baker's essay entitled Meaningful Relationships. I said, It discusses the modern approach to love. Are you crazy? she asked me. Why would I waste my time reading about love when I can see a movie about love? Look, I replied, Reading is good for you. I left the room thinking to myself, What a superficial person you are. You probably don't even read the Baltimore Sun, your local newspaper.

Unit Talk-Write Assignment

For this assignment, you are a fly on the wall listening to a conversation between two students about their older relatives. Your job is to correct each sentence by putting in the appropriate punctuation marks that can't be heard, all of which have been covered in this chapter. Be sure to insert quotation marks and to put other marks where they belong in the quotation. Some sentences may be punctuated in more than one way.

TALK	WRITE
1. I have a special aunt Jimmy said who is something of an artist she does macramé	
2. Roberta replied and I have a special uncle who is missing a leg however that doesn't stop him from being a blue water sailor	
3. My aunt is crotchety she's 87 but strong furthermore she still has a sense of humor and often likes to tell off-color jokes Jimmy added	
4. This is amazing gushed Roberta my uncle is much the same way he was in the war which war I don't know but he didn't like it much too noisy dirty disorganized and regimented he said	
5. My aunt's macramé is much in demand said Jimmy for all the work she does on her pieces it takes her nearly a week to finish one she sells them for very little	
6. My uncle has no hobby like that said Roberta he just likes to talk a lot about the good old days otherwise he's likely to be found on the lake he goes there a lot sailing by himself. He says sailing is a good hobby it has action danger the outdoors and the feeling of the wind in his hair	
7. You wouldn't catch my aunt dead on the lake said Jimmy she's afraid of the water she won't even take baths, only showers	
8. Jimmy then went on to talk about the special things he loves in his aunt her sharp tongue	

her individuality her strong will she's afraid of nothing he added but water

9. Roberta added some of her uncle's traits 1 his sense of adventure 2 his eagerness to learn and 3 his willingness to take risk even at his age she told the story of the time her uncle capsized his sailboat on the lake, and when the park police tried to help, he asked them don't you have anything better to do

10. Jimmy sighed I'm going to miss my aunt when I move on to a four-year college she'll be too far away for a drop-in visit

11. Gosh my uncle already lives far away from me he's in the next state and I hardly ever see him replied Roberta

12. My aunt is a special person in my life remarked Jimmy I hope she lives long enough for my own kids if I have any to get to know her

Unit Collaborative Assignment

A. Choose a partner to whom you will dictate the following sentences. See if your partner can write them down with the correct punctuation.

1. Whose book is this? she asked Tom.
2. Ten years ago we heard, Learn word processing. Now we hear, Get on the Internet.
3. You backed into my car! she cried.
4. Did you see the movie Face/Off?
5. The title of the poem is, How Tall Is the Mountain?

B. Reversing the process, have your partner dictate the following sentences to you. Write them down with correct punctuation.

1. I did a report on the book Cold Mountain.
2. We knew who he meant when he said, She's gone.

3. The title of the essay is I Want a Wife.
4. What is her real name? he muttered to himself.
5. Who said, Give me liberty or give me death?

Unit Writing Assignment

Imagine that you are disturbed about a critical remark someone made about your best friend. Recreate the incident, and include an imaginary conversation between you and your friend's critic. The point is to punctuate correctly. Be especially careful to use quotation marks where they belong. Use the Revising Checklist inside the front cover of this book to help you revise.

Photo Writing Assignment

The following photo shows someone reading intently. Write a paragraph about the importance of books or the importance of good reading skills. You might ask yourself if television is a hindrance to developing reading skills. If you have read a good book lately, write about it and tell your reader what the book meant to you. When you have finished writing, get together with a classmate and check each other's punctuation. Use the Revising Checklist to help you revise.

21 CAPITALIZATION

"Jimmy, will you please jimmy open the door?"

Because uppercase (capital) and lowercase letters sound the same, your ear cannot help you with capitalization: *Jimmy,* the name, sounds the same as *jimmy,* the verb (which means to force open). To capitalize correctly, you must know the following rules:

- Capitalize the first word in a sentence or direct quotation.
- Capitalize after a colon if what follows is a complete sentence.
- Capitalize the names of individual persons and the word *I.*
- Capitalize family relationships used as names.
- Capitalize the names of nationalities, religions, races, tribes, and languages.
- Capitalize the names of companies, clubs, political groups, and other official organizations.
- Capitalize the names of commercial products.
- Capitalize the names of specific places, including monuments.
- Capitalize the names of areas of the country.
- Capitalize the abbreviations of familiar organizations, corporations, people, countries, time, and titles.
- Capitalize the names of the days of the week, months, holidays, and religious occasions.
- Capitalize historical eras and events.
- Capitalize the titles of books, magazines, essays, poems, stories, plays, articles, films, television shows, songs, and cartoons.

- Capitalize titles used in front of a person's name.
- Capitalize the names of specific college courses.
- Capitalize the opening and the first word of the closing of a letter.

We will discuss each rule of capitalization separately.

Rules of Capitalization

Capitalize the first word in a sentence or direct quotation.

Jimmy was 17 years old.

He said, "My dad's the greatest."

"They realized," she admitted, "that they were wrong."

Notice that in the third example, *They* is capitalized because it begins a new sentence; however, *that* remains lowercase because it is part of the first sentence.

PRACTICE 1

Correctly capitalize the following sentences.

1. He set several goals. first, he would get his degree. then he would buy a new car.
2. "Perhaps," she suggested, "your father could help you. he has money."
3. He scoffed, "my dear fellow, you must have been living on the moon."
4. an open mind can lead to indecision. it can be worse than a closed mind.
5. Get out of my way! don't just stand there!

Capitalize after a colon if what follows is a complete sentence.

These are the words he spoke: "We must love our country."

but

These are the items we need: a wheelbarrow, a shovel, and a large sack.

Note: See also Unit 20, p. 000

PRACTICE 2

Correctly capitalize the following sentences. Cross out any unnecessary capitals and replace them with lowercase letters.

Example: Dear Sir: we have never met, but I am interested in your product.

1. Do the following: get some ice, set out some glasses, and pour some lemonade.
2. Listen to me carefully: don't swim immediately after eating.
3. He has many talents: playing the accordion, tap dancing, and singing the blues.
4. This is the program for today: we take out the garbage and clean up the cabins.
5. To become a freelance writer, here is what you need: talent, an agent, and luck.

Capitalize the names of individuals and the word I.

It was Mary, not Miss Muffet, who had a little lamb.

The name of my sociology teacher is Mathilde Johnson.

Nicknames are also capitalized:

He was known in the neighborhood as Big Thumb Bob.

PRACTICE 3

Capitalize the names of individuals in the following sentences.

1. Even foreigners are familiar with the name george washington.
2. Because of his large size, his own mother called him jumbo.
3. Henry hadley, marguerite woolley, and isabelle lopez gave speeches in favor of recycling.
4. George herman ruth was babe ruth's real name.
5. All of a sudden, billy kissed erika. I know because i saw him.

Capitalize family relationships used as substitutes for proper names.

I'm glad that Uncle Bryan is happily married.

Every Saturday, I take a box of cookies to Grandmother Trudy.

Don't make so much noise, or you'll wake up Mother.

If you tell Dad, he'll feel hurt.

However, do not capitalize *mother, father, grandmother, grandfather, uncle, aunt, cousin,* and so forth when these terms are preceded by *my, your, our,* or any other possessive word.

Hand Grandpa his walking stick.

but

Hand your grandpa his walking stick.

Give Aunt Lilly a call.

but

Give Lilly, your aunt, a call.

IN A NUTSHELL

- Capitalize the names of nationalities, religions, races, tribes, and languages.
- Capitalize the names of companies, clubs, political groups, and other official organizations.
- Capitalize the names of commercial products.
- Capitalize the names of specific places, including monuments.

PRACTICE 4

Capitalize the sentences below as needed. If the sentence is correct, write a *C* in the blank provided.

1. ____ My dad is a completely self-made man.
2. ____ He looked at aunt Martha's purse and wondered what was in it.
3. ____ My grandmother came over from Ireland in 1920.
4. ____ My cousin Gerty never speaks to my cousin Bob.
5. ____ Please give mom my love and tell her to quit working so hard.

Capitalize the names of nationalities, religions, races, tribes, and languages.

The nationalities of my three best friends are Korean, Armenian, and Brazilian.

He is Roman Catholic, and she is Buddhist.

Carolyn Mazloomi is a famous African American artist.

The patterns in Navajo rugs have specific meanings.

Which language sounds more beautiful to you—Italian or French?

PRACTICE 5

Fill in the blanks as indicated.

Example: In high school, I took (language) ***Spanish***.

1. My neighbors are (nationality) ________.
2. I was brought up in the (religion) ________ faith.
3. I can't imagine ever learning (language) ________.
4. Occasionally, a questionnaire will ask me my race. I am (race) ________.
5. The (nationalities) ________, ________, and ________ create a melting pot of family businesses in many large cities.

Capitalize the names of companies, clubs, political groups, and other official organizations.

I prefer to buy gas from Union Oil.

The May Company has huge sales every year.

My father's family has always belonged to the Democratic Party.

My parents encouraged me to join the Girl Scouts.

"Olé" is the name of our Spanish Club.

My car is insured with Allegiance Insurance Company, and my medical plan is with Kaiser.

Al-Quaeda is a world-wide terrorist organization.

PRACTICE 6

Capitalize as necessary in the following sentences.

1. My mother wants me to pledge alpha sigma, a sorority that stresses grades.
2. The advantage of working for a company like lincoln savings is that you get benefits.
3. My parents' building is controlled by the los feliz towers homeowners association.
4. Sometimes extreme democrats are the same as extreme republicans.
5. My history professor has decided to run for the new york state assembly.

Capitalize the names of commercial products.

Why not buy Dove soap? It is as good as the more expensive soaps.

Do not capitalize types of products.

A good breakfast consists of oatmeal, fruit, and skim milk. **(These are merely types of products, not brand names.)**

but

Quaker Oats cereal is low in fat. **(Quaker Oats is a brand name, but cereal is a type of food.)**

PRACTICE 7

Capitalize the names of commercial products in the following sentences.

1. I love reese's candy because the peanut butter and chocolate combination is delicious.
2. If I have to have breakfast, then give me jimmy dean sausages and eggs.
3. Dandruff is helped by head and shoulders shampoo.
4. In the 1940s, fords and chevrolets were the most popular cars.
5. On a hot day, nothing tastes better than carnation strawberry ice cream and snapple iced tea.

Capitalize the names of specific places, including monuments.

It was a small town in the Imperial Valley called El Centro.

Let's visit the Grand Canyon and Yellowstone National Park.

The Taj Majal is one of the world's great wonders.

I attend Glendale Community College, which has about 15,000 students.

Just walk straight down Broadway; then turn right on Monroe Boulevard, and look for Virgil's Hardware Store.

Do not capitalize the names of places that are not specific:

He walked down the street toward the hardware store.

but

He walked down Elm Street toward Ace Hardware.

IN A NUTSHELL

- Capitalize the names of areas of the country.
- Capitalize the abbreviations of familiar organizations, corporations, people, countries, time, and titles.
- Capitalize the days of the week, months, holidays, and religious occasions.
- Capitalize historical eras and events.

PRACTICE 8

Correct the capitalization errors in the following sentences.

Examples: I love murietta because it's such a sleepy little town.

I love ~~m~~*M*urietta because it's such a sleepy little town.

1. The capital of jamaica is kingston.
2. Keeping grant's tomb beautiful is not as easy as it sounds.
3. A millionaire once wanted to buy the famous rock of gibralter.
4. President kennedy was killed by a sniper in dallas, texas.
5. Once I had a job as a busboy at the hilton hotel in new york.

Capitalize the names of areas of the country.

When we lived in the South, I spoke with a drawl.

The Southwest has become a popular source of interior decor and food.

They moved to the East Coast.

Do not capitalize compass directions or areas of the country used as adjectives.

Drive south on Hill Street until it crosses Allen Drive, and then turn west on Allen.

She has a southern drawl.

We like southwestern food.

PRACTICE 9

In the blank provided, fill in an area of the country or a compass direction. Capitalize correctly.

Example: My favorite poet lives in the ***South***. (or Midwest, or East, etc.)

1. To the ______ of us were three steep, muddy hills.
2. Our wagons crept along slowly, always moving toward the ______.
3. In December, we moved to ______.
4. I'd like to live in the ______.
5. Head ______ on Maple, then ______ on Elm Road.

Capitalize the abbreviations of familiar organizations, corporations, people, countries, time, and titles.

Organizations:	CIA, FBI, IRS, AEC
Corporations:	IBM, NBC, ITT, CNN
People:	JFK, FDR, LBJ, GWB
Things:	ICBM, WMD (Weapons of Mass Destruction)
Countries:	USA, UK (United Kingdom)
Time:	10:00 A.M., 1:15 P.M.
Titles:	Milton Freedman, Sr.
	Jean Smith, M.D.
	Ana Chang, D.D.S.
	Becky Winkler, Ph.D.
	Sean H. Cotton, Esq.

PRACTICE 10

Complete the following sentences with an appropriate abbreviation.

1. President John F. Kennedy was called ______.
2. Under Stalin, Russia was part of the ______.
3. The Young Women's Christian Association is referred to as the ______.
4. If you're a dentist, you will place ______ after your name.
5. An intelligence quotient is also called ______.

Capitalize the days of the week, months, holidays, and religious occasions.

My birthday falls on Tuesday this year.

The best time to see the fall colors is in October or November.

Have you picked out your Halloween costume yet?

We celebrate both Christmas and Hanukkah.

The seasons of the year, however, are not capitalized.

I'm always joyful in the spring.

PRACTICE 11

In the blank provided, write a *C* if the sentence is properly capitalized or an *NC* if it is not. Then correctly capitalize the sentence.

1. _____ The african american holiday known as kwanza is celebrated from december 26 to january 1.
2. _____ I get confused because february has only 28 days except for leap year.
3. _____ On monday, wednesday, and friday, I have a body-building class.
4. _____ Do we get the day off on veteran's day?
5. _____ I gain three pounds every easter

Capitalize historical eras and events.

During the Middle Ages, women were adored but were given no legal power.

The Modern Era has given us some great jazz musicians.

The Depression of the 1930s left my grandparents poor.

No one wants to have World War III.

The Battle of Little Big Horn was an important event in history.

IN A NUTSHELL

- Capitalize the titles of books, magazines, essays, poems, stories, plays, articles, films, television shows, songs, and cartoons.
- Capitalize the titles used in front of a person's name.
- Capitalize the names of specific college courses.
- Capitalize the first word of the opening and the closing of a letter.

PRACTICE 12

Correctly capitalize the following sentences.

1. My personal favorites are poets from the romantic age.
2. Would you have been happy as a woman in the victorian age?
3. The battle of fort sumter officially began the civil war.
4. Many famous movies have been made about world war II.
5. The sixties were a crazy time.

Capitalize the titles of books, magazines, essays, poems, stories, plays, articles, films, television shows, songs, and cartoons.

Book:	I enjoyed *Tom Sawyer* by Mark Twain.
Magazine:	I always read *Time* magazine.
Essay:	My essay is entitled "Women in Politics: Onward and Upward."
Poem:	The poem "The Waltzer in the House" is about a mouse.
Story:	"Flowering Judas" is Katherine Anne Porter's best short story.
Play:	He was very good in *Death of a Salesman*.
Article:	I read an article entitled "Coming to Grips with Kingston."
Film:	Each year, the film version of *Gone with the Wind* is shown without losing its popularity.
Television show:	We always watch *Law and Order* on Mondays.
Song:	I love the way Nat King Cole sings "Mona Lisa."
Cartoon:	People complain that "Peanuts" has gotten stale.

Note: For more on the use of italics and quotation marks in titles, see Unit 20, pp. 000–000.

Notice how words are capitalized in titles. The beginning word is always capitalized. The first word after a colon is also always capitalized. Certain words are not capitalized, however, unless they come at the beginning of a title.

Do not capitalize:

- The article *a, an,* or *the* unless it is the first word.
- The coordinating conjunctions *and, but, yet, or, nor, so, for.*
- Short prepositions such as *of, from, by, in, up,* and *out.*

Capitalize, however, prepositions of five or more letters, such as *about, among, between, behind, through, though,* and *without.*

PRACTICE 13

In the following sentences, capitalize all words that should be capitalized, and change any incorrect capitals to lowercase.

Example: I wish that the cartoon "Calvin ~~And~~ *and* Hobbes" appeared in the *New York* ~~times~~ *Times,* but unfortunately that comic strip is no longer active.

1. On the back page of today's newspaper was a mysterious article, titled "A Car Is born—again."

2. My sister wrote a song about rock climbing— "Take Me With You Up To The Top."
3. You can learn much about nature by watching The discovery channel on television.
4. KCBS is showing a television special— "Travels With Chuck Henry."
5. In the eleventh grade, we were asked to write a report on Hemingway's *For Whom The bell Tolls.*

Capitalize titles used in front of a person's name.

Mrs. Milford, Mr. Franklin, Ms. Hightower, Dr. Dorsey

President Abraham Lincoln, Mayor Cheryl Dixon, Senator Dianne Feinstein, Secretary of State Colin Powell, General George B. McClellan

but

Abraham Lincoln, the sixteenth president of the United States; Cheryl Dixon, the mayor of Cedartown; Dianne Feinstein, the senator from California; Colin Powell, retired general; George B. McClellan, chief commander of the northern forces

PRACTICE 14

In the blank provided, write a *C* if the sentence is correct or an *NC* if the sentence is not correct. Write the correction above the error.

1. ____ President Lincoln was called "Honest Abe."
2. ____ Pass the message to Mr. Brown and miss Hurst.
3. ____ I wish that a strong woman would become governor of our state.
4. ____ I greatly admire Vice President Al Gore.
5. ____ Perhaps assemblywoman Waters would give the speech.

Capitalize the names of specific college courses.

I'm hoping for a passing grade in Calculus 101.

but

Most freshmen find calculus a difficult subject.

The Introduction to Marine Biology course includes a field trip to Baja.

but

Courses in marine biology are popular today.

Language courses are always capitalized.

I'm taking Spanish C22.

I'm taking French again this year.

PRACTICE 15

Capitalize the names of specific college courses.

1. If I fail economics 103, I cannot graduate next June.
2. Charles loves astronomy, but he hates the night labs.
3. He is majoring in english.
4. I am taking geography, russian, and theater.
5. Professor Jenkins teaches a humanities course called the human struggle C421.

Capitalize the first word of the opening and the closing of a letter.

Dear Sir,

My dear Lily,

Dear Dr. Lopez,

Sincerely,

Sincerely yours,

Best regards,

Love and kisses,

PRACTICE 16

Write a brief letter to an imaginary bank, reporting that someone is using your credit card without permission. Capitalize correctly the opening and closing and the sentences in the body of the letter.

____

____

____

____

____

____

____

IN A NUTSHELL

- Capitalize the first word in a sentence or direct quotation.
- Capitalize after a colon if what follows is a complete sentence.
- Capitalize the names of individual persons and the word *I*.
- Capitalize family relationships used as substitutes for proper names.

Unit Test

Correct all the capitalization errors in the following paragraphs.

I want to say something about glenacre, my home town. picture in your mind a middle-class neighborhood in california, nestled against the san rafael mountains. my parents moved here on a bright monday in may. i was ten years old and happy as a clam to be out of new york. from our house, malibu beach is one hour west; mt. baldy is one hour east; beverly hills is one hour north.

glenacre is an international neighborhood, filled with armenians, iranians, vietnamese, koreans, and hispanics. The most famous monument, standing on a bank patio, is a bronze statue entitled "wild horses." the u.s. post office is always crowded with people standing in line to buy stamps or pick up packages because we are a town of people with relatives living elsewhere.

In an election year, the republican candidate always gets more support than the democratic one. I suppose that this is because we are conservative property boosters who value private enterprise. a handful of people run the city—from the city council to the chamber of commerce. they all know each other and get reelected when it's time to choose the local politicians.

we have an old movie theater, called "the capitol," that features classics like *casablanca* and it happened one night. you might say that my town is old-fashioned and out-of-step with modern ways. well, maybe so, but I'm happy here. as my mother said just the other day, "it's a safe place to bring up a family."

Unit Talk–Write Assignment

When students were asked, "What has the computer contributed to society?" most spoke glowingly about the magic of word processing, doing research through the Internet, and communicating by e-mail. But one student worried that computers were causing a generation gap. His ideas, are expressed in the *Talk* column. Rewrite his comments in the blanks provided in the *Write* column. Be sure to capitalize correctly throughout. Then write a short paragraph agreeing or disagreeing with this student's ideas. Using the Revising Checklist to help you revise

TALK	WRITE
Sorry, guys, but I see a black cloud on the horizon. Hey, sure computers are awesome for us, but what about for mom, dad, grandma, and grandpa? You can bet that I don't want to go back to typewriters, library shelves, and letters sent only through post offices. I'm with you when you rave about how it is to order paperbacks through Amazon.com and how much time is saved by surfing the internet for sources on your History or Psychology paper. But do your parents or, for that matter, your grandparents know how to use a computer? Here's my point: I'd hate to see technology divide young from old. We're not talking about the problem like at the early part of the last Century when some women could drive while others couldn't. That's peanuts compared to the rift computers are causing. My mom can't even use the ATM. Her sis, aunt Birdie, sits at the computer and practically has the shakes from being so nervous. One of our elderly neighbors, dr. Manley, sees the computer as satan trying to	

destroy the world—or something. My point is that some older people are unbelievably threatened by computers. Not all of them sit right down, learn it, and then go on their merry way to use the software quicken for paying bills, excel for keeping track of business, and the latest microsoft word version for writing things. All kinds of things have come between people—religion, politics, race. The computer is doing the same. It's making a society of knows and know-nots. What needs to happen is that the older generation needs to be talked into learning how to use computers. Once they have, there'll be no stopping them. They'll see how hot it is.

Unit Collaborative Assignment

A. Dictate the following sentences to a partner. Then check to see if there are any capitalization errors.

1. I always wished that I could meet Jerry Lewis in person.
2. Yesterday I read a newspaper article entitled, "Be Kind to Your Neighbor."
3. My maternal grandparents are Baptists, but my mother converted to Islam when she married Dad.

4. My gas credit card is with Wells Fargo Bank.
5. When it's cold, I love to sit and sip Hershey's hot cocoa.
6. My favorite junk food is Coke and Twinkies.
7. Photographers love Rainbow Ridge in Arizona.
8. The second Sunday in May is important because it is Mother's Day.
9. Dear Mr. Nolan: Thank you for your order. Sincerely yours, Janet Johnson
10. Jerry failed geography but did very well in Spanish.

B. Now, turn the tables and have your partner dictate the following sentences to you. Try to avoid any capitalization errors.

1. Why would anyone send greeting cards for Groundhog Day?
2. My family is taking a trip to Montana, where we plan to visit Glacier Park.
3. Dear Mrs. Grant, Please excuse Jeffrey from gym class. Yours truly, Frank Alpert
4. Sometimes I have nothing but a can of Campbell's soup for dinner.
5. My sister gave me her old Honda as a birthday gift.
6. We hiked through the Blue Ridge Mountains.
7. My grandmothers tells us stories about the Roaring Twenties.
8. If you're in business, it is important to join the Rotary Club.
9. I love my Angora cat.
10. Promise that you will not tell Grandpa George.

Unit Writing Assignment

Write a paragraph describing your last vacation or school outing. Describe what you saw, including all towns, parks, mountains, lakes, monuments, or other memorable places. Tell how the experience affected you. Be sure to capitalize correctly. Use the Revising Checklist inside the front cover of this book to help you revise.

Photo Writing Assignment

This national landmark, carved into Mount Rushmore in South Dakota, portrays the following U.S. presidents: George Washington, Thomas Jefferson, Teddy Roosevelt, and Abraham Lincoln. Add to this list of great presidents another U.S. president whom you consider worthy of being carved into a mountain ridge. Offer specific reasons for your choice. Be sure to use proper capitalization. Use the Revising Checklist to help you improve your work.

22 How to Use the Dictionary

"dic · tion · ar · y (dik' shän er' ë), n., pl. -aries. 1. a book containing a selection of the words of the language, usually arranged alphabetically, giving information about their meanings, pronunciations, and origins."

The modern dictionary is a useful tool for the writer. It tells not only what words mean, but how they are used, spelled, hyphenated, pronounced, and often how they came into being. For anyone who writes in standard English, the dictionary is vital.

Among the good desk dictionaries are the following:

American Heritage Dictionary

The Random House Dictionary of the English Language

The Random House Unabridged Dictionary: Print and Electronic Versions

New Webster's Dictionary

The New International Webster's Dictionary of the English Language: Encyclopedic Edition

Most good dictionaries give more or less the same kind of information about words. Typically, this information includes the following:

- Spelling
- Word division
- Pronunciation

- Grammatical uses
- Meanings
- Usage labels
- Origin
- Synonyms

Here is a sample dictionary entry from the *American Heritage Dictionary* (Houghton Mifflin Company):

> **sand·wich (san'wich) n.** 1. Two or more slices of bread with meat, cheese, or other filling placed between them. 2. An arrangement resembling an edible sandwich; for example, two slabs of one material holding a slab of different material between them, as in certain electronic devices. **tr. v.** *sandwiched, -wiching, -wiches*. 1. To insert tightly between two things. 2. To place in tight, alternating layers. 3. To fit between two other things that allow little time: *sandwich a meeting between two others*. [After the Fourth Earl of Sandwich (1718–92), for whom sandwiches were made so that he could stay at the gambling table without interruptions for meals.]

Spelling

A prime function of the dictionary is to tell us how a word is spelled. If there is more than one acceptable spelling, the preferred spelling is given first. Next comes the plural spelling of irregular nouns and verbs. If the noun or verb is regular, no spelling is given. Because *sandwich* has a regular plural—*sandwiches*—no spelling is given. On the other hand, if you look up the word *goose*, you will find that the plural—*geese*—is given because it is irregular. If a verb is irregular, the dictionary will also list its principal parts. For instance, our dictionary lists the principal parts of the irregular verb *to go* as follows: present participle, *going*; simple past, *went*; past participle, *gone*.

If you do not know how to spell a word, pronounce it slowly, even in several ways, and then look them all up. Chances are that one will be right. If you are a really bad speller, you might check *The Bad Speller's Dictionary*, published by Random House, whose entries are organized to help bad spellers find words they can pronounce but can't spell.

PRACTICE 1

The words listed are spelled incorrectly. Pronounce them first and then look up each word in the dictionary. Write the correct spelling in the blanks provided.

1. accidently ____________
2. potatos ____________
3. Febuary ____________
4. labratory ____________

5. lightening ____________
6. disasterous ____________
7. heighth ____________
8. mischeivous ____________
9. goverment ____________
10. sophmore ____________

Word Division

A good dictionary will show how a word is divided into syllables. The end of each syllable is marked by a dot (·). Look again at the word *sandwich.* It has two syllables: **sand·wich.** The word *preparation*, on the other hand, has four syllables: **prep·a·ra·tion.**

Knowing how a word is divided helps you to pronounce it correctly and tells you how to break it at the end of a line. You may break any word by inserting a hyphen at the end of a convenient syllable.

sand-wich

not

sa-ndwich

prepara-tion or prep-aration or prepa-ration

not

pre-paration

If you must break a word that won't fit at the end of a line and don't know where to put the hyphen, check your dictionary.

PRACTICE 2

Draw a vertical line between the syllables of the words listed below.

Example: sau/sage

1. decent
2. brutality
3. anatomy
4. calculate
5. controversial
6. foliage
7. glimmer
8. gunfight
9. likelihood
10. penalty

Pronunciation

Another basic function of the dictionary is to give the pronunciation of words. Pronunciation is given in parentheses after the listing of the word. For example, the dictionary tells us that *sandwich* is pronounced this way:

san' wich **(the *d* is silent)**

Pediatrician is pronounced this way:

pe' de æ trish' an

Two recurring sounds in English are the *æ* combination and the *schwa*, ə (an upside-down *e*). The combined *æ* sound is what we find in words like P*a*t, fl*a*t, and s*a*ck. The *schwa* is the unaccented sound in words like *a*bout, gall*u*p, and circ*u*s. You will find these symbols on many pages of your dictionary.

PRACTICE 3

Copy the pronunciation information given in your dictionary for the following words. Then pronounce the words out loud.

1. mahogany ____________
2. telegraph ____________
3. commentary ____________
4. realtor ____________
5. spaghetti ____________
6. voluntary ____________
7. lieutenant ____________
8. silicone ____________
9. pachyderm ____________
10. realization ____________

Grammatical Uses

Dictionaries also list the various grammatical uses of a word. Our example lists *sandwich* as a noun (*n.*) and a transitive verb—a verb requiring an object (*tr. v.*). Here are the grammatical labels commonly used:

adj.	adjective	*pl.*	plural
adv.	adverb	*prep.*	preposition
conj.	conjunction	*pron.*	pronoun
interj.	interjection	*sing.*	singular
intr. v.	intransitive verb	*tr. v.*	transitive verb
n.	noun	*v.*	verb

PRACTICE 4

Consult your dictionary and list the various grammatical uses for the following words. Then use each word correctly in a sentence.

Example: quake ***intransitive verb, noun***

Louis quakes every time he speaks in public.

1. quarrel ______________________________

   ____
2. skid ______________________________

   ____
3. talkative ______________________________

   ____
4. for ______________________________

   ____
5. inmate ______________________________

   ____
6. nest ______________________________

   ____
7. record ______________________________

   ____
8. tonight ______________________________

   ____
9. tomato ______________________________

   ____
10. too ______________________________

    ____

Meanings

A chief function of the dictionary is to define words. If a word has more than one meaning—many words do—each meaning is numbered and listed, starting with the most common.

The most common meaning of our example, *sandwich*, is *two or more slices of bread with meat, cheese, or other filling placed between them.* Another meaning is *an arrangement resembling an edible sandwich.* For example, one of the last steps in making a quilt is to make a sandwich (that is the term that quiltmakers use) by putting cotton batting between the finished quilt top and the fabric that will be the quilt bottom; now the quilt is ready to be sewn together. A third meaning is *to fit tightly between two things.* Thus, a car between two trucks on the highway may be said to be *sandwiched* between them.

The primary meaning of *cricket* is *an insect*, a secondary one is *a low wooden footstool*, and a third meaning is *a game played with a ball and a bat.*

PRACTICE 5

Look up in your dictionary the primary and secondary meanings of the words listed below. Give only the meanings for the part of speech listed, not all of the meanings for the word.

Example: fleece, n.

Answer: 1. the coat of wool covering a sheep, 2. any of various soft or woolly coverings.

1. grade, tr. v.

____

____

2. costly, adj.

____

____

3. governess, n.

____

____

4. leotard, n.

____

____

5. nervous, adj.

____

____

6. persist, intr. v.

____

____

7. red herring, n.

____

____

8. simple, adj.

____

____

9. tattle, n.

____

____

10. whimper, n.

____

____

Usage Labels

College writing requires the use of standard English. By now, you know that standard English is accepted as universal by dictionaries and respected authorities. In other words, dictionaries have the final say on whether words are standard or nonstandard. Sometimes a dictionary simply labels a word *nonstandard.* Other times, it also tells us specifically in what way a word is nonstandard. These are the other labels that dictionaries use:

nonstandard:	word not accepted by most educated people
Example:	irregardless (Irregardless of the weather, we'll stay home. Instead, use *regardless.*)
informal or colloquial:	conversational, appropriate for casual communication
Example:	gonna (I'm gonna go for a walk. Instead, use *going to*.)
slang:	informal, often humorous, words used by various groups
Example:	flunk (Pete flunked math. Instead, use *failed.*)
regional:	words limited to a particular region
Example:	goober for peanut (in the South)
usage problem:	a word that is often misused
Example:	snuck (The cat snuck into the room. Instead, use *sneaked.*)

Because language is always changing, you should consult a recent dictionary for any word you think might not be standard English.

PRACTICE 6

Use your dictionary to label each italicized word below as *standard, nonstandard, informal* or *colloquial, slang*, or *regional.*

Example: My problem with studying is that I love to *goof* around.

<u>*Slang*</u>

1. His car is a *heap*. ______
2. I *ain't* scared of the dark. ______
3. They *reckon* that by tomorrow it will rain. ______
4. The plumber *repaired* the leaking faucet. ______
5. Many neighbors *brung* food to the family. ______
6. That bike *rocks*! ______
7. Mary looks *real* pretty in her graduation picture. ______
8. What kind of *pop* do you want? We have Pepsi and Diet Coke. ______
9. Americans *sure* like football. ______
10. He's such a *dude*. ______

PRACTICE 7

In the blank provided, rewrite the following sentences to avoid any slang, informal, regional, or other nonstandard English.

1. Listen, you sucker, you ain't goin' to get by with that lie.

____

____

2. They talks as if they was mean as hell.

____

____

3. Is that y'all's hat?

____

____

4. The computer I bought was a bummer and a rip-off.

____

____

5. The bunch of us knocked off early to watch the playoffs.

____

____

6. It seem wrong to me that yesterday she work only one hour.

____

____

7. That don't matter much noways.

____

____

8. It's a downer to read about innocent kids being molested by grown-ups.

9. What an old bag my landlady turned out to be!

10. I wish my old man would quit hassling me about getting a job.

Origin

A good desk dictionary (not a portable one) will often include the origin or **etymology** of a word. For example, we learn from the entry that *sandwiches* were first made for the British Earl of Sandwich, after whom they were named, to allow him to continue gambling without breaking for meals.

PRACTICE 8

Using a desk dictionary, look up the origins of the following words.

1. silhouette, n.

2. lunatic, n.

3. sinister, adj.

4. pasteurized, adj.

5. magnanimous, adj.

6. peer, n.

____

____

7. paradise, n.

____

____

8. cabbage, n.

____

____

9. arrowroot, n.

____

____

10. cute, adj.

____

____

Synonyms

The **synonym** of a word is another word whose meaning is similar. For example, *chilly, cool, frigid,* and *frosty* are listed in the dictionary as synonyms for *cold.* In most dictionaries, the synonyms of a word are listed after its definition and are labeled *syn.*

Sandwich has no synonyms listed. *Erase*, however, does. Its synonyms in our dictionary are listed as *expunge, efface, delete, cancel*, and *blot.* Synonyms can be helpful, but you must use them carefully. After all, a *cool* morning is hardly the same as a *frosty*—or a *frigid*—one.

PRACTICE 9

With the help of a dictionary, list two synonyms for the following words.

1. dark (adj.) ______________ ______________
2. inflexible (v.) ______________ ______________
3. careful (adj.) ______________ ______________
4. fat (adj.) ______________ ______________
5. lawyer (n.) ______________ ______________
6. circle (v.) ______________ ______________

7. fault (n.) ______ ______
8. glib (adj.) ______ ______
9. promise (n.) ______ ______
10. sour (adj.) ______ ______

IN A NUTSHELL

A good dictionary gives the following information about words:

- Spelling
- Word division
- Pronunciation
- Grammatical uses
- Meanings
- Usage labels
- Origin
- Synonyms

Unit Test

The paragraph that follows contains words that are nonstandard, colloquial, and slang. It also contains some words that are misspelled. Rewrite all sentences that aren't in standard English and correct all misspellings. If a sentence is correct, write *C* on the corresponding line.

1. Fred irritiates the heck out of me. 2. He is forever bragging about his grades. 3. But yesterday I gave him something to worry about: I whipped him good in a biology examination. 4. Once he even ripped me off a dollar by not paying up when we made a bet that I won. 5. Sometimes I wonder why I bother to remain his friend and to socialice with him on campus and at parties. 6. He ain't never going to become the sort of friend I respect and admire. 7. So why do I hang out with him? 8. Fred doesn't give a hoot about me, and I should distence myself from him. 9. My mom agrees with me; she don't like Fred. 10. Here comes Fred. Who's that cute chick with him?

1. ______

______

2. ______

______

3. ______

______

4. ______

______

5. ______________________________

6. ______________________________

7. ______________________________

8. ______________________________

9. ______________________________

10. ______________________________

Unit Talk–Write Assignment

What follows in the *Talk* column is an ungrammatical, incomplete attempt at defining "glass ceiling." Your assignment has several parts. First, turn the text in the *Talk* column into complete sentences written in standard English and spelled and punctuated correctly. Use your dictionary if you need help. (Every sentence has at least one misspelled word.) Then, find out—from the dictionary, teachers, friends, and any other available source—just what the term "glass ceiling" means. Finally, write a paragraph on "glass ceilings." Begin with a one-sentence definition, which will function as your topic sentence. Then, expand on your definition with reasoning and examples. If you need help with spelling or word meaning, check your dictionary.

TALK	WRITE
1. What's this "glass ceiling" busness I keeps hearing about?	
2. Beets me what it means.	

3. I know it has something to do with womin's jobs.

4. Something about being shovved back down by men when they gets too hotsy totsy.

5. Can you imagine someone trying to get through a glass cieling?

6. Maybe that be the point; glass cielings are tricky, man.

7. I wish peoples wouldn't use words like them without splaining.

8. The reason this come to mind is that yestday I hear someone say that some Air Force woman had gone through the glass cieling because she was to be the pilat on a space shuttle.

9. I guess the glass cieling is what keep women in jobs where they make less money.

10. But why not call it an iron cieling or a sement cieling?

Unit Collaborative Assignment

Pair up with a partner. Working together, use your dictionaries to turn these paragraphs into standard English. Also, find and correct the spelling errors (there are eight).

Most college campuses are filled with various personality types. There are the jocks, the nerds, the party animals, the lab rats/the do-gooders. My favorit is the nerd. Computer sceince programs seem to grow nerds. My theory is that nerds spend so much time at a keyboard that they beccome isolated. They turn into geeks that aint got no social contact with people outside their computer circle.

A sure way of identifing a nerd is by appearence. A nerd just does not know how to dress cool. His pants are always too short, usually hitting just above the ankle. His shirts are buttoned up to the collar, but the buttons are never in the right button holes. Then, too, the nerd's shirts are never stuck inside his pants, but hang half in and half out, looking quite sloppy. (I say "his," but there are just as many femmale nerds today.) A nerd never inquires about the wether before dressing. You can count on the fact that if it is a hot day, he will wear a sweater; whereas if it is a cold day, he will wear shorts. Nerds wear tee-shirts that say "My parents went to Disneyland, and all I got was this lousy tee-shirt." This, of course, is the nerd's yucky attempt at being cool.

Nerds always dress opposite to the established styles. They don't do this to rebel the way that punks do. They just don't know better. When the surfer look is popular, they wear leather jackets. When the preppy look is in, they wear disco clothes. Most important of all, though, a nerd is always comfortable in polyester. Sometimes, I'm a nerd, but then that's a diffrent story.

Unit Writing Assignment

In a good dictionary, find a word with an interesting origin (etymology). In a paragraph, explain this origin and tell how knowing the origin helps you better understand the word. Use the Revising Checklist inside the front cover of this book to help you revise.

Photo Writing Assignment

The following photo shows a baseball game in progress. Write a paragraph explaining the basic rules of the game to someone who has never even heard of the game. Or, if you wish, you can explain the basic rules of another sport or any board or card game. Be sure to explain any words that are unique to the sport or game or that have a different meaning from their meaning in common usage. For example, in discussing baseball, you should explain the special meanings of *ball* and *strike.* Use the Revising Checklist to help you revise.

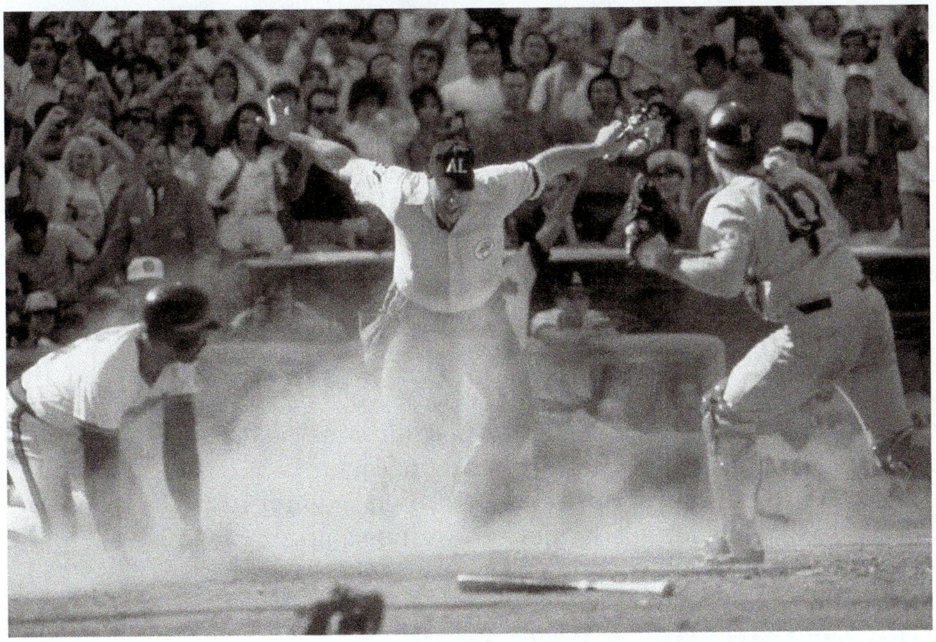

23 Spelling Rules

"Spelling is a p-a-i-n! Or is it p-a-n-e?"

Before the existence of dictionaries, words were spelled entirely by ear or by whim. *Slow* might be spelled *sloe, slo,* or *slough.* With the appearance in the eighteenth century of the first English dictionary, however, spelling gradually became standardized to the point that children today compete in spelling bees.

Even if we are never sufficiently skilled to enter a spelling bee, we can all become better spellers by observing some simple rules.

Tips for Improving Your Spelling

1. Sound out words. For instance, the word *government* contains an *n* if you say it aloud slowly. The word *find* has a final *d* sound and should not be spelled *fine.* Saying a word out loud can definitely help you to spell it correctly.
2. Make up your own memory tricks for remembering the spelling of problem words. For example, *cemetery* is spelled with all *e*'s because it is so eerie; the *principal* is your *pal*; after-dinner *dessert* has two *s*'s because it is doubly good.
3. Use a dictionary regularly. Looking up a word not only helps you with the spelling of that particular word, but also it helps you develop a sense of how words are spelled. That is, you begin to develop a feeling for the English language and for its spelling rules and exceptions. (See the list of dictionaries on page 406.)
4. Keep a list of words that you often misspell and use it when you proofread your writing. For some reason, everyone has trouble with certain words. Make a list of your particular

spelling weaknesses—words you often misspell—and put it in your dictionary. Be sure to check the spelling of these words when you proofread your paper.

Using a Spell Checker

If writing with a computer, as you most likely are, the first rule of spelling is simply this: Use the Spell Checker. The second rule is this: Remember that Spell Checkers go only so far. Although they catch such misspellings as *heighth* for *height,* and *ocasion* for *occasion,* they don't tell you if you've incorrectly used *its* for *it's* or *their* for *there* or *they're.* Neither do they tell you whether you've spelled a name correctly. Yet, if you're writing a letter of application for a job, the last thing you want to do is to misspell the name of the company.

PRACTICE 1

The following paragraph contains a number of words that are incorrectly spelled. Find the words and correctly spell them, using context as your guide.

Spell checkers are useful but they can all so make miss steaks. If you depend on spelling checkers too much, your writing will contain many arrows. These will be very hard to fine. The individual words may be correctly spelled, but in the context of your right in they will be wrung. For example, I've already maid several bad spelling errors in this paragraph, yet my spelling checker tells me that there are no missed takes. Can you sea watt I've done rung? If you have a sharp aye, ewe should find thirteen misspelled words.

Rules for Spelling

You will become a better speller if you follow certain simple spelling rules. However, spelling in English is not always as clear-cut as we would like; nearly every rule has an exception. Nevertheless, learning the rules and the exceptions can still help you become a better speller.

As you go over the rules, bear in mind the difference between vowels and consonants.

Vowels: *a, e, i, o, u,* and sometimes *y*

Consonants: All other letters of the alphabet

Using *ie* and *ei*

Remember the age-old rule: "*i* before *e* except after *c* or when sounded as *ay* as in *neighbor* or *weigh*":

niece

relieve

believe

but

ceiling
receive
deceive

EXCEPTIONS

either	leisure	species
caffeine	neither	their
financier	seize	weird
foreigner	science	
height	society	

ESL Advice!

If your background is British, remember that there are significant differences between American and British rules of spelling, for example, in the use of the final *-our* or *-or* (Br. *colour,* Am. *color*).

PRACTICE 2

Place a check mark in front of the correct spelling in each word pair.

1. ____ (a) reign
   ____ (b) riegn
2. ____ (a) yeild
   ____ (b) yield
3. ____ (a) perceive
   ____ (b) percieve
4. ____ (a) preist
   ____ (b) priest
5. ____ (a) recieve
   ____ (b) receive
6. ____ (a) weigh
   ____ (b) wiegh
7. ____ (a) chief
   ____ (b) cheif
8. ____ (a) society
   ____ (b) soceity

9. ____ (a) vein
   ____ (b) vien

10. ____ (a) breif
    ____ (b) brief

PRACTICE 3

Underline the correct spelling of the word in parentheses.

1. Drinking too much (caffeine, caffien) makes you jittery.
2. His (conciet, conceit) makes him unpopular.
3. Every one of our (nieghbors, neighbors) is quiet after 10 P.M.
4. The (weight, wieght) of the fruit does not determine its taste.
5. (Niether, Neither) Paula nor Manuel was at the scene.
6. He was (heir, hier) to a huge fortune.
7. Were you (relieved, releived) to see her leave?
8. It is difficult to (beleive, believe) him.
9. A good (freind, friend) is like pure gold.
10. How could they have (decieved, deceived) us so thoroughly?

Changing *y* to *i*

When you add an ending to a word that ends in a consonant plus *y*, change the *y* to *i*:

fry + ed = fried

worry + es = worries

happy + ness = happiness

merry + ly = merrily

EXCEPTIONS

decry	decrying (but decried)
horrify	horrifyingly
lady	ladylike
carry	carrying
cry	crying (but cried, crier)
worry	worrying (but worried, worrier)

PRACTICE 4

Combine the following words with the endings to their right and write the correct spellings in the blanks provided.

Example:	study	+	es	=	***studies***
1.	marry	+	ed	=	________
2.	hazy	+	ily	=	________
3.	hurry	+	ed	=	________
4.	terrify	+	es	=	________
5.	purify	+	ing	=	________
6.	bury	+	ing	=	________
7.	stay	+	ed	=	________
8.	copy	+	es	=	________
9.	worry	+	ing	=	________
10.	cry	+	ed	=	________
11.	marry	+	ing	=	________
12.	happy	+	ily	=	________
13.	delay	+	ed	=	________
14.	mercy	+	ful	=	________
15.	juicy	+	er	=	________

The Final Silent e

When you add endings that start with a vowel, such as *-al, -able, -ence,* or *-ing,* drop the final *e.* When you add an ending that starts with a consonant, such as *-ment, -less,* or *-ly,* keep the final *e.* Here are some examples for you to study:

bride + al = bridal

like + able = likable

true + ly = truly

emerge + ence = emergence

take + ing = taking

nine + th = ninth

manage + ment = management

love + less = loveless

polite + ly = politely

EXCEPTIONS

argue + ment = argument
courage + ous = courageous
judge + ment = judgment
manage + able = manageable
notice + able = noticeable

PRACTICE 5

Write a *C* next to the word that is spelled correctly.

Example: pleasureable	_____	pleasurable	__C__
1. desirable	_____	desireable	_____
2. endureable	_____	endurable	_____
3. abatment	_____	abatement	_____
4. measureless	_____	measurless	_____
5. dosage	_____	doseage	_____
6. writing	_____	writeing	_____
7. forcful	_____	forceful	_____
8. believable	_____	believeable	_____
9. exerciseing	_____	exercising	_____
10. completely	_____	completly	_____
11. excitement	_____	excitement	_____
12. sameness	_____	samness	_____
13. hopless	_____	hopeless	_____
14. continuous	_____	continueous	_____
15. arrangment	_____	arrangement	_____

Doubling the Final Consonant in One-Syllable Words

To add *-ed, -ing, -er,* or *-est* to a one-syllable word, double the consonant if it is preceded by a single vowel:

pin + ed = pinned
trim + ing = trimming
thin + er = thinner
sad + est = saddest

PRACTICE 6

Add the indicated endings to the words listed below and spell them correctly in the blanks provided.

Example: drop (ed) ***dropped***

1. dip (ing) ____________
2. top (ing) ____________
3. trim (ing) ____________
4. big (est) ____________
5. knit (ing) ____________
6. run (er) ____________
7. stop (ed) ____________
8. hot (est) ____________
9. slap (ed) ____________
10. beg (ed) ____________
11. skip (ing) ____________
12. fit (ed) ____________
13. clip (ing) ____________
14. flip (ed) ____________
15. strip (ing) ____________

Doubling the Final Consonant in Multisyllable Words

To add *-ing* or *-ed* to words of more than one syllable, double the final consonant if the following is true:

- The stress is on the final syllable:

  ad-mit´

  be-gin´

  de-fer´

- The last three letters consist of a consonant/vowel/consonant pattern:

  admit

  begin

  defer

Therefore,

admit + ed = admitted

begin + ing = beginning

defer + ed = deferred

Now, consider these words:

tra´vel = traveling	**(Do not double the consonant because the accent is on the first syllable: tra´vel.)**
ben´efit = benefited	**(Do not double the consonant because the accent is on the first syllable: ben´-e-fit.)**
repeat = repeating	**(Do not double the consonant because the last three letters do not fit the consonant/vowel/consonant pattern.)**

PRACTICE 7

In the blanks provided, add *-ed* and *-ing* to the following words.

	-ed	-ing
Example: commit	*committed*	*committing*
1. deter	______	______
2. label	______	______
3. expel	______	______
4. omit	______	______
5. travel	______	______
6. evict	______	______
7. occur	______	______
8. rebel	______	______
9. begin	______	______
10. control	______	______

PRACTICE 8

Underline the correct word in parentheses.

Example: Twice John (travelled, <u>traveled</u>) across the country by motorcycle.

1. John politely (deferred, defered) to those in authority.
2. He (predictted, predicted) sunshine, but it rained.

3. Believe me, they were all (profiting, profitting) from the experiment.
4. While we were (unwrapping, unwraping) the box, they left.
5. If he had (returned, returnned) on time, the fire would have been detected.
6. (Submiting, Submitting) meekly to mean bosses is difficult.
7. The new puppy (resisted, resistted) anyone who came near his bone.
8. The short-order cook was (refered, referred) to Burger King by my mom.
9. Jim did not believe in (enlistting, enlisting) in the army.
10. Have you (relented, relentted) after your decision to leave?

Forming Plurals

1. Most words form their plurals by simply adding *-s*:

SINGULAR	PLURAL
dog	dogs
umbrella	umbrellas
mother	mothers
book	books

However, there are a few exceptions that you should master. For example, words ending in *-s, -ss, -z, -x, -sh,* or *-ch* form their plurals by adding *-es,* an extra syllable for easier pronunciation.

SINGULAR	PLURAL
lens	lenses
kiss	kisses
buzz	buzzes
box	boxes
wash	washes
church	churches

PRACTICE 9

Form the plurals of the following words.

1. boy ______________
2. peach ______________
3. bump ______________
4. fox ______________
5. business ______________
6. fix ______________

7. bush ______________
8. wish ______________
9. sun ______________
10. letter ______________
11. lurch ______________
12. bus ______________
13. flash ______________
14. tax ______________
15. farmer ______________

2. If a word ends in an *o* preceded by a vowel, add *-s*:

rodeo	rodeos
patio	patios
zoo	zoos
radio	radios
video	videos

If a word ends in an *o* preceded by a consonant, add *-es*:

hero	heroes
potato	potatoes
echo	echoes
buffalo	buffaloes

EXCEPTIONS

alto	altos
grotto	grottos
memo	memos
motto	mottos
photo	photos
piano	pianos
solo	solos

PRACTICE 10

Form the plurals of the following words.

1. zero ______________
2. rodeo ______________
3. mosquito ______________
4. halo ______________

5. zoo ______________

6. tomato ______________

7. domino ______________

8. radio ______________

9. tornado ______________

10. motto ______________

PRACTICE 11

Write a sentence using the plurals of the following words.

1. buffalo

____

____

2. photo

____

____

3. antipasto

____

____

4. soprano

____

____

5. hero

____

____

6. potato

____

____

7. memo

____

____

8. video

____

____

9. patio

____

____

10. lingo

____

____

3. For most words ending in *f* (or *fe*), change the *f* to *v* and add *-es:*

SINGULAR	PLURAL
half	halves
calf	calves
leaf	leaves
wife	wives

EXCEPTIONS

roof	roofs
safe	safes
chief	chiefs
proof	proofs

PRACTICE 12

Form the plurals of the following words.

1. brief ______________
2. hoof ______________
3. yourself ______________
4. knife ______________
5. wife ______________
6. thief ______________
7. chief ______________
8. proof ______________
9. leaf ______________
10. mastiff ______________
11. self ______________
12. wolf ______________
13. life ______________

14. wharf ____________
15. half ____________

4. Some words form irregular plurals:

SINGULAR	PLURAL
woman	women
foot	feet
ox	oxen
mouse	mice
index	indices
appendix	appendices
criterion	criteria
analysis	analyses

PRACTICE 13

Form the plurals of the following words.

1. tooth ____________
2. child ____________
3. goose ____________
4. louse ____________
5. man ____________
6. foot ____________
7. ox ____________
8. mouse ____________
9. species ____________
10. alumnus ____________

5. Compound nouns—made up of two or more words—form their plurals by adding *-s* to the main word. If a compound noun is written as a single word, make the ending word plural:

SINGULAR	PLURAL
boyfriend	boyfriends
eyeglass	eyeglasses
grandchild	grandchildren
bookshelf	bookshelves

EXCEPTION	
passerby	passersby

If the compound noun is written as separate or hyphenated words, make the main word plural:

SINGULAR	PLURAL
bus stop	bus stops
jump shot	jump shots
rule of the road	rules of the road
mother-in-law	mothers-in-law
man-of-war	men-of-war

PRACTICE 14

Form the plural of the following compound nouns.

1. rule of thumb ______________
2. right-of-way ______________
3. sergeant major ______________
4. attorney general ______________
5. attorney-at-law ______________
6. secretary of state ______________
7. eyesore ______________
8. daughter-in-law ______________
9. storybook ______________
10. storm window ______________
11. jumping jack ______________
12. son-in-law ______________
13. jack-of-all-trades ______________
14. home plate ______________
15. jukebox ______________

6. Some words have the same spelling for singular and plural:

SINGULAR	PLURAL
deer	deer
fish	fish
sheep	sheep
species	species
series	series
moose	moose

PRACTICE 15

Turn the following words into plurals and then write a sentence using the plural.

Example: fish ______ ***fish*** ______

The boys caught three fish with their homemade rods.

1. series ______________

____

2. sheep ______________

____

3. person ______________

____

4. moose ______________

____

5. tie ______________

____

6. deer ______________

____

7. virus ______________

____

8. species ______________

____

9. virtue ______________

____

10. household ______________

____

PRACTICE 16

The following announcements were taken from actual church bulletins. Correct the misspelled or mistyped words.

1. The pastor would appreciate it if the women of the congregation would lend him their electric girdles for the pancake breakfast next Sunday morning.
2. The audience is asked to remain seeded until the end of the recessional.

3. Deacon Clark is on vacation. Massages can be given to the church secretary.
4. The third verse of "Blessed Assurance" will be sung without musical accomplishment.
5. A song fest was hell at the Methodist church on Wednesday.
6. Prayer and medication will follow Wednesday's potluck supper.
7. The choir director invites any member who enjoys sinning to join the choir.

IN A NUTSHELL

Most words form their plurals by adding *-s*. Many exceptions exist. When in doubt, check the dictionary.

Unit Test

Circle the word in each pair that is correctly spelled.

1.	leafs	leaves
2.	receive	recieve
3.	committed	commited
4.	expeled	expelled
5.	potatos	potatoes
6.	benefited	benefitted
7.	gooses	geese
8.	feets	feet
9.	echoes	echos
10.	writing	writting
11.	noticable	noticeable
12.	admitted	admited
13.	sliming	slimming
14.	yield	yeild
15.	saddest	sadest

Unit Talk–Write Assignment

In the *Talk* column is a conversation between two students, Jan and George, on whether it's better to live in a small town or a big city. First, rewrite the *Talk* column into complete sentences in standard English. Be sure to correct all the spelling errors you find. Then write a well-developed paragraph stating your opinion and supporting it with evidence from your own experience.

TALK		WRITE
Jan:	Living in a small town is so wierd.	
George:	No weigh! I used to live in a town so small that I knew the names of all the dogs. I loved it.	
Jan:	No, in small towns, the soceity is too pusshy. Everyboudy nose your bussiness.	
George:	I don't think so. I like the way people in small towns percieve each other. Nobody's a chief. Everyone's a bottle washer.	
Jan:	Yeah, wright! Like living in a restaurant. You said it!	
George:	That's not what I meant. I meant that the nieghbors are friendly.	

Jan: There's just a samness that's borring. Plus, everybody's chucked together like potatos in a sack. I destest it.

George: So, what'd you get in a city? Greif on the streets, not nowing the person next door?

Jan: Yeah, but at least you can come and go as you please. Their's something to be said for that.

George: There's something to be said for feeling foriegn where you live?

Jan: Well, a big city makes me feel free, not penned up and surounded by a bunch of watchdogs. Sorry, but that's my openion.

George: A small town makes me feel loved, not penned up. Listen, I gotta go. You're too crochety today, anyhow.

Jan: Yeah, later. Meantime, I'll just sit here and enjoy being ignored by all the passerbys. City life! It's fabuluous! Look at me! I'm unknown! I'm free!

George: Bye!

Jan: Bye!

Unit Collaborative Assignment

Working with a partner, first read the spelling rule, and then think of examples of the rule. Use one of your examples in a sentence.

Example: "*I* before *e* except after *c*."

Answer: Tomorrow, I will *receive* my history grade.

1. When you add an ending to a word that ends in a consonant plus *y*, change the *y* to *i*.

2. When you add *-ed, -ing, -er,* or *-est* to one-syllable words, double the consonant if it is preceded by a single vowel.

3. To add *-ing* or *-ed* to words of more than one syllable, double the final consonant if (1) the stress is on the final syllable, or (2) the last three letters consist of a consonant/vowel/consonant pattern.

4. Most words form their plurals by simply adding -s.

5. Words ending in *-s*, *-ss*, *-z*, *-x*, *-sh*, or *-ch* form their plurals by adding *-es*, an extra syllable for easier pronunciation.

6. When you add endings that start with a vowel, such as *-as*, *-able*, *-ence*, or *-ing*, drop the final *e*. When you add an ending that starts with a consonant, such as *-ment*, *-less*, or *-ly*, keep the final e.

7. Some words ending in *o* form their plurals by adding *-es*.

8. For most words ending in *f* (or *-fe*), change the *f* to *v* and add *-es*.

9. Some words have the same spelling for singular and plural.

10. Some words form irregular plurals.

Unit Writing Assignment

Write a paragraph about the person you hope to be 10 years from now. What sort of life would you be leading? What kind of ideal job would you have? Do you picture yourself as the boss or as a worker? Would you be married? Would you have children? Would you want a wife or husband who also has a career, or would you prefer a stay-at-home partner? What kind of social life would appeal to you? Most importantly, what would be the basis of your belief system? Be sure to follow the spelling rules in this unit. Use the Revising Checklist inside the front cover of this book to help you revise.

Photo Writing Assignment

The following photo shows students campaigning for their causes on campus. What cause do you support? Write a paragraph explaining why one of your causes is important to you. What do you do to support this cause? Make sure your spelling follows the rules outlined in this unit. Use the Revising Checklist to help you revise.

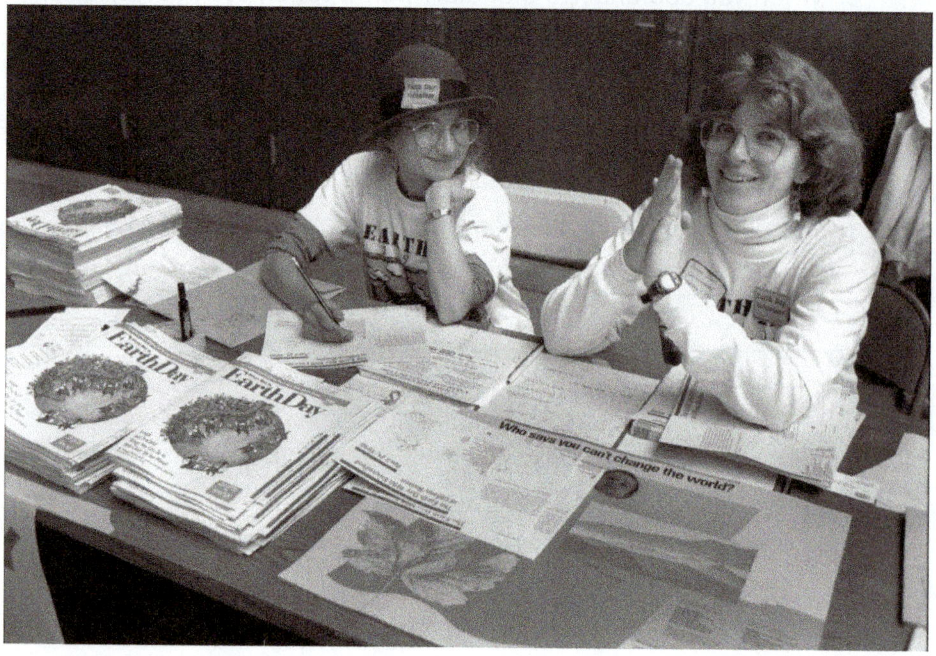

24 Commonly Misspelled Words

"Are you quite quiet?"

EAR ALERT

English spelling is difficult. Words are often not spelled the way they sound. *Raccoon* sounds like it should have a *k,* but doesn't. *Threw* sounds like *through,* but is spelled differently. *Though, cough,* and *through* look like rhyming words, but are actually not pronounced at all alike. Given that English has a vocabulary of more than 400,000 words, it's a wonder that we spell as well as we do.

Some words—called **homonyms** (also called **homophones**)—sound exactly alike, but have different spellings and meanings. Other words are not exact homonyms, but are similar enough to often be confused. Study the following examples:

Homophones:	altar (a raised platform in church)	alter (to change)
	The minister stood at the *altar.*	I can *alter* your jacket.
	it's (short for "it is")	its (possessive pronoun)
	It's getting late.	The rabbit is in *its* nest.
Confusing words:	accept (to receive with consent)	except (excluded)
	I *accept* your money.	Everyone left *except* Fred.
	advice (a noun)	advise (a verb)
	She asked for *advice.*	They *advised* her to study.

Homophones and Frequently Confused Words

Learn the meaning and spelling of these homophones and frequently confused words. Errors in spelling can change the meaning of writing. *Angel* spelled correctly will still confuse your reader if you really meant *angle.*

- **accept**—to take or receive/**except**—excluding, other than, but for

  I *accept* the gifts.

  Everyone was there, *except* you.

- **access**—a means of approach/**excess**—too much

  He had *access* to the computer.

  Ann wore an *excess* of jewelry.

- **advice**—recommendation (noun)/**advise**—to caution, to warn (verb)

  My *advice* is to remain silent.

  We *advise* you to remain silent.

- **affect**—to influence, to change/**effect**—to bring about (verb); consequence, result (noun)

  Breaking up with Barry *affected* my grades.

  They were able to *effect* some improvements in the hospital kitchen.

  One *effect* of regular exercise is increased energy.

- **alter**—to change/**altar**—a raised platform in a church

  She will *alter* the dress.

  At the *altar,* they said, "I do."

- **bare**—without covering or clothing/**bear**—to bring forth; to endure (verb); an animal (noun)

  The trees were *bare* of leaves.

  Please *bear* with me for one more minute.

  The *bear* strolled past the campground.

- **berry**—a kind of fleshy fruit/**bury**—to place in the ground

  My favorite *berry* is the raspberry.

  Let's *bury* the garbage in the back yard.

- **capital**—value of goods, money; a principal city/**capitol**— a building in which lawmakers meet

  My grandfather would not part with any of his *capital.*

  The *capital* of Ohio is Columbus.

  The students toured the new state *capitol.*

- **cite**—to quote/**site**—place or scene/**sight**—ability to see

    The lawyer could *cite* a dozen laws.

    What a perfect *site* for a public park!

    At seventy, she had the *sight* of a youngster.

- **course**—a path; subjects taken in school/**coarse**—rough in texture

    He followed a different *course* through the woods.

    Helen signed up for two *courses* in history.

    The texture of the linen was *coarse.*

- **desert**—a dry land (noun); to abandon (verb)/**dessert**—something sweet served at the end of a meal

    I spent the weekend in the *desert.*

    He vowed that he would never *desert* his troops.

    I always check the *dessert* menu first.

- **fairy**—a tiny superhuman being/**ferry**—a boat used for transportation across water

    A *fairy* helped Cinderella go to the ball.

    They crossed the Sacramento River in a *ferry.*

- **forth**—forward/**fourth**—next after third

    He said, "Go *forth* and play hard."

    I am the *fourth* child.

- **gulf**—deep chasm/**golf**—game

    We could see across the *gulf.*

    My grandfather loves to play *golf.*

- **hole**—an opening through something/**whole**—complete

    They hid the money in a deep *hole.*

    Max ate the *whole* lemon pie.

- **its**—possessive form of *it*/**it's**—contraction of *it is*

    The dog chased *its* tail.

    It's a hot day.

- **lose**—to misplace or come to be without/**loose**—to be free from restraint

    You're going to *lose* your hat in this wind.

    The cattle were let *loose* on the range.

- **passed**—went by/**past**—an earlier time; beyond

    I *passed* her in the hall.

    Forget the *past*; live for today.

    I drove *past* your house.

- **personal**—private, intimate/**personnel**—employees

  This is my *personal* diary.

  Go directly to the *personnel* office.

- **piece**—part of a whole/**peace**—opposite of war

  Would you like a *piece* of chocolate cake?

  Everyone wants *peace* in the world.

- **principal**—first in rank; the chief or head/**principle**—an accepted rule or belief

  She's the *principal* of our elementary school.

  I have my *principles.*

- **quiet**—making no noise; peaceable/**quite**—completely or entirely

  They were *quiet* all night.

  I am *quite* confused.

- **right**—correct, fitting, proper (adj.); privilege, prerogative (noun)/**write**—to form letters on a surface/**rite**—a formal or ceremonial act or practice

  Don't bother unless you expect to be *right.*

  To see your bank balance is your *right.*

  Please *write* me a postcard.

  The *rite* of Baptism is observed in many churches.

- **sole**—only; the bottom of the foot/**soul**—the spirit

  I was the *sole* member of the team to go.

  The *soles* of my feet itch.

  Music is good for the *soul.*

- **their**—ownership/**there**—in that place/**they're**—contraction of *they are*

  This is *their* boat.

  My car is over *there.*

  They're friendly people.

- **to**—a preposition; part of any infinitive/**too**—also, excessively/**two**—number after the number one

  He went *to* the beach.

  I'm going *to* walk the dog.

  First Julie wept; then Meg wept, *too.*

  Don't eat *too* much ice cream.

  I have *two* dogs.

- **who's**—contraction of *who is*/**whose**—the possessive case of *who*

    Who's talking about us?

    I know *whose* coat that is.

- **your**—the possessive case of *you*/**you're**—contraction of *you are*

    This is *your* choice.

    You're quite welcome.

These are, of course, not the only homophones—English is riddled with many others. These are just some that you are most likely to encounter.

IN A NUTSHELL

Watch out for homophones–words that sound exactly alike but have different spellings and meanings–and words that are easily confused.

PRACTICE 1

Underline the correct word in the parentheses.

Example: Mr. Murphy is the (forth, <u>fourth</u>) person in line.

1. They cut down all the trees, making the plot look (bear, bare).
2. He was the (sole, soul) survivor of the airplane crash.
3. All I want is a (quite, quiet) evening at home by the fire.
4. All of (there, their) relatives showed up for the wedding.
5. They were forced to (except, accept) 20 extra guests.
6. They must hire extra (personnel, personal) for the job.
7. If they only understood (their, they're) limitations.
8. The (passed, past) is behind us; don't worry about it.
9. I had apple pie for (desert, dessert).
10. Don't (lose, loose) your place in line.

PRACTICE 2

In the blank provided, write a *C* if the sentence is correct or an *NC* if it is not correct. Write the correct word over any italicized word that is incorrect.

Example: ***<u>NC</u>*** As a mother, she could not bare to watch her son being punished.

1. ____ Everyone is going to the game *except* Joe.
2. ____ My sister always gives me good *advice*.

3. ____ The nuts should be *coarsely* chopped.
4. ____ We're going hiking in the *desert.*
5. ____ Was I happy that I *past* accounting!
6. ____ We went to *they're* open house last Sunday.
7. ____ I'm afraid *its* too late for that.
8. ____ Don't make the knot too *loose.*
9. ____ If *you're* not the owner, who is?
10. ____ *Who's* jacket is this?

PRACTICE 3

Each sentence below is preceded by a pair of homonyms. Insert the correct word in each blank in the sentence.

1. witch/which

   ____ ____ in *The Wizard of Oz* was the good ____?

2. plain/plane

   The ____ landed on the ____.

3. warn/worn

   Let me ____ you that those socks are ____ and may have holes in them.

4. wore/war

   The general ____ the medals that he won during the ____.

5. heal/heel

   She is hoping that the cut on her ____ will ____ soon.

PRACTICE 4

Write a sentence for each of these homophones.

1. piece

   ____

   ____

   peace

   ____

   ____

2. advice

   ____

   ____

advise

3. affect

effect

4. bare

bear

5. site

sight

6. gulf

golf

7. berry

bury

8. fairy

____

____

ferry

____

____

9. right

____

____

write

____

____

10. hole

____

____

whole

____

____

Commonly Misspelled Words

Below is a list of words that are commonly misspelled. If you regularly have trouble with any of the words on this list, memorize the correct spellings.

accidentally
acquaintance
acquire
address
already (not to be confused with *all ready*)
all right (always two words, just like *all wrong*)
answer
anxious
arithmetic
athletics
attendance
awful
awkward
believe (not to be confused with *belief*)
breathe (not to be confused with *breath*)
business
calendar
cemetery
changeable
chief
choose (not to be confused with *chose*)
conscience (not to be confused with *conscious*)
daily
definite
dependent
design
device (not to be confused with *devise*)
disappearance
embarrass
environment
especially
exaggerate
exercise
existence
familiar
fascinate

finally
foreign
forty
fragrant
friend
fulfill
government
harass
height
hindrance
incredible
independent
interesting
irresistible
judgment
library
literature
maintenance
mathematics
medicine
million
miracle
miscellaneous
mischief
necessary
neighbor
noticeable
nuisance
occasion
occur/occurrence/occurred
offered
parallel
peculiar
politics
possess
practically
precede
preferred
prejudice
preparation
privilege
proceed
receive
recognize
referred/referring
relieve/relief
resemblance
restaurant
reverence
ridiculous
sandwich
seize (not to be confused with *size*)
separate
several
similar
sincerely
succeed
surprise
temperature
than (not to be confused with *then*)
thorough
tragedy
truly
unnecessary
until
usually
vegetable
visitor
weird
writing

IN A NUTSHELL

You should memorize any words that you often misspell. Repeatedly writing these words will help.

PRACTICE 5

Each of the following sentences contains a misspelled word from the list above. Write the corrected version in the blank provided.

Example: He has a definate plan for getting a career in broadcast journalism. ***definite***

1. She looked akward giving the speech. ________
2. The baby suffered from a high temparature. ________
3. It's January 1, so I need a new calandar. ________
4. The Senate voted to expand our aid to foriegn nations. ________
5. Why did you refuse to fulfil your promise to a good friend? ________

6. By speaking so crassly, he does embarass our class. _______
7. His judgment of people has been sharpened by litareture. _______
8. He claimed that thousands of people attended the parade—an exageration. _______
9. Stop being such a baby and take your medecine. _______
10. His driving priviledges were taken away. _______
11. Don't be rediculous! That's a fake orange. _______
12. In preperation for the swim meet, she ate lots of pasta. _______
13. The restoraunt that serves the best fries is McDonald's. _______
14. Broadway and Lincoln are paralell streets. _______
15. The hero siezed the controls and safely landed the spaceship. _______

PRACTICE 6

Cross out the incorrectly spelled word in parentheses in each of the following sentences.

1. Spinach is my favorite (vegetable/vegtable).
2. Wait (untill/until) late afternoon to go to the beach.
3. I have better grades in English than I do in (mathmatics/mathematics).
4. It's (all right/alright) to cry when you're sad.
5. Her (temprature/temperature) was normal, but she felt warm.
6. Evelyn runs a successful (business/busness).
7. She has (definite/defnite) ideas about how to manage her money.
8. Joan has been my (freind/friend) since second grade.
9. Don't complain about the (government/goverment) if you don't vote.
10. Use your good (judgment/judgement) when you vote.
11. A (pecular/peculiar) smell is coming from the refrigerator.
12. I think it's coming from the (vegetable/vegitable) bin.
13. Let's (seperate/separate) the twins in school so that their teachers won't be confused.
14. For the sake of peace, the neighbors will have to overcome their (prejudice/predjudice) against newcomers.
15. You have (finaly/finally) completed this exercise.

PRACTICE 7

Circle the correctly spelled word in each of the following pairs.

1. fourty/forty
2. literature/litrature
3. practically/practicly
4. receive/recieve
5. sevral/several
6. sincerly/sincerely
7. calendar/calender
8. address/adress
9. necessry/necessary
10. nieghbor/neighbor
11. precede/preceed
12. truely/truly
13. ridiculous/rediculous
14. pratically/practically
15. noticeable/noticable

Words Spelled with One or Two Words

After years of being repeatedly used together, some separate words have blended into one. The list below will help you learn which of these words are commonly used as one and which may be used separately.

Words that *cannot* be combined into one word:

a lot	in front
all right	high school
each other	no one
even though	

Words that *must* be combined into one word:

already	nearby
another	newspaper
bathroom	rooommate
bedroom	schoolteacher
cannot	throughout
downstairs	worthwhile
good-bye	yourself

Words that are combined or not combined, depending on the meaning.

One word: *already,* meaning "previously"

The minister had *already* finished his sermon by the time they arrived.

Two words: *all ready,* meaning "prepared"

We're *all ready* for the flag ceremony.

One word: *altogether,* meaning "entirely"

The policeman was *altogether* right.

Two words: *all together,* meaning "as a complete group"

The children were asked to meet *all together* on the platform.

One word: *always,* meaning "every time" or "forever"

My parents will *always* love each other.

Two words: *all ways,* meaning "every aspect" or "every phase"

Before paying for a new bike, check *all ways* the old one could be repaired.

One word: *anymore,* meaning "any longer"

Please don't eat pork *anymore.*

Two words: *any more,* meaning "extra"

They shouldn't have *any more* children.

One word: *everyone,* meaning "all the people"

Everyone at work was included in the pay raise.

Two words: *every one,* meaning "all of the items or people in a particular group"

We had to use *every one* of the knives in the drawer.

PRACTICE 8

Underline the correct word in each pair listed

1. I found the dirty rags in a basket downstairs/down stairs.
2. Jeremy all ways/always wants to eat the pizza crust.
3. Tell the dog to fetch Dad's newspaper/news paper.
4. Tonight we'll eat in the formal dining room/diningroom.
5. She is all together/altogether too negative in her thinking.
6. Can you get anymore/any more tickets to the game?
7. Will you attend your high school/highschool reunion this year?
8. Cleaning the park is a worth while/worthwhile project.
9. The rosebush was planted infront/in front of the shed.
10. Every one/everyone of the dogs was checked for rabies.

Unit Test

The paragraph that follows contains 19 spelling errors mentioned in this unit. Correct each error.

In the passed, my relationship with my teachers was always quiet hostile. They always seemed to treat me like a criminal instead of just the insecure, akward schoolboy that I was. For instance, my arithmatic teacher once told my parents that they might consider chosing a diffrent school for me since I was so difficult to handle. At the time, I found that suggestion incredable. I didn't think that my teachers were using there best judgement and most compassionate instincts to help me ajust to school. It seemed that I couldn't do anything to please my teachers. Even my perfect attendence didn't altar the fact that just the site of me annoyed them. My very existance seemed to be a threat to their way of teaching. I truly beleived that they were predjudiced against me and prefered the more pleasant and agreeable students who simply sat at their desks and treated the teachers with great reverance. But today, I look back and realize that, in actuality, I was just a pecular, cynical student while my teachers were conscientious and commited to their jobs. Today, I like most of my teachers because I understand what a difficult task they have.

Unit Talk–Write Assignment

Asked to say what they thought were life's simple pleasures (romance excluded), students in an English class came up with the list reproduced in the *Talk* column. First, rewrite each item as a complete sentence, correcting any misspelled words. Then choose one of the topics listed or a simple pleasure of your own and write a paragraph about it.

1. State what the pleasure is (e.g., "I love to play pick-up basketball.").
2. Describe the pleasure in detail.
3. State why it gives you pleasure.
4. Check your paragraph for spelling errors.

TALK	WRITE
1. Sleeping grate at knight.	______________________

2. Playing ketch with my dog.

3. Picking while flours.

4. Riding in my ant's convertible.

5. Having a bear with a friend.

6. Shearing secrets with a girlfriend.

7. Going cite seeing in a new city.

8. Eating my favorite desert.

9. Excepting a challenge.

10. Watching a knew program on TV

11. Walking in the rein without an umbrella.

12. Fixing my family there dinner.

13. Laying on the grass and watching the clouds.

14. Eating a hot fudge Sunday topped with nuts.

15. Watching my wife comb her blonde hare.

16. Celebrating the forth of July.

17. Enjoying a quite day in my garden.

18. Watching my brother moe the lawn.

19. Taking a coarse in night school.

20. Watching Monday nite football.

Unit Collaborative Assignment

A. Read the following sentences aloud, asking a partner to spell the words in italics. Confirm that the spelling is right or correct it.

1. Jane's *past* work has always been excellent.
2. I have had *quite* enough trouble from you.

3. We had cookies for *dessert.*
4. *They're* over *their* limit of credit.
5. You have a hole in the *sole* of your shoe.
6. She has red hair, and she is *awkward.*
7. Lately the weather has been *changeable.*
8. What is your *height* and weight?
9. They were guilty of more than *mischief.*
10. Although they were twins, they always chose *separate* friends.

B. Now reverse your roles.

1. You give me *too* much trouble.
2. If she does not *accept* this time, I will still ask her out again.
3. I could not *bear* so much pain again.
4. This is the *fourth* football game we've won!
5. I hated the big *hole* in John's sock.
6. The dance floor looked *irresistible.*
7. Our *neighbor* picks up our newspaper when we're gone.
8. A camping trip requires much *preparation.*
9. *Seize* the next opportunity to do a kind deed.
10. She always tries to *fulfill* her promises.

Unit Writing Assignment

Your neighborhood action committee wants to raise money to buy children's playground equipment for the park. You have been asked to write a description of the project and ask for donations. Your letter will be mailed to everyone in town, so you'll want to watch your spelling. Use the Revising Checklist on the inside front cover of this book to help you revise.

Photo Writing Assignment

The following photo shows a graduation exercise. Write a paragraph discussing the value of this ceremony. You might ask yourself these questions: What is the value of the tradition? What would happen if it were discontinued? Is the tradition worth the time and effort that it requires? Begin with a discussible topic sentence, which you should then prove. Check your spelling carefully and use the Revising Checklist to help you revise.

READINGS

In these readings, you will see put into practice many of the techniques and principles you have learned so far in this book. We strongly advise you to read the headnote that precedes each reading, and to take the comprehension test, Understanding What You Have Read, before going on to the questions under Thinking About What You Have Read and Writing Assignments.

Help for Your Reading

You can improve your reading with a few commonsense techniques. Here are some suggestions to help you read the selections in this book.

1. Scan the whole piece before you read.

Before you begin to actually read an essay, short story, or poem, casually look it over. Pay attention to the title—especially in the case of poems and short stories. The title is often a clue to the meaning of the piece. Turn the pages of an essay to see its major divisions, if any. Some essays are subdivided by headings, others appear as solid blocks of print. Scanning the headings as you turn the pages will tell you what an essay is about and what points it covers. Note the number of pages. What you are doing is looking over the essay as if it were a map for an upcoming trip. You are finding out how far you have to go and what kind of ground you have to cover.

2. Read the headnote first.

The **headnote** is the paragraph that precedes each writing selection. It gives you a general idea of what the reading is about and any surprises or twists you should look for. The headnote may also alert you to the work's main points. Through the headnote, the editors can whisper advice in your ear as you get ready to tackle the selection.

3. Write your reactions in the margins of the pages.

Get rid of the old-fashioned idea that writing in a book is a sin. If the book belongs to someone else or to the library, writing in it is *definitely* a sin. Otherwise, writing in a book is not sinful, but useful. Feel free to underline words or ideas. Scribble your reactions in the margin as you read. Writing down your reactions helps you become an active, rather than a passive, reader. When you react to a piece of writing, you involve yourself in it and are likely to get its point better than if you simply sit and read between snores. If a description is particularly sad, you might note: "This passage is gloomy." If the author's opinion annoys you, show your irritation by jotting down your reaction, whether it be, "That's a typical closed-minded opinion," or simply, "Rubbish." Another good use of marginal writing is to summarize in a phrase what the whole paragraph is about, so that when you reread, you can go straight to your summaries.

4. Underline key ideas.

All writing consists of two parts—a point and its proof. As shown in this text, most nonfiction paragraphs make a point and then try to prove it, using facts, examples, or reasons. To understand a paragraph, you must know its main point, usually found in the topic sentence. The topic sentence can be the opening sentence of a paragraph or, less commonly, the closing sentence. An alert reader learns, therefore, to pay special attention to opening and closing sentences. Underlining the topic sentence is an excellent way to help you keep the main idea in mind as you read the rest of the paragraph. Consider this passage:

> <u>The best way to make sure that you don't die a pauper is to begin a systematic savings account early in life.</u> Even if you put away only $10 a month at the

> start, the act of saving some money every month starts a habit that, if continued, can eventually make you, if not wealthy, at least secure. With no savings, a person usually is unable to retire. It is a pathetic situation in our country that people who have earned good wages all of their working days often retire without a penny. They become dependent on their children or the state for food and board. If you have a pension plan, so much the better, but even then, an additional nest egg of savings will give added comfort in your retirement.

The topic sentence is the key to the meaning of the paragraph. The rest of the paragraph supports and explains the topic sentence.

Also pay close attention to *signal words,* words that announce some important idea. Here are some examples, with the signal words underlined:

> Most important, however, is the temperature of the metal.
>
> Particularly relevant is how the mother gorilla shows affection to her baby.
>
> A major reason for the country's downfall was love of luxury.
>
> Above all, we recommend exercises to strengthen the muscles of the abdomen.
>
> Most noteworthy is the senator's stand on the tobacco industry.

These signal words are clues to ideas that the author considers particularly important.

5. Think about what you have read.

Every paragraph or so, stop and think about what you have just read. Make a mental summary—preferably aloud—to be sure that you fully understand what you are reading. If you have trouble doing this, read the passage again, and perhaps even a third time, until you understand it.

6. Look up unfamiliar words in the dictionary.

Often **context**—surrounding words or sentences—will suggest a word's meaning. In the paragraph below, notice how context tells what the word *interloper* means:

> Just a few days after the police barricaded Pennsylvania Avenue to car traffic, in order to protect the White House from dangerous intruders after the Oklahoma City bombing, the first of two *interlopers*—a psychologist—climbed the White House fence. In front of dozens of shocked tourists, the man rushed across the White House lawn. A few days later, another intruder hoisted himself over the fence and was immediately handcuffed and hustled into a guard house. While neither man seemed to have a clear motive and did not seem intent on assassinating the President, the incident caused concern among the White House police.

What is an *interloper?* The context of the paragraph tells us that it means the same as *intruder*—one who barges into a place uninvited.

Sometimes context tells us all we need to know about the meaning of a word. Consider this sentence: "The cows had to be herded back to their *byre* for milking." Although you may have no idea what the word *byre* means if you see it standing alone, in the context of this sentence, you are sure that it must mean something like "barn," "stable," or "cowshed."

7. Reread.

Your first reading of an essay, short story, or poem will provide a general picture of the work. You will understand its broad outline, get its main idea, and absorb its general point of view. But in order to become a better writer, you must read, and reread, line by line, and even word by word. Poems, especially, need rereading because so much meaning is contained in relatively few words. So rid yourself of the idea that five minutes before class starts you can skim the reading assignment and know it. Good writing requires careful rereading.

AN OBJECT

Tortillas

José Antonio Burciaga

In Burciaga's words, the common tortilla takes on the life of a theater prop, a piece of clothing, and—most importantly—a symbol of Mexican life. Burciaga not only describes the most familiar use of the tortilla, but also informs us of its important history, reaching back to the Mayan civilizations and their mythology. The author even suggests ways of eating tortillas and creating works of art with them. In addition to serving as a basic food staple over the centuries, the tortilla has risen to the high rank of a cultural badge for the Mexican people. As you read, think about what details the author uses to give the tortilla such cultural importance.

My earliest memories of tortillas is my Mamá telling me not to play with them. I had bitten eyeholes in one and was wearing it as a mask at the dinner table. 1

As a child, I also used *tortillas* as hand warmers on cold days, and my family claims that I owe my career as an artist to my early experiments with *tortillas.* According to them, my clowning around helped me develop a strong artistic foundation. I'm not so sure, though. Sometimes I wore a *tortilla* on my head, like a *yarmulke,* and yet I never had any great urge to convert from Catholicism to Judaism. But who knows? They may be right. 2

For Mexicans over the centuries, the *tortilla* has served as the spoon and the fork, the plate and the napkin. *Tortillas* originated before the Mayan civilizations, perhaps predating Europe's wheat bread. According to Mayan mythology, the great god Quetzalcoatl, realizing that the red ants knew the secret of using maize as food, transformed himself into a black ant, infiltrated the colony of red ants, and absconded with a grain of corn. (Is it any wonder that to this day, black ants and red ants do not get along?) Quetzalcoatl then put maize on the lips of the first man and woman, Oxomoco and Cipactonal, so that they would become strong. Maize festivals are still celebrated by many Indian cultures of the Americas. 3

When I was growing up in El Paso, *tortillas* were part of my daily life. I used to visit a *tortilla* factory in an ancient adobe building near the open *mercado* in Ciudad Juárez. As I approached, I could hear the rhythmic slapping of the *masa* as the skilled vendors outside the factory formed it into balls and patted them into perfectly round corn cakes between the palms of their hands. The wonderful aroma and the speed with which the women counted so many dozens of *tortillas* out of warm wicker baskets still linger in my mind. Watching them at work convinced me that the most handsome and *deliciosas tortillas* are handmade. Although machines are faster, they can never adequately replace generation-to-generation experience. There's no place in the factory assembly line for the tender slaps that give each *tortilla* character. The best thing that can be said about mass-producing *tortillas* is that it makes it possible for many people to enjoy them. 4

In the *mercado* where my mother shopped, we frequently bought *taquitos de nopalizos,* small tacos filled with diced cactus, onions, tomatoes, and *jalapeños.* Our friend Don Toribio showed us how to make delicious, crunchy *taquitos* with dried, salted pumpkin seeds. When you had no money for the filling, a poor man's *taco* could be made by placing a warm *tortilla* on the left palm, applying a sprinkle of salt, then rolling the *tortilla* up 5 quickly with the fingertips of the right hand. My own kids put peanut butter and jelly on *tortillas,* which I think is truly bicultural. And speaking of fast foods for kids, nothing beats a *quesadilla,* a *tortilla* grilled-cheese sandwich.

Depending on what you intend to use them for, *tortillas* may be made in various ways. Even a run-of-the-mill *tortilla* is more than a flat corn cake. A skillfully cooked homemade *tortilla* has a bottom and a top; the top skin forms a pocket in which you put the filling that folds your *tortilla* into a taco. Paper-thin tortillas are used specifically for *flautas,* a type of taco that is filled, rolled, and then fried until crisp. The name *flauta* means *flute,* which probably refers to the Mayan bamboo flute; however, the only sound that comes from an edible *flauta* is a delicious crunch that is music to the palate. In México *flautas* are sometimes made as long as two feet and then cut into manageable segments. The opposite of *flautas* is *gorditas,* meaning *little fat ones.* These are very thick small *tortillas.* 6

The versatility of *tortillas* and corn does not end here. Besides being tasty and nourishing, they have spiritual and artistic qualities as well. The Tarahumara Indians of Chihuahua, for example, concocted a corn-based beer called *tesgüino,* which their descendants still make today. And everyone has read about the woman in New Mexico who was cooking her husband a *tortilla* one morning when the image of Jesus Christ miraculously appeared on it. Before they knew what was happening, the man's breakfast had become a local shrine. 7

Then there is *tortilla* art. Various Chicano artists throughout the Southwest have, when short of materials or just in a whimsical mood, used a dry *tortilla* as a small, round canvas. And a few years back, at the height of the Chicano movement, a priest in Arizona got into trouble with the Church after he was discovered celebrating mass using a *tortilla* as the host. All of which only goes to show that while the *tortilla* may be a lowly corn cake, when the necessity arises, it can reach unexpected distinction. 8

Vocabulary

yarmulke (2)
maize (3)
infiltrated (3)
absconded (3)
aroma (4)
bicultural (5)
concocted (7)
whimsical (8)
host (8)

Understanding What You Have Read

Check the correct answer in the blank provided.

1. The author's earliest memory of tortillas is
   ____ (a) the odor they produced while baking.
   ____ (b) his mother telling him not to play with them.
   ____ (c) using them as flying saucers.
   ____ (d) that they tasted terrible.

2. Tortillas predate
   ____ (a) horses.
   ____ (b) the wheel.
   ____ (c) the founding of Mexico City.
   ____ (d) the Mayan civilizations.

3. What do the author's children place on their tortillas?
   ____ (a) Peanut butter and jelly
   ____ (b) Chocolate syrup
   ____ (c) Ice cream
   ____ (d) The hottest jalapeños

4. What is a *flauta?*
   ____ (a) A girl who flouts customs
   ____ (b) A flirtatious girl
   ____ (c) A tortilla that is filled, rolled, and fried until crisp
   ____ (d) An act of disobedience

5. What segment of society has used tortillas when they were short of materials?
   ____ (a) Artists
   ____ (b) Nurses
   ____ (c) Football players
   ____ (d) Cleaning women

Thinking About What You Have Read

1. What is the author's formal definition of a tortilla? In which paragraph does he state it?
2. Why do you think the author uses terms like *mercado, masa, deliciosas,* and *jalapeños*? Do these terms make the essay difficult to understand for readers who do not know Spanish? Why or why not?
3. Besides serving as a basic food, what other functions have tortillas served over the centuries of Mexican history? Why does the author mention these other functions?
4. What does the author have against machine-made tortillas? Do you agree or disagree? Give reasons for your answer.
5. What humor does the author use throughout his essay? Point to some specific instances. What does the humor add?

Writing Assignments

1. Write about a food that is particularly representative of your ethnic background. Describe the food and explain how it is used among your family and friends. Use details that allow your reader to see the food and taste it.
2. Describe your favorite food with details that will show your reader why you like it.

Beautiful Music

Dana Wall

This story is written from the point of view of a son whose father once crafted a violin with the magnificent tone of a Stradivarius, the world's most celebrated stringed instrument. We are reminded that many of the objects we encounter in life may vanish, never to be seen again; yet, we may imagine their existence, or long for a key to unlock the mystery that caused their disappearance.

When I was a boy, my father told me he could do anything he wanted to do. I believed him. Dad said he wanted to become the first photographer in Sioux City to develop color prints. He did, and his prints were displayed for weeks at the local Eastman Kodak store. **1**

When I was 13, I said I wanted an "Olson-60" gasoline engine for my balsa-wood model airplanes. Dad said he could build it for me. He borrowed my friend's motor, took measurements, made wooden parts, cast them in aluminum and turned the pieces on his lathe until they fit. He purchased only a spark plug, the gas tank and a rubber fuel line. **2**

When I was 16, Dad looked closely at the violin I played and announced that he wanted to make one. He read about violinmaking, then became a violinmaker at the age of 43. He bought the tools and materials from a local stringed-instrument repairman, leased a small storefront and set Mom up as the shopkeeper, while he worked until 3 p.m. at the local Bell Telephone Co. **3**

From 3:15 p.m. until he decided to quit for the day, Dad was at his shop. He retired from the phone company 17 years later and continued to make violins, violas, and at least one cello. He sold and rented his instruments to students and repaired stringed instruments for area musicians. **4**

Dad often speculated about the superiority of Stradivarius violins. He'd occasionally read a magazine or newspaper article in which an expert claimed it was the unique varnish that gave those instruments their beautiful sound. Dad argued that chemists could analyze and duplicate the varnish —if that were the answer. **5**

Other experts believed the sound was in the craftsmanship, but Dad said if that were the case, modern technology would allow us to fashion exact duplicates of Stradivari's works. **6**

One of Dad's friends once asked him which kinds of woods were used in making a fiddle. When Dad explained that the top of a violin was made of spruce, his friend said he had an old chunk of spruce he might be interested in. The friend explained that this was not just any piece of wood. He had found it when he was fighting below an ancient monastery at Monte Cassino in Italy during World War II. He had lain in the mud for days and watched numerous buddies die before the Allies, reluctantly, bombed the fortified abbey to root out the last of the enemy. **7**

As my dad's buddy scrambled up the mountain and through the ruins, he picked up a section of timber less than two feet long to keep as a souvenir, shoved it under the straps of his pack and carried it throughout the rest of the war. When he returned home, he put the wood on a storage shelf in his basement, where it had stayed for the last 20 years. **8**

Dad's eyes widened when he heard the story. **9**

He worked for the next 12 months making a violin from the wood that his friend had given him. The first time I heard it, Dad played the soothing, repetitive melody of a barcarole, a Venetian boatman's song. The instrument had a mellow sound that lost little resonance in the higher notes, the mark of a superior violin. The violin with the Monte Cassino spruce top was **10**

Dad's masterpiece. He had discovered on his own what many experts now agree is the secret of the Stradivarius sound: It was the wood itself that resonated so beautifully. The abbey at Monte Cassino was first built in 529; the last reconstruction had been done in 1349. Dad reasoned old Stradivari had access to spruce that had cured for centuries, perhaps ancient timbers from a ruined medieval castle or cathedral.

Leo Kucinski, the venerable conductor of the Sioux City Symphony Orchestra, was one of Dad's many musician friends. The maestro stopped at the violin shop almost weekly to talk and to play the Monte Cassino violin. So did others. But Dad would never sell it. **11**

In the early 70's, knowledgeable burglars broke into Dad's shop one night and stole the instrument along with other quality violins. The thieves left starter fiddles, inexpensive factory reproductions and the like. Dad never saw the violin again. **12**

Dad's spirit was broken by the robbery. He stopped making instruments. He kept the music shop until he was 80 years old, selling guitars and violins and occasionally working on a repair, charging too little for everything. **13**

Dad has been gone for 14 years now. The Monte Cassino violin has been missing for more than 25. Somewhere a musician plays a late-20th-century violin with a remarkable tone. If a thief did not remove the maker's tag, a light shined into the curved hole on that ancient spruce top will show the violin was made by Harold A. Wall, Sioux City, Iowa. But the owner today may never understand why the violin sounds so much like a Stradivarius. **14**

Vocabulary

displayed (1)
lathe (2)
speculated (5)
unique (5)
varnish (5)
craftsmanship (6)
monastery (7)
reluctantly (7)
fortified (7)
abbey (7)
root (7)
barcarole (10)
resonance (10)
cured (10)
venerable (11)
maestro (11)
reproductions (12)

Understanding What You Have Read

Check the correct answer in the blank provided.

1. The main subject of this essay is a
   ____ (a) rare spruce tree.
   ____ (b) spectacular violin.
   ____ (c) loyal son.
   ____ (d) photographer who developed colored print.

2. What role did World War II play in this story?
   ____ (a) The writer was a captain in the army during WW II.
   ____ (b) The Nazis looted the abbey during WW II.
   ____ (c) WW II is the setting for the entire story.
   ____ (d) The father's buddy found the chunk of wood while fighting in WW II.

3. Which of the following factors is NOT suggested as a reason why the Stradivarius is such a fine violin?
    ____ (a) The varnish
    ____ (b) The craftsmanship
    ____ (c) The strings
    ____ (d) The wood

4. What is the first melody the writer heard his father play on the violin?
    ____ (a) A Venetian boat song
    ____ (b) "America the Beautiful"
    ____ (c) "Taps"
    ____ (d) A Viennese waltz

5. What happened to the father's masterpiece?
    ____ (a) It was stolen by burglars.
    ____ (b) It was sold at an auction.
    ____ (c) It was destroyed during a fire.
    ____ (d) It has been recently found in an antique shop.

Thinking About What You Have Read

1. How do you feel about the way the writer admired his dad and thought of him as all powerful? Do you think it is healthy for a son to admire his father to that extent? Would it be better if a son always had a realistic view of his father, including the father's faults? Explore the reasons for your answer.
2. Why was the father's spirit broken (paragraph 14)? Is his broken spirit justified or is the father being self-centered? Why couldn't the father find a new challenge for his enormous creativity?
3. In telling this story about his father, what characteristics of the writer's presentation strongly demonstrate the intimacy and love that once existed between the two?
4. How was the wood that the father turned into the violin discovered? Explain why you find that story far-fetched or believable.
5. What is your opinion of the end of the story? Do you find the ending satisfactory or do you think it is lacking in some way? How can the author justify such a gloomy ending?

Writing Assignments

1. Write a paragraph about something your father (or mother) made or owned that you loved. Explain your attraction.
2. Pretending that this is a work of fiction, write a paragraph in which you propose a different ending to the story.

The Cello

Lorena Bruff

"The Cello" is a modern poem. As you can see, it has no traditional rhyme or poetic rhythm. It is short and to the point. Yet it has a haunting quality to it. As you read this poem, ask yourself these questions: What is the poet actually talking about? Is she talking about a cello or about a person? How can you tell? What point is she really trying to make?

The Cello

To tell you
the truth
I never
wanted to be
a cello.
When I was
wood
I had
my own song.

Understanding What You Have Read

Check the correct answer in the blank provided.

1. What is a cello?
   ____ (a) It is a musical instrument played with the lips.
   ____ (b) It is a percussion instrument.
   ____ (c) It is something used in chemistry experiments.
   ____ (d) It is a musical instrument played with a bow.
2. Who is speaking in this poem?
   ____ (a) The cello
   ____ (b) We can't tell
   ____ (c) A person who plays the cello
   ____ (d) None of the above
3. What is a cello made of?
   ____ (a) Metal
   ____ (b) Wood
   ____ (c) Clay
   ____ (d). Cotton
4. What would you say is the mood of the cello?
   ____ (a). It is happy.
   ____ (b). It is optimistic.
   ____ (c). It is sad.
   ____ (d). It is in love.

Thinking About What You Have Read

1. What do you think that the stanza "When I was /wood /I had /my own song" means?
2. What was the cello before it became a cello? How can "wood" have its own song?
3. What is this poem actually about? About whom do you think it was written? A cello, or a person?
4. How could the complaint of the cello be summed up in a single sentence? Write a single-sentence explanation of the meaning of this poem.

Writing Assignments

1. Write a paragraph comparing yourself to any musical instrument you think you are like.
2. Write a paragraph about a time you had to sing a song (or play a role) you felt was really someone else's, not your own.

A PLACE

How the Lawyers Stole Winter

Christopher B. Daly

The title of this opening essay may seem oddly inappropriate for writing that is intended to be descriptive of a place. But in fact, when you read the essay, you'll quickly understand what place the author has in mind. As you read, try to see things from the point of view of the town fathers and mothers who are responsible for any accidents that might occur during the winter on public property. Ask yourself whether the writer is not perhaps a trifle optimistic in thinking that adolescents will take the proper precautions to ensure accident-free skating. What is your opinion of his argument that risk is a natural condition of living?

When I was a boy, my friends and I would come home from school each day, change our clothes (because we were not allowed to wear "play clothes" to school), and go outside until dinnertime. In the early 1960s in Medford, a city on the outskirts of Boston, that was pretty much what everybody did. Sometimes there might be flute lessons, or an organized Little League game, but usually not. Usually we kids went out and played. 1

In winter, on our way home from the Gleason School, we would go past Brooks Pond to check the ice. By throwing heavy stones on it, hammering it with downed branches, and, finally, jumping on it, we could figure out if the ice was ready for skating. If it was, we would hurry home to grab our skates, our sticks, and whatever other gear we had, and then return to play hockey for the rest of the day. When the streetlights came on, we knew it was time to jam our cold, stiff feet back into our green rubber snow boots and get home for dinner. 2

I had these memories in mind recently when I moved, with my wife and two young boys, into a house near a lake even closer to Boston, in the city of Newton. As soon as Crystal Lake froze over, I grabbed my skates and headed out. I was not the first one there, though: the lawyers had beaten me to the lake. They had warned the town recreation department to put it off limits. So I found a sign that said DANGER, THIN ICE. NO SKATING. 3

Knowing a thing or two about words myself, I put my own gloss on the sign. I took it to mean *When the ice is thin, there is danger and there should be no skating*. Fair enough, I thought, but I knew that the obverse was also true: *When the ice is thick, it is safe and there should be skating*. Finding the ice plenty thick, I laced up my skates and glided out onto the miraculous glassy surface of the frozen lake. My wife, a native of Manhattan, would not let me take our two boys with me. But for as long as I could, I enjoyed the free, open-air delight of skating as it should be. After a few days others joined me, and we became an outlaw band of skaters. 4

What we were doing was once the heart of winter in New England—and a lot of other places, too. It was clean, free exercise that needed no Stair-Masters, no health clubs, no appointments, and hardly any gear. Sadly, it is in danger of passing away. Nowadays it seems that every city and town and almost all property holders are so worried about liability and lawsuits that they simply throw up a sign or a fence and declare that henceforth there shall be no skating, and that's the end of it. 5

As a result, kids today live in a world of leagues, rinks, rules, uniforms, adults, and rides—rides here, rides there, rides everywhere. It is not clear that they are better off; in some ways they are clearly *not* better off. 6

When I was a boy skating on Brooks Pond, there were no grown-ups around. Once or twice a year, on a weekend day or a holiday, some parents might come by with a thermos of hot cocoa. Maybe they would build a fire (which we were forbidden to do), and we would gather round. 7

But for the most part the pond was the domain of children. In the absence of adults, we made and enforced our own rules. We had hardly any gear—just some borrowed hockey gloves, some hand-me-down skates, maybe an elbow pad or two—so we played a clean form of hockey, with no high-sticking, no punching, and almost no checking. A single fight could ruin the whole afternoon. Indeed, as I remember it, thirty years later, it was the purest form of hockey I ever saw—until I got to see the Russian national team play the game. 8

But before we could play, we had to check the ice. We became serious junior meteorologists, true connoisseurs of cold. We learned that the best weather for pond skating is plain, clear cold, with starry nights and no snow. (Snow not only mucks up the skating surface but also insulates the ice from the colder air above.) And we learned that moving water, even the gently flowing Mystic River, is a lot less likely to freeze than standing water. So we skated only on the pond. We learned all the weird whooping and cracking sounds that ice makes as it expands and contracts, and thus when to leave the ice. 9

Do kids learn these things today? I don't know. How would they? We don't let them. Instead we post signs. Ruled by lawyers, cities and towns everywhere try to eliminate their legal liability. But try as they might, they cannot eliminate the underlying risk. Liability is a social construct; risk is a natural fact. When it is cold enough, ponds freeze. No sign or fence or ordinance can change that. 10

In fact, by focusing on liability and not teaching our kids how to take risks, we are making their world more dangerous. When we were children, we had to learn to evaluate risks and handle them on our own. We had to learn, quite literally, to test the waters. As a result, we grew up to be savvier about ice and ponds than any kid could be who has skated only under adult supervision on a rink. 11

When I was a boy, despite the risks we took on the ice no one I knew ever drowned. The only people I heard about who drowned were graduate students at Harvard or MIT who came from the tropics and were living through their first winters. Not knowing (after all, how could they?) about ice on moving water, they would innocently venture out onto the half-frozen Charles River, fall through, and die. They were literally out of their element. 12

Are we raising a generation of children who will be out of their element? And if so, what can we do about it? We cannot just roll back the calendar. I cannot tell my six-year-old to head down to the lake by himself to play all afternoon—if for no other reason than that he would not find twenty or thirty other kids there, full of the collective wisdom about cold and ice that they had inherited, along with hockey equipment, from their older brothers and sisters. Somewhere along the line that link got broken. 13

The whole setting of childhood has changed. We cannot change it again overnight. I cannot send my children out by themselves yet, but at least some of the time I can go out there with them. Maybe that is a start. 14

As for us, last winter was a very unusual one. We had ferocious cold (near-zero temperatures on many nights) and tremendous snows (about a hundred inches in all). Eventually a strange thing happened. The town gave in—sort of. Sometime in January the recreation department "opened" a section of the lake, and even dispatched a snowplow truck to clear a good-sized patch of ice. The boys and I skated during the rest of winter. Ever vigilant, the town officials kept the THIN ICE signs up, even though their own 15 truck could safely drive on the frozen surface. And they brought in "life-guards" and all sorts of rules about the hours during which we could skate and where we had to stay.

But at least we were able to skate in the open air, on real ice. 16

And it was still free. 17

Vocabulary

domain (8)
meteorologists (9)
connoisseurs (9)
ordinance (10)
vigilant (15)

Understanding What You Have Read

Check the correct answer in the blank provided.

1. What big city did the author live near as a boy and man?
   ____ (a) New York
   ____ (b) Boston
   ____ (c) Pittsburgh
   ____ (d) Detroit

2. How did the boys know that a frozen pond was safe to skate on?
   ____ (a) They asked the coach.
   ____ (b) They called up the television weatherperson.
   ____ (c) They formed a committee to check out the weather.
   ____ (d) They subjected the pond to various tests.

3. What meaning did the writer give to the sign posted against skating?
   ____ (a) If the ice was thin, don't skate; if thick, skate.
   ____ (b) All skating was banned.
   ____ (c) Only roller skating was allowed.
   ____ (d). Skating was permitted if properly supervised.

4. As a boy, what role did adults play in the skating of children?
   ____ (a). They closely supervised the boys.
   ____ (b). They established leagues for the boys.
   ____ (c). They mandated the hours for skating.
   ____ (d). None. Occasionally they brought a thermos of cocoa.

5. What group is, according to the author, most likely to drown during winter?
   ____ (a). Foreign students from the tropics
   ____ (b). Unsupervised students
   ____ (c). Gang members
   ____ (d). Single girls who can't swim

Thinking About What You Have Read

1. On what does the author blame the attempts of small towns to overregulate ice-skating? How do you think a small town municipal official would explain this tendency? What is your own opinion of what or who is to blame?
2. The author portrays the kids as being highly responsible in checking the thickness of the ice before attempting to skate on it. Say why you believe him or why you don't.
3. What kind of example do you think the author is setting for his two sons in his attitude toward authority?
4. What does the author mean in paragraph 13 when he speaks about the "collective wisdom about cold" not inherited by the children of today? What is your opinion of this "collective wisdom?"
5. How would you characterize the author's attitude towards authority? What is your opinion of this attitude?

Writing Assignments

1. Write a paragraph about anything risky you used to do as a child when not under the supervision of adults.
2. Write a paragraph giving your opinion about who is right in this dispute, the author or the town authorities. Make a case for your point of view.

Letter from Tokyo

Michael A. Lev

Every country has its own way of adapting to and dealing with the world—its own culture. The episode that Lev, the Tokyo foreign correspondent for the Chicago Tribune, recounts here is a classic example of what can happen when the expectations of two cultures clash. Lev, with the point of view of a typical American, cannot understand why he can't get lettuce and tomato on his cheeseburger. On the other hand, the Japanese restaurant owner cannot understand why Lev doesn't follow the rules. As you read this piece, try to imagine how Lev must have seemed to the Japanese, with their entirely different way of looking at things.

TOKYO—The day of the naked cheeseburger could have turned ugly. The ex-New Yorker in me wanted to scream and yell. But the journalist in me recognized a chance to gain insight into Japanese society, or at least to have a classic native experience—like being in Manhattan and getting accosted by an arrogant panhandler. **1**

It was lunch time, and my Japanese interpreter, Naoko Nishiwaki, and I were in a Tokyo hamburger restaurant called One's. Naoko ordered the One's burger, and I picked the cheeseburger. **2**

When our food came, Naoko's hamburger looked fabulous—a thick, juicy patty heaped with fresh lettuce and tomato. My cheeseburger was naked. It looked sad. In halting Japanese, I called over the proprietor. **3**

"Excuse me." I said. "My cheeseburger doesn't have lettuce or tomato. Can I have some, please?" **4**

She gave me a quizzical look. **5**

"No." **6**

No? My pulse immediately quickened beyond my Japanese fluency level, and Naoko was forced to begin interpreting. "Just bring some lettuce and tomato. I'll pay for it." **7**

"Sorry. The cheeseburger doesn't come with lettuce and tomato." **8**

I didn't back down, so she got tough. "Cheeseburgers don't get lettuce and tomato; that's not how they come," she said, adding, "Even for a child, we wouldn't do anything different." **9**

Her final offer: "If you don't want the cheeseburger, I'll take it back and make you a One's burger." **10**

"That's absurd. Just cut me some tomato slices and bring them on a napkin." **11**

The woman got so excited that even Naoko had trouble deciphering her. The tomato and lettuce aren't the right size for the cheeseburger, she argued. They won't mesh properly with the cheese. **12**

She grabbed my cheeseburger from me. She returned later with a freshly cooked One's burger and a dirty look. **13**

I label this run-in with Japanese inflexibility the "kir effect" because of what happened to Masao Miyamoto, an author and social critic I know. **14**

Miyamoto went to a hotel bar, saw an open bottle of white wine on display and ordered a glass. Sorry, he was told, white wine isn't on the menu. It's used to make kir, a wine cocktail with cassis. Thinking quickly, Miyamoto ordered a kir—hold the cassis. **15**

Long negotiations ensued with the waiter, with the maitre d', with the assistant manager. Finally, he got his drink, but he was told to please never come back. **16**

These moments of exasperation reflect a culture in which order reigns. It is a cliché, but it's true: Japan is a group-oriented society. If everyone did **17** their own thing, this tiny overpopulated archipelago would descend into chaos, the thinking goes.

In some ways, it's a great system. Riding a bicycle in Tokyo is a pleasure, even on crowded sidewalks. The rule is, ring your bicycle bell once and pedestrians ahead will step to the side. Works every time. **18**

Just don't question the rules. While buying an expensive cellular telephone, the salesman asked for my Japanese residency card. I had my temporary card with permanent ID number but had not yet received the credit-card-size permanent card with photograph. **19**

"Sorry," he said. "Come back when you have it." **20**

"But it's the correct ID number," I explained. "I just have it on a sheet of paper instead of on a credit card." **21**

He continued to pack up the paperwork. I insisted that he call headquarters. I needed the phone, didn't he need the sale? He returned sucking his teeth and shrugging. "It would be a little difficult," he said, using the Japanese phrase for "impossible." **22**

If I were Japanese, I would have been expected to apologize and leave the store for causing trouble. Instead, Naoko, who has lived in America and understands our strange ways, went to work. There were belabored discussions by telephone with several parties and then a visit to the local telephone company office. Proposals. Counteroffers. Liberal use of the phrase "a little difficult." But I finally got my phone. **23**

Miyamoto sees the issue in harsh terms: Japanese society does not teach or tolerate independent thinking. All decisions are reached by consensus. Everything is done by the book. **24**

I was stopped for speeding not long ago. Instead of producing a Japanese or an American driver's license, I showed my international driver's license. The cop had never seen one before. I knew he was impressed with how official it looked. But he was confounded by the identification numbers. They didn't correspond with the number of blank spaces on his speeding-ticket form. **25**

Would he risk filling out a messy ticket with numbers that didn't fit in the boxes? **26**

No way. He let me go. **27**

Vocabulary

accosted (1)
quizzical (5)
deciphering (12)
exasperation (17)
archipelago (17)
belabored (23)
consensus (24)
confounded (25)

Understanding What You Have Read

Check the correct answer in the blank provided.

1. What did the author want that caused such a scene in the restaurant?
    ____ (a). He wanted a bottle of ketchup.
    ____ (b). He wanted sushi.
    ____ (c). He wanted Jamaican pepper sauce.
    ____ (d). He wanted lettuce and tomato on his cheeseburger.

2. What name does the author give to Japanese inflexibility?

____ (a) Mulishness
____ (b) The kamikaze principle
____ (c) The kir effect
____ (d) The anti-American practice

3. What, according to the author, is a cliché, but true?

____ (a) That Japan is a group-oriented society
____ (b) That there is a streak of wildness in the Japanese
____ (c) That the Japanese love sports
____ (d) That the Japanese emphasize individual rights

4. What is the rule for riding a bicycle on the sidewalk in Tokyo?

____ (a) Bicyclists have the right-of-way.
____ (b) Ring your bicycle bell once and pedestrians will step to the side.
____ (c) Shout, "Look out!"
____ (d) Hire a guide to go ahead of you.

5. Why did the Japanese cop not give the author a speeding ticket?

____ (a) Because he felt sorry for the author
____ (b) Because the author's license number would not fit on the speeding ticket form
____ (c) Because the author was unfamiliar with the rules of the road
____ (d) Because the author talked him out of it

Thinking About What You Have Read

1. The author writes in the first paragraph that the "ex-New Yorker" in him wanted to scream and yell. What do you suppose an ex-New Yorker is like? Why do you think he mentions where in the United States he used to live?

2. What basic rule of American business did the author's experience at the hamburger restaurant run counter to?

3. The author writes, "While buying an expensive cellular telephone, the salesman asked for my Japanese residency card." The sentence contains a grammatical error that this book has taught you how to correct. What is it? How would you correct the sentence?

4. What is your opinion of the author's complaints about Japanese society? Do you think that they are reasonable, or do you think that he is fussy? Explain your answer.

5. In paragraph 23, the author writes that his interpreter had lived in America and understood "our strange ways." What does he mean by "strange ways"?

Writing Assignments

1. Write a paragraph about a time someone did not behave the way you thought he or she would.
2. Write about any unpleasant encounter you had with a difficult salesperson.

An Animal

Snakes

Michael Ondaatje

What makes this brief essay fascinating is the mystery associated with it. Why did the grey cobra lead such a charmed life? Snake stories tend to interest most readers because secret powers have been attributed to this reptile by many ancient myths and folklore. As you read, look for humor as well as mystery.

The family home of Rock Hill was littered with snakes, especially cobras. The immediate garden was not so dangerous, but one step further and you would see several. The chickens that my father kept in later years were an even greater magnet. The snakes came for the eggs. The only deterrent my father discovered was ping-pong balls. He had crates of ping-pong balls shipped to Rock Hill and distributed them among the eggs. The snake would swallow the ball whole and be unable to digest it. There are several paragraphs on this method of snake control in a pamphlet he wrote on poultry farming. 1

The snakes also had the habit of coming into the house and at least once a month there would be shrieks, the family would run around, the shotgun would be pulled out, and the snake would be blasted to pieces. Certain sections of the walls and floors showed the scars of shot. My stepmother found one coiled asleep on her desk and was unable to approach the drawer to get the key to open the gun case. At another time one lay sleeping on the large radio to draw its warmth and, as nobody wanted to destroy the one source of music in the house, this one was watched carefully but left alone. 2

Most times though there would be running footsteps, yells of fear and excitement, everybody trying to quiet everybody else, and my father or stepmother would blast away not caring what was in the background, a wall, good ebony, a sofa, or a decanter. They killed at least thirty snakes between them. 3

After my father died, a grey cobra came into the house. My stepmother loaded the gun and fired at point blank range. The gun jammed. She stepped back and reloaded but by then the snake had slid out into the garden. For the next month this snake would often come into the house and each time the gun would misfire or jam, or my stepmother would miss at absurdly short range. The snake attacked no one and had a tendency to follow my younger sister Susan around. Other snakes entering the house were killed by the shotgun, lifted with a long stick and flicked into the bushes, but the old grey cobra led a charmed life. Finally one of the old workers at Rock Hill told my stepmother what had become obvious, that it was my father who had come to protect his family. And in fact, whether it was because the chicken farm closed down or because of my father's presence in the form of a snake, very few other snakes came into the house again. 4

Vocabulary

magnet (1)
deterrent (1)

pamphlet (1)
poultry (1)
ebony (3)
decanter (3)
absurdly (4)

Understanding What You Have Read

Check the correct answer in the blank provided.

1. What at the family home of Rock Hill was a greater magnet to the snakes than the garden?
   ____ (a) The turtles
   ____ (b) The geese
   ____ (c) The fireplaces
   ____ (d) The chickens

2. Certain sections of the walls at Rock Hill showed signs of
   ____ (a) splattered food.
   ____ (b) earthquake damage.
   ____ (c) shotgun holes.
   ____ (d) pink paint.

3. Once the author's stepmother saw a snake coiled asleep
   ____ (a) on her desk.
   ____ (b) in her washing machine.
   ____ (c) on her bed.
   ____ (d) on her ironing board.

4. What happened each time the stepmother would shoot at the grey cobra?
   ____ (a) The snake would slither out of range.
   ____ (b) She would miss or the gun would jam.
   ____ (c) Someone could be heard praying.
   ____ (d) She would faint from fear.

5. Finally, one of the old workers decided that the grey cobra
   ____ (a) had no taste for eggs.
   ____ (b) was too old to do any harm.
   ____ (c) was really the author's father returning from the dead to protect the family.
   ____ (d) deserved to be handed over to the local zoo.

Thinking About What You Have Read

1. What does the ping-pong ball incident indicate about the author's father?

2. What incident, other than finding a snake in your house, could cause the same kind of family excitement described in paragraphs 2 and 3? Give a specific example.

3. Judging from the details offered by the author, what kind of woman was the author's stepmother? List some of her traits.

4. What do you suppose gave the old worker the idea that the snake was the father returned from the grave?

5. Why do you think few other snakes came into the house again?

Writing Assignments

1. Write about something that happened in your life that you have never been able to fully explain.

2. Write a paragraph describing how you feel about snakes. Do they frighten you? Are you repulsed by them? Do you like them? Do you consider them interesting? Do they have a special meaning for you?

The Revolt of the Elephants

Ingrid E. Newkirk

This is an argument in favor of freeing captive elephants. The author argues with the passion of a true believer. Her point is simple: It is wrong to hold elephants in captivity solely for the entertainment of humans. She tries to convince us that the elephant is not just a dumb animal, but a sensitive creature capable of almost human feelings. As you read, notice her use of examples and the contrast she draws between the lives of a wild elephant and one that has been captured, trained, and put to work in a circus.

The elephants are mad and they're just not going to take it anymore. **1** Three times this summer a "circus elephant" has run amok and hurt her captors. In New York, an elephant named Flora crushed the skull of a Moscow Circus interpreter minutes before a planned appearance on the "Live With Regis and Kathy Lee" show. In Honolulu, a 21-year-old African elephant named Tyke trampled her trainer to death and injured a dozen spectators as she tore out of the Circus International tent. She was shot dead in the street.

Last summer, Janet, an old elephant who had been kept on repeated **2** doses of drugs to calm her down, tore out of the Great American Circus ring in Florida, carrying a box full of children on her back, and was shot 47 times by an off-duty police officer before she died. These spectacularly hideous attacks made headlines; many others did not.

Circus proprietors have been too busy counting their money to do more **3** than slug or drug uppity elephants. Now the pachyderms' polite protestations have turned nasty. How much human blood will mingle with that of the elephants before their struggle for freedom is successful?

Sound far-fetched? Consider this. Elephants have the largest brains of **4** any mammals on Earth. They are creative and altruistic. Imagine what it must be like for them to be told what to do, courtesy of a bullhook, every moment of their lives. They live more than 70 years in their homelands but their average life in captivity is reduced to 14 years; because of stress, traveling in boxcars and being stabled in damp basements, many captive elephants have arthritis, lame legs, and tuberculosis.

Left to their own devices in their homelands, elephants are highly social **5** beings; aunts babysit, mothers teach junior life skills such as how to use leaves and mud to ward off sunburn and insect bites, babies play together under watchful eyes, lovemaking is gentle and complex, and elephant relatives mourn their dead. They draw pictures in the dirt with twigs and rocks.

Life under the big top means: Pay attention to your trainers, don't falter **6** even if you feel tired or ill, obey, obey, obey. It means leg chains between acts, the loss of warmth from your father and mother, no long-term friends.

Behaviorists tell us elephants cry from loss of social interaction and from **7** physical abuse. If you wonder how they keep from going mad, they don't.

Rani was the first captive elephant I ever met. Every single day for **8** years she stood outside the Asoka Hotel in New Delhi, India, from sunrise to late at night, waiting to be prodded into action whenever a tourist fancied a ride. One day I asked Ram, her owner, where Rani had come from, and he explained that young elephants are taken from their families and "broken." He described how they must be chained and beaten until they learn to listen and behave. Several years ago, a National Geographic television special about elephants in the wild and in servitude showed men carrying out exactly that barbaric, inhumane system.

Rani died long before I had learned that elephant calves in the wild stay at their mothers' sides for a decade or longer; the elephants grieve and mourn, cradling their lost relatives' skulls in their trunks and swaying back and forth; that they communicate subsonically at frequencies so low humans cannot detect them without sophisticated equipment. **9**

There are 2,000 to 3,000 "Ranis" held captive in the beast wagons of circuses and in private collections. Sometimes, they stop behaving like windup toys and crush the bones and breath out of a keeper, make a break for it, go berserk. Most simply endure. **10**

It is now a criminal offense to confine elephants, big cats, and, in most cases, primates in circuses visiting the Australian Capital Territory. Seven municipalities in Western Australia have banned circuses from using government land. Animal acts have also been banned or restricted in Sweden, Denmark, and the United Kingdom. **11**

What are we waiting for before we grant elephants the freedom we have taken from them? Perhaps the tragedies of the summer will be lesson enough for us to demand that legislators ban captive animal performances and to redirect our children's attention to entertainments that avoid exploitation. As a society that prides itself on being civilized, we would be far richer for the "loss" of captive beasts. **12**

Vocabulary

amok (1)
proprietors (3)
pachyderms (3)
altruistic (4)
bullhook (4)
falter (6)
behaviorists (7)
servitude (8)
subsonically (9)
berserk (10)
exploitation (12)

Understanding What You Have Read

Check the correct answer in the blank provided.

1. What has happened to elephants "three times this summer"?
   ____ (a) Elephants have escaped.
   ____ (b) Elephants have run amok.
   ____ (c) Elephants have been freed by animal rights activists.
   ____ (d) Elephants have died of loneliness.

2. What is the average life span of an elephant in captivity?
   ____ (a) Ten years
   ____ (b) Fourteen years
   ____ (c) Seventy years
   ____ (d) Five years

3. Left alone in their homeland, what are elephants like?
   ____ (a) They are highly social beings.
   ____ (b) They are disorganized.
   ____ (c) They are loners.
   ____ (d) They long for the company of people.

4. How are elephants broken for servitude?
   ____ (a) They are chained and beaten.
   ____ (b) They are given electric shocks.
   ____ (c) They are deprived of food.
   ____ (d) They are treated with great kindness.

5. How do elephants communicate with one another?
   ____ (a) They do not communicate.
   ____ (b) They communicate subsonically.
   ____ (c) They bellow.
   ____ (d) They tap on the ground with their feet.

Thinking About What You Have Read

1. The author opens her essay by declaring that "The elephants are mad and they're just not going to take it anymore." What evidence does she provide for this statement?
2. In paragraph 5, the author talks about the behavior and lifestyle of elephants in the wild. How does this discussion help in her argument against the captivity of elephants?
3. Do you agree that animals should be treated humanely? Give reasons for your answer.
4. In some countries, it is now a criminal offense to confine elephants, big cats, and primates in circuses. What is your opinion of this regulation?
5. What do you think is the obligation, if any, of humans toward animals?

Writing Assignments

1. Write a paragraph about the way circus animals should be treated and why.
2. If you have a pet, write a paragraph on how you treat that pet. If you have no pet, write a paragraph on how you would treat one if you had one.

Sport

Jimmy Carter

This poem, by a former president of the United States, is a moving last farewell to a beloved pet. Some readers have criticized the way the dog's life was ended. However, no one has questioned the writer's sincere affection for his friend. He most certainly loved his dog. As you read the poem, ignore the fact that it is written in poetic form and concentrate only on the meaning and feelings expressed.

Yesterday I killed him. I had
known
for months I could not let
him live. I might
have paid someone to end it,
but I knew
that after fifteen years of
sharing life
the bullet ending his must
be my own.
Alone, I dug the grave,
grieving, knowing
that until the last he trusted
me.
I placed him as he'd been
some years ago
when lost, he stayed in place
until I came
and found him shaking,
belly on the ground,
his legs too sapped of
strength to hold him up,
his nose and eyes still
holding on the point.
I knelt beside him then to
stroke his head—
as I had done so much the
last few days.
He couldn't feel the tears
and sweat that fell
with shovelfuls of earth.
And then a cross—
a cross, I guess, so when I
pass that way

I'll breathe his name,
and think of him alive,
and somehow not remember
yesterday.

Vocabulary

sapped (21)

Understanding What You Have Read

Check the correct answer in the blank provided.

1. How did the speaker put the dog to death?
   ____ (a) By lethal injection
   ____ (b) By drowning
   ____ (c) By poisoning
   ____ (d) By shooting
2. Who witnessed this act of euthanasia?
   ____ (a) The speaker's mother
   ____ (b) No one
   ____ (c) His sister
   ____ (d) A visiting uncle
3. Why didn't the speaker pay someone to do it?
   ____ (a) Because he loved the dog
   ____ (b) Because no one was available
   ____ (c) Because he wanted to save the expense
   ____ (d) Because his mother ordered him to do it
4. What did the speaker do after he euthanized the dog?
   ____ (a) He wept on his wife's shoulder.
   ____ (b) He offered a prayer.
   ____ (c) He dug a grave.
   ____ (d) He visited his minister.
5. What had the speaker done to the dog many times lately?
   ____ (a) He had scolded him.
   ____ (b) He had taken walks with him.
   ____ (c) He had watched birds with him.
   ____ (d) He had stroked his head.

Thinking About What You Have Read

1. How does the title of this poem relate to its content?
2. What does the anecdote about losing the dog and finding him later, "his nose and eyes still/holding on the point," say about the animal?

How does the speaker seem to regard this behavior? How do you regard it?

3. What would have happened to the speaker if he had done to a suffering human being what he did to the dog? What is your view of this double standard?
4. What are the speaker's feelings during this final act he is performing? How do you know?
5. The speaker says he put a cross over the dog's grave. What is your view of the appropriateness of this gesture?

Writing Assignments

1. Write a paragraph about the real or imagined loss of a pet. Try to describe your feelings at the time.
2. Write a paragraph agreeing or disagreeing with the idea of mercy killing for people who are painfully and hopelessly sick.

A Person

A Brotherly Bond That Beat the Odds

Bill Paschke

Many of us regard sports either as a waste of time or as the couch potatoes' favorite excuse for idleness. But sometimes sports can also be the glue cementing two people together. This article, by a sportswriter, describes a relationship that grew between a little boy and his "Big Brother." Along the way, we meet two memorable characters whose only thing in common was a mutual love for sports.

He was so small. Expecting to meet a little boy, I had just been introduced to a stick figure. **1**

His jeans hung loosely around dental-floss legs. His T-shirt swallowed the rest. **2**

I reached for his hand, and grabbed him clear up to his elbow. I had just agreed to be Andrew's "Big Brother," yet there was nothing there. **3**

A commitment of three hours a week, each week, for the next year? **4**

What could an active 22-year-old man possibly do with a 7-year-old shadow? **5**

What could we ever share besides an awkward stare? **6**

I had been told that Andrew was suffering from cystic fibrosis, a genetic predator that kills young. But an overeager counselor whispered, "Don't worry, you can't tell." **7**

One look at Andrew's stunted growth and I could tell. One ugly cough, and I could hear. **8**

I had just met a boy to whom I was morally bound for the next year, yet I couldn't figure out how to spend the first minute. **9**

"So, um, what do you like?" I finally asked this little thing hugging his mother's legs. **10**

It was then I realized I had missed something, two eyes, flickering under a mop of blond hair, eyes now bigger than all of him. **11**

"Sports," he said, his small voice booming, and I'll remember this as long as I remember anything. "I like sports." **12**

We like it, hate it, embrace it, denounce it, talk about it for hours, watch it for weekends, rip it for days. We teach with it, blame it, try fruitlessly to play it and hopelessly to understand it. **13**

The one thing we never do, it seems, is pause and be thankful for it. **14**

For me, for sports, this day works as well as any. **15**

This is trying to be a Thanksgiving sports story, but not about sports as names and numbers, winners and losers. **16**

It's about sports as language, as one of this country's most important means of communication, spanning generations, crossing economic classes, giving our diverse people something in common. **17**

It's about how sports connected me with Andrew. **18**

I wasn't trying to save the world. I was trying to save myself. **19**

I had just graduated from college and was working in the swamp bureau for a newspaper in Fort Lauderdale, Fla. I was covering bowling and **20** shuffleboard and hoping for the day when somebody would consider me good enough to cover high school football.

I lived in a one-room apartment with a bed in the wall and roaches on the ceiling. My life lacked any sense of order or importance. I figured the Big Brothers and Sisters program would give that to me. 21

I met Andrew Fishbein at a Christmas party in 1980. 22

He said he liked sports. 23

"What do you know?" I said. "So do I." 24

On our second visit, I tentatively dumped a pile of baseball cards on the floor. He dropped to his knees and ran them through his hands like money. 25

"Do you know how to play?" I asked. 26

He didn't, so I taught him a game I had learned when I was young. Soon we were sprawled out on the carpet, shouting together at little pieces of cardboard, big and little now shoulder to shoulder. 27

And so the language of our relationship had been established, the currency set. 28

We played soccer as long as his clogged little lungs could handle it. We pitched baseball until it was time to go home for his medicine. 29

I was promoted to covering high school basketball, so he attended his first live sports event, Boyd Anderson High versus Dillard High, sitting next to me in the stands, cheering as if it was the Bulls and the Jazz. 30

Sports was like this for us. A language of laughter and lessons, a bridge between distant lives. 31

A year passed, my formal commitment to Andrew ended, but our visits continued. Sports had given us a new world—big enough for only two—that neither was willing to leave. There was always another miniature golf course to play, another pretend Super Bowl to enact with a rubber football on the scrubby field behind his townhouse. 32

Then in the fall of 1983, I landed a job as far from that world as Andrew thought possible. I was going to cover the Seattle Mariners, 3,500 miles away, 33

I still remember watching Andrew collapse in tears on the floor of his mother's townhouse. To him, I was just another man who had come and gone. 34

"You'll come see me, I'll stay in touch, I promise," I said quickly. "I'm covering baseball, remember?" 35

I'm sure he didn't believe it. I don't know if I believed it. 36

But it was baseball, remember? Within a year, Andrew, by then 10, had worked up the courage to fly cross-country by himself to spend long summer days with me and my wife. 37

Or more to the point, to spend an afternoon with the Mariners, running the outfield during batting practice, hanging out in the clubhouse, chaperoned by an unforgettable pitcher named Roy Thomas. 38

As we grew older, through vastly different situations on different sides of the country, it was sports that gave us both the incentive to keep our relationship strong. 39

At least three times a year, we would get together, seemingly always to watch a sporting event or to hang out near a sporting event I was covering. Our reunions were, therefore, usually marked by big happy crowds, and our separations usually occurred against the echoes of cheers. 40

When Andrew was 13, a basketball assignment took me close enough to Florida so I could give the toast at his bar mitzvah, a wonderful celebration of manhood for a child not expected to live long past his 18th birthday. 41

When Andrew graduated from high school, another milestone for a kid whose lungs and digestive system were weakening by the day, he received a congratulatory phone call from Orel Hershiser. 42

I've never asked an athlete for anything like that before or since. But Hershiser never held it over my head because he understood the death sentence hanging over Andrew's. 43

Cystic fibrosis is a genetic, terminal disease affecting about 30,000 children and adults. It causes the body to produce an abnormally thick mucus that clogs the lungs and obstructs the pancreas, affecting everything from breathing to digesting. 44

The language of sports, of course, includes none of those words. It's about life, and I privately rejoiced that the topic of Andrew's prognosis never came up. We were too busy arguing who was better, the Dolphins or Seahawks, the Heat or Lakers. 45

Many times, for a boy who underwent daily chest-pounding therapies and biannual lengthy hospital stays, sports was also the language of healing. 46

Despondent over his situation as a freshman at the University of Florida, Andrew once swallowed enough pills to kill himself. Fortunately, a fraternity brother found him in time. 47

When I was finished being furious, I bought him World Series tickets, and we stayed up all night in Atlanta, talking about comebacks. 48

It was his first of three World Series games, one baseball All-Star game, one Super Bowl, one national college football championship, one NCAA regional basketball championship. 49

He has been with me everywhere from Seattle to St. Petersburg, with stops in places like Cincinnati, New Orleans, Charleston, S.C., and even Dodgertown. 50

He has survived two major surgeries—half of his lungs have been removed—with that same language. 51

Sitting at his hospital bedside, I would read him the sports pages. 52

Phoning his room, from across the country, I would ask which game he was watching, and turn my TV to the same game, and we would shout at it together, even if he couldn't always shout. 53

The years passed, and I became a balding middle-ager, and the stick figure became a strong, handsome adult. Yet we stayed together until, at some point, it stopped being all about sports and started being somewhat about us. 54

That point was reached this fall, when I was scheduled to fly to Boston to cover what became one of the most dramatic Ryder Cup golf tournaments in history. 55

I flew to Jamaica instead. It was there, on a beach, that his mother and I gave Andrew away at his wedding. 56

On Wednesday, he flew to join me for this Thanksgiving with his new bride, Sigrid. Sure enough, the little guy has finally rumbled his way out of the corner and back up field. 57

Andrew is 26. He is a successful real estate agent. He undergoes countless daily therapies and painstaking hospital stays, but he works out at a gym, and is cut like a body builder. Scientific advancements have pushed the median age of an individual with CF to 31, and here's betting he doubles it. 58

Today he will hug my wife as if she is his second mother, which she is. He will roll around the floor with my three children like one of their favorite uncles, which he is. 59

And with me? What do you think? 60

Today we'll watch football, eat turkey, watch football, watch more football, then fall asleep in front of the TV while watching everything replayed in 30-second video bites on the highlight show. 61

Some might call us lazy sports nuts. We just call ourselves brothers. 62

Vocabulary

predator (7)
denounce (13)
diverse (17)
tentatively (25)
currency (28)
scrubby (32)
chaperoned (38)
incentive (39)
congratulatory (42)
prognosis (45)
biannual (46)
despondent (47)
painstaking (58)
median (58)

Understanding What You Have Read

Check the correct answer in the blank provided.

1. What was the writer's initial impression of the boy?
   ____ (a) That he was big for his age
   ____ (b) That he had startling red hair
   ____ (c) That he was uncommonly bold
   ____ (d) That he was a stick figure
2. What disease did the boy suffer from?
   ____ (a) Parkinson's disease
   ____ (b) AIDS
   ____ (c) Multiple sclerosis
   ____ (d) Cystic fibrosis
3. What useful function does the writer see in sports?
   ____ (a) It provides employment for many people.
   ____ (b) It helps make some star athletes very rich.
   ____ (c) It gives a diverse people something in common.
   ____ (d) It contributes to the renewal of old neighborhoods.
4. What baseball team was the writer assigned to cover?
   ____ (a) The New York Yankees
   ____ (b) The Seattle Mariners
   ____ (c) The Atlanta Braves
   ____ (d) The Texas Rangers
5. What did the boy do that enraged the writer?
   ____ (a) He tried to kill himself.
   ____ (b) He eloped.
   ____ (c) He disobeyed his mother.
   ____ (d) He tried to kill the writer.

Thinking About What You Have Read

1. This piece came from a newspaper. What characteristic of its paragraphing makes its journalistic origin obvious?

2. What does the author mean in paragraph 20 that he was "working in the swamp bureau?"

3. Aside from describing the relationship that emerged over the years between the writer and the boy, what else does this article do?

4. In paragraph 31, the author writes: "Sports was like this for us. A language of laughter and lessons, a bridge between distant lives." What is wrong with this paragraph? How could you fix this error with different punctuation?

5. What main point about sports does the writer prove in the extended example of his relationship with Andrew?

Writing Assignments

1. Write a paragraph about any personal hobby or passion that would work to bond you to someone else.

2. Write a paragraph about the importance of sports either in your own life or in the life of your family.

Two Roads Converged in a Wood

Jenijoy La Belle

The essay that follows was written as a newspaper column for Father's Day. A daughter paints a loving portrait of the father about whom no "greeting card can speak." Ask yourself what greeting cards are likely to say about a father as opposed to what the author actually says. Do you think the writer is romanticizing her father—picturing him as better than he is—or telling the truth? What does she find admirable about her father? How does she express this in a way that no greeting card could? A tribute to a father on Father's Day can easily become sticky with sentimentality. How does the writer avoid that trap?

It was easy to choose a card for Mother's Day. I knew the one my mother would like because I'm like my mother. Now, I stand perplexed in front of the Father's Day display. 1

My father, Joy La Belle, was a meter reader for 25 years. Most meter readers finally move into office positions, but my father liked being outdoors. He retired in 1976. By that time, he figured he'd walked around the world twice (more than 50,000 miles) on his job. He weighed 125 pounds when he started, 125 when he stopped. He was bitten by dogs only four times. You can still see German shepherd teeth marks on his right arm. 2

Once he retired, my father could turn his full attention to his real career. Almost 60 years ago, he bought a tract of wooded land near Olympia, Wash. He began building a house on a hill overlooking a waterfall. But a winter storm crushed the unfinished frame. My newly married parents moved into a tiny cabin and lived there for several years without electricity or running water. When my brother and I were born, my father added rooms and handcrafted furniture. Eventually, my father built five dwellings in the woods. For each, he cleared just enough for construction. The green light of the forest filters through the windows. Since several houses have walls of glass, the woods almost move into the living rooms. My father has no use for curtains. Like Thoreau* at Walden, he has "no gazers to shut out but the sun and moon." What they gaze in on is beautiful and true, in harmony with nature. 3

I came to appreciate my father's life more fully when I met him in literature. I found him in Robert Frost's† poems and Thomas Hardy's‡ novels—a straightforward, hard-working man with a quiet wisdom deeper than that of more articulate men. My father watches and waits. He doesn't talk much, but his silence is wonderful to listen to. 4

I work with words, my father with wood. And yet we communicate. He doesn't write me letters, but sometimes in the fall I receive a large envelope full of yellow maple leaves. When my favorite madrona tree died, he carved from it a "writer's block" to keep on my desk. In days when no words come, I pick it up, feel its smoothness and know that somewhere my father is driving nails or patiently planing and sanding. These are also ways of giving form to ideas. 5

What is unspoken is not unexpressed. One morning when he thought I was asleep, I heard my father walk softly into the kitchen near my room and begin slowly unloading the dishwasher. I lay in bed, listening to how gently 6

*Henry David Thoreau (1817–1862), American author and novelist who escaped the city to spend more than two years in a cabin on Walden Pond in Concord, Massachusetts.

†Robert Frost (1874–1963), American poet.

‡Thomas Hardy (1840–1928), English novelist and poet.

he lifted out each pan, each glass. Like the stealthiest thief in reverse, he returned the silverware to its drawer. He took 20 minutes to do what he could have done in 5, just to let me dream. Once in a while, we are lucky enough to be awake when love performs its silent testaments.

My father is 81. Not only do he and my mother still live quietly in the woods; they belong to it. Slender as is his frame, my father remains a powerful man. His arms are sinewy from years of chopping trees and raising roof beams. He works every day, digging stumps, laying a brick floor with precision, repairing the steps to the waterfalls, creating a bridge from a white fir that had fallen over the creek. 7

Knowing what to leave alone is as important as knowing what to do. Every few months, someone offers my father a small fortune to timber his forest. "Why would I want to cut down the trees?" my father asks. A doctor tells him about an operation for his fingers, which have become gnarled into a fist. "I can still hold a hammer," my father says. And he can. 8

My father is a happy man—not from trying to be, but because he lives at the center. He understands how to simplify the complexities of life. He does something each day toward clearing his own path through the wilderness, within and without. There is at the core of his being a mysterious strength I will never fully comprehend, nor to which any greeting card can speak. 9

Vocabulary

perplexed (1)
tract (3)
articulate (4)
planing (5)
stealthiest (6)
testaments (6)
sinewy (7)
gnarled (8)
timber (8)
comprehend (9)

Understanding What You Have Read

Check the correct answer in the blank provided.

1. What did the author's father do for a living before he retired?
   ____ (a) He was a lawyer.
   ____ (b) He was a physician specializing in elder care.
   ____ (c) He flew planes for a large business.
   ____ (d) He was a meter reader.

2. What can you see on the right arm of the author's father?
   ____ (a) Bite marks from a German shepherd dog
   ____ (b) A burn scar from a plane crash
   ____ (c) A tattoo of Uncle Sam
   ____ (d) A Nazi death camp identification tattoo

3. When did the author first come to appreciate her father's life?
   ____ (a) When she saw how hard he had to work
   ____ (b) When she met his brother
   ____ (c) When she met him in literature
   ____ (d) When she joined the Air Force

4. What testament of love did the author witness her father perform?
   ____ (a) He shot a bear for her.
   ____ (b) He bought her a car for her graduation.
   ____ (c) He threw himself between her and a rattlesnake.
   ____ (d) He unloaded the dishwasher silently so that she could sleep.

5. What offer does the father receive every few months?
   ____ (a) Someone offers him a small fortune for his timberland.
   ____ (b) Someone offers him a job in the home office.
   ____ (c) Someone offers to marry him.
   ____ (d) Someone offers him a million dollars for his life story.

Thinking About What You Have Read

1. The author admits that she finds it easy to buy a greeting card for her mother, but hard to buy one for her father. What explanation can you give for this difference? What impact do you think being a daughter rather than a son has on this dilemma?

2. The author says that she is like her mother. Reading between the lines, what do you think her mother is like?

3. Why did the father build walls of glass without curtains? What is your reaction to his attitude? Do you agree or do you prefer to feel protected by walls and curtains? Explain your answer.

4. In your own words, how would you describe the author's father? What does the author mean when she states that her father's "silence is wonderful to listen to"?

5. What fact about the author's father seems at odds with her portrayal of him as a man who lived off the woods and was a source of "mysterious strength"?

Writing Assignments

1. Write a paragraph about a "silent testament" of love you have witnessed.

2. Write a paragraph about someone you admire.

Barbie Doll

Marge Piercy

The title of a poem must never be ignored because a poem begins with its title, not its first line. Since this poem is about society's unhappy tendency to judge people, especially women, solely by their looks, the reader who does not know what a Barbie doll is misses the biting commentary of its title. Notice the ironic—opposite of what is expected—ending of the poem and the description, at the end, of the unhappy "girlchild" as a made-up doll.

This girlchild was born as usual
and presented dolls that did pee-pee
and miniature GE stoves and irons
and wee lipsticks the color of cherry candy.
Then in the magic of puberty, a classmate said:
You have a great big nose and fat legs.
She was healthy, tested intelligent,
possessed strong arms and back,
abundant sexual drive and manual dexterity.
She went to and fro apologizing.

Everyone saw a fat nose on thick legs.
She was advised to play coy,
exhorted to come on hearty,
exercise, diet, smile and wheedle.
Her good nature wore out
like a fan belt.
So she cut off her nose and her legs
and offered them up.
In the casket displayed on satin she lay

with the undertaker's cosmetics painted on,
a turned-up putty nose, dressed in a pink and white nightie.
Doesn't she look pretty? everyone said.
Consummation at last.
To every woman a happy ending.

Vocabulary

puberty (5)
dexterity (9)
coy (12)
exhorted (13)
wheedle (14)
putty (23)
consummation (23)

Understanding What You Have Read

Check the correct answer in the blank provided.

1. What did someone say to the "girlchild" that made her defensive?
   ____ (a) That she looked powerful
   ____ (b) That she had a potbelly
   ____ (c) That she had two different colored eyes
   ____ (d) That she had a great big nose and fat legs
2. What did the "girlchild" do after that remark?
   ____ (a) She went around apologizing.
   ____ (b) She went on a strict diet.
   ____ (c) She saw a psychiatrist.
   ____ (d) She moved out of town.
3. When was the damaging remark made?
   ____ (a) At the senior prom
   ____ (b) During puberty
   ____ (c) At a birthday party
   ____ (d) By her first date
4. What aspect of the girl wore out "like a fan belt"?
   ____ (a) Her sense of humor
   ____ (b) Her patience
   ____ (c) Her faith
   ____ (d) Her good nature
5. What did everyone say about her in the casket?
   ____ (a) That she looked asleep
   ____ (b) That she looked unnatural
   ____ (c) That she had on too much makeup
   ____ (d) That she looked pretty

Thinking About What You Have Read

1. What is the significance of the toys given to the "girlchild"?
2. Had the girl been born a boy, what do you think would have been an equivalent cutting remark to "You have a great big nose and fat legs"?
3. In lines 7–9, the poet tells that the girl was "healthy, tested intelligent/possessed strong arms and back,/abundant sexual drive and manual dexterity." Why do you think she tells us all this?
4. We are told that the girl was advised to "play coy," "come on hearty,/exercise, diet, smile and wheedle," but we are not told who gave her this advice. Why do you think this information is omitted?

5. It is sometimes said that the type of sexist pressure exerted on this girl simply doesn't occur anymore. What is your opinion of this view?

Writing Assignments

1. Write about the most cutting criticism you ever suffered.
2. Write about the pressures to which males are subjected nowadays.

AN EVENT

The War Prayer

Mark Twain

Mark Twain, pseudonym for Samuel Clemens, wrote this short piece sometime in 1904–05. Twain was frequently at odds with the popular thinking of his day and had a strong pacifistic streak in him. Toward the end of his life—he died in 1910—Twain became very bitter and openly scornful about the stupidity of mankind. This fable is from this last period of his life and contrasts sharply with the gentle humor found in The Innocents Aboard *(1869) or* The Adventures of Huckleberry Finn *(1885)*

It was a time of great and exalting excitement. The country was up in arms, the war was on, in every breast burned the holy fire of patriotism; the drums were beating, the bands playing, the toy pistols popping, the bunched firecrackers hissing and spluttering; on every hand and far down the receding and fading spread of roofs and balconies a fluttering wilderness of flags flashed in the sun; daily the young volunteers marched down the wide avenue gay and fine in their new uniforms, the proud fathers and mothers and sisters and sweethearts cheering them with voices choked with happy emotion as they swung by; nightly the packed mass meetings listened, panting, to patriot oratory which stirred the deepest deeps of their hearts, and which they interrupted at briefest intervals with cyclones of applause, the tears running down their cheeks the while; in the churches the pastors preached devotion to flag and country, and invoked the God of Battles, beseeching His aid in our good cause in outpouring of fervid eloquence which moved every listener. It was indeed a glad and gracious time, and the half dozen rash spirits that ventured to disapprove of the war and cast a doubt upon its righteousness straightway got such a stern and angry warning that for their personal safety's sake they quickly shrank out of sight and offended no more in that way. **1**

Sunday morning came—next day the battalions would leave for the front; the church was filled; the volunteers were there, their young faces alight with martial dreams—visions of the stern advance, the gathering momentum, the rushing charge, the flashing sabers, the flight of the foe, the tumult, the enveloping smoke, the fierce pursuit, the surrender—then home from the war, bronzed heroes, welcomed, adored, submerged in golden seas of glory! With the volunteers sat their dear ones, proud, happy, and envied by the neighbors and friends who had no sons and brothers to send forth to the field of honor, there to win for the flag, or, failing, die the noblest of noble deaths. The service proceeded; a war chapter from the Old Testament was read; the first prayer was said; it was followed by an organ burst that shook the building, and with one impulse the house rose, with glowing eyes and beating hearts, and poured out that tremendous invocation **2**

"God the all-terrible! Thou who ordainest, Thunder thy clarion and lightning thy sword!" **3**

Then came the "long" prayer. None could remember the like of it for passionate pleading and moving and beautiful language. The burden of its supplication was, that an ever-merciful and benignant Father of us all would watch over our noble young soldiers, and aid, comfort, and encourage them in their patriotic work; bless them, shield them in the day of battle and the hour of peril, bear them in His mighty hand, make them strong and confident, **4** invincible in the bloody onset; help them to crush the foe, grant to them and to their flag and country imperishable honor and glory—

5 An aged stranger entered and moved with slow and noiseless step up the main aisle, his eyes fixed upon the minister, his long body clothed in a robe that reached to his feet, his head bare, his white hair descending in frothy cataract to his shoulders, his seamy face unnaturally pale, pale even to ghastliness. With all eyes following him and wondering, he made his silent way; without pausing, he ascended to the preacher's side and stood there, waiting. With shut lids the preacher, unconscious of his presence, continued his moving prayer, and at last finished it with the words, uttered in fervent appeal, "Bless our arms, grant us the victory, O Lord our God, Father and Protector of our land and flag!"

6 The stranger touched his arm, motioned him to step aside—which the startled minister did—and took his place. During some moments he surveyed the spellbound audience with solemn eyes, in which burned an uncanny light; then in a deep voice he said:

7 "I come from the Throne—bearing a message from Almighty God!" The words smote the house with a shock; if the stranger perceived it he gave no attention. "He has heard the prayer of His servant your shepherd, and will grant it if such shall be your desire after I, His messenger, shall have explained to you its import—that is to say, its full import. For it is like unto many of the prayers of men, in that it asks for more than he who utters it is aware of—except he pause and think.

8 "God's servant and yours has prayed his prayer. Has he paused and taken thought? Is it one prayer? No, it is two—one uttered, the other not. Both have reached the ear of Him Who heareth all supplications, the spoken and the unspoken. Ponder this—keep it in mind. If you would beseech a blessing upon yourself, beware! lest without intent you invoke a curse upon a neighbor at the same time. If you pray for the blessing of rain upon your crop which needs it, by that act you are possibly praying for a curse upon some neighbor's crop which may not need rain and can be injured by it.

9 "You have heard your servant's prayer—the uttered part of it. I am commissioned of God to put into words the other part of it—that part which the pastor—and also you in your hearts—fervently prayed silently. And ignorantly and unthinkingly? God grant that it was so! You heard these words: "Grant us the victory, O Lord our God!" That is sufficient. The whole of the uttered prayer is compact into those pregnant words. Elaborations were not necessary. When you have prayed for victory you have prayed for many unmentioned results which follow victory—must follow it, cannot help but follow it. Upon the listening spirit of God the Father fell also the unspoken part of the prayer. He commandeth me to put it into words. Listen!

10 "O Lord our Father, our young patriots, idols of our hearts, go forth to battle—be Thou near them! With them—in spirit—we also go forth from the sweet peace of our beloved firesides to smite the foe. O Lord our God, help us to tear their soldiers to bloody shreds with our shells; help us to cover their smiling fields with the pale forms of their patriot dead; help us to drown the thunder of the guns with the shrieks of their wounded, writhing in pain; help us to lay waste their humble homes with a hurricane of fire; help us to wring the hearts of their unoffending widows with unavailing grief; help us to turn them out roofless with their little children to wander unfriended the wastes of their desolated land in rags and hunger and thirst, sports of the sun flames of summer and the icy winds of winter, broken in spirit, worn with travail, imploring Thee for the refuge of the grave and denied it—for our sakes who adore Thee, Lord, blast their hopes, blight their lives, protract their bitter pilgrimage, make heavy their steps, water their way with their tears, stain the white snow with the blood of their wounded

feet! We ask it, in the spirit of love, of Him Who is the Source of Love, and Who is the ever-faithful refuge and friend of all that are sore beset and seek His aid with humble and contrite hearts. Amen."

(After a pause) "Ye have prayed it; if ye still desire it, speak! The messenger of the Most High waits." **11**

It was believed afterward that the man was a lunatic, because there was no sense in what he said. **12**

Vocabulary

exalting (1)
receding (1)
oratory (1)
invoked (1)
fervid (1)
martial (2)
invocation (2)
benignant (4)
invincible (4)
uncanny (6)
import (7)
elaborations (9)
unavailing (10)
travail (10)

Understanding What You Have Read

Check the correct answer in the blank provided.

1. What was the occasion of the prayer?
    ____ (a) The celebration of a victory in battle
    ____ (b) The outbreak of war
    ____ (c) The launching of a battleship
    ____ (d) The dedication of a military academy
2. What did the people pray for?
    ____ (a) Horses
    ____ (b) Boats to launch an invasion
    ____ (c) The founding of Mexico City
    ____ (d) Victory over their enemies
3. What did those opposed to war do?
    ____ (a) They kept out of sight for their own safety.
    ____ (b) They muttered curse words.
    ____ (c) They formed a committee.
    ____ (d) They demonstrated with anti-war placards.
4. Who delivered a message to the people?
    ____ (a) A girl who flouted customs
    ____ (b) A flirtatious girl
    ____ (c) An extremely old man
    ____ (d) An old woman
5. How did the people react to the message?
    ____ (a) They thought that it was the message of a madman.
    ____ (b) They began to weep.

____ (c) They rioted in anger.

____ (d) They cleaned up the altar.

Thinking About What You Have Read

1. What kind of language does Twain use to characterize the mood of the time?
2. In his description of the behavior of the congregation, how does Twain portray their attitude toward war?
3. Which of the two sexes has a better and more realistic attitude toward war? How can you explain the different attitude, if there is one, between the sexes on warfare?
4. What is the main point being made by the old man about war? Why does the congregation consider him mad?
5. How would you characterize the difference between the congregation's view of war and the old man's?

Writing Assignments

1. Write a paragraph on the difference between the old man's view of war and the congregation's.
2. In a straightforward paragraph, express your opinion on women's attitudes about war. Try to explain why they feel as they do.

Shame

Dick Gregory

Because most of us can remember someone from our youth who represented the fairy tale life we desired, we can understand the writer's experience even though we may never have been as poor as he was. Allow yourself to soak in all of the details that make this narration so moving and heartrending. Try to imagine yourself in the narrator's place—to understand how his pride was hurt because of a teacher's lack of sensitivity.

1 I never learned hate at home, or shame. I had to go to school for that. I was about seven years old when I got my first big lesson. I was in love with a little girl named Helene Tucker, a light-complected little girl with pigtails and nice manners. She was always clean and she was smart in school. I think I went to school mostly to look at her. I brushed my hair and even got me a little old handkerchief. It was a lady's handkerchief, but I didn't want Helene to see me wipe my nose on my hand. The pipes were frozen again, there was no water in the house, but I washed my socks and shirt every night. I'd get a pot, and go over to Mr. Ben's grocery store, and stick my pot down into his soda machine. Scoop out some chopped ice. By evening the ice melted to water for washing. I got sick a lot that winter because the fire would go out at night before the clothes were dry. In the morning I'd put them on, wet or dry, because they were the only clothes I had.

2 Everybody's got a Helene Tucker, a symbol of everything you want. I loved her for her goodness, her cleanliness, her popularity. She'd walk down my street and my brothers and sisters would yell, "Here comes Helene," and I'd rub my tennis sneakers on the back of my pants and wish my hair wasn't so nappy and the white folks' shirt fit me better. I'd run out on the street. If I knew my place and didn't come too close, she'd wink at me and say hello. That was a good feeling. Sometimes I'd follow her all the way home, and shovel the snow off her walk and try to make friends with her Momma and her aunts. I'd drop money on her stoop late at night on my way back from shining shoes in the taverns. And she had a Daddy, and he had a good job. He was a paper hanger.

3 I guess I would have gotten over Helene by summertime, but something happened in that classroom that made her face hang in front of me for the next twenty-two years. When I played the drums in high school it was for Helene and when I broke track records in college it was for Helene and when I started standing behind microphones and heard applause I wished Helene could hear it, too. It wasn't until I was twenty-nine years old and married and making money that I really got her out of my system. Helene was sitting in that classroom when I learned to be ashamed of myself.

4 It was on a Thursday. I was sitting in the back of the room, in a seat with a chalk circle drawn around it. The idiot's seat, the troublemaker's seat.

5 The teacher thought I was stupid. Couldn't spell, couldn't read, couldn't do arithmetic. Just stupid. Teachers were never interested in finding out that you couldn't concentrate because you were so hungry, because you hadn't had any breakfast. All you could think about was noontime, would it ever come? Maybe you could sneak into the cloakroom and steal a bite of some kid's lunch out of a coat pocket. A bit of something. Paste. You can't really make a meal out of paste, or put it on bread for a sandwich, but sometimes I'd scoop a few spoonfuls out of the paste jar in the back of the room. Pregnant people get strange tastes. I was pregnant with poverty. Pregnant with dirt and pregnant with smells that made people turn away,

pregnant with cold and pregnant with shoes that were never bought for me, pregnant with five other people in my bed and no Daddy in the next room, and pregnant with hunger. Paste doesn't taste too bad when you're hungry.

The teacher thought I was a troublemaker. All she saw from the front of the room was a little black boy who squirmed in his idiot's seat and made noises and poked the kids around him. I guess she couldn't see a kid who made noises because he wanted someone to know he was there. **6**

It was on a Thursday, the day before the Negro payday. The eagle always flew on Friday. The teacher was asking each student how much his father would give to the Community Chest. On Friday night, each kid would get the money from his father, and on Monday he would bring it to the school. I decided I was going to buy me a Daddy right then. I had money in my pocket from shining shoes and selling papers and whatever Helene Tucker pledged for her Daddy I was going to top it. And I'd hand the money right in. I wasn't going to wait until Monday to buy me a Daddy. **7**

I was shaking, scared to death. The teacher opened her book and started calling our names alphabetically. **8**

"Helene Tucker?" **9**

"My Daddy said he'd give two dollars and fifty cents." **10**

"That's very nice, Helene. Very, very nice indeed." **11**

That made me feel pretty good. It wouldn't take too much to top that. I had almost three dollars in dimes and quarters in my pocket. I stuck my hand in my pocket and held onto the money, waiting for her to call my name. But the teacher closed her book after she called everybody else in the class. **12**

I stood up and raised my hand. **13**

"What is it now?" **14**

"You forgot me." **15**

She turned toward the blackboard. "I don't have time to be playing with you, Richard." **16**

"My Daddy said he'd . . ." **17**

"Sit down, Richard, you're disturbing the class." **18**

"My Daddy said he'd give . . . fifteen dollars." **19**

She turned around and looked mad. "We are collecting this money for you and your kind, Richard Gregory. If your Daddy can give fifteen dollars you have no business being on relief." **20**

"I got it right now, I got it right now, my Daddy gave it to me to turn in today, my Daddy said . . ." **21**

"And furthermore," she said, looking right at me, her nostrils getting big and her lips getting thin and her eyes opening wide, "we know you don't have a Daddy." **22**

Helene Tucker turned around, her eyes full of tears. She felt sorry for me. Then I couldn't see her too well because I was crying, too. **23**

"Sit down, Richard." **24**

And I always thought the teacher kind of liked me. She always picked me to wash the blackboard on Friday, after school. That was a big thrill, it made me feel important. If I didn't wash it, come Monday the school might not function right. **25**

"Where are you going, Richard?" **26**

I walked out of school that day, and for a long time I didn't go back very often. There was shame there. **27**

Now there was shame everywhere. It seemed like the whole world had been inside that classroom, everyone had heard what the teacher had said, everyone had turned around and felt sorry for me. There was shame in going to the Worthy Boys Annual Christmas Dinner for you and **28** your kind, because everybody knew what a worthy boy was. Why couldn't they just call it the Boys Annual Dinner, why'd they have to give it a name? There was shame in wearing the brown and orange and white plaid mackinaw the welfare gave to 3,000 boys. Why'd it have to be the same for everybody so when you walked down the street the people could see you were on relief? It was a nice warm mackinaw and it had a hood, and my Momma beat me and called me a little rat when she found out I stuffed it in the bottom of a pail full of garbage way over on Cottage Street. There was shame in running over to Mister Ben's at the end of the day and asking for his rotten peaches, there was shame in asking Mrs. Simmons for a spoonful of sugar, there was shame in running out to meet the relief truck. I hated that truck, full of food for you and your kind. I ran into the house and hid when it came. And then I started to sneak through alleys, to take the long way home so people going into White's Eat Shop wouldn't see me. Yeah, the whole world heard the teacher that day, we all know you don't have a Daddy.

Vocabulary

relief (20)
mackinaw (28)

Understanding What You Have Read

Check the correct answer in the blank provided.

1. Where did the narrator say he learned shame?
    ____ (a) In church
    ____ (b) At home
    ____ (c) On the baseball field
    ____ (d) At school
2. Helene Tucker is a symbol of
    ____ (a) everything you have ever wanted.
    ____ (b) academic achievement.
    ____ (c) power.
    ____ (d) girlish modesty.
3. The teacher thought that the narrator was stupid when in actuality he was
    ____ (a) lonely.
    ____ (b) ashamed.
    ____ (c) hungry.
    ____ (d) stubborn.
4. "The eagle always flew on Friday" means that
    ____ (a) a political rally is about to start.
    ____ (b) it's payday.
    ____ (c) people were taking off for vacation.
    ____ (d) Friday is a time to observe eagles flying in the sky.

5. What did the narrator plan to do in order to impress Helen Tucker?
   ____ (a) Give her some red roses
   ____ (b) Take her to the Worthy Boys Annual Christmas Dinner
   ____ (c) Attend church regularly
   ____ (d) Pretend that his father asked him to pledge $15 to the Community Chest

Thinking About What You Have Read

1. How does his crush on Helen Tucker affect the narrator? Do you consider his reaction believable? Cite a similar experience you or someone you know has had.
2. What about the classroom experience that kept the narrator remembering Helene Tucker for decades to come? Do you consider this long-term remembrance healthy? Give reasons for your view.
3. What are some of the details used by the narrator to prove that his family was poor? Point to specific passages.
4. What technique does the narrator use to make the "shame" scene come to life so that you, the reader, can feel the complete humiliation of the event?
5. What seems to be the most shameful aspect of all for the narrator? Why would that be so shameful? Give specific reasons for your answer.
6. How does the narrator maintain a consistent voice and point of view?

Writing Assignments

1. Write about an event in your life that made you feel ashamed and humiliated. Make sure that the details of your narration support your point.
2. Write a paragraph about the importance of elementary school teachers being sensitive to their students' home lives and lifestyles.

A Problem

Señor Payroll

William E. Barrett

Look for the main conflict in "Señor Payroll." Decide who is fighting whom. Once you have clarified the battle lines, concentrate on the story, which is about Mexican gas plant laborers and the two American engineers who are their paymasters. Notice that it is both serious and humorous. As you read, try to identify the major ch aracter traits of the laborers and the managers. Compare and contrast these traits.

Larry and I were Junior Engineers in the gas plant, which means that we were clerks. Anything that could be classified as paperwork came to the flat double desk across which we faced each other. The Main Office downtown sent us a bewildering array of orders and rules that were to be put into effect. 1

Junior Engineers were beneath the notice of everyone except the Mexican laborers at the plant. To them we were the visible form of a distant, unknowable paymaster. We were Señor Payroll. 2

Those Mexicans were great workmen; the aristocrats among them were the stokers, big men who worked Herculean eight-hour shifts in the fierce heat of the retorts. They scooped coal with huge shovels and hurled it with uncanny aim at tiny doors. The coal streamed out from the shovels like black water from a high-pressure nozzle, and never missed the narrow opening. The stokers worked stripped to the waist, and there was pride and dignity in them. Few men could do such work, and they were the few. 3

The Company paid its men only twice a month, on the fifth and on the twentieth. To a Mexican, this was absurd. What man with money will make it last fifteen days? If he hoarded money beyond the spending of three days, he was a miser—and when, Señor, did the blood of Spain flow in the veins of misers? Hence, it was the custom of our stokers to appear every third or fourth day to draw the money due to them. 4

There was a certain elasticity in the Company rules, and Larry and I sent the necessary forms to the Main Office and received an "advance" against a man's pay check. Then, one day, Downtown favored us with a memorandum: 5

"There have been too many abuses of the advance-against-wages privilege. Hereafter, no advance against wages will be made to any employee except in a case of genuine emergency." 6

We had no sooner posted the notice when in came stoker Juan Garcia. He asked for an advance. I pointed to the notice. He spelled it through slowly, then said, "What does this mean, this 'genuine emergency'?" 7

I explained to him patiently that the Company was kind and sympathetic, but that it was a great nuisance to have to pay wages every few days. If someone was ill or if money was needed for some other good reason, then the Company would make an exception to the rule. 8

Juan Garcia turned his hat over and over slowly in his big hands. "I do not get my money?" 9

"Next payday, Juan. On the twentieth." 10

He went out silently and I felt a little ashamed of myself. I looked across the desk at Larry. He avoided my eyes. 11

In the next hour two other stokers came in, looked at the notice, had it explained and walked solemnly out; then no more came. What we did not 12 know was that Juan Garcia, Pete Mendoza, and Francisco Gonzalez had spread the word, and that every Mexican in the plant was explaining the order to every other Mexican. "To get money now, the wife must be sick. There must be medicine for the baby."

The next morning Juan Garcia's wife was practically dying, Pete Mendoza's mother would hardly last the day, there was a veritable epidemic among children, and, just for variety, there was one sick father. We always suspected that the old man was really sick; no Mexican would otherwise have thought of him. At any rate, nobody paid Larry and me to examine private lives; we made out our forms with an added line describing the "genuine emergency." Our people got paid. 13

That went on for a week. Then came a new order, curt and to the point: "Hereafter, employees will be paid ONLY on the fifth and the twentieth of the month. No exceptions will be made except in the cases of employees leaving the service of the Company." 14

The notice went up on the board, and we explained its significance gravely. "No, Juan Garcia, we cannot advance your wages. It is too bad about your wife and your cousins and your aunts, but there is a new rule." 15

Juan Garcia went out and thought it over. He thought out loud with Mendoza and Gonzalez and Ayala, then, in the morning, he was back. "I am quitting this company for a different job. You pay me now?" 16

We argued that it was a good company and that it loved its employees like children, but in the end we paid off, because Juan Garcia quit. And so did Gonzalez, Mendoza, Obregon, Ayala and Ortez, the best stokers, men who could not be replaced. 17

Larry and I looked at each other; we knew what was coming in about three days. One of our duties was to sit on the hiring line early each morning, engaging transient workers for the handy gangs. Any man was accepted who could walk up and ask for a job without falling down. Never before had we been called upon to hire such skilled virtuosos as stokers for handy-gang work, but we were called upon to hire them now. 18

The day foreman was wringing his hands and asking the Almighty if he was personally supposed to shovel this condemned coal, while there in a stolid, patient line were skilled men—Garcia, Mendoza, and others—waiting to be hired. We hired them, of course. There was nothing else to do. 19

Every day we had a line of resigning stokers, and another line of stokers seeking work. Our paperwork became very complicated. At the Main Office they were jumping up and down. The processing of forms showing Juan Garcia's resigning and being hired over and over again was too much for them. Sometimes downtown had Garcia on the payroll twice at the same time when someone down there was slow in entering a resignation. Our phone rang early and often. 20

Tolerantly and patiently we explained: "There's nothing we can do if a man wants to quit, and if there are stokers available when the plant needs stokers, we hire them." 21

Out of chaos, Downtown issued another order. I read it and whistled. Larry looked at it and said, "It is going to be very quiet around here." 22

The order read: "Hereafter, no employee who resigns may be rehired within a period of 30 days." 23

Juan Garcia was due for another resignation, and when he came in we showed him the order and explained that standing in line the next day would do him no good if he resigned today. "Thirty days is a long time, Juan." 24

It was a grave matter and he took time to reflect on it. So did Gonzalez, Mendoza, Ayala and Ortez. Ultimately, however, they were all back—and all resigned. 25

We did our best to dissuade them and we were sad about the parting. This time it was for keeps and they shook hands with us solemnly. It was very nice knowing us. Larry and I looked at each other when they were gone and we both knew that neither of us had been pulling for Downtown to win this duel. It was a blue day. 26

In the morning, however, they were all back in line. With the utmost gravity, Juan Garcia informed me that he was a stoker looking for a job. 27

"No dice, Juan," I said. "Come back in thirty days. I warned you." 28

His eyes looked straight into mine without a flicker. "There is some mistake, Señor," he said. "I am Manual Hernandez. I work as the stoker in Pueblo, in Santa Fe, in many places." 29

I stared back at him, remembering the sick wife and the babies without medicine, the mother-in-law in the hospital, the many resignations and the rehirings. I knew that there was a gas plant in Pueblo, and that there wasn't any in Santa Fe; but who was I to argue with a man about his own name? A stoker is a stoker. 30

So I hired him. I hired Gonzalez, too, who swore that his name was Carrera, and Ayala, who had shamelessly become Smith. 31

Three days later the resigning started. 32

Within a week our payroll read like a history of Latin America. Everyone was on it: Lopez and Obregon, Villa, Diaz, Batista, Gomez, and even San Martín and Bolívar. Finally Larry and I, growing weary of staring at familiar faces and writing unfamiliar names, went to the Superintendent and told him the whole story. He tried not to grin, and said, "Damned nonsense!" 33

The next day the orders were taken down. We called our most prominent stokers into the office and pointed to the board. No rules any more. 34

"The next time we hire you hombres," Larry said grimly, "come in under the names you like best, because that's the way you are going to stay on the books." 35

They looked at us and they looked at the board; then for the first time in the long duel, their teeth flashed white. "Sí, Señores," they said. 36

And so it was. 37

Vocabulary

array (1)	gravely (15)
stokers (3)	transient (18)
Herculean (3)	virtuosos (18)
retorts (3)	stolid (19)
elasticity (5)	tolerantly (21)
veritable (13)	ultimately (25)
epidemic (13)	dissuade (26)
curt (14)	solemnly (26)
significance (15)	prominent (34)

Understanding What You Have Read

Check the correct answer in the blank provided.

1. In the story, management functions as

____ **(a)** a cruel tyrant.

____ **(b)** supporters of communism.

____ **(c)** a benevolent dictator.

____ **(d)** cold and remote headquarters in the United States.

2. The ending of the story is satisfying because
____ (a) the cruel boss was assassinated.
____ (b) all of the laborers became rich overnight.
____ (c) Larry and the narrator were promoted.
____ (d) the hardworking laborers got their way.

3. The morality of the laborers is based on
____ (a) pure and instant needs.
____ (b) their Catholic upbringing.
____ (c) what their loving mothers had taught them.
____ (d) their hatred for their employers.

4. How did the laborers first respond when management informed them that there would be no more pay advances except in a case of emergency?
____ (a) They formed a picket line and refused to work.
____ (b) They worked shorter hours.
____ (c) They all came in with emergencies.
____ (d) They fled to the United States.

5. What was the reputation of the stokers?
____ (a) They were known to be lazy.
____ (b) They were excellent workers who performed without mistakes.
____ (c) They were frail men who did their best.
____ (d) They were arrogant and demanding.

Thinking About What You Have Read

1. How does the author achieve humor?
2. The ending of the story is ironic; it does not end the way we expected it to under the circumstances described. Why? How would you have expected the story to end?
3. The narrator is himself a character in the story. What does this dual role add to the narrative?
4. How do you feel about the morality of the laborers? About the morality of management? Explain the reasons for your views.
5. How is the passing of time indicated? Point to specific passages.

Writing Assignments

1. Write a paragraph describing the work of someone you know. It can be physical work, such as that of a car mechanic, bus driver, firefighter, or carpenter. Or, it can be mental work, such as that of a teacher, lawyer, accountant, or psychologist. Describe the worker's duties and attitude toward the job.
2. Write a paragraph answering the question, "Why are some laborers so poorly paid in our country?"

Talkin' White

Wayne Lionel Aponte

When the author wrote this essay, he was an English major at the University of Rochester in New York. He felt compelled to put down his thoughts because so many Blacks were accusing him of denying his African American heritage by using what they considered "white talk." His point is that there are many kinds of English, and pride in African American heritage doesn't require the exclusive use of street slang.

Recently, during a conversation on film at a dinner party, when I was using my best college-educated English, I was asked where I was born. I received a curious look when I replied, with pride, "Harlem." The questioner, whom I had met through a mutual friend, looked at me as if I were a brother from another planet and immediately wanted to know whether I'd lived in Harlem all my life. When I responded, "Yeah, man, I been cold chillin' on Lenox Avenue ever since I was rockin' my fly diapers," he laughed, and I realized his was a nervous laughter, the kind folks use to mask their thoughts. Has he really lived in Harlem all his life? He talks white was the thought behind his laughter, and the follow-up question asked after my departure. 1

While growing up in Harlem during my not-so-long-ago elementary and middle-school days, I often encountered the phrase "talkin' white." It was usually thrust on people who were noticed because they were speaking grammatically correct English in a community that did not. I've also heard the term applied to people who place themselves above others by verbally showboating with the elocution of a Lionel Trilling or a Sir Laurence Olivier. 2

Nevertheless, I've always loved those folks who have mastered the art of manipulating words. Eloquent oratory and masterful writing have stimulated my mind for as long as I can remember. I took great pride in my ability to mimic and to slowly transform the styles of my favorite writers and orators into my own voice. In this sense language is a form of intellectual play for me. 3

When I was a child, my reaction to the question "Why do you talk so white?" was to alter my spoken English drastically (once "Ask yo mama" became less effective and after I ran out of money for candy bribes to make the kids like me). Like most children, I wanted to be liked and wanted to blend into each new social circle. But speaking as I did made blending difficult since it brought favorable attention from teachers that, outside the classroom, evoked fierce verbal attacks from my peers. I never could quite understand how talking slang proved I was Black. Nor did I understand why I couldn't be accepted as a full-fledged, card-holding member of the group by speaking my natural way. 4

Hearing the laughter, though, and being the butt of "proper" and "Oreo" jokes hurt me. Being criticized made me feel marginal—and verbally impotent in the sense that I had little ammunition to stop the frequent lunchtime attacks. So I did what was necessary to fit in, whether that meant cursing excessively or signifying [goading, often good-naturedly]. Ultimately I somehow learned to be polylingual and to become sensitive linguistically in the way animals are able to sense the danger of bad weather. 5

The need to defend myself led me to use language as a weapon to deflect jokes about the "whiteness" of my spoken English and to launch harsh verbal counterattacks. Simultaneously language served as a mask to hide the hurt I often felt in the process. Though over time my ability to "talk 6 that talk"—slang—gained me a new respect from my peers, I didn't want to go through life using slang to prove I am Black. So I decided "I yam what I yam," and to take pride in myself. I am my speaking self, but this doesn't mean that I'm turning my back on Black people. There are various shades of Blackness; I don't have to talk like Paul Laurence Dunbar's dialect poems to prove I'm Black. I don't appreciate anyone's trying to take away the range of person I can be.

"Talkin' white" implies that the English language is a closed system owned exclusively by whites. But my white friends from Chattanooga, Ventura, California, and New York City don't all speak the same way. Nor do the millions of poor whites working below the poverty line "talk white," as that phrase is interpreted. **7**

But the primary reason I question this peculiar euphemism for "speaking well" is that it has been used tyrannically to push to the periphery of the race people who grew up in the West Indies and attended English schools or who lived in predominantly white environments: They are perceived as not being Black enough, or as somehow being anti-Black. **8**

It hurts to know that many people judge me and others on whether or not we break verbs. If we follow this line of thought, maybe we'll also say that W. E. B. DuBois wasn't Black because he matriculated at Harvard and studied at the University of Berlin. Or perhaps that Alain Leroy Locke wasn't Black because he earned a degree from Oxford University. Or, to transfer the logic, maybe we're not all of African descent since we don't speak Swahili and some "real" Africans do. **9**

If we can take pride in the visual diversity of the race, then surely we can transfer this diversity and appreciation to spoken English. Because all of us don't be talkin' alike—ya know what I'm sayin'? **10**

Vocabulary

encountered (2)	signifying (5)
elocution (2)	polylingual (5)
manipulating (3)	linguistically (5)
oratory (3)	deflect (6)
evoked (4)	euphemism (8)
marginal (5)	periphery (8)
impotent (5)	diversity (10)

Understanding What You Have Read

Check the correct answer in the blank provided.

1. The author of the essay grew up in
   ____ (a) the West Indies.
   ____ (b) Africa.
   ____ (c) Harlem.
   ____ (d) Chicago.

2. According to the essay, what did "talkin' white" mean?
   ____ (a) Socializing with white people rather than Blacks
   ____ (b) Speaking in a dull monotone
   ____ (c) Speaking with a British accent
   ____ (d) Speaking grammatically correct English

3. For some time, the author used Black slang outside of school because
   ____ (a) he wanted to fit in and be liked by fellow Blacks.
   ____ (b) his teachers advised him to do so.
   ____ (c) it made him seem physically tough.
   ____ (d) he knew it well.

4. What does the author mean when he says he became "polylingual"?
   ____ (a) He used a polished kind of slang.
   ____ (b) He was always polite.
   ____ (c) He had more than one wife.
   ____ (d) He could use different kinds of English.

5. What is the main reason the author disapproves of the term "talkin' white"?
   ____ (a) It angers the white community because their language is attacked as inferior.
   ____ (b) It is used as a label to exclude people from the West Indies or Black people who grew up in predominantly white environments.
   ____ (c) Blacks can never learn to "talk white."
   ____ (d) Blacks should continue to keep their own slang and resist "talkin' white."

Thinking About What You Have Read

1. What does the author mean when he states (paragraph 3) that "language is a form of intellectual play for me"?
2. Children and teens often ridicule anyone who is different. Did this happen to you or to someone you know? For what reason? Looking back, how do you react to such behavior in yourself or in others?
3. Why do you think the author's classmates ridiculed him and were angry with him when he spoke educated English? Try to put yourself in the classmates' shoes.
4. Do you believe that the English language is a closed system, or that it allows for a wide range of spoken English? Give reasons for your answer.
5. What, if any, advantage is there in learning to speak and write grammatically correct English?

Writing Assignments

1. Write an imaginary letter to Wayne Lionel Aponte telling him your reaction to the experience he had with fellow Blacks who disapproved of his language.
2. Write a paragraph about the diversity of spoken English in our country. Use specific examples.

An Argument

Welcome Our Planet, Ourselves

Dominique Browning

Global warming is in the news practically every day with predictions ranging from the catastrophic to the merely inconvenient. At least once a week, some talk show host will make a yuk-yuk joke about the subject. Some comedians have regular routines that include a skit on global warming. But as the author tells us, this is no joking matter. Global warming is a fact of life and nature, and while none or only a few of us may live to see it, the Earth is getting warmer, the ice caps on the ends of the Earth are shrinking, and the effects on all life-forms on the planet are incalculable. If global warming struck like an avalanche or earthquake, we would all sit up and listen intently. Instead, it is growing slowly everywhere around us like a deadly poisonous mushroom, and no one is paying attention.

I pulled into the parking lot in front of the yoga studio in January and found a space next to a supersized SUV. It was a frigid evening; I noticed that the SUV was running, but no one was inside. I was early for class, so I went into the market for some weekend supplies. When I returned 15 minutes later, the SUV's engine was still going, exhaust pouring from the tailpipe. The previous class had just ended, and people were heading for their cars; a young woman began climbing into the SUV. 1

"You left your car running," I said. "Did you know that?" 2

"Of course." She looked at me as if I were an idiot. "I didn't want my car to be freezing when I got in." 3

"Don't you know how wasteful that is?" I admit it. I was not minding my own business; my inner calm was about as woeful as her enlightenment. "All those emissions, poison pouring into the air? Haven't you heard about global warming?" 4

"Global warming? I don't believe in all that global warming stuff." 5

I spent Christmas in Rhode Island last year. It was a balmy week, and I took long walks along deserted lanes by the ocean. Most of the houses in this seaside town were closed for the winter. But the gardens were not. In one, cherry trees were in full bloom. In another, the peonies had begun to push up out of the earth, and their waxy, blood red stems stood a good nine inches tall. Go back, I wanted to say. You're here too early. You'll be killed. The newspapers were full of strange reports: schools of dolphins off Long Island; bears in the Catskills unable to hibernate, foraging in people's trash; 2006, the warmest year in U.S. history. 6

Normally, my children's eyes roll back when I begin to go on about climate change and what we have done to our planet. But not this winter. 7

"I'm beginning to believe in all this global warming stuff, Mom." 8

Believe? As if this were like a belief in God or Santa Claus? We seem to have lost the distinction between matters of faith and matters of fact, which is frightening enough. But this kind of willful confusion is now accompanied by a flagrant disregard for responsibility in the face of impending catastrophe; it is, in short, immoral. 9

Some of us console ourselves with the idea that the truly terrible consequences of climate change will happen long after we—and our children—are dead. Why worry about something we won't be around to see? I walk 10 the beach and think about the wonders of this coast: the pools and eddies that swirl at the foot of the granite cliffs; the tide lines that mat the grasses; the plover's nest full of brindled eggs; the marsh ponds dotted with mute swans. I love this landscape. Of course, the coastline changes, daily, and I accept that as part of its natural rhythm. But to have it disappear? I maintain a fantasy about what my children's lives will be like; how they will live in the house I've built with their children, how they'll walk the same lanes and explore the same shoreline. It is a fiction, of course, but comforting. I can't indulge it at all without some certainty about the natural world we now inhabit together.

When I was in high school, I read several books that altered the course **11**
of my life: Plato's *Symposium*; *Our Bodies, Ourselves*; and Simone de Beauvoir's *The Second Sex*. You can see instantly the absurdity in such a list. You can also feel what I now understand to have been that touching openness and vulnerability to big, if not overblown, ideas that is one of the earmarks of adolescence.

The memory of reading this constellation of books has been much on **12**
my mind lately—and I never think of one without all of them bubbling up together. They are somehow inextricably linked, and they somehow seem very important again.

There was no philosophy class in my public high school in Stamford, **13**
Connecticut, until one of the history teachers decided to pull together a little seminar of students who might be interested. I signed up. On the first day of class, Mr. Falcone handed out an index card to each of us and asked us to write, in one word, what we considered the most important thing in life.

I confess that this is the sort of exercise that I still find excruciatingly **14**
unpleasant. I always feel there is a trick—that there is a correct answer, and that I will be humiliated by whatever I have come up with. I had my answer immediately, but I was sure it was wrong—simplistic, stupid; I tried to find a better one. I stared at my little white blank card, and it reflected my blank mind. Finally, time up, I wrote down: HAPPINESS. The goal in life is to find happiness.

I was not kicked out of the class, and we began at what was then con- **15**
sidered to be the beginning, with Plato, and went on to spend a pleasurable and momentous semester talking about what motivates people to act the way they do; what is important in life; what makes for a whole individual; what is the nature of love; all the wonderful treasures in any philosophical tract worth the time.

Now, the pursuit of happiness obviously tied into feminism; how could **16**
any woman be happy when she was being discriminated against, treated unfairly, held back, etc. I was wholehearted in my feminism; it defined me. There was absolutely nothing I did that wasn't informed by thoughts of justice, equity, fairness. A friend of mine made me a silver charm of an equal sign inside the symbol for female and I wore it on a chain around my neck every waking moment. I wanted to proclaim to the world that feminism was the most important cause—and I wanted to convert people to it.

I have held firm to both ideals—feminism, and the need to live in a **17**
society that guarantees us the pursuit of happiness. The feminism has taken many turns, as I've dealt with the corporate world, and marriage, and motherhood.

But what I want to get to here is the underlying sense of urgency I felt **18**
about the feminist cause—an urgency that is now absorbed by another sense of urgency having to do with the condition of our planet. It is hard to say that this is a feminist issue, but perhaps it is worth considering our contribution to climate change from the point of view of motherhood, community, and consciousness.

When I read *Our Bodies, Ourselves* as a young woman, I suddenly, electrically, felt connected to women everywhere. I felt as though we were a community, whether we knew it or not, of like-minded people, simply because we were like-bodied. The book managed to do two contradictory things at once: strip away the mystery of our bodies, and glorify the magic of our selves. **19**

Science has taken us to a place in which much of the mystery about how things work is gone. And still we remain dazzled by the wonder of our natural world—that poetry at the heart of science. **20**

I've been thinking about the connection I felt as a feminist—the sense of community in the world, as I've been reading the increasingly terrifying news about climate change. It is as clear as day that we are dramatically altering our planet, and that the results of our polluting ways will be disastrous for the world we are leaving our children. There is absolutely no serious scientific controversy about this state of things. (In fact, scientists are wondering—among themselves, sadly—why "citizens" aren't more upset about global warming. And this citizen is wondering why our scientists haven't been more vocal, dynamic, impassioned with their grave warnings.) **21**

Indeed, where is our communal sense of urgency about climate change? Where is our sense of moral responsibility—as a country? Where is our leadership? Are we all sleepwalking, stirring sporadically with the drift of oil prices? **22**

We are in a crisis of democracy. Climate scientists are testifying about Bush administration interference in their research. NASA's mission "to understand and protect our home planet" was quietly canceled months ago. Activist Laurie David has reported that high school science teachers are not allowed to accept free copies of Al Gore's *An Inconvenient Truth*, although they do accept oil industry involvement in curriculum funding. The opposition—those whose interest is not served by an informed public—is fierce. Intelligent, well-educated people say to me all the time, oh, do you believe all this stuff about global warming? Or, as one 25-year-old put it recently, I guess we'll have some really nice weather in the future. Even now, newly elected politicians, with environmental concerns and credentials, arrive in Washington talking about moderation, taking it easy, so as not to alienate voters—next time around. But wait! We put you there for this time around! We need leadership now. **23**

We no longer have the excuse that we don't know how serious the problem is. We may differ on whether it is the most important problem the world faces—just as we once differed on whether civil rights, or feminism, say, was more important. To my way of thinking, climate change is the gravest issue we face—it will cause great poverty, disease, homelessness, famine, drought. **24**

There is something so overwhelming about the magnitude of the disaster facing us that the temptation to look at the sunny side is understandable. Why not enjoy a North Carolina climate in once snowy New York? But to enjoy it, as an individual simply enjoying warmth and the shedding of a heavy winter coat, is to operate in a manner that is oblivious to the greater good of our world. **25**

We are, of course, all in this together—whether we like it or not. These times feel much like the nascent days of the feminist movement, or the civil rights movement. As has happened in the past, we are at a crossroads. We have a decision to make, and we have to use our collective power for change. We have to decide what kind of world we want to live in—a world that wastes and pollutes, or a world that cherishes our resources and safeguards the future. We have to decide to change our **26** ways. We have to assert our rights as consumers; we have to demand to know what is in everything we buy—because it is now clear that products are laced with toxic chemicals, from the plastic toys we give our babies to chew, to the fire retardants in the furniture in which we cuddle them, to the food we spoon into their trusting mouths. We have to decide that we love our children enough to give them the same right to pursue their happiness that we have taken—and are now squandering—for ourselves. We cannot expect the next generation to clean up our mess. There isn't the time. The time is now.

Vocabulary

balmy (6)
foraging (6)
willful (9)
flagrant (9)
brindled (10)
vulnerability (11)
inextricably (12)
momentous (15)
oblivious (25)
nascent (26)
squandering (26)

Understanding What You Have Read

1. Why did the young woman leave her SUV running?
   ____ (a) Because her starter did not work
   ____ (b) Because her ignition was bad
   ____ (c) Because she wanted to keep the car warm
   ____ (d) Because she forgot to turn it off

2. According to the author, which was the warmest year on record?
   ____ (a) 2006
   ____ (b) 2007
   ____ (c) 2008
   ____ (d) 1999

3. What philosophical view did the author convert to as a young woman?
   ____ (a) She became a feminist.
   ____ (b) She became a logical positivist.
   ____ (c) She became a believer in Aristotle.
   ____ (d) She adopted the principles of Hinduism.

4. What did the author's children come to believe?
   ____ (a) That steam engines were good for the environment
   ____ (b) That global warming was a lie
   ____ (c) That global warming was true
   ____ (d) That flatulent cattle was the cause of global warming

5. According to the author, why don't people take global warming seriously?
    ____ (a) They fear the loss of their jobs.
    ____ (b) They welcome warmer weather.
    ____ (c) They think that it is God's plan.
    ____ (d) They don't believe it.

Thinking About What You Have Read

1. What does the theory about global warming seem to imply about human life and its relationship with nature?
2. What does the opening anecdote about the SUV say about global warming? What is the author trying to imply?
3. What is wrong with this sentence found in paragraph 10? "I maintain a fantasy about what my children's lives will be like; how they will live in the house I've built with their children, how they'll walk the same lanes and explore the same shoreline."
4. What evidence does the author cite to prove her case for the reality of global warming? Quote some of this evidence.
5. The author wonders why scientists have not been more impassioned and dynamic in warning us about global warming. What possible answers can you give her?

Writing Assignments

1. Go to your library and look up the topic of global warming. In a paragraph, sum up at least three reasons for us to believe that global warming is a reality.
2. Write a paragraph on how, if ever, global warming might affect your personal life.

Cheating

Iyah Romm

Having grown up in Canton, tutored privately at home, the author had never encountered cheating until he enrolled in an American university and witnessed many instances of cheating on exams. In this opinion essay, the writer analyzes why students cheat and who is to blame.

Have you ever cheated? You know who you are. Remember when you whispered, asking for the definition of *correr* (to run) during the Spanish quiz, or when you asked the name of the Soviet official behind the Cuban missile crisis during the history final? By the way, it was Nikita Khrushchev. **1**

As a home-schooled student, cheating was never a viable option for success. Whom was I competing against? Did I want to be top in my class? Certainly. That wouldn't be hard. I was the only student. **2**

But when I enrolled at a state university in metro Atlanta at the age of 16, I was shocked at the prevalence of cheating. Friends asked, "You never cheated in high school?" **3**

Virtually all of them had once duped a teacher. For example, one student entered key formulae into a TI 20000 personal "calculator" before a crucial calculus midterm. **4**

Top students are frequently tagged as targets for such covert operations. Students come in droves asking to cheat during a test: from the student who "just cannot understand the material," to the venerated senior class officer who offers $200 to sneak a peek at another student's test in order to maintain his honors status. **5**

Honors? During exams and quizzes, cheaters pull out all the stops. Last semester during a quiz, I observed students passing a cheat sheet back and forth, brazenly marked in two columns, "Test Form A" and "Test Form B." I have managed to get through 18 months of college without being directly affected by the cheating, though I am acutely aware it occurs. **6**

I thought I had become somewhat numb to the phenomenon, but recently, during an exam, a student whom I thought of as a friend cheated off my paper. I caught on at the beginning, and by the time I reached the third problem, I was so irritated I had to sit in front of the classroom to finish my test in peace. Later, another student asked me why I had moved. **7**

Upon completion of my story, he replied, "I thought that it [the cheating] was mutual." This comment represents a common student mentality, simply accepting the prevalence of this issue. **8**

However, I wouldn't passively drop the subject. I went and talked to my professor. During our meeting, I was struck by my lack of options. My only recourse was to name the student, accuse him of the crime and take him before the Honor Committee, where the minimal sentence was suspension. As one student put it, "you either rat out or shut up." **9**

While I wanted vindication, I certainly did not want this student to be suspended. While he committed an egregious act, he is a good student. Yet good students are not exempt from this crowd of rule-breakers. **10**

Indeed, according to a recent survey conducted among students at a local university, 84 percent admitted to having cheated at least in high school, if not in college. Of those students, 63 percent had at least a B average. **11**

Why do students cheat? From income taxes to marital infidelity, the impetus for cheating is all around us. We have become an outcome-based society, focused on the goal rather than the process. The impulse to cheat is well recognized, as evidenced by numerous articles on the topic and even **12** the recently released motion picture *The Perfect Score,* in which a group of students attempts to "defeat" the SAT.

What can we do to fix this problem? School administrations and honor codes can only have so much influence. Unfortunately, all too often, the responsibility falls solely on the shoulders of the professor. Classes in which professors ignore cheating statistically have a higher occurrence of it. This portion of faculty trivializes the core values of academic life: honor and hard work. **13**

However, we cannot hold our teachers entirely accountable. We, as students, must take responsibility for our actions and for those of our fellow classmates even if it means the full measure, taking a student in front of an honor board. **14**

Moreover, we must remember, as Sen. Elizabeth Dole (R–N.C.) told Duke University students, "In the final analysis, it is your moral compass that counts far more than any bank balance, any resume and, yes, any diploma." **15**

Vocabulary

viable (2)
option (2)
prevalence (3)
virtually (4)
duped (4)
formulae (4)
covert (4)
venerated (5)
brazenly (6)
acutely (6)
phenomenon (7)
recourse (9)
vindication (10)
egregious (10)
exempt (10)
impetus (12)
evidenced (12)
trivializes (13)

Understanding What You Have Read

Check the correct answer in the blank provided.

1. Who, according to the author, trivializes the core values of academic life?
   ____ (a) Foreign students who cheat for political reasons
   ____ (b) Faculty members who ignore cheating in their classes
   ____ (c) Parents who ignore their offspring cheating
   ____ (d) Clergymen who do not preach against cheating

2. What are the two most important groups who can help cure the problem of cheating?
   ____ (a) Teachers and students
   ____ (b) Registrars and school counselors
   ____ (c) Campus bookstores and copy machines
   ____ (d) The college president and dean of students

3. Whom do students often ask to help them cheat?
   ____ (a) Students who have already graduated
   ____ (b) The teacher's secretary who has access to the tests
   ____ (c) Students who already have a record of cheating
   ____ (d) Honor students

4. What did the author do to stop a friend from cheating off his paper during an exam?
   ____ (a) He whispered to the friend to stop copying.
   ____ (b) He moved to the front of the classroom.
   ____ (c) He raised his hand to get the teacher's attention.
   ____ (d) He did nothing and just ignored the friend's action.
5. What viable recourse did the author have concerning the friend who cheated?
   ____ (a) The author could move to another school.
   ____ (b) The author could angrily rebuke his friend, the cheater.
   ____ (c) The author could name the cheater and take him in front of the Honor Committee.
   ____ (d) The author could hire a lawyer to take the cheater to civil court.

Thinking About What You Have Read

1. What specific examples of cheating have you encountered in your education so far? What was your reaction to this cheating?
2. This writer was homeschooled, which means that a parent taught him at home. What do you think are the advantages of homeschooling? What are some possible disadvantages? What kind of schooling would you prefer for your own children? Why?
3. Why did the author refuse to name the friend who had cheated? How do you regard his refusal? What would you have done in his situation?
4. Why, according to the author, do students cheat? Do you agree with his reasoning? Why or why not?
5. What do you think is a suitable punishment for someone caught cheating on a test? Justify your answer.

Writing Assignments

1. Write a paragraph in which you narrate an incident of cheating in one of your classes, indicating how you felt about this act.
2. Write a paragraph offering your opinion on what punishment should be handed out to students caught cheating.

CREDITS

TEXT CREDITS

Dana Wall, "Beautiful Music" from *Newsweek* (October 28, 2002). Copyright © 2002 Newsweek, Inc. All rights reserved. Reprinted by permission.

Michael Ondaajte, "Kegalle (ii)" from *Running in the Family* by Micheal Ondaajte, pp. 98-99. Copyright © 1982 by Michael Ondaatje. Used by permission of W.W. Norton & Company, Inc.

Ingrid E. Newkirk, "The Revolt of the Elephants". Reprinted by permission.

Jimmy Carter, "Sport" from *Always Reckoning and Other Poems* by Jimmy Carter. Copyright © 1995 by Jimmy Carter. Used by permission of Crown Publishers, a division of Random House, Inc.

Bill Paschke, "A Brotherly Bond that Beat the Odds" from *Los Angeles Times* (November 25, 1999).

Jenijoy La Belle, "Two Roads Converged in a Wood". Reprinted by permission.

Marge Piercy, "Barbie Doll" from *Circles on the Water* by Marge Piercy. Copyright © 1982 by Marge Piercy. Reprinted by permisson of Alfred A. Knopf, a division of Random House, Inc.

Dick Gregory, "Shame" from *Nigger: An Autobiography* by Dick Gregory, pp. 43-46. Copyright © 1964 by Dick Gregory Enterprises, Inc. Used by permission of Dutton, a division of Penquin Group (USA) Inc.

William E. Barrett, "Senor Payroll". Copyright © 1943 Southwest Review. Reprinted by permission of Harold Ober Associates, Inc.

Dominique Browning, "Our Planet, Ourselves". Copyright © 2007 Conde Nast Publications. All rights reserved. Originally published in House and Garden, April 2007. Reprinted by permission.

Iyah Romm, "Cheating". The Atlanta Journal Constitution (April 20, 2004).

Christopher B. Daly, "How the Lawyers Stole Winter". Reprinted by permission.

Lorena Bruff, "The Cello," a poem by Lorena Bruff. Reprinted by permission.

Michael A. Lev, "Letter from Tokyo" from *The Chicago Tribune* (March 31, 1998). Originally titled, "Lunch Served in 5 Easy Pieces." Copyright © 1998 Chicago Tribune. Reprinted by permission.

Wayne Lionel Aponte, "Talkin' White" from *Essence* (January 1989). Copyright © 1989 Essence Communications, Inc. Reprinted by permission.

PHOTO CREDITS

p.18, Tom Stewart Corbis/Bettmann; p.32, Dave Martin/AP Wide World Photos; p.48, Getty Images, Inc.-PhotoDisc; p.71 and p.90, Spencer Grant/Stock Boston; p.120, Randy Matusow; p.142, Myrleen Ferguson/PhotoEdit Inc.; p.165, Spencer Grant/Photo Researchers, Inc.; p.186,

Megan Garvin/Retna Ltd.; p.200(left), Pete Byron/PhotoEdit Inc.; p.200 (right), Jeff Greenberg/PhotoEdit Inc.; p.221, Corbis/Bettmann; p.242, Michael Newman/PhotoEdit Inc.; p.267, Jeff Greenberg/ Omni-Photo Communications, Inc.; p.279, Cindy Charles/PhotoEdit Inc.; p.292, Jean-Claude LeJeune/Stock Boston; p.312 (left), Gary Hershorn/Corbis/Reuters America LLC; p.312 (right), Adam Nadel/AP Wide World Photos; p.332, Rick Friedman/CORBIS- NY; p.344, AP Wide World Photos; p.369, (c) Chris Pizzello /CORBIS All Rights Reserved; p.388, Esbin/Anderson/Omni-Photo Communications, Inc.; p.405, National Archives and Records Administration; p.421, PCN Photography; p.442, Nita Winter/The Image Works; p.460, John Coletti/Stock Boston.

INDEX

H

I

J

K

L

M

N

O

P

Y

NOTES

NOTES

NOTES

Notes